A TRAUMA ARTIST

Mark A. Heberle   *A TRAUMA ARTIST*

TIM O'BRIEN and the Fiction of *VIETNAM*

University
of Iowa Press

Iowa City

University of Iowa Press, Iowa City 52242
Copyright © 2001 by the University of Iowa Press
All rights reserved
Printed in the United States of America

http://www.uiowa.edu/~uipress

The publication of this book was generously supported by the University of
Iowa Foundation.

Printed on acid-free paper

Design by Omega Clay

Library of Congress Cataloging-in-Publication Data
Heberle, Mark A.
  A trauma artist: Tim O'Brien and the fiction of Vietnam / by Mark A. Heberle.
    p.   cm.
  Includes bibliographical references and index.
  ISBN 0-87745-760-3 (cloth), ISBN 0-87745-761-1 (pbk.)
  1. O'Brien, Tim, 1946—Criticism and interpretation. 2. Vietnamese Conflict,
1961–1975—Literature and the conflict. 3. Post-traumatic stress disorder—
United States. 4. War stories, American—History and criticism. 5. Postmodern-
ism (Literature)—United States. 6. Psychic trauma in literature. 7. Soldiers in
literature. I. Title.

PS3565.B75 Z65   2001
813'.54—dc21   00-067478

01 02 03 04 05 P 5 4 3 2 1
01 02 03 04 05 C 5 4 3 2 1

CONTENTS

PREFACE

I began work on this book more than twenty years after my own military service in Viet Nam, ten years after teaching a course on "Representations of Vietnam" at the University of Hawai'i, and about seven years after giving talks at American Popular Culture Association conferences that resulted in articles on journalist fiction of the war in Viet Nam from Graham Greene to Gustav Hasford and on Takeshi Kaiko's Vietnam novels. The return of Vietnam in my personal and professional life might be regarded as an instance of the persistence of trauma that I find represented in all of Tim O'Brien's works; but it is certainly a result of my admiration for O'Brien's fiction, which has grown over the years as, through his remarkable career, he has continued to rewrite what he has called "the war of life itself."

I am indebted first to Tim O'Brien for his responses to questions and inquiries over the past two decades, from Cambridge, Massachusetts, to Honolulu, but beginning more particularly in October 1989 during a series of readings in Honolulu sponsored by the Hawai'i Committee for the Humanities, the Hawai'i Literary Arts Council, the University of Hawai'i English Department, and *Mānoa: A Pacific Journal of International Writing*. Since then, whether in Honolulu, Cambridge, or most recently in Ann Arbor, his patience and tolerance in addressing my further inquiries has helped to make this book possible and worth pursuing. I am grateful as well for his permission to quote excerpts from "The Vietnam in Me" in my own work and for his willingness to have another book written about his books. I am at least just as grateful for those books themselves, which have continuously educated me in the resources and pleasures of narrative fiction and also brought something redemptive and permanently valuable out of the war that has shaped the past thirty years for so many of us in so many ways.

Most of the original manuscript was accepted for consideration by Holly Carver, the director of the University of Iowa Press, and her encouragement helped me to finish the final two chapters and submit a manuscript that the press, and its outside readers, found worth publishing. Prasenjit Gupta, the acquisitions editor for the press, was accommodating and helpful throughout the months of moving the manuscript through the evaluation process. I am profoundly grateful to both Holly and Prasenjit for their faith in this book. Charlotte Wright, managing editor, and Sarah Walz, marketing manager, provided valuable assistance as well. Jessie Dolch was the perfect copyeditor for this book as well as a wonderful reader of Tim O'Brien's work and saved the original manuscript from numerous blunders.

I am also deeply and happily indebted to my colleague at Michigan, Elizabeth Goodenough, another admirer of Tim O'Brien's stories. She encouraged me to undertake this project initially, knowing how much more important it was to me than a belated attempt to revise my dissertation on *The Faerie Queene*, and she later gave me the direction I needed to substantially revise and complete *A Trauma Artist* as well as valuable last-minute help. I am grateful as well to Peter Widdowson and other colleagues in England, who found that I had taught a course on Vietnam at Hawai'i and encouraged me to give a public lecture on Vietnam War literature in spring 1995, when I was teaching John Milton and metaphysical poetry while on exchange at Cheltenham and Gloucester College of Higher Education. I ended up rereading and discussing Tim O'Brien's works, and that talk became the starting place for this study. Some of my research for the book was done in the Bodleian Library that spring, and most of the initial draft was written during a sabbatical two years later in London. I am very thankful to the University of Hawai'i for the release time and to David Grant and Thames Valley University for the office space and word-processing resources that helped me to complete the first version of the work. I owe an additional debt of gratitude to the University of Hawai'i Office of Research Relations for a travel grant from the National Endowment for the Humanities that allowed me in October 1998 to interview Tim O'Brien in Ann Arbor during a fall reading tour for *Tomcat in Love.*

Although additional research was done at Harvard's Widener Library in 1995 and 1997, most of my work was made possible by the resources of the University of Hawai'i's Hamilton Library, including relevant books, articles, on-line bibliographies and reviews, and several important articles and books obtained through interlibrary loans. Professor Stephen O'Harrow and Kimthu Nguyen Ton, my classroom teacher, were helpful in allowing me to audit Introductory Vietnamese at UH in 1996–97. Several of my colleagues in the English Department at Hawai'i have been valuably supportive, whether through giving me information and references, providing opportunities for Vietnam-related talks or articles, or directly encouraging this project: They include Chip Hughes, Paul Lyons, Pat Matsueda, Barry Menikoff, Rodney Morales, Joan Peters, Kathy Phillips, Todd Sammons, Robbie Shapard, Frank Stewart, and Valerie Wayne. Gayle Nagasako and Tammy Carroll helped greatly in enabling me to process and format the final manuscript within the department. Glenn Man and Cristina Bacchilega, the English Department chair and associate chair, respectively, helped provide me with needed time over two consecutive summers so I could complete and revise the manuscript, and I am deeply indebted to Mark Lawhorn, who taught summer school courses for which I would otherwise have been responsible. I am particularly grateful for the suggestions and recommendations of Craig Howes, whose magisterial book on American POW narratives (Oxford: 1993) is a model of Vietnam scholarship and criticism.

My book draws heavily on earlier criticism of American Vietnam literature and of O'Brien himself, as well as interviews with the author and reviews of his books. It could not have been written without using others' work as a resource, and I am grateful to all of the texts on Vietnam and O'Brien that I have used or cited, especially the work of Philip Beidler, the bibliographies of Catherine Calloway and of Philip K. Jason, and the earlier book-length studies of O'Brien by Tobey C. Herzog and Steven Kaplan. Lynn Warton graciously forwarded from England her recent interview with O'Brien, and earlier interviews by Herzog, Larry McCaffery, Brian McNerney, and Eric James Schroeder have been particularly valuable. My attempt to view O'Brien's works within the framework of abnormal psychology and posttraumatic narratives is most indebted, however, to the authoritative studies of trauma and culture by Kirby Farrell, Judith Herman, Jonathan Shay, and Kali Tal. I would also like to thank the American Psychiatric Association for its permission to reproduce, as an appendix, "Diagnostic Criteria for Posttraumatic Stress Disorder" from its *Diagnostic and Statistical Manual of Mental Disorders*, fourth edition (DSM-IV).

This book is dedicated to my wife, Kyoko, and son, Jacob Akira, who in February 2000 both went through the trauma that brings all of us into this world while I was awaiting readers' evaluations of *A Trauma Artist*. May Jacob and his peers everywhere enjoy a Pacific Century that is free at least of another American war, hot or cold.

INTRODUCTION

Vietnam as Figure and Symptom: "We've All Been There"

"Vietnam Vietnam Vietnam, we've all been there."

These final words of Michael Herr's *Dispatches* served as title in 1978 to an important review by Elizabeth Pochoda of two recent works: Herr's brilliant stoned-age journalism account of the American war in Viet Nam and Tim O'Brien's second novel, *Going After Cacciato*, the story of a soldier who tries to fantasize an escape from it. Published within a year of each other, each is among the handful of narratives of the war that have also become canonical works of American literature. My own edition of *Dispatches* includes lavish testimonials from John le Carré ("The best book I have ever read on men and war in our time"), William S. Burroughs, David Halberstam, Tom Wolfe, Robert Stone, and Hunter S. Thompson. *Cacciato* won the National Book Award for fiction in 1979, and later printings include lavish praise from Herr himself, already a venerated author. In a 1982 interview, O'Brien praised Herr as one of the contemporary writers he most admired (Schroeder 1984: 147), and his later masterpiece *The Things They Carried* echoes his contemporary's use in *Dispatches* of strangely resonant war anecdotes. Looking back over his career in 1995, O'Brien quoted another famous line from Herr's work to explain his imaginative reworkings of the war: "Vietnam's what we had instead of happy childhoods" (Lee 201).[1]

The connection between Herr and O'Brien is not limited to a common subject, mutual admiration, and superb writing, however. As Herr's phrase suggests, the war was an ironic site of growth for both men, enabling them to become authors through experiences that were personally damaging. Although Herr was later to write the screenplays for *Apocalypse Now* and *Full Metal Jacket*, his career as a Vietnam author ended with *Dispatches*. O'Brien, on the other hand, has become America's most celebrated Vietnam novelist; yet, in a 1982 interview with Larry McCaffery, he insisted, "No, I'm not a Vietnam writer. Although Vietnam was the impetus and spark for *becoming* a writer, I do not consider myself a war writer" (131). O'Brien's resistance to being labeled and even canonized so has become stronger with time, even as *The Things They Carried* (1990) and *In the Lake of the Woods* (1994) have enhanced that reputation. With the publication in 1998 of *Tomcat in Love*, which takes place in Minnesota and Florida but revises Vietnam yet again, it is time to redefine this extraordinary career more accurately by placing it at the center of what Kirby Farrell has recently called "post-traumatic culture."

The problem and peril of continuing to write about the war, as well as O'Brien's success in reusing it to center on trauma and to formally replicate its symptoms, are suggested by Michael Herr's farewell to Tim O'Brien's putative subject. "Vietnam Vietnam Vietnam, we've all been there": Like most of *Dispatches*, Herr's final mantra as he "breathes out" the last of his untranquil recollections is deliberately overstated. Its very tone is unstable, intimating impatient dismissal of something that has gone on long enough or too long to be continued or repeated on the one hand ("been there, done that") and comprehensive, satisfying closure on the other. But who are all of us, and how did we end up in "Vietnam"? In 1978, the collective "we" would have united the writer and his American readers, few of whom would have been to Viet Nam, but all of whom would have been exposed to the media spectacle that the war had become during the 1960s and 1970s. Two decades later, the text can still assume that we've all "been there," either literally as one of the 3 million Americans who served in-country or as consumers of one of the war's endless representations.

But "Vietnam" is also being used as a synecdoche, a signifier for one of the most significant public policy catastrophes in American history, naming but also extending beyond the war to include its political, historical, and cultural ramifications for the nation and all of its citizens. In Herr's memorable phrases: "You couldn't use standard methods to date the doom; might as well say that Vietnam was where the Trail of Tears was headed all along, the turnaround point where it would touch and come back to form a containing perimeter; might just as well lay it on the proto-Gringos who found the New England woods too raw and empty for their peace and filled them up with their own imported devils" (49). Defining it as a cultural and historical tragedy, all Americans will always already have been to Vietnam, and *Dispatches* ends by calling upon us to recognize our collective identity.

In another sense, "Vietnam" is the book itself, a compilation, revision, and postwar supplement to Herr's quasi-fictional evocations of the war that had been published to great acclaim in *Esquire* between 1968 and 1970. Assuming that we have read *Dispatches* from beginning to end, we have been to Vietnam insofar as Herr has provided a truer and more authoritative account than anyone else has. *Dispatches* then becomes synecdoche for Vietnam, replacing the outdated battlefield maps, official reports, mere journalism, and linear views of history that are included and derided within its account. Herr has variously compared his work to a novel or to Edward Gibbon's *Decline and Fall of the Roman Empire* (Heberle 13), and his self-congratulation has been vindicated by reviewers and critics of *Dispatches*. Even James Webb, Ronald Reagan's onetime secretary of the navy, a Marine officer in Viet Nam, and a successful war novelist himself who does not share Herr's antiwar perspective, has acknowledged the superior power of works of the imagination to represent Vietnam, which he defined at a 1985 literary conference as the most important event in American life since World War II: "Only a good book or painting or play or movie can conjure the emotions and ambiguities . . . and through such exorcism affect attitudes that shape consciousness. . . . [T]hrough literature we can explore ambiguities and work toward synthesizing an enormously complex and painful experience" (Lomperis 15). For better or worse, most Americans in the twenty-first century and thereafter will come to understand Vietnam through *Dispatches* or *Going After Cacciato* —or through *Rambo* and its imitations.

At least one more consciousness-shaping product of Vietnam is intimated by Herr's final incantation, but for O'Brien's work it is the most important. Herr suffered a post-Vietnam breakdown in the years after his months in the war (Schroeder 1992: 35–36, 40–41), prompted and exacerbated by the memories of experiences that were difficult to put behind him. The final, postwar section of *Dispatches* is titled "Breathing Out," a counterpart to the first, "Breathing In," as if Vietnam were an inspiration that threatened the author with suffocation. These metaphoric bookends define *Dispatches* as a psychosomatic recovery of earlier experiences by the author, locating "Vietnam" within his own memory and imagination and giving it posttraumatic release. Indeed, Herr's recollections of the bad times after the war culminate "unforgettably" in experiences that are symptomatic of posttraumatic stress disorder: "I was once in such a bad head about it that I thought the dead had only been spared a great deal of pain. Debriefed by dreams, friends coming over from the other side to see that I was still alive. Sometimes they looked exactly as I'd known them, but standing in a strange light; the light told the story, and it didn't end like any war story I'd ever imagined" (259). The final sentence suggests not only that Herr's hauntings tell a story that transcends war but also that, unlike wars and their stories, this one is interminable. Perhaps, then, Vietnam is not only a war or a book but also an arena of psychic wounding and its posttraumatic aftermath—and we've *all* been "there." The trace of such disorder is mimicked by Herr's fragmented, frenetic, psychedelic discourse, much praised by his admirers, which resembles the traumatic symptom of hyperarousal. Indeed, one of the earlier published fragments of *Dispatches* was titled "High on War," and Pochoda, typically, praises Herr's skill in "tapping into a general psychosis" and the "drug-induced sharpness" (345) of his descriptions. For Herr, only when the national nightmare awakened as a shameful part of American history could the personal nightmares be finally released and Vietnam fully dispatched: "The war ended, and then it really ended, the cities 'fell,' I watched the choppers I'd loved dropping into the South China Sea as their Vietnamese pilots jumped clear, and one last chopper revved up, lifted off and flew out of my chest" (259–60). Like Philip Caputo's *A Rumor of War, Dispatches* achieves personal, literary, and historical closure with the [North] Vietnamese victory in 1975, freeing Caputo to pursue a series of postwar novels about male fortitude and violence and Herr to write books on Las Vegas and Walter Winchell.

O'Brien's works make explicit the psychic terrain that *Dispatches* merely suggests, a site of traumatization that is variously linked to the war but not defined by it. Indeed, although Tim O'Brien actually fought in the war, while Herr was a freelance correspondent, *Dispatches* presents its author as a more active participant than are O'Brien's various authorial surrogate/protagonists. Herr dresses as a grunt, accompanies troops into the field, claims to be their "intimate," and even throws himself into combat at

one point. Even in his own combat memoir, *If I Die in a Combat Zone,*
O'Brien remains largely on the sidelines, replacing combat experiences or
events with personal reflections that frequently leave the war behind altogether. Herr seems to have said all that he needed or wanted to say about
Vietnam in one book, gotten over it, and left us with what purports to be a
literally authoritative representation; O'Brien's career, on the other hand,
has parceled Vietnam out over seven books, belying the notion that there
is some conclusive account to be realized.

The view that any American book about the war can satisfactorily represent Vietnam has been rightly questioned by recent cultural and literary
critics. After all, "Vietnam," the usual English spelling for the nation where
the American war was fought, is the French transliteration for the native
spelling Viet Nam (literally, the Viet people to the South, as seen from the
perspective of China [see Reischauer and Fairbank 60; Buttinger 306, n. 3]).
A convenient adoption of the French spelling, our borrowing is ideological
as well as lexical, a symptom of how we view Viet Nam through the Western perspective that we share with the French.[2] In *The Viet Nam War/The
American War,* Renny Christopher has decried the American mythologiza-
tion of the war implicit in the usual readings, writings, and spellings,
which "make it almost impossible for that discourse to break from the idea
of 'Vietnam' the war in order to consider the participation in that war of
Viet Nam the country" (2). Her own title signifies a new reading of discourses concerning Viet Nam and the American war, one that commends
noncanonical works, especially those by Vietnamese exiles, while damning
most of the critically celebrated Euro-American writers. Tim O'Brien, an
important target for her critique, is criticized for ethnocentricity, for stress-
ing the suffering of himself and his comrades and ignoring the Vietnamese; for "the minutiae of individualism" (230), simply recirculating first reactions to the war twenty years after its end; for, conversely, universalizing
personal experiences and the particulars of the conflict in Viet Nam into
the transcendent category of "warfare"; and for being apolitical in his fiction, despite his own judgments of American criminality in Viet Nam.
Christopher's reconsideration of O'Brien focuses on *Going After Cacciato,*
but her strictures would probably not be satisfied by the subsequent
works either. And despite the overwhelmingly laudatory criticism in full-
length studies of Vietnam literature by John Hellmann, Philip Beidler,
Thomas Myers, and Don Ringnalda and in the full-length studies of

O'Brien by Steven Kaplan (1995) and Tobey Herzog (1997), O'Brien has also come under fire by feminist critics for his representations of women characters in the wake of Susan Jeffords's important Reagan-era study of *The Remasculinization of America* (although she does not herself deal with O'Brien's work). We will consider such critiques of O'Brien in the conclusion, along with hypotheses about what directions his career might take after *Tomcat.* In the meantime, this study will follow Renny Christopher's important and valuable distinction between "Vietnam"—an ideological signifier for the futilely destructive American military, political, and economic intervention in Southeast Asia and its cultural and political ramifications within the United States and elsewhere; and "Viet Nam"—the nation that won the war and has a history and culture that transcends "Vietnam."

A Trauma Artist

Like Herr and other American authors, O'Brien uses "Vietnam" as a synecdoche for the U.S. war in Viet Nam and its effects on Americans. But he also uses it metaphorically as a psychic condition characterized by traumatization, a condition derived from his own experiences that is variously rewritten in his works. "Nam lived on inside me," he told John Mort in 1994, "and I just called it by another name—I called it life. Nam, divorce, your father's death—such things live on even though you think you're over them. They come bubbling out" (1990). In a 1992 interview (Bourne 76), O'Brien referred to Vietnam as "an essential metaphor or a life-given metaphor that, for me, is inescapable. And I'm grateful for it in a sense. I've used it in the way that Conrad writes about the sea. . . . But Conrad is no more writing about the sea than I am writing about war." Vietnam is thus a figure for something else in O'Brien that he associates with traumatic experiences, and his writing is a fictional representation of such experiences and often mimics its symptoms.

In its Greek form, $\tau\rho\alpha\nu\mu\alpha$ is a physical wound, reflecting quite directly the circumstances of organized male violence in warfare that have helped to define constructions of virtue, philosophy, government, and literature, from the *Iliad* and *The Republic* to the American Revolution and Kosovo. O'Brien's concern with the issue of courage in his earlier works reflects that tradition but also moves beyond it by considering the unhealed psychic wounds that we have come to associate with traumatization in the twentieth century and that are not limited to conventional warfare. "[W]hen I read a good piece of literature," O'Brien told Daniel Bourne in 1992, "[I am reminded] that in fact all of us, in all our lives, whether we're personally serving in a war or not, have gone through the threat of war, the threat of annihilation, the threat of human violence, . . . which is around all of us. It's in our genes, this sense that we're all going to die some day" (83). The "threat" of violence is not just a psychic phenomenon but a reality of American political and social culture, from violence-saturated media to school massacres to real or imagined terrorists and what has been labeled "the neurotic-sounding military-industrial 'complex'" itself (Farrell xiii). And trauma-generated awareness of our mortality, which may be exacerbated by such threats as well as the actual experience of rape, child abuse, natural or manmade catastrophe, and the like, acknowledges the tenuousness of our identity and integrity as well. O'Brien's works are thus among the richest and most complex expressions of American posttraumatic culture, as examined in Kirby Farrell's recent study of cultural phenomena ranging from the novels of Don DeLillo to *Schindler's List* to "tropes of berserking and the apocalypse" in popular movies and novels (318). Although Farrell does not consider O'Brien, his characterization of what happens when we are removed from "the magic circle of everyday life" reflects the situation faced by all of the writer's protagonists: "Natural catastrophe or human violence readily breaks the circle, but under the right conditions any pileup of stresses, any mortal terror, can do it. In trauma, terror overwhelms not just the self, but the ground of the self, which is to say our trust in the world" (xii).

Although Vietnam was both a site of traumatization and the origin of O'Brien's subsequent career, his resistance to being characterized as a war writer suggests that "trauma writer" is a more pertinent label. In fact, as his life and his works have moved beyond the war in Viet Nam, traumatic psychic conditions have become more widespread and explicit. In *Tomcat in Love*, his most recent book, the word "trauma" and its derivatives appear more frequently than in any previous book, even though the ostensible subject of the work is a marital crisis and its physical settings are Minnesota and Florida. Conversely, O'Brien has identified the period *before* his induction into the army as "a horrid, confused, traumatic period—the trauma of trying to decide whether or not to go to Canada" (Myers 1995: 140). Here trauma is an ethical crisis, an agonizing prewar decision first described in his combat memoir *If I Die in a Combat Zone* (1973). O'Brien feared dying or killing in what he regarded as an immoral war, and the bad choice that he made, to participate in Vietnam, is the most pervasive and recurrent source of trauma in his works, recalled in the personal essay "The Vietnam in Me" (1994); revised in the story "On the Rainy River" (1990); and more drastically rewritten in *Going After Cacciato*, *The Nuclear Age* (1985), and *In the Lake of the Woods* (1994). Warfare is not just physically and psychically traumatizing but morally devastating for combatants, and what Jonathan Shay has labeled "the undoing of character," ethical breakdown, is at the heart of O'Brien's trauma writing.

Although the war and its ramifications may be the effective cause of this writing, they constitute only part of what we can now identify as a traumatic triad. During an Ann Arbor reading of *Tomcat in Love*, O'Brien defined the focus of his entire career in terms that would be surprising if we were to view him primarily as a Vietnam war writer: "Although this book has been described as a departure, . . . I'm writing about the same subject I've always written about in every single book, which is a simple one—it has to do with the things we do for love." But just as the fear of embarrassing those he loved prevented the writer from deserting to Sweden (*Combat Zone* 70), the trauma of Vietnam has been supplemented and extended by private wounds in *Northern Lights*, *The Nuclear Age*, *In the Lake of the Woods*, and *Tomcat in Love*: a son's need to be loved and respected by his father on one hand, and the obsessive need to fill what O'Brien has called "a hole in the heart" (telephone interview, November 3, 1998) through marital love on the other. The domestic trauma of childhood and marriage implicitly or explicitly (*The Nuclear Age*, *In the Lake of the Woods*) complement Vietnam as antecedent and consequent: Sons become or fail to become soldiers while trying to satisfy paternal expectations, while soldiers or protagonists who have avoided the war desperately seek love to heal the wounds that have resulted. One effect of O'Brien's focus on traumatized protagonists in need of love has been what we might label a feminization of virtue, revising and even subverting the virtue of militarized male fortitude.

Although O'Brien has scrupulously avoided overt political engagement, his traumatic fictions serve both as figures and as symptoms of public as well as psychic breakdowns. As Farrell asserts in his analysis of *Fearless*, Peter Weir's airplane disaster film of 1993, "Trauma exposes not only the ultimate nothingness of the self, but also the sickening falseness of the social world" (185). Peter Schwenger notes of O'Brien's traumatized, shelter-digging protagonist in *The Nuclear Age* that "the very title of [the] novel reminds us that we are not dealing with one case history; rather, history is the case" (108). Similarly, in O'Brien's great Vietnam War story of the same name, "the things they carried" include overwhelming psychic burdens and "sparklers for the Fourth of July, colored eggs for Easter . . . the fruits of science, the smokestacks, the canneries, the arsenals at Hartford, the Minnesota forests, the machine shops, the vast fields of corn and wheat" (*Things* 16) as well as the full complement of GI military gear.

O'Brien's fictional narratives are organized as retrospective meditations or reflections by deeply traumatized figures trying to revisit the sources of their breakdowns so that they can recover themselves. With the exception of *In the Lake of the Woods*, these traumatic fictions also function as therapy for their subjects and provide some redemption for what has been suffered; in short, they replicate trauma therapy, which relies on an attempt to communicate to others an ineffable wounding so that the posttraumatic survivor's life can be repaired and resumed. "Trauma" is also at least phonologically echoed by "Traum," the German word for "dream," and O'Brien's stories can be seen as *traumwerk*, fabricating dreams out of wounds. In doing so, O'Brien rewrites not only his own experiences but himself. Beginning a 1998 reading in Ann Arbor, he asserted that what made him most satisfied about his latest novel, *Tomcat in Love*, was his creation of a new persona: "It's the first book I've written in a career that's almost thirty years old now where the narrator's voice, or the storyteller's voice, whether it is first- or third-person, is not my own. Almost everything else I've done, except for a couple of short stories, comes more or less out of the voice of a Midwestern guy like me and in this case it's a Midwestern guy, yeah, but not too much like me." As we will see, however, even Thomas Chippering, the insufferable tomcat of the title, is a revised version of the author.

Trauma is not so much the subject of O'Brien's works as it is the medium within which and out of which his protagonists are impelled to revisit and rewrite their life experiences, and, as Chapter 1 will more fully detail, the writing mimics the phenomena of constriction, intrusion, hyperarousal, and the like that are characteristic of traumatized survivors and the experiences they have lived through. The stories thus both figur-

ally represent trauma and are symptomatic of that experience—whether in
Viet Nam, in revising Vietnam, or in the fissile nuclear families in O'Brien's
work that are still stereotypically associated with the American dream despite our 50 percent divorce rate. The self-conscious figuration and formal
structuring of the books, what O'Brien himself especially prizes in his
work, make evident the gap between the author—the trauma artist—and
those rewritings of the author that constitute the fictional protagonists.
What separates O'Brien from them is the creation of fictional narratives
through which the protagonists mimic O'Brien's activity but remain traumatized subjects. Whatever recovery is possible is realized as psychological catharsis for the protagonist, but as the closure of a fiction for the
trauma artist.

The border between the two is strikingly permeable, however. "[S]tories
can save lives," asserts the narrator of "The Lives of the Dead" (*Things* 255),
not least because our identity itself is a construct, a fabrication that
trauma survivors are forced to recognize and reassemble through narratives. This posttraumatic slippage between "authentic" self and fiction is at
the center of Tim O'Brien's life as a writer, and it is often dramatically incarnated at public readings. At the beginning of his 1998 Ann Arbor appearance, for example, O'Brien illustrated an overt theme of *Tomcat*—that
words have unstable, idiosyncratic meanings—by citing a personal example: "The word for me, from my youth, for example, might be the word
'Pontiac,' because at age sixteen or seventeen I made first love on the hood
of my dad's Pontiac in a cornfield in southern Minnesota, in late October,
with a light frost on the hood, and to this day the word 'Pontiac,' when I
hear it, doesn't mean Pontiac, it means 'will this get any better'?" But that
ironically traumatic scenario is "actually" an experience narrated by
Thomas Chippering in the thirteenth chapter of *Tomcat in Love* ("Pontiac").
Moreover, O'Brien had also described the same experience as his own
while introducing a reading from *The Things They Carried* in Honolulu
two years earlier! That reading seemed to be an account of his failure to
desert to Canada after receiving his draft notice in 1968; but at the end of
what seemed to be an autobiographical confession ("one story I've never
told before. Not to anyone. Not to my parents, not to my brother or sister,
not even to my wife"), O'Brien revealed that everything in his apparent
confession was made-up except its shameful secret: "I was a coward. I
went to the war." This riveting narrative of moral cowardice appears as "On

the Rainy River," the fourth fiction in *The Things They Carried*. During an appearance in Hawai'i in 1989, shortly before publication of the book, O'Brien had presented the same account as a personal confession, adding the same coda, and Don Ringnalda has noted similar performances in other readings (102–3). The boundaries between personal traumatization and retrospective narrative, authorial and fictional identity, actual experience and literary figuration are nearly dissolved in all of these instances, reflecting an enigmatic remark by O'Brien in my own phone interview with him in November 1998: "I'm not even sure that my own life even happened any more."

These rereadings of fictions presented as personal experiences dramatize characteristics of O'Brien's work that will be analyzed more fully in Chapter 1, "Fabricating Trauma": trauma witnessing, the uncertain border between actual experience and fictions, the revision of self and previous texts, the fabrication of self-consciousness. Both the readings and the works are characterized by repetition, the primary feature of posttraumatic survivorhood, whether in the form of bad dreams and intrusive reexperiencing or the more dispersed anxiety of paranoia, an imaginary fear of terrible things repeating themselves. O'Brien's works rewrite the same primal scenes and experiences, and the repetitions are so numerous and recurrent that the works have become an endless refiguration of trauma writing that constantly revises itself—or a symptom of trauma that is never healed. As noted above, every book except *Tomcat* rewrites O'Brien's perception of moral cowardice in going to Viet Nam as a soldier. The first girl that O'Brien fell in love with, a nine-year-old named Lorna Lou (telephone interview, November 3, 1998), has been most obviously refigured as the nine-year-old Linda in *The Things They Carried* ("The Lives of the Dead") and as Thomas Chippering's former wife, Lorna Sue, in *Tomcat*, both of which present posttraumatic love stories. But she has also reappeared in Indochina as the child-woman Sarkin Aung Wan, Paul Berlin's fantasy beloved in *Going After Cacciato*, and as Kathy Wade, the forever lost, too-much-loved wife of the protagonist of *In the Lake of the Woods*. Even less expansive signifiers recur in significantly changed forms throughout the books. Thus, Mount Rainier, a symbol of "freedom" in *Combat Zone* (40), looming over Fort Lewis as O'Brien completes the advanced infantry training that will lead to self-imprisonment in a bad war, comes back to haunt the bad dreams of John Wade (*In the Lake of the*

Woods) after his political career has been obliterated in a primary election "landslide" prompted by revelation of his participation in the My Lai Massacre: "The thought formed as a picture in his head, an enormous white mountain that he had been climbing all his life, and now he watched it come rushing down on him, all that disgrace" (5).

The Fiction of Vietnam

An art that so expansively and intrusively rewrites itself cannot and has not defined its purpose as the representation of Vietnam; hence O'Brien's objections to having his writing so characterized. "Vietnam" is a deliberate fiction in O'Brien, one artist's imaginative re-creation of a reality that always remains "Other" and escapes final realization. His works do not even attempt the arrogant and impossible task of presenting the final truth about the war or Vietnam, let alone Viet Nam, nor do they presume to speak for the Vietnamese. Accusations of ethnocentricity derive from an assumption that literature represents or should represent some authoritative truth that would summon universal assent—or at least the assent of the right readers—and they ignore O'Brien's own recognition of the problem. As he noted in a 1991 interview with Ronald Baughman:

> The way one handles the enemy is a big question for people who write about Vietnam in particular and about war in general. People often ask why not treat the enemy with the same detail and richness as you treat your protagonists, the American soldiers. And the answer is, of course, that you often simply *cannot*. You don't *know* the enemy. You are pretty much stuck with your own point of view. Beyond that, of course, you'd end up doing stereotypical sorts of things. The enemy is *almost always* rendered in fiction in predictable ways. In my own fiction I've tried to handle this problem by offering quick little glimpses of the Vietnamese—snapshots, images, and so on. (206–7)

Not only the "enemy" but the supportive, pacified, or indifferent Vietnamese among whom O'Brien's platoon lived and fought were also strangers to the writer and other Americans, and his treatments of their lack of understanding are among the most powerful episodes in his representations of Viet Nam. Awareness of one's ignorance may be less desirable than full and sympathetic understanding of or even identification with another people and culture, but at least it has the virtue of honesty and may be less presumptuous, perhaps even wiser.

As the last of the colonialist inheritors of "Indochina," the United States misread Viet Nam, and with devastating consequences for the people of both nations. Both *Dispatches* and *Cacciato* record that misreading, but O'Brien's is the more valuable recognition. Another of Herr's celebrated aphorisms, "reading . . . the Vietnamese . . . was like trying to read the wind" (5), stylishly locates the origin of ignorance in stereotypical Asian inscrutability. O'Brien finds it in a well-meaning bewilderment and arrogance that is prototypically American. In the Baughman interview, O'Brien called attention to his study in ethnocentricity, "The Things They Didn't Know" (Chapter 39 of *Going After Cacciato*), as one of the passages by which he would like to be remembered, "a kind of listing that I hope has a poetic feel, a certain lyricism, a haunting ode to ignorance [that] seem[s] to me to go to the heart of my writerly concerns" (211). O'Brien's ode to ignorance ends with an eloquently understated catalog, one of his most distinctive stylistic devices:

> They did not know even the simple things: a sense of victory, or satisfaction, or necessary sacrifice. They did not know the feeling of taking a place and keeping it, securing a village and then raising the flag and calling it a victory. No sense of order or momentum. No front, no rear, no trenches laid out in neat parallels. . . . They did not have targets. They did not have a cause. . . . They did not know the names of most villages. They did not know which villages were critical. . . . They did not know how to feel. Whether, when seeing a dead Vietnamese, to be happy or sad or relieved; whether, in times of quiet, to be apprehensive or content; whether to engage the enemy or elude him. They did not know how to feel when they saw villages burning. Revenge? Loss? Peace of mind or anguish? They did not know. They knew the old myths about Quang Ngai—tales passed down from old-timer to newcomer—but they did not know which stories to believe. Magic, mystery, ghosts and incense, whispers in the dark, strange tongues and strange smells, uncertainties never articulated in war stories, emotion squandered on ignorance. They did not know good from evil. (320–21)

Here, the double trauma of victimizing and victimization of both Americans and Vietnamese is turned into something terribly beautiful, the final sentence climactically articulating the truth that we have come to know

by reading through the rest of them: cultural ignorance breeds moral ignorance. The bemusement recorded here is not primarily cognitive or discursive, but psychological and spiritual, a loss of familiar ideological and
ethical terrain that unsettles one's own identity and is registered as traumatic emotional constriction through the dispassionate accumulation of
defamiliarizing details.

O'Brien begins this favorite chapter with a less discursive dramatized
example of bewilderment, one that is generated by literally misreading
Vietnamese. Stink Harris is awkwardly and unsuccessfully using a Vietnamese-English dictionary to order civilians out of a village being
searched by the platoon. He can read the letters, but his mind and tongue
cannot produce anything meaningful.[3] Frustrated by the villagers' amuse-
ment and incomprehension of his incompetent braying of their language
("'Lui lai, lui lai!' Stink would scream, pushing them back. '*Lui lai*, you
dummies . . . Back up, move!'" [308]), accusing *them* of ignorance or willful
hostility, he finally resorts to the only language that he can command: "Re-
loading, he would keep firing and screaming, and the villagers would
sprawl in the dust, arms wrapped helplessly around their heads. And when
they were all down, Stink would stop firing. He would smile. He would
glance at Doc Peret and nod. 'See there? They understood me fine. *Nam
xuong dat* . . . it means to lie down. You just got to punctuate your sentences'" (309). Appallingly funny, the passage allows us to share the befud-
dlement of everyone involved, while suggesting how misreading might
lead to murder under the wrong circumstances. Everyone is dangerously
hyperaroused, including Stink. Threatening his captives with a barbaric
distortion of their own language, he can gain their attention and respect
only with the coercion of a rifle.

Since Vietnam, the United States has nearly perfected the art of immac-
ulate intervention, from Grenada and Haiti to Iraq and the Balkans, but
such triumphs have been merely military and no less dependent upon gun
barrels than Stink Harris's temporary enforcement of order. Whether or
not O'Brien actually observed such an incident in the war is irrelevant to
the truth of the scene, which paradigmatically represents the American
misreading of Viet Nam that was intended to win hearts and minds but
could only expand organized violence. "The Things They Didn't Know"
uses the trauma of the war to articulate and dramatize our own naïve and
ignorant arrogance. Even in *Cacciato*, the most fully Viet Nam–sited of his

novels, O'Brien is using the war for purposes that acknowledge but try to transcend its futile devastation. Most of the work is literally located within the imagination of an almost archetypally bewildered and well-meaning GI who both mimics and anticipates the career of the author himself by re-creating Vietnam as a fiction. The fictional redemption of the trauma of Vietnam, including such deadly ignorance, began with O'Brien's first work, a combat memoir that is less an account of his own experience than a quasi-fictional paradigm of tragic misreadings. Ultimately, Vietnam has metamorphosed into an imaginative site in O'Brien, a place of sometimes agonized, sometimes ironic meditation not limited to the terrible misadventure in Viet Nam, a postwar world of "uncertainties never articulated in war stories . . . no front, no rear, no trenches laid out in neat parallels."

A TRAUMA ARTIST

CHAPTER 1

FABRICATING TRAUMA

"The Vietnam in Me"

Just after publication of his fifth novel, *In the Lake of the Woods*, the cover story of the October 2, 1994, *New York Times Magazine* presented an autobiographical piece by Tim O'Brien that attested to his cultural status as America's leading Vietnam War writer. "The Vietnam in Me" alternates an account of O'Brien's return to Viet Nam in February 1994, accompanied by his companion Kate Phillips, with his reflections later that summer in Cambridge, Massachusetts, concerning the subsequent breakup of their relationship. The magazine's cover reproduces a 1969 photograph of a shirtless and helmetless O'Brien in Quang Ngai Province, Viet Nam, where he was serving as a combat soldier in a battalion of the Americal Division. Filling the entire page, the image fashions O'Brien as the archetypal grunt, the American soldier in Viet Nam, but it also authenticates the writer as an experienced combatant: This is not simply any Vietnam veteran but, for the magazine's readers, the most well-known and admired novelist of the war. The photo is reproduced in miniature throughout the article, alternating with photos of Vietnamese whom O'Brien met during his 1994 return. This iconic juxtaposition reflects the written account, in which the author describes meeting residents of Quang Ngai at peace while remembering how he and his comrades died and killed on the same ground during his year in the war. "Dear God. We should've bombed these people with love," he writes after being told that he is the first American soldier to visit here in the 24 years since his former firebase was abandoned to the weeds (50). But O'Brien's return to Viet Nam is not just an atonement; it is also a return to the site of his constitution as a writer, a career that the publication of this piece extends.

"The Vietnam in Me" appeared again in the Sunday *Observer* magazine for April 2, 1995, as part of a special issue devoted to the twentieth anniversary of the end of the American war in Viet Nam. This cover page reproduces a shot by the legendary British Vietnam War photojournalist Tim Page of an otherwise anonymous GI smoking a hash pipe in the field. O'Brien's is the first piece of writing in the issue and is preceded by a series of famous combat photos and followed by three articles that discuss in turn the continuing effect of the war on the United States and on Viet Nam, the British antiwar movement, and the role of the Ho Chi Minh Trail. (The series concludes more pragmatically with a review of Vietnamese restaurants in London.) Even more tellingly than in its original appearance, this reprinting of O'Brien's double narrative reflects his status as America's canonical Vietnam War writer. A note at the end, referring to O'Brien's previous works and announcing the imminent publication of *In the Lake of the Woods* in Britain on April 24, identifies the author of the preceding personal narrative as America's most celebrated writer of Vietnam War fiction. Published barely a month before media celebrations of the fiftieth anniversary of the end of World War II, the issue commemorates America's failure in Viet Nam, largely ignored officially by the U.S. political establishment that spring, as a resonant political and cultural event of the post-1945 world. While the Victory in Europe observances of May provided nostalgic last rites for an increasingly distant "good" war, the Vietnam conflict is, according to the magazine cover blurb, "the war that goes on forever seen through the eyes of soldiers, civilians, and photographers." Except for a black GI whose traumatic response to a white buddy's death is captured in a haunting photograph by Larry Burrows, O'Brien is the only American soldier, and only American writer, whose name appears in the issue. His voice thus carries a doubled authority, and it is in his personal account that the war's lack of closure for Americans is most decisively dramatized. Conversely, for the Vietnamese presented both in O'Brien's piece and in the others, the war seems an event of history.

Although both magazines acknowledge O'Brien's special status as a Vietnam writer, "The Vietnam in Me" represents the celebrated author as a traumatized survivor of a war that will not end. O'Brien's return to Viet

Nam is deeply unsettling, reawakening terrible memories as he revisits former battlefields in Quang Ngai Province, where he served as an infantryman in 1969: the terror of combat, the deaths of former comrades, homicidal fear and dread directed at the Vietnamese themselves, the destruction of their villages, small brutalities and large atrocities perpetrated by American soldiers. The scenes in Cambridge present an abandoned writer who is taking medication against a suicidal despondency that threatens his life. His companion goes to Viet Nam in the spirit of "adventure" but is horrified by what she discovers when they visit the site of the My Lai Massacre at the subhamlet of Thuan Yen; by the time of the scenes in Cambridge, she has left him for someone else. O'Brien's self-revelation shocked many of his readers because, unlike many combat veterans, he had seemed to be relatively unaffected psychologically by his experiences in Viet Nam. In a 1990 interview, he confessed that "for the rest of my life I'll probably be writing war stories" but "not out of any obsession with war," and claimed that he had experienced no postwar adjustment problems (Coffey). But here O'Brien was presenting himself as a deeply troubled figure who had suffered for more than two decades from bad dreams that had been reawakened to the point of self-destruction by the return to Viet Nam. Nor is the near-breakdown simply a result of the war. The loss of the woman he loves also seems to be a life-threatening experience: It is unclear whether he is tempted to kill himself because he can't leave Vietnam behind or because the woman he loves has left him. And O'Brien's double trauma is darkened further by guilt: "I have done bad things for love, bad things to stay loved. Kate is one case. Vietnam is another" (52).

Although O'Brien has been criticized for exploiting intimate secrets in publishing this piece, he has pronounced himself more than satisfied with his apparent self-revelation: "I reread it maybe once every two months, . . . just to remind myself what writing's for," he told Don Lee (196). In finding his confession a piece of good writing, whatever its value as personal therapy, O'Brien joins two categories that we normally regard as distinct. To facilitate recovery, trauma survivors are normally encouraged to tell their story to fellow survivors, therapists, or other sympathetic audiences. Such narratives have as their goal the cathartic re-creation of the original scene or scenes of horror, not literary achievement. O'Brien's piece is certainly not therapy in the normal sense because the community to whom he reveals himself is a dispersed audience of readers. Nor does his memoir or personal testimony simply recall events that occurred in the past in a particular place. "The Vietnam in Me" reduces but also intensifies the American war as a psychic reality within O'Brien's memory and imagination. Thus, "Vietnam" is a continuing trauma but also a literary representation of that trauma created by a particular American author.

That this personal testimony is carefully contrived is most evident in its structure. The piece is organized into eighteen separately titled sections, fourteen headed by the location and date of the scene that is re-created within each (e.g., "LZ Gator, Vietnam, February 1994"; "Cambridge, Mass., June 1994"). Nine of these occur in Viet Nam, five back in Cambridge four months after the return to Viet Nam. The juxtaposition of these two different locations and times deliberately links yet separates past and present, Viet Nam and America, the writer as victimizer and the writer as victim, other American and Vietnamese casualties of the war and O'Brien himself, the trauma of war and the trauma of love, being with his companion and being separated from her. The turning point from Vietnam to domestic trauma is the couple's visit to the site of the My Lai Massacre. Not only is this the longest single series of scenes (three) in a single place ("My Lai, Quang Ngai Province, February 1994," 52–53), but the first My Lai scene is the seventh of the fourteen sited and dated sections, while the final one is the ninth of the eighteen sections as a whole. My Lai is thus literally situated at the center of O'Brien's revelation of double trauma. Formal patterning is also metaphorically significant elsewhere: The final scene of personal desolation in Cambridge takes place on the Fourth of July, and the final scene in Viet Nam is Ho Chi Minh City, which the lovers find hatefully Americanized and which O'Brien invests with a split personality that verbally reflects his own breakdown and reinvokes the war, not the present peace: "Even the names—Saigon, Ho Chi Minh City. A massive identity crisis. Too loud, too quiet. Too alive, too dead. . . . An hour in the Chinese market district . . . is like an hour in combat" (57). The alternation of the two interwoven chronologies of Viet Nam and Cambridge is itself carefully fabricated to reflect traumatization. The resulting fragments parody the linear narrative suggested by the chronological headings; they formally enact a series of flashbacks from a present state of grief over the loss of Kate to the devastating visit to Vietnam when they were still together.

Besides its dual chronology, O'Brien's piece reorganizes his direct experiences in less obvious ways. As noted above, the hinge of the transition from one trauma to the other is the couple's visit to Thuan Yen, a series of scenes that ends with a cold rain coming down over the ditch where American soldiers murdered "maybe 50, maybe 80, maybe 100 innocent human beings."

> The guilt has turned to a gray, heavy sadness. I have to take my leave but don't know how.
> After a time, Kate walks up, hooks my arm, doesn't say anything, doesn't have to, leads me into a future that I know will hold misery for both of us. Different hemispheres, different scales of atrocity. I don't want it to happen. I want to tell her things and be understood and live happily ever after. I want a miracle. That's the final emotion. The terror at this ditch, the certain doom, the need for God's intervention. (53)

In this account, My Lai has been translated (and diminished?) from an unspeakable war crime into an unspoken anxiety between two lovers that will lead to their separation four months later. The narrator finds it difficult to "take leave" not only of Thuan Yen but of the woman he loves. The grave site of the My Lai Massacre and of America's own righteous pretensions becomes a tomb for their relationship as well, poisoning love with its terrible influence. Yet O'Brien's emotions at the grave have been written into the moment from a later perspective, after Kate has left him. O'Brien has revised his earlier self, investing the visitor to Viet Nam with the awareness of the suicidal survivor of the Fourth of July: "The future will hold misery for both of us." On the other hand, this scene may be regarded as an intrusive memory that reemerges as O'Brien grieves over losing his beloved in July 1994. "The Vietnam in Me" is thus not direct self-revelation but a refashioning of actual experiences in which O'Brien represents himself as a double trauma survivor. That "The Vietnam in Me" straddles the border between confession and contrivance, nonfiction and fiction, has been recognized by the *New York Times Magazine* editors themselves, who characterize it as a "fractured love story."

O'Brien's Endless War

"The Vietnam in Me" is O'Brien's only explicitly autobiographical work since *If I Die in a Combat Zone, Box Me Up and Ship Me Home*, his first published book. It belies his previous complacency about recovering from

the war psychologically, and its publication precisely twenty-five years after his year in Viet Nam intimately testifies to his own traumatization. Despite its direct personal details, however, it is of a piece with all his previous work in its self-conscious fabrication of traumatic phenomena.
Ultimately, "The Vietnam in Me" and traumatic recovery have been the
dominant subjects of O'Brien's entire life as a writer. To date, the shape of
his career is a series of reimaginings of the war in Viet Nam alternating
with works in which it resides as an experience that is variously evaded.
As in the traumatic memoir, the physical sites of the books have alternated
between Viet Nam and the United States, but the ultimate settings are psychic, and Viet Nam and America have come to merge within the minds of
O'Brien's later protagonists. Thus, the antihero of *Tomcat in Love*, O'Brien's
most recent novel, is a professor of linguistics at the University of Minnesota who remains haunted by traumatic experiences in Viet Nam, retells
them to others, and eventually puts on his old uniform as he prepares to
avenge himself upon his ex-wife. The three "war" books include his first
work and the odd-numbered novels that followed it: *Combat Zone* (1973),
Going After Cacciato (1978), and *The Things They Carried* (1990). The first is
a war memoir, the second a novel, the third a collection of short fictional
narratives—three different genres, yet in a sense they all retell the same
stories. The works set outside Viet Nam—*Northern Lights* (1975), *The Nuclear Age* (1985), and *In the Lake of the Woods* (1994)—are equally varied in
literary type: a circumstantially realist adventure tale; a cartoonlike black
satire; and a bleakly inconclusive detective story that mixes psychobiography, history, and war story. Like *Tomcat*, however, each focuses on a figure
damaged by the war in Viet Nam: a returning wounded veteran, a draft
dodger, and a participant in war crimes.

Taken as a whole, the seven major works not only re-create America's
involvement in Viet Nam but represent it within the larger context of what
Alan Sinfield has called "the hegemony of U.S. Man" (267). Like the author
himself in *Combat Zone* and "The Vietnam in Me," O'Brien's protagonists
are embarrassed witnesses to the last half of the "American Century," traumatized by what they have gone through as observers of its violence or as
willing or unwilling participants. Even as the war has receded into history
from 1973 to the millennium and has increasingly become part of his characters' past lives, the extent of traumatization has increased from book to
book, as if both remembrance and amnesia were psychically dangerous.

Ironically, the character who seems to be least affected by Vietnam is O'Brien himself in his initial combat memoir. "The Vietnam in Me" thus appears to confirm Kali Tal's observation that "survival literature tends to appear at least a decade after the traumatic experience in question" (1996: 125). The progressively greater emphasis on such experiences in O'Brien's works suggests a personal working out of trauma through refabrication. Indeed, each of O'Brien's protagonists is a version of the author, and in two of the later works, the author's fictional personae are nearly indistinguishable from himself: The narrator and chief protagonist of *The Things They Carried* is even named "Tim O'Brien," and the unnamed narrator of *In the Lake of the Woods* is a former combat soldier in Viet Nam who has just re-visited Thuan Yen as part of his research for writing the book that we are reading. Furthermore, just as Tim O'Brien lost Kate Phillips after she had seen the site of the My Lai Massacre, the novel's traumatized protagonist, John Wade, loses his wife—whose name is Kathy—after she discovers that her husband had participated in the crime. Besides this merging of O'Brien with his own characters, many distinctive episodes and even details in later books are revisions of earlier ones (a full list of parallel passages would run into the hundreds); such recursive scenes mimic the intrusion of past experiences that is one of the symptoms of continued traumatiza-tion. More pointedly, several repeated motifs in the books are symptomatic of trauma survivors' behavior. Like the author himself in "The Vietnam in Me," for example, one or more characters in each of the novels except *Go-ing After Cacciato* becomes suicidal after falling into despair and grief. Norman Bowker in "Speaking of Courage" (*The Things They Carried*) fi-nally does kill himself, and John Wade self-destructively vanishes.

But O'Brien's psychically disturbed characters are not limited to survi-vors of combat in Viet Nam. In *Northern Lights*, his first novel, Harvey Perry has been physically and spiritually wounded in Viet Nam, but his brother Paul, who neither went to the war nor has any interest in it, is the novel's central character. Paul Perry seems to have been emotionally chilled by a terrifying childhood experience, and his life is marked by the alienation and anomie characteristic of trauma survivors. Childhood trau-matization also persists in *The Nuclear Age, In the Lake of the Woods*, and the final story in *The Things They Carried*, and it fatefully determines the twisted triangular relationship that lies at the heart of *Tomcat in Love*. Do-mestic security is threatened by survivor trauma in that work as well as in the three even-numbered novels, and in all of O'Brien's works after *Cacci-ato*, broken marriages or love relationships are as traumatizing as anything suffered by his characters in Viet Nam. Thus, the destructive merging of Vietnam with intimate relationships in "The Vietnam in Me" is found throughout O'Brien's works as they explore the private sources and rever-berations of public catastrophes.

After finishing *In the Lake of the Woods*, O'Brien was reported to be con-sidering giving up fiction altogether; and although *Tomcat* marks a wel-come return to storytelling, he has suggested that *this* might be his last novel. If the books are a working out of O'Brien's personal recovery from his own traumatization, then the body of work created may at some time be sufficient—at least insofar as fiction may be compensation or therapy for unresolved guilt, fear, anger, and shame. Regardless of any personally therapeutic purpose for the works, however, trauma is both their fictional source and condition, mimicked by form and style and at the heart of their power as narratives. Nonetheless, previous critics have largely left O'Brien's focus on trauma unexplored. There are only a few brief refer-ences to the writer in *Worlds of Hurt*, Kali Tal's authoritative study of Viet-nam- and other trauma-generated literature, for example. Indeed, al-though O'Brien has been celebrated as a Vietnam War author, it is a label that he strongly resists and that his trauma-saturated fiction calls into question. There have been more studies of O'Brien's individual works than any other American writer on the war, but relatively little attention has been paid to the non-Vietnam novels *Northern Lights* and *The Nuclear Age*, and the development of O'Brien as a traumatist from *Combat Zone* to his latest novel has not been considered. In earlier book-length studies of Vietnam writers, his works have been handled separately within generic or thematic brackets devised by the critic (Beidler 1982, Hellmann 1986, Myers 1988). When analyzed together, they have been part of a larger study of American Vietnam writers: Philip Beidler (1991) deals with all of O'Brien's works and those of five other writers under a generic rubric, "The Life of Fiction," but provides little more than a description of the non-Vietnam books; Don Ringnalda (1994) gives O'Brien a chapter in his study of experimental Vietnam writers but omits *Northern Lights* and *The Nu-clear Age*, as does Mats Tegmark in his 1998 reader-response analysis of *Combat Zone, Cacciato*, and *Things*. The recent full-length introductions to O'Brien's work by Steven Kaplan (*Understanding Tim O'Brien*, 1995) and

Tobey Herzog (*Tim O'Brien*, 1997) deal with all of the works through *In the Lake of the Woods*. Kaplan considers him primarily as a fiction writer rather than as a Vietnam author, a valuable correction of received opinion, and Herzog provides valuable biographical information based on his extensive 1995 interview of O'Brien. His bracketing together of *Going After Cacciato* and *Things* in a single chapter and his interesting perspective on O'Brien as son, soldier, and author reinforce O'Brien's status as a Vietnam writer, however. Neither deals with the shape of the career as a whole, the repetition and refabrication of incidents from one book to the next, and the role of trauma in all of the books. Nor does either consider why Vietnam seems to be both an inescapable subject for O'Brien and one that his books are constantly trying to escape, a paradoxical perspective epitomized by "The Vietnam in Me." Although each of O'Brien's narratives has its own form and purpose, the relationships and parallels between them, and the author's revision of himself in his protagonists, call for more attention than they have been given. O'Brien's most important source is not the war in Viet Nam but his own writing, which has created a fictional world of compelling integrity that reflects the self-absorbed anxiety of the generation that passed through Vietnam but has not left it behind.

Posttraumatic Stress Disorder and Vietnam

O'Brien's fictional world is both generated by trauma and also effectively rewrites it. As Dr. Judith Herman has noted in her authoritative study *Trauma and Recovery*, until recently the history of trauma and its treatment have been largely hidden, like the psychological ailment itself. In "A Forgotten History," she traces the three major issues that have generated professional research and treatment up to the present: female hysteria at the end of the nineteenth century, out of which Freudian psychoanalysis was born; shell shock during and in the immediate aftermath of World War I; and domestic abuse within the past two decades. Each was linked to an important political movement, and while fin de siècle French anticlericalism and post–Great War pacifism have passed away, the rights of women and children remain at the heart of contemporary feminism. Just as the related therapy is a revised and reformed version of the earlier work on hysteria, so shell shock therapy, initially intended to get soldiers back into the trenches as quickly as possible, has been more humanely advanced in the wake of Vietnam, starting in 1970 when the psychiatrists Robert Jay Lifton and Chaim Shatan began working with antiwar veteran discussion groups. Lifton's seminal *Home from the War: Vietnam Veterans: Neither Victims nor Executioners* (1973) brought public attention to the widespread rage, guilt, and self-disgust of many former combat soldiers and was part of a larger movement within the medical profession that recognized, researched, and attempted to treat a mental disorder far more widespread than the term "shell shock" could accurately define. In 1980, the American Psychiatric Association (APA) officially recognized "posttraumatic stress disorder" (PTSD) in its *Diagnostic and Statistical Manual of Mental Disorders*, third edition, revised in 1987 (DSM-III-R) and 1994 (DSM-IV). Concurrently, the Veterans Administration established an outreach program for former soldiers, and in 1981 Congress brought out *Legacies of Vietnam*, a five-volume, 900-page study that comprehensively documents widespread PTSD symptoms among combat veterans. Updated in 1992, the *National Vietnam Veterans Readjustment Study* (NVVRS) demonstrates the prolongation of the disorder well beyond the initial trauma (Kulka et al. 51). Work with Vietnam veterans has mutually benefited study of other victims of PTSD, and the International Society for Traumatic Stress Studies, founded in 1985, and its *Journal of Traumatic Stress* (first published in 1987) are devoted to advancing work in the field.

Today, PTSD is recognized as a disorder not limited to those who have survived combat only to be psychologically harmed by it. It also includes victims of industrial accidents and natural and manmade disasters; of rape, incest, and spousal abuse; and of violent crime; survivors of Hiroshima, Nagasaki, and the Holocaust; former political prisoners or POWs; and victims of torture. In short, PTSD seems a characteristic product of life in the century in which it was first diagnosed, which began with the Great War; continued with concentration camps, gulags, and nuclear terror; and has ended with genocide in East Africa, ethnic cleansing in central Europe, and the bombing of Serbia. A recent review essay by Judith Kitchen on *In the Lake of the Woods* juxtaposes O'Brien's novel with the Oklahoma City federal building bombing, itself a deranged response to the 1993 Branch Davidian conflagration at Waco. In her study of the literature of trauma, Kali Tal (1996) treats Vietnam narratives along with testimonies of Holocaust victims and recent survivors of incest. But the disorder is not limited in time or place. In *Achilles in Vietnam: Combat Trauma and the Undoing of*

Character, Dr. Jonathan Shay juxtaposes episodes from the *Iliad* and analogous situations encountered by American soldiers in Viet Nam, drawn
from his sessions with PTSD patients; and the epilogue to the NVVRS (284
ff.) identifies examples of the three chief PTSD phenomena—re-experienc-
ing, avoidance, and arousal—in Lady Percy's characterization of Hotspur's
behavior in Shakespeare's *Henry IV, Part I.* Shay convincingly identifies
eleven distinct symptoms of PTSD (165–66) in her speech, and Kirby Farrell's study of posttraumatic culture in the 1990s cites Shakespeare even
more extensively, as well as the St. George legend, Sherlock Holmes, H. G.
Wells, and Oscar Wilde's *De Profundis.*

The first DSM-III-R diagnostic criterion for PTSD is that the victim has
gone through an experience "that is outside the range of usual human experience and that would be markedly distressing to almost anyone" (cited
in Davidson and Foa 245). This paradoxical combination of the abnormal
and the universal obviously makes trauma a powerfully dramatic subject
for representation and suggests one reason for O'Brien's resonance with
his readers. "Usual human experience" can become something alien for
those who have gone through extensive distress, of course. Anyone who
survived Auschwitz or the obliteration of Hiroshima became part of a radically devastated community separated from the expectations and experiences of normal human society. Traumatization may thus become the
"usual experience" for certain groups of people: for example, survivors of
racial cleansing and threatened minorities, unwelcome refugees from civil
warfare, or children who have lost their parents to violence. Vietnam combat veterans, who may have been no more than 20 percent of the total
American military personnel in Southeast Asia, constitute another such
group: By the late 1980s, 35.8 percent met all the APA diagnostic criteria for
PTSD, and more than 70 percent had suffered at least one of the primary
symptoms (Shay 168).[1] Feminists would argue that for many women and
children in the United States, traumatic stress is not an unusual experience. Herman suggests that "rape and combat might . . . be considered
complementary social rites of initiation into the coercive violence at the
foundation of adult society" (61). O'Brien's traumatized protagonists thus
speak of a condition that extends beyond war stories and that complicates
the usual male paradigms of power, self-control, and purposeful violence
that Richard Slotkin's studies of American frontier mythology have inter-
rogated.

Traumatization, the individual response to the terrible experience, is both immediate and long-term. Faced with sudden, threatening, and unbearable stress, victims may black out, go berserk, or otherwise turn off part of themselves to survive. But delayed reactions of at least one month's duration—posttraumatic stress disorder—are even more disabling, inappropriately and often destructively repeating the initial responses to trauma once "usual human experience" has been resumed, and in complicated, displaced forms. The symptoms of long-term traumatization are complex, various, and multiple, and their overlap with symptoms of clinical personality disorders as well as schizophrenia has led to frequent misdiagnosis (Herman 122–24). A Veterans Administration list for use at outreach centers, cited by Kali Tal (1996: 270–71), includes psychic or emotional numbing; apathy; repressed anger, rage, and hostility; anxiety and fears associated directly with combat; sleeplessness and recurrent nightmares; irritability; suicidal thoughts and feelings; self-destructive behavior; survivor guilt; flashbacks to traumatic events; self-deceiving and self-punishing patterns of relating to others, inability to discuss war experiences with them, and fear of losing them; fantasies of retaliation and destruction; negative self-image; alienation and feeling "different"; and a sense of meaninglessness. The APA criteria for PTSD classifies these and the other symptoms into three general categories that Herman defines as *hyperarousal, constriction,* and *intrusion.* The chronic and debilitating nervousness, irritation, and sleeplessness of the first reproduces states of self-protective vigilance associated with the original trauma but now maladaptive; at its most destructive, hyperarousal can trigger frenzied homicidal and suicidal episodes. This disorder directly contrasts with the shutting down of physiological, emotional, and cognitive responses typical of constriction, which resembles affectless hypnotic trance states in which time and self-consciousness seem to dissolve. While constriction blocks painful and unbearable trauma-related responses and even effaces memory of the trauma itself, intrusion breaks through the repression, forcing the survivor to relive the horror through fragmentary, asynchronous images and sensations of the original experience, often in the form of nightmares. Constriction and intrusion are intimately linked, as trying to bury a soul-shattering event simply increases the pressure to resolve it. Shay notes that "a cycle of alternating states of numbness and intrusive reexpe-

riencing is common enough in PTSD for most authorities in the field to regard it as intrinsic to the disorder" (169).

Intrusive trauma typically appears in prenarrative, iconic fragments of
the original experience, and treating PTSD relies crucially on the subject's
being supported and encouraged to recollect what happened as fully as
possible so that it can take its place in the interrupted story of his or her
own life and enable that life to be revised and resumed. Psychological recovery thus depends on narrative recovery: The survivor must feel safe to
fully share his or her story with others, an audience that will not be incredulous or dismissive or feel threatened by the unspeakable horror that
has left the narrator with unresolved feelings of grief, anger, guilt, shame,
or disgust. Despite recent advances in pharmacotherapy, Shay notes that
traumatization cannot be treated simply as an individual pathology: "The
essential injuries in combat PTSD are moral and social, and so the central
treatment must be moral and social. The best treatment restores control to
the survivor and actively encourages communalization of the trauma.
Healing is done *by* survivors, not *to* survivors" (187). But he also stresses
that there is no quick or certain cure and that complete healing may not
be possible.

Trauma does not include every overwhelmingly distressful human experience but those that constitute a threat to the victim's life or physical
integrity or situations in which he or she becomes a witness to the destruction, real or potential, of others (DSM-IV criterion A1; see the appendix). Its poststress symptoms are the evidence of traumatization, but its essence is a radically bewildering and painful change in one's self-identity:
"[T]raumatic events destroy the victim's fundamental assumptions about
the safety of the world, the positive value of the self, and the meaningful
order of creation" (Herman 51). Tal notes that "trauma is a transformative
experience, and those who are transformed can never entirely return to a
state of previous innocence" (1996: 119). The self-shattering, dark enlightenment of traumatic events is intimately linked to the literal or figurative
death of the self, an awareness that can be more productively displaced
but may never be effaced. Although trauma recovery involves working beyond self-destructive fixation upon past experiences, seeing the death of
others or being threatened with one's own violently illuminates the survivor's destiny, which is everyone's. Therefore, traumatic events can never

be completely consigned to what *has* happened, because they anticipate what *will* and *must* happen, providing an illumination that can be difficult to accept. Witnessing the sudden and unexpected death of others anticipates one's own, and life as usual cannot be easily resumed after the survivor has seen the end of his or her own story. In *The Nuclear Age*, William Cowling foresees thermonuclear annihilation, and he knows that the world will eventually come to an end. He is right to be concerned, and he is cosmologically correct as well, but his trauma-induced enlightenment leads him only toward the futile destruction of himself and his family.

While trauma produces an individual existential crisis, it also raises larger questions about the ultimate responsibility for victimization and the lethal indifference to violence and injustice that may characterize social and political institutions. When an airliner blows up, friends and family of the victims demand that those responsible be punished, even though the only manageable response may be a redesign of aviation fuel tanks by the manufacturer. The treatment of rape victims often puts the American criminal justice system on trial, and to rescue the victims of ethnic cleansing and official terror, governments may have to fall and leaders be jailed or executed. Responding fully to the victim of trauma may require reforming the world in which he or she has been wounded. Jonathan Shay ends *Achilles in Vietnam* with a conclusion that recommends changes in U.S. military training and attitudes; Judith Herman notes that "the study of war trauma becomes legitimate only in a context that challenges the sacrifice of young men in war" (9). Governmental fabrication of traumatic scenarios is itself an effective means of validating and increasing militarization, whether the perceived threat is nuclear holocaust, terrorism, or foreign spies. The originating myth of Serbian national identity, we have come to learn, is a traumatic defeat by the Turks in 1389 in Kosovo. O'Brien's traumatic fictions certainly prompt us to consider the larger context of individual breakdowns, although his most explicitly polemical book, *The Nuclear Age*, has been regarded by many readers and reviewers as his least successful.

Although traumatization has intensified in O'Brien's later works, each of his protagonists is characterized by specific traumatic symptoms. The sometimes manic narrative voices of William Cowling and Thomas Chippering nearly parody hyperarousal; the narrator of *The Things They Carried* moves from one intrusive memory to another; in John Wade, who is nearly a textbook case of PTSD, constriction has become a way of living. O'Brien's fiction does not simply represent traumatized characters, however; it mimics traumatization through style, organization of narrative, and point of view. Among the characteristic devices of such enactments are repetition; fragmentation; violation of temporal sequence; lack of affect, understatement, irony, and other markers of emotional constriction; and images and actions resonant of unspeakable violence. Moreover, figurative manifestations of trauma are also recurrent. For example, Paul Perry in *Northern Lights*, Paul Berlin in *Going After Cacciato*, John Wade in *In the Lake of the Woods*, and Norman Bowker ("Speaking of Courage"), Jimmy Cross ("In the Field"), and the narrator Tim O'Brien ("Field Trip") in *The Things They Carried* all immerse themselves in bodies of water after terrible experiences that have left them feeling guilty or ashamed, as if they were trying to expiate, cleanse, or wash away a hidden wound or stain. But circumstances and outcomes differ significantly. Perry and Wade are initially suicidal, and each survives his deadly plunge beneath a Minnesota pond; however, whereas Perry immerses himself in summer, emerging from the richly organic slime to recovery and personal regeneration, Wade plunges into icy waters that reflect his inner state, and reemergence simply prolongs his misery. In *Tomcat*, O'Brien initially parodies these earlier instances of posttraumatic baptism. After his wife Lorna Sue has divorced him, Thomas Chippering returns one late night to his childhood home, where he "lay beside the birdbath and made fists and blubbered at the moon." (50). But his minibreakdown is interrupted by Mrs. Robert Kooshof, the present owner and his future lover, who is puzzled and suspicious to find a strange man crying in her backyard and threatens him with a garden spade.

Since all of O'Brien's main characters are survivors of trauma and all of the works are generated through first-person or intimate third-person points of view, the narratives are both products of trauma and vehicles of recovery. Although each character is a persona of the author, however, we cannot simply identify their traumatization with O'Brien's own. The allusiveness, elaborate formal structuring, and stylistic distinction of each story calls attention to the difference between the trauma artist and his subjects. Beyond the writerliness of the texts, moreover, O'Brien's fiction is deliberately marked with the very repression, amnesia, and displacement that characterize traumatization and that make a full and clear account so difficult to assemble. In trauma therapy, recovery of the primary experiences precedes and makes possible recovery of the damaged self and thus psychological reintegration. O'Brien's narratives mimic such therapeutic revelations of the truth, but each book refabricates the trauma of its predecessors as well as anything that may have happened to or been observed by the author himself. O'Brien's writing thus "recovers" whatever personal experience may lie behind it by covering it up again and again. "Recovering" and revealing the truth never achieve closure because the works are simultaneously engaged in re-covering and reveiling whatever may have happened through the endless displacement and fabrication of fiction.

PTSD and Writing

Philip Caputo, another important Vietnam writer who was also a combat veteran, has noted that no one who has intimately experienced combat can ever experience life in the same way. In her pathbreaking 1991 essay on Vietnam War literature and trauma (revised and incorporated within *Worlds of Hurt*), Kali Tal points out that the deepest source of much writing by veterans is the shattering experience of deadly combat and its attendant fear, grief, guilt, and sense of helplessness. Her argument valuably distinguishes the work of battlefield participants from that of other Vietnam writers. Her analysis also links Vietnam combat writing to accounts of other personal trauma: the Holocaust, the atomic bombings, rape, incest, and combat in earlier wars. According to Tal, all such literature shares three common elements: "the experience of trauma, the urge to bear witness, and a sense of community" (1991: 217–18). The incommensurability of such overwhelming catastrophes with normal experience determines a fundamental contradiction of all trauma literature, which "defines itself by the impossibility of its task—the communication of the traumatic experience" (1991: 218). Critics of American Vietnam War literature frequently note the sense of contradiction and confusion that marks many works, viewing it as a trope or symbol for intellectual, political, or moral judgments of the war by the writer (shared or illuminated by the critic). Such a hermeneutics may be relevant to writers who are making up experiences that they have not undergone themselves, but, as Tal notes (1991: 226), it ignores the directly personal stake of the combat survivor.

His need to bear witness to a personal trauma that must be unintelligible to the rest of us may account for discursive incoherencies rather than some ideological closure perceived, invented, or desired by the critic.

Tal's salutary emphasis on the phenomenological and psychological roots of much Vietnam literature may be extended further. Trauma on the battlefields of Viet Nam was not simply a solitary violation of self, like rape or incest, but a shared experience of grief and terror by men whose lives and deaths depended on each other. The collective "we" governing the narrative point of view in so many Vietnam memoirs and fictions attests to an experience that many veterans have later described, sadly enough, as the closest communal intimacy they have ever experienced. But Vietnam trauma was not simply a function of innocent victimhood either, such as the suffering of violated women or children or the agony of Auschwitz or Hiroshima. The abuse, killing, or even murder of civilians has been part of every war fought anywhere by anybody since the United States became a nation, but it was peculiarly distinctive in Viet Nam, where it had not yet been refined into the category of "collateral damage." The strategy of attrition and the tactic of search and destroy carried out among the rural Vietnamese; the peculiarly political objectives of the war, nation building and "pacification," so dramatically at odds with operational realities; the resulting meaninglessness of distinctions between Vietnamese who were enemies and Vietnamese who were supporters; and the increasing realization of all Americans that we were destroying Viet Nam while trying to "save" it—all these phenomena helped produce an unprecedented self-awareness of their own brutalities and atrocities by many American soldiers that coupled explosively with their own sense of victimhood. As a result, battlefield comrades might be doubly linked by ties of shared trauma: that which they suffered and that which they inflicted on noncombatants. Unlike other groups of trauma survivors, therefore, Vietnam veterans may have shared a guilt for their own actions that went beyond the guilt of survival itself. Finally, the trauma of Vietnam combat veterans was additionally complicated and extended by the outcome of the war and national attitudes toward their participation in it. None of the violence that they suffered and inflicted had any purposeful outcome because the U.S. effort was so destructively unsuccessful. Their comrades' lives were "wasted," to use the GI combatants' own telling phrase for death in Viet Nam. Another ubiquitous articulation, "it don't mean nothing," affectlessly recorded not just the horrors of combat but could serve as an epitaph for the American intervention in general. And for returning combat survivors, neither the civil war in the United States concerning the value and justness of what they had done nor subsequent national indifference, amnesia, or ignorance could provide a satisfactory resolution for their own trauma.

Beyond being the source of many individual crises, of course, Vietnam, the major failure of the American century, was also a national trauma. Because it was so spectacularly brought home through omnivorous media attention, the war engaged all Americans for at least a decade and its effects have continued to excite controversy, from charges about Bill Clinton's draft dodging to the furor over Robert McNamara's 1994 memoirs to the temporary elevation of John McCain as the only "hero" among Republican presidential candidates in 1999. Because it produced both personal and national trauma, reactions to and resolutions of Vietnam have been both private and public, and Vietnam literature has been especially susceptible to the mythic and ideological interpretations that Tal criticizes.

The national or collective trauma has expressed itself in various cultural forms as well, some of them redemptive, some pathological. For example, the great success of Bobbie Ann Mason's *In Country* (1985) among critics and readers alike, not to mention its successful translation into a Hollywood film, illustrates that Vietnam literature can attempt both to express and to heal the national trauma, like Maya Lin's epochal Wall in Washington, D.C., the setting of the novel's conclusion. The common expressions of national posttraumatic pathology, on the other hand, have been denial and amnesia or compensatory fantasy. Such symptoms of unresolved trauma were particularly evident in postwar American political mythmaking. While other veterans returned individually and anonymously, most of them to public indifference or embarrassment, some to public hostility, the release of elite officer POWs by Hanoi in 1973 occasioned a well-orchestrated public celebration for these heroic victims (Howes 7–9). And what H. Bruce Franklin has labeled the "myth" of abandoned POWs, a final cruel fantasy of enemy sadism and American suffering, senselessly and petulantly blocked political normalization for twenty years while perpetuating futile shame, guilt, and recriminations within the United States. The American failure to recognize Viet Nam was not simply a political gesture or economic punishment but also a nearly delusional continuation of the war by other means that refused to accept either defeat or peace, had outlived any political or economic rationale years before the 1995 normalization, and assumed that incarcerating Americans had some punitive or political value for the Vietnamese government. Even the insistence on a proper accounting of Americans lost in Southeast Asia placed more value on the dead than the living on both sides that would have benefited from peace and reconciliation. The continuation of our trauma also helped to spawn a series of Hollywood films in which Rambo and his avatars won a final triumph over the enemy at home and in Viet Nam.

A literary work such as *In Country* more honestly acknowledges and achieves imaginative healing of national trauma. But its ability to do so may depend crucially on the removal of its author, if not her characters, from participation in or direct witness of combat and death in Viet Nam. That detachment is not limited to women, Vietnam-era civilians, or Americans who grew up after the war. It includes soldiers who never went to the war in Viet Nam, such as the Vietnam literary critic Don Ringnalda, as well as those who did but never saw combat, such as myself and Albert Gore, Jr., together with those who rejected or protested it from afar, such as Bill Clinton. All of us have the idle privilege of either considering or ignoring what Tal (1991) has labeled "Other People's Trauma" (246) as well as the Vietnam experience more generally. For the combat trauma survivor who becomes a writer, however, the experience cannot be forgotten nor can it be as satisfactorily resolved in fiction as it has been for Mason and her readers. The memoirs of W. D. Ehrhart, a Vietnam Marine combat veteran, provide an instructive contrast to works that deal with Other People's Trauma. Ehrhart's narratives also help to define the distinctiveness of O'Brien as a trauma artist.[2]

W. D. Ehrhart is one of the finest of American Vietnam War poets, the editor of several collections of others' war poems, an important Vietnam War essayist, and the author of four Vietnam memoirs. Between February 1967 and February 1968 he served as a Marine in the war and saw action in some of its heaviest battles. In his introduction to *Unaccustomed Mercy: Soldier Poets of the Vietnam War* (1989), Ehrhart noted that "Vietnam has been a permanent fact of my life, a chronic condition, a shadow companion as welcome as a tattoo with an ex-girlfriend's name on it" (1), a statement that suggests how the trauma of Vietnam continued to afflict this former combatant many years after leaving Viet Nam. Its persistence is particularly evident in the memoirs. The first of them, Ehrhart's straightforward battlefield narrative *Vietnam–Perkasie*, was published relatively late (1983), after seven volumes of poetry. It represents the author as a flag-waving seventeen-year-old Marine volunteer from Perkasie, Pennsylvania, pursuing dreams of heroism in Viet Nam and finding only meaningless violence punctuated by the loss of comrades and the increasing callousness of himself and those who survived. *Passing Time* (1986) interweaves Ehrhart's final year in the Marines after returning from Viet Nam, his experiences as a student-veteran at Swarthmore College, his passionate involvement with Vietnam Veterans Against the War, and a period of aimless wandering and traveling after graduation, culminating in his service as a deckhand on an American oil tanker in 1974. *Busted* (1995) picks up Ehrhart's narrative from there. He is charged by the Coast Guard with shipboard possession of marijuana; simultaneously, Richard M. Nixon is twisting slowly in the toils of Watergate, and the book combines an account of Ehrhart's prosecution with comments on Nixon's. Both defendants are guilty, but both escape legal punishment at the end of the book, which invites us to compare the crimes of the pot-smoking, working-class, antiwar veteran dropout and the architect of Vietnamization, the invasion of Cambodia, and the Christmas bombing, during whose administration more Southeast Asians and American soldiers died than in all the previous years of America's war in Viet Nam.

Ehrhart's trilogy is a nearly paradigmatic representation of extended combat veteran trauma. The appearance of each of the volumes at least fifteen years after the events they narrate indicates the continued personal presence and influence of the agony of Vietnam and the need to bear witness. The last volume appeared twenty years after the end of the war and six years after Ehrhart's confession that Vietnam was an inescapable obsession. And by ending in the summer of 1974, its narrative literally leaves the subject in the middle of his posttraumatic condition. *Vietnam–Perkasie* graphically and plentifully records both the grief and fear of soldiers who are victims and the brutality and guilt of soldiers who are victimizers. The two later books extend the trauma of the war to America more generally through Ehrhart's experiences among antiwar protesters and their opponents, dropouts, and former veterans. The subtitle of the third book, *A Vietnam Veteran in Nixon's America*, intimates its evocative re-creation of the collective paranoia that characterized that era of American history, with Vietnam continuing as unresolved national trauma.

All three books nakedly present detailed symptoms of trauma-influenced behavior by Ehrhart, including sexual dysfunction, frequent outbursts of rage, actual or verbal violence against friends and lovers, and recklessly self-destructive acts. Furthermore, the protagonist in *Passing Time* directly recalls his own actions in Viet Nam, many of them acts of brutality against Vietnamese civilians that fill him with shame and self-disgust despite his combat decorations. Even his movement from unexamined chauvinism to dismissive contempt toward America and most of his fellow citizens in *Busted* is so extreme and without nuances that Ehrhart's ideological reversal seems somewhat pathological. Finally, the traumatic symptoms identified in DSM-IV are reflected in the style and form as well as the content of the memoirs. In *Vietnam–Perkasie*, horrific moments of lethal violence are presented matter-of-factly, with a curious lack of affect and reflection that suggests the emotional constriction necessary for them to be experienced without guilt or grief. The recurrence of these moments in *Passing Time*, often simply reproduced from the earlier book and juxtaposed with the other chapters of the thus interrupted postwar narrative, strikingly suggests the intrusion of repressed trauma into later experiences. And both the repression and the compulsive repetition contribute to the narrator's sense of now being someone other than who he once was, alienated from family, former friends, and fellow students; even the Swarthmore antiwar activists, whom Ehrhart eventually joins, often seem shallow and ignorant to one who has directly experienced and participated in the horror and evil of the war.

In writing and publishing these memoirs, of course, Ehrhart is relatively unengaged with Other People's Trauma because he is trying to give significance to his own, healing himself by making his experiences meaningful for readers. In contrast to the full resolution of Mason's *In Country*, however, the trilogy presents gestures of closure that leave the trauma unresolved. Thus, Ehrhart's public acknowledgments of guilt in having devastated Viet Nam represent moral enlightenment but give him no satisfaction. The guilt generates extensive reading by the student veteran and ultimately produces his own historical and political critique of American society and the institutions that allow the war to continue, killing Vietnamese and Americans for the benefit of an ideology that he has come to reject. American history is seen as a series of power plays and atrocities against indigenous peoples, whether Native Americans or Vietnamese, and

Nixon's fall is seen not as a vindication of the constitutional system but as an abrogation of the punishment that he justly deserved. Ehrhart's speeches, poems, and conversations gain supportive audiences among fellow Vietnam veterans who have rejected the war and help to create the sense of community that Tal defines as one of the three factors necessary to trauma literature. Yet the strident political radicalism of the memoirs seems as futile as it is necessary, since Ehrhart's political activism and his jeremiads against America have no practical effect that he finds satisfying.

Busted presents one final resolution of trauma into productive activity through the recurrent appearance of three ghosts of fellow Marines whose deaths in Viet Nam were recorded in *Vietnam–Perkasie.* These spectres share Ehrhart's enlightenment about the war in which their lives were wasted, and at the very end of the memoir they link their stories to his own by urging him to write for all of them. Ehrhart's first volume of poetry, *A Generation of Peace*, was published in 1975, the year the war ended but also one year after this imagined haunting in *Busted.* By re-creating and memorializing the coming-to-be of his own literary career in this final memoir, Ehrhart suggests that writing itself may heal the trauma of Vietnam. Yet even this resolution is problematic. The appearance of these three ghosts exemplifies traumatic intrusion, but their dialogues with the narrator violate the otherwise consistently mundane, realistic detail of his memoirs. These figures call attention to their literary re-creation, unlike the other friends, acquaintances, and historical figures whom Ehrhart presents. They are fictional characters, imaginative tropes for his memories of the dead, who may be the most important community that the Vietnam trauma writer continues to inhabit. While this fantasy seems appropriate for a trilogy that proposes writing as a way to resolve trauma, it also suggests that the resolution possible for the Vietnam combat survivor will be *only* literary. That resolution, as we have noted, has simply recycled the trauma found in *Vietnam–Perkasie*, and the power of Ehrhart's war-related poetry depends on the anger, guilt, and alienation that mark the persistence of Vietnam as a "chronic condition, a shadow companion" for the writer.

A more satisfactory healing of personal trauma for the combat veteran writer may be found in *Going Back*, Ehrhart's relatively neglected account of his return to Viet Nam in 1985. This is a mature, nuanced account of Socialist Viet Nam that reconfirms the war as an American crime without

idealizing or demonizing either nation. "I love my country," Ehrhart af-
firms at the end of the book (181), where he also registers the differences
between Vietnam and Viet Nam and his own movement from traumatized
survivor to politically engaged writer: "The Vietnamese have burdens of
their own to bear; they have no need and no use for my anguish or my
guilt. My war is over. It ended long ago" (180). Returning to Viet Nam
has helped to end the war for other American participants, including Vietnamese Americans and combat veteran writers such as the journalists William Broyles and retired Col. David Hackworth, the poet Bruce Weigl
(Schroeder 1992: 193–94), and the novelists Larry Heinemann and Philip
Caputo, among others (Baughman 135). Indeed, Heinemann, author of the
powerful Vietnam combat novel *Close Quarters* (1977) and the National
Book Award–winning posttraumatic novel *Paco's Story* (1986), is currently
(1998) writing a study of American and Vietnamese culture through the
prism of the Vietnamese railroad system. Such returns to Viet Nam, as
Renny Christopher argues, not only provide personal healing but may por-
tend an end to national trauma as well, which must involve Americans'
coming to peace with Viet Nam (and Vietnam) by acknowledging the suffering on both sides (309).

O'Brien's Art of Trauma

Like Ehrhart's trilogy and other writings by combat veteran writers,
O'Brien's works both represent and have been generated by Vietnam
trauma. But O'Brien does not simply reproduce or re(-)collect his own experiences; rather, trauma becomes a resource for further writing that both
replaces and elaborates with imaginative refabrication whatever might
have happened to the author. Furthermore, O'Brien uses Vietnam itself as
a resource to refigure trauma as a domestic and private wounding that
leaves the war behind. "The Vietnam in Me," which purports to be autobiographical, provides a striking example of such refabrication. The *New
York Times Magazine* text exhibits many of the features of Vietnam combat veteran testimony that we have seen in Ehrhart's memoirs. O'Brien's
experiences are both painfully repeated and repressed; the reader becomes the writer's intimate as O'Brien recalls horrible battlefield events,
yet he cannot or dares not reveal these secrets to Kate. His psychic detachment from her and from the Vietnamese whom he meets produces an

effect of alienation and dissociation from others as a result, and dissociation from self is evident in the suicidal impulses terribly present in Cambridge. During the scenes in Viet Nam, O'Brien summons memories of comrades who were killed in Quang Ngai, including a black friend named Chip who had been memorialized earlier in *Combat Zone*, just as Ehrhart continues to live with the dead whom he has survived.

"The Vietnam in Me" differs from other trauma testimonies in ways that are distinctive of O'Brien's work, however. Most recountings of Vietnam's horror are relatively straightforward accounts of personal experiences shared with other soldiers that try to reproduce traumatic circumstances as clearly as possible. Even a fiction like Heinemann's *Paco's Story* fully details the traumatic battlefield catastrophe that its protagonist has either repressed or can recover only as nightmare. Despite its figuration of intrusive memories in *Passing Time* and of muselike ghosts in *Busted*, Ehrhart's powerful trilogy, like most nonfiction memoirs, is concerned with clearly reproducing the circumstances of inexpressible trauma. "The Vietnam in Me," on the other hand, is meticulously organized and beautifully written in order to convey trauma unclearly even as it extends and complicates O'Brien's actual experiences. His agony has many sources: the deaths and brutalities of his comrades, the sufferings of the Vietnamese, personal guilt and shame over other undefined bad memories that have left him suicidal, estrangement and separation from his companion, and, at the literal center of all these desolations, his visit to My Lai with Kate. O'Brien did not participate in that massacre, but in the spring of 1969, one year after it had occurred, his unit regularly patrolled the My Lai area. Moreover (as recounted in Chapter XXII of *Combat Zone*), he had later been a clerk under the battalion officer who shepherded journalists to the site in 1970, when the atrocity had been publicly revealed. In "The Vietnam in Me," O'Brien reflects that he and his comrades had been as capable of such atrocities as Calley's men but never crossed the line to cold-blooded murder. Instead of providing any personal self-validation or moral resolution, however, My Lai becomes a climactic site of trauma for O'Brien, one that spreads its obscene revelation to Kate and helps destroy their relationship. It is also the vehicle through which O'Brien's personal crisis reinvokes the larger national trauma, since "My Lai" has become a metonym for all that was shameful and criminal in America's Viet Nam intervention. Yet even as the memoir extends its private agony, it also obscures it: Only by analogy or through imagination does O'Brien become a participant in or witness to My Lai, and exactly why this visit destroys the lovers' relationship is never explained, since Kate is largely silent in Viet Nam and absent in Cambridge.

Indeed, it is difficult to think of his companion's being in Viet Nam in the same way as O'Brien himself. In the scenes describing their experiences in the country, her immediate and direct reactions to people and places contrast with his own more complex and traumatic meditations. During a feast in the village of Nuoc Man, situated just below O'Brien's old firebase, she adroitly spits out a local delicacy into a Kleenex while he takes it down as if it were a private ceremony of atonement: "[O]ur hosts are among the maimed and widowed and orphaned, the bombed and re-bombed, the recipients of white phosphorus, the tenders of graves. Chew, they say, and by God I chew" (50). As he ingests, O'Brien tries to imagine that the repulsive food is herring, which leads to a series of contradictory memories, including herring snacks prepared by his father during half-times of Minnesota Vikings games on TV and his firebase's mortaring of "this innocent, impoverished, raped little village." The local food is "foul, for sure, but things come around. Nuoc Man swallowed plenty" (50). By contrast, partly because she was a child when the war was fought, Kate is ignorant as well as innocent: "Kennedy, Johnson, Nixon, McNamara, Bunker, Rogers, Bundy, Rusk, Abrams, Rostow—for her, these names are like the listings on a foreign menu. Some she recognizes not at all, some she recalls from books or old television clips. But she never tasted the dishes. She does not know ice cream from Brussels sprouts" (50). O'Brien's metaphors casually suggest Milton's *Paradise Lost*, representing Kate as an Eve who has not yet suffered the "mortal taste" that illuminates even as it brings "death into the world" (I.2–3). Similarly, when they visit the site of the My Lai Massacre, observe the Vietnamese memorial to the dead, and interview survivors, Kate weeps along with one of them while O'Brien takes notes and empathizes more authoritatively:

I'm exhausted when Mrs. Quy finishes. Partly it's the sheer magnitude of horror, partly some hateful memories of my own. . . .

Years ago, ignorant of the massacre, I hated this place, and places much like it. Two miles away, in an almost identical hamlet, Chip was blown into his hedge of bamboo. A mile or so east, Roy Arnold was shot dead, I was slightly wounded. A little farther east, a kid named McElhaney died. . . . It goes on.

I despised everything—the soil, the tunnels, the paddies, the poverty, and myself. . . . This is not to justify what occurred here. Justifications are empty and outrageous. Rather, it's to say that I more or less understand what happened on that day in March 1968, how it happened. . . . I know what occurred here, yes, but I also feel betrayed by a nation that so widely shrugs off barbarity, by a military judicial system that treats murderers and common soldiers as one and the same. Apparently we're all innocent— those who exercise moral restraint and those who do not, officers who control their troops and officers who do not. In a way, America has declared *itself* innocent. (53)

The final adjective may also remind us of Kate, whose innocence separates her from her companion's fuller knowledge of good and evil.

The employment of figures like the metaphor of swallowing or the paradox of bombing Viet Nam with love invests the account with stylistic flourishes that also evade clear explanations: for example, "I have done bad things for love, bad things to stay loved. Kate is one case. Vietnam is another" (52). What seems naked honesty is conveyed through formal and figural means that call attention to the writer's art and resonate beyond the details of O'Brien's private circumstances but also keep them covered. Moreover, although his internal obsessions are revealed to the reader, they remain unspoken to Kate. The dramatic situation at My Lai thus represents traumatic constriction—O'Brien cannot tell his partner what he feels and knows—even as the writing constitutes a therapeutic narrative that fails to achieve closure.

O'Brien's writerly self-consciousness is reflected by the roles that he plays in his self-revealing and self-reveiling memoir. Always meditating, reflecting, or omnisciently observing in Viet Nam, he registers the physical and emotional destruction of others, past and present. More tangibly, he takes notes at My Lai and elsewhere, thus becoming a researcher into Other People's Trauma rather than simply presenting his own, as Ehrhart does. And even though his own suffering is the subject of the Cambridge scenes, O'Brien explicitly enacts the role of writer in them—for example: "Now it's 4 A.M., June the 5th. The sleeping pills have not worked. I sit in my underwear at this unblinking fool of a computer and try to wrap words around a few horrid truths" (50). While Ehrhart and other combat veterans like Ron Kovic and Caputo narrate the circumstances and outcomes of their trauma transparently, as if writing were a vehicle for full representation of unspeakable experiences, O'Brien's account calls attention to its own writing and the difficulty and contrivance of representation, even as his identity as author of "The Vietnam in Me" usurps his former identity as combat soldier. Such writerly self-consciousness distinguishes O'Brien's work from most American Vietnam War narratives, and "The Vietnam in Me" is a particularly radical example because it seems to be so nakedly confessional. Of course, only a writer well-aware of his own authority and the certainty of his already having an audience can postulate, as he does here, the contingency of his being heard.

Ehrhart's trilogy dramatizes several stages of trauma recovery, including self-blame and guilt, education and enlightenment, and political activism; but whatever resolution is achievable resides in writing the trauma out through poetry and memoir (*Busted*) and returning to Viet Nam at peace (*Going Back*). Unlike Ehrhart's and other narratives of revisiting Viet Nam, however, O'Brien's represents a retraumatization, one that infects his relationship with Kate and inscribes itself in "The Vietnam in Me." Indeed, he asserts that returning was fundamentally against his will: "[I]t was Kate who insisted we come here. I was more than reluctant—I was petrified, I looked for excuses. Bad dreams and so on" (50). The deliberate indefiniteness of the final phrase, which vaguely gestures at stereotypical traumatic symptoms, is itself symptomatic of traumatization. But the encounter with surviving Vietnamese provides no closure, nor is it redemptive; it reignites private nightmares that are offered to the reader but concealed from everyone else around the speaker. Nor can O'Brien offer solace or even full understanding of the suffering endured by the Vietnamese, their words translated to him by an ever-present interpreter. Of the idea of "brothers in arms" suggested in William Broyles's title there is no trace. Ho Chi Minh City/Saigon was the lovers' final destination during their visit, but placing that scene last also accentuates the desolation ultimately produced by Viet Nam—"We hate this place," the final entry of O'Brien's morbid travelogue begins.

Although the Fourth of July back in Cambridge brings certainty that he has lost Kate, it also offers a resolution to move beyond trauma, which O'Brien expresses with opaque eloquence:

The hardest part, by far, is to make the bad pictures go away. On war time, the world is one long horror movie, image after image, and if it's anything like Vietnam, I'm in for a lifetime of wee-hour creeps.

Meanwhile, I try to plug up the leaks and carry through on some personal resolutions. For too many years I've lived in paralysis—guilt, depression, terror, shame—and now it's either move or die. Over the past weeks, at profound cost, I've taken actions with my life that are far too painful for any public record. But at least the limbo has ended. Starting can start.

There's a point here: Vietnam, Cambridge, Paris, Neptune—these are states of mind. Minds change. (56)

This riveting self-portrait has the form and function of trauma and recovery, yet it leaves undefined and unexplained the particulars of O'Brien's own—the symptoms, the causes, the resolutions, and the change that has been initiated. It is not even clear what the "new start" means: Is it perhaps new writing that leaves Vietnam behind, or the abandonment of writing altogether? O'Brien's "states of mind" transform places actually visited or inhabited physically into imaginative creations. "The Vietnam in Me" literally turns Viet Nam, as well as O'Brien's current hometown, into a fiction. We could only visit Neptune in a story, just as Paul Berlin's trip to Paris in *Going After Cacciato* occurs only in his own mind. O'Brien's indefiniteness contrasts markedly with Ehrhart's much clearer narrative of his own traumatic cycle and the final resolution to make his trauma meaningful and productive by writing it out for others. *Busted* was published in 1995, "The Vietnam in Me" in 1994, yet while Ehrhart looks back with implicit satisfaction on a career that has rewritten the trauma of Vietnam, O'Brien, the most successful of Vietnam writers, represents himself as needing to start over.

On the one hand, no *writing* could dramatize the inexpressibility of a Vietnam veteran's trauma more tellingly than "The Vietnam in Me." On the other, the confident strength of the writing itself represents a mastery of the discourse of trauma that "The Vietnam in Me" is practicing. If we ask what has produced the hopefulness amid suicidal depression of the Fourth of July, therefore, the answer must be the writing of the piece. In both revealing and covering up, clarifying and complicating his personal agony, O'Brien has given it a purely formal closure that seems to announce its end. Yet some undefined actions are still "too painful" to uncover.

Moreover, "Cambridge, July 1994" is followed by two final scenes that took place earlier in Viet Nam and extend O'Brien's elaboration of trauma. The first is a visit to a former battlefield near My Khe, now a rice field again, where he tries to recapitulate the details, unsuccessfully: "I doubt Kate remembers a word. Maybe she shouldn't. But I do hope she remembers the sunlight striking that field of rice. I hope she remembers the feel of our fingers. I hope she remembers how I fell silent after a time, just looking out at the golds and yellows, joining the peace, and how in those fine sunlit moments, which were ours, Vietnam took a little Vietnam out of me" (57). The final paradox relocates "Vietnam" as a psychic category, capable of a reformulation and persistence that counter its apparent closure on July 4. But the difference between the O'Brien presented there and the O'Brien presented here makes us aware of the artist behind all of the self-revelations, the re-coverer of his own trauma. O'Brien's last words in Saigon provide a final trompe l'oeil: "For now, Kate lounges at the pool. She writes postcards. She catches me watching. She snaps pictures to show her children someday." For Kate in Saigon, those children might have been O'Brien's. For O'Brien now, those children will be somebody else's. The poignant conundrum is a product of the writing that has allowed it to be produced, not the actual scene in Viet Nam, in which "her children" would have been the author's.

I have been arguing that "The Vietnam in Me" is not simply powerful self-revelation but deliberately contrived trauma writing. Insofar as all autobiography is produced by selective self-characterization and arranges particular life events in some purposeful order, it employs the means of fiction to represent real events and real people. In O'Brien, however, style, form, and self-representation are so self-consciously controlled that the trauma sufferer seems largely a product of the trauma artist's fabrication. At the same time, the sleepless writer who sits before his word processor at 4 A.M. on June 5 is also enacting traumatization. If we compare "The Vietnam in Me" with *In the Lake of the Woods,* the novel that O'Brien published in the same year, the slippage between the writer and fictional characterization becomes even more striking. O'Brien's protagonist, John Wade, has covered up his participation in the My Lai Massacre from the public and from his wife Kathy. When this dark secret is revealed, it not only ruins his political career but also threatens to destroy his marriage. In the course of the novel, he suffers PTSD intrusions and loses his wife—and perhaps his life. Whether the novel fertilized the essay or vice versa, the trauma of John Wade and the trauma of Tim O'Brien are closely related. Indeed, passages from one text are rewritten in the other. Thus, O'Brien claims in the memoir that he had himself felt the motivations that must have contributed to the My Lai Massacre: "the wickedness that soaks into your blood and heats up and starts to sizzle. I know the boil that precedes butchery" (53). These same feelings infect O'Brien's fictional veteran of My Lai in *Lake*: "Late at night an electric sizzle came into his blood, a tight pumped-up killing rage, and he couldn't keep it in and he couldn't let it out. He wanted to hurt things. Grab a knife and start cutting and slashing and never stop" (5). A passage in "The Nature of Love," the tenth chapter in the novel, replicates the memoir's paradoxical coupling of fighting in Viet Nam and the need to be loved, for John Wade goes to Viet Nam "not to hurt or be hurt, not to be a good citizen or a hero or a moral man. Only for love. Only to be loved. . . . Sometimes he did bad things just to be loved, and sometimes he hated himself for needing love so badly" (59–60). The fictional passage represents remorseful feelings no less truly, and actually explains them more clearly, than does the personal memoir's relatively obscure revelation.

In sum, the border between conventional fiction and autobiography is thin in these two works: Both narratives seem authentic, and it would be difficult to determine which influenced the other because both are partly derived from O'Brien's reimagining of the My Lai Massacre. Both texts correct the name of My Lai, the American military designation, to its Vietnamese name, Thuan Yen, information that O'Brien derived either from his trip to Viet Nam or from the research that went into the writing of both the memoir and the novel. Moreover, the novel includes an account by its intermittent narrator of his own trip to Thuan Yen, which echoes the explanation cited in the autobiographical memoir almost precisely:

> I arrived in-country a year after John Wade, in 1969, and walked exactly the ground he walked, in and around Pinkville, through the villages of Thuan Yen and My Khe and Co Luy. I know what happened that day. I know how it happened. I know why. It was the sunlight. It was the wickedness that soaks into your blood and slowly heats up and begins to boil. Frustration, partly. Rage, partly. . . . This is not to justify what occurred on March 16, 1968, for in my view such justifications are both futile and outrageous.

> Rather, it's to bear witness to the mystery of evil. Twenty-five years ago, as a
> terrified young PFC, I too could taste the sunlight. I could smell the sin. I
> could feel the butchery sizzling like grease just under my eyeballs. (203)

This passage seems to recall O'Brien's feelings as a combat soldier at My
Lai more directly and more fully than his testimony in the memoir. But we
would be wrong to think that such an explanation represents his actual
experiences any more than the memoir does. For one thing, this text is a
footnote that ends Chapter 20 of the novel, a collection of "Evidence" being assembled by the narrator to explain John Wade's tragedy. Is this
O'Brien speaking as himself or as a fictional version of himself posing as
the investigator of Wade's story? And in what sense did John Wade arrive
in-country in 1968? If he is a fictional character, what does that make the
narrator, who walked in his footsteps? Just like O'Brien in "The Vietnam in
Me," the narrator has also visited My Lai "in the course of research for this
book" (*Lake* 149), but his reaction has little of the traumatic resonance of
that rewriting of O'Brien's actual trip to the site: "Thuan Yen is still a quiet
little farming village, very poor, very remote, with dirt paths and cow dung
and high bamboo hedgerows. Very friendly, all things considered: the old
folks nod and smile; the children giggle at our white foreign faces. The
ditch is still there. I found it easily. Just five or six feet deep, shallow and
unimposing, yet it was as if I had been there before, in my dreams, or in
some other life" (149). With the exception of the final clause, the account is
matter-of-fact, simply part of another mere footnote to another collection
of "Evidence" (Chapter 16). O'Brien is representing the same trip in both
texts, but using it as the centering experience of trauma in one and as a
casual piece of documentation in the other. Because the narrator characterizes himself very differently in each, we can regard both self-representations as artful fabrications. But the reciprocity of fiction and personal experience here antedates the works of 1994. Four years earlier, "Field Trip,"
the nineteenth piece in *The Things They Carried*, described how Tim
O'Brien had returned to Viet Nam and visited an old battle site at My Khe
with his daughter Kathleen, where he laid to rest the trauma associated
with the death there of a beloved comrade. But O'Brien has no daughter;
no actual trip took place until 1994; and instead of providing solace, that
visit reopened and extended O'Brien's trauma—if we are to trust the testimony of "The Vietnam in Me" as being more factual than the fiction of

"Field Trip." Moreover, the imaginary daughter Kathleen resembles in both name and function O'Brien's companion Kate, who did look at My Khe with him later in 1994, and both figures' names and identities are rewritten in Kathy Wade, the wife of the protagonist in *Lake.*

But just as "Field Trip" both anticipates O'Brien's actual trip to My Lai in 1994 and is refabricated in "The Vietnam in Me" and *In the Lake of the Woods,* O'Brien's most recent novel reechoes the works of 1994. In the memoir, O'Brien revealed that he had considered killing himself after Kate had left him. In *Tomcat in Love,* Thomas Chippering is so traumatized when his wife walks out on him that he also nearly kills himself. His subsequent desire for revenge reechoes phrases and ideas from O'Brien's earlier reflections on the trauma of My Lai. John Wade's case is extended by Chippering, who claims human compulsions are "all for love. All to *be* loved" (160). Anticipating vengeance upon Lorna Sue and her second husband, his movement toward traumatic breakdown literally recalls Wade's and the author's own: "I could taste the ions. A fried-out feeling. An electric sizzle behind the eyeballs" (209).

O'Brien's reimagining of such experiences symptomatizes traumatic intrusion and repetition, but it also constitutes his traumatic art. "To bear witness to the mystery of evil" would refashion the actual trauma of Vietnam in order to illuminate a darkness that O'Brien's phrase deems universal. Thus, he refashions both his experiences and his works, transforming them into fictions that may achieve a more lasting truth than the particulars of one soldier's war. Among her case studies of traumatic symptoms in *Trauma and Recovery,* Judith Herman cites only one Vietnam writer, extensively quoting passages from *The Things They Carried.* Did she know that the whole work is fiction?—that the wounded, vengeful, and traumatized "Tim O'Brien" she quotes (137) is made-up, like the rest of the story "The Ghost Soldiers"?; that another "Vietnam veteran" cited as an example of traumatic contamination by the war (66) is a character named Norman Bowker, speaking in a revised version of a story titled "Speaking of Courage"?; that in the original, Norman Bowker was Paul Berlin, the protagonist of *Going After Cacciato*?; that some of Berlin's experiences recapitulate O'Brien's own in the summer *before* he went to the war, experiences represented in his first book, *If I Die in a Combat Zone*? Does fiction make O'Brien's representations any less or more authentic or true, after all, when they can be cited as cases by a leading psychotherapist? Although his canonicity might account for Herman's using O'Brien, the narrator "Tim O'Brien" is cited simply as "a Vietnam veteran" at one point in her text (70). Thus, O'Brien's stories in *The Things They Carried* are allowed to speak for all survivors of combat in Viet Nam. In turn, his next novel, *In the Lake of the Woods*, was to cite Herman's descriptions of PTSD symptoms as part of its "Evidence." In sum, whether confirming or incarnating Herman's paradigms of trauma, O'Brien's fiction, revising and thus transcending his own story, *has* achieved a certain universality. The blurring of literature and personal experience, fiction and fact, has seldom been so deliberate, so successful, or so productive as it is in the work of this trauma writer. But O'Brien's work differs radically from that of other combat veteran narratives, whether fictional or nonfictional, in that trauma is constantly recirculated in different forms with different outcomes, without linear progression or closure. This is writing that refabricates personal experience in order to transcend it through or re-create it as fiction, an art of trauma of which O'Brien is a supreme practitioner.

Writing Beyond Vietnam

O'Brien's brief Viet Nam memoir illustrates features that are distinctive of his longer works. Like the author of "The Vietnam in Me," his protagonists typically are meditative observers of themselves and the actions of others rather than actors. Each takes on the witness function of a trauma survivor, a subject position that also aligns them with the perspective of the author. As the very title of the Viet Nam–Cambridge chronicle indicates, O'Brien's Vietnam stories move inward, demilitarizing them and enabling a stylistic elaboration and muted lyricism that would be out of place in more conventionally action-driven narratives. That the distinction between fiction and nonfiction is irrelevant to American Vietnam literature has become nearly a cliché for critics and writers alike (see, for example, McInerney and Kuberski), but O'Brien's effacing of such distinctions is so self-consciously practiced that it becomes the central theme of many of his works. The interchangeability of fiction and experience supports two other notable features of O'Brien's work. First, he constantly refigures himself as his own subject, not simply to effect self-expression but to translate or even empty out his identity into other possibilities. The contrast here with a self-dramatizing writer such as Ehrhart is striking, just as O'Brien's relatively withdrawn and passive protagonists differ markedly from the usual figures of American Vietnam fiction and memoir. Second, just as he revises himself, O'Brien constantly rewrites his earlier work, so that an event narrated in *Combat Zone*, for example, will be refashioned in subsequent works. As we have seen, he can travel back to Viet Nam in three different works, all with different outcomes and perspectives. Within individual works, moreover, repetition is a formal and thematic device that also reflects symptomatic traumatization and reaches a condition of near-pathology in *Lake of the Woods*. Finally, the writerliness of O'Brien's trauma work is evident in its formal, stylistic, and rhetorical patterns and allusions but also in its awareness of itself as writing, a species of truth somewhere between mere facts and mere fantasies. The increasing meta-fictionality of O'Brien's novels makes explicit what was evident as early as *Cacciato* (1979): The most common subject of O'Brien's writing is writing itself.

As Steven Kaplan (1995: 9) and many other readers and critics have noted, the power of imagination is a recurrent theme in O'Brien, but it is more than just a theme—it is a way of redeeming the author's own life. In this writer, we encounter a radically self-absorbed and powerful imagination feeding on itself to produce a fictive world that has its origin in the trauma of Vietnam but tries to convert it into something more valuable and permanent. In fact, although the war is the raw material out of which O'Brien's career has been generated, it is not a comfortable or satisfying subject in itself for him. The former soldier's reluctance to return to Southeast Asia in 1994 betrays the writer's unease with Vietnam as a subject, even though he has capitalized on it. As noted above, O'Brien's "war" books (*Combat Zone, Cacciato, The Things They Carried*) have alternated with works that explicitly leave the war behind in various ways that will be detailed in subsequent chapters. The three even-numbered narratives may register the significance of Vietnam within American history and myth, but they are also attempts to get beyond the war, not only for their protagonists but also for their author. Yet O'Brien's most recent novel parodically revisits Vietnam through Thomas Chippering's actions, revelations, and imaginary obsessions. Rather than repressing or attempting to forget the war, O'Brien's Tomcat tries to bring it back home even as he is being pursued by its ghosts.

The conflict between leaving Vietnam behind and revisiting it is reflected in many of O'Brien's comments about his own writing and his attitudes about war literature generally. He has strongly emphasized that his first work, *If I Die in a Combat Zone,* is autobiographical and records his direct experiences in the war, although names have been changed, dialogues re-created, and scenes refashioned (Schroeder 1984: 135–36). This insistence on its experiential authenticity not only identifies his war memoir as nonfiction; it defines all the rest of his work as fictional, made-up, literally untrue to the facts of whatever happened to him, even though O'Brien seems to appear as a character and/or narrator in propria persona in two of them. He has also claimed that everything worth writing about his personal experience of the war is found in *Combat Zone,* which he was glad to have gotten out of his system so that he could avoid publishing "autobiography cast as fiction" thereafter (Schroeder 148). He has called *Cacciato,* which many readers and critics regard as the finest American Vietnam War novel, a "*peace* novel" and denied that its subject is the war (Schroeder 143–44). Such statements betray O'Brien's unease about being characterized or even canonized as a Vietnam writer, just as through his career since *Combat Zone* he has either tried to leave the war behind or to rewrite it as something else.

His personal aims as a writer illuminate this paradoxical stance toward the subject with which he has become virtually identified. O'Brien has been critical of what he regards as the triviality of much modern fiction (McCaffery 148, Schroeder 145). He claims to be interested in ethically significant ideas, and his common themes—"[W]hat's courage and how do you get it? What's justice and how do you achieve it? How does one do right in an evil situation?" (Schroeder 145)—sound almost old-fashioned and may reflect his background both as a soldier and as a student of political philosophy (he majored in political science at Macalester College and was a graduate student in government at Harvard after his year in Viet Nam). He holds to a similarly traditional view of the value of literature: "[S]tories can save us," the narrator asserts at the beginning of "The Lives of the Dead," the final part of *The Things They Carried,* and he has defined "the true core of fiction" as "the exploration of substantive, important human values" (McCaffery 138). He admires and has variously emulated Conrad, Hemingway, Faulkner, and Joyce—modernist masters who regarded fiction as a high vocation and their own works as metonyms of the contemporary world invested with higher significance. O'Brien's emphasis on ideas is facilitated by having his traumatized protagonists predominantly involved in meditation rather than action, typically reflecting on what they have experienced in order to make sense of it. Formally, too, O'Brien is nominally a traditionalist. "I don't like novels that seem arbitrary," he told Larry McCaffery in 1982, and he has a passion for well-ordered writing—"I like my chapters to have beginnings, middles, and ends" (137), he asserted. He rewrites sentences over and over until they are stylistically right; has published rewritten versions of *Combat Zone, Cacciato,* and *The Things They Carried*; and would like to find time to revise *Northern Lights.*

War is virtually the material origin of Western literature, the *Iliad*, the wellspring of all serious public narrative to follow, including history itself. Vietnam would thus seem to offer rich possibilities for a writer interested in handling the great themes of courage and its corollaries in carefully constructed fictions that extend the Western literary tradition. Given the military, political, and social disaster that characterized the Vietnam War, however, the conventional masculinist discourse of war literature is difficult to sustain. Furthermore, the mimetic, cultural, and ideological imperatives of Vietnam writing and criticism of it threaten the autonomy of literature that would use the war merely as its source. O'Brien's entire career, including even his war memoirs, has involved recycling Vietnam into something more significant than personal experience or information about a particular war. His own comments about Vietnam War literature are critical of writers and readers who are simply satisfied with therapy, information, or final moral judgments. At the same time, as noted above, he has been unable to efface the war from any of his works. Instead, he has endlessly recirculated his experience of Vietnam in forms that both disguise and refigure their traumatic origins.

In an early chapter of *Combat Zone* that anticipated the writing career to come, O'Brien simply characterized himself as a teller of "war stories" (32). The narrator Tim O'Brien was to comment more explicitly on the nature and value of war stories in *The Things They Carried.* "How to Tell a True War Story," the seventh of the twenty-two fictions that make up the larger work, combines a number of brief stories involving members of Alpha Company, many of them narrated by the soldiers, with the narrator's own commentary on war literature. The intersection of apparent fact and apparent fiction in this essay with multiple stories is only one of a number of deliberate ambiguities, beginning with the title, which has the appearance of a series of recommendations both for writers—those who "tell" war stories—and readers—those who are trying to "tell" whether a story is true. But in what sense, after all, can a "story" be "true"—and why is truth important anyway? The narrator's most explicit statement appears after the first story that is told: "A true war story is never moral," he asserts:

> It does not instruct, nor encourage virtue, nor suggest models of proper human behavior, nor restrain men from doing the things men have always done. If a story seems moral, do not believe it. If at the end of a war story you feel uplifted, or if you feel that some small bit of rectitude has been salvaged from the larger waste, then you have been made the victim of a very old and terrible lie. There is no rectitude whatsoever. There is no virtue. As a first rule of thumb, therefore, you can tell a true war story by its absolute and uncompromising allegiance to obscenity and evil. (76)

O'Brien's caution, both a denunciation of war and a guide to reading and evaluating its representations, suggests why he has resisted being categorized as a war writer. Any story suggesting that war itself has any redeeming value, the narrator asserts, is a lie; therefore, if such fictions seem uplifting, they are both factually and morally untrue or else their true subject is not war. Given such judgments, the only literally true war story would seem to be an account of human wastage, but would such a work be worth reading? It wouldn't correspond to O'Brien's narratives, which are more meditative, more deliberately artful, and more restrained in their reproduction of violence and anomie than most American fiction of the war in Viet Nam. Thus, the narrator is questioning the value of literature that passively accepts the reality of war either by falsely valorizing its obscenity or by simply reproducing it, although the two can amount to the same thing. For O'Brien, it is their very fictiveness that keeps the best war stories from being mistaken for the reality of war and allows them to transcend the filth that has generated them. "The obsession is not with horror," he told an interviewer after the publication of *The Things They Carried,* "but with making *art* out of the horror. Understanding. Beauty. In my case, the real obsession involves storytelling, exploring, re-exploring the past as a means of forging a new *present.* Which is the story itself: the art" (Baughman 211). Here the distinction between writing literature and recovering (whether through revelation and integration of trauma or through further concealment) nearly disappears.

"Absolute occurrence is irrelevant" the narrator Tim O'Brien notes at the end of "How to Tell a True War Story" (89): "A thing may happen and be a total lie; another thing may not happen and be truer than the truth." These paradoxes help explain why apparent realism is disrupted by fantasy and self-conscious fictiveness in O'Brien's war writing and why he is uncomfortable with being classified as a Vietnam writer or having his work limited to or validated by Vietnam. First, the subject of a "true story" is "war," a move that transforms actual combat in Viet Nam into a more universalized subject whose significance is conferred by fictional means. O'Brien has argued against the uniqueness of the war in Viet Nam by citing representations of war in *The Red Badge of Courage* and World War I poetry, a perspective that is literary rather than military, political, or historical. Second, war itself does not confer value upon a true war story; it is an embarrassing human reality transformed by literary shaping into something more valuable, such as the *Iliad* or *The Red Badge of Courage, Catch-22* or *Regeneration*. Finally, "truth" is not fidelity to direct experience but is closer to what Keats called "the holiness of the Heart's affections, and the truth of imagination" (letter of November 22, 1817). For O'Brien, imaginative truth is also moral truth, a reservoir of deeper or higher consciousness that he summons in his readers through the art of transforming facts into fiction. O'Brien wrote *Cacciato*, he has said, "so I could free myself from making authorial judgments and instead present a story. Let the reader make the judgments" (Schroeder 1984: 142). Citing the destruction of a water buffalo that he witnessed in Viet Nam and its transformation into a scene in *Cacciato*, O'Brien notes that the written version "takes on a quality of its own; you remove the preaching, the moralizing, and it becomes its own event. The reader has to figure out what it means, if anything: how it fits into the whole fabric of the book." The writing is "true" not because O'Brien actually witnessed his platoon obliterate a water buffalo in 1969 but because when we read the episode in *Cacciato*, we may imaginatively identify what is narrated as a little crime within the larger crime of the war, a "symbol," O'Brien has called it, that "represents something beyond that which it is." Like trauma itself, the episode enlightens even as it leaves all observers speechless.

O'Brien has rewritten the water buffalo experience many times, as the narrator of "How to Tell a True War Story" coyly acknowledges. But his purpose is not to re-create the war, his own or anyone else's; it is to produce imaginatively engaging literature that transcends the particulars of Vietnam through a resonant traumatic fiction. Because each retelling occurs in a different context within different books, O'Brien is not simply repeating himself but summoning us to read the symbol anew. His works have their own truth, he would appear to hope, and judging them by reference to fidelity to personal experience, the "real" war, or that even larger abstraction, "Vietnam," is a mimetic fallacy. "The Vietnam in Me" is one writer's refabrication of his own experiences, as the title alerts us. And none of O'Brien's novels or stories pretends to provide anything more or less than a literary transformation of Vietnam into writing that will speak truly to every reader. O'Brien's Vietnam is a fiction, a recurrently recreated imaginative world, like that of Faulkner's Yoknapatawpha County, in which the author and his former comrades and loved ones reappear in new guises. It is a country in which trauma is converted into art, whether in the place that the GIs called "Nam," or the Minnesota that O'Brien left in 1969 but continues to revisit in his works, or the Fiji that Thomas Chippering imagines in *Tomcat in Love* as the site where the dreams of each of us have been lost: "But realize this: Fiji is not Fiji. Fiji is Pittsburgh. Fiji is Boston or London or Santa Fe or wherever else your faith has gone" (243).

CHAPTER 2

A BAD WAR

Origins of *If I Die in a Combat Zone*

Writing a lasting book about the American war in Viet Nam does not depend on combat experience, as Bobbie Ann Mason's *In Country* and the more recent example of Susan Fromberg Schaeffer's *Buffalo Afternoon* indicate (Jason 1993). Conversely, such experience does not in itself produce significant literature. As O'Brien has noted, too much combat fiction is merely experiential: "[M]any published novels should have been written as nonfiction because their *content* is nonfiction: the authors are not trying to imagine; they're writing purely from memory. . . . Good novels don't work on that principle" (Schroeder 1984: 147). Nonetheless, as O'Brien and other writers have noted, Vietnam nonfiction has been more popular than Vietnam novels, probably because most readers of books about the war in Viet Nam proceed under an assumption of mimetic authenticity that they would never apply to subjects such as love, mystery, or science fiction: The value of the account depends on its being true to actual experience. Jacqueline Lawson, who has categorized the enormous variety of nonfiction Vietnam narratives, has noted that most have been generated out of the simple personal need to articulate what the writer found the most significant experience of his or her life.

Of the few nonfiction combat narratives that have received extensive literary and cultural criticism and are among the critically acclaimed works of Vietnam literature (i.e., Caputo's *A Rumor of War*, Ron Kovic's *Born on the Fourth of July*, and Robert Mason's *Chickenhawk*), O'Brien's *If I*

Die in a Combat Zone, Box Me Up and Ship Me Home was the first to be published (1973), and it has remained among the most permanently valuable literary treatments of the war. Like all of O'Brien's works except *Northern Lights*, what became *If I Die in a Combat Zone* first appeared as a smaller piece that was later incorporated into the larger work. This earliest fragment of O'Brien's war memoir was published in 1969, even before he had survived his tour in Viet Nam, and was followed by additional pieces in 1970 and 1972 before Delacorte brought out the completed work in 1973.[1] *Combat Zone* thus includes O'Brien's only writing contemporaneous with his residence in the war, and all of it was completed before the culminating catastrophe of America's intervention, the North Vietnamese victory in 1975, and the reunification of the country. As John Clark Pratt has noted (Lomperis 124), the provenance of any Vietnam work—chronological as well as geographical—affects its attitude and themes. There are fewer representations of traumatic combat circumstances in this work than in *Going After Cacciato, The Things They Carried, In the Lake of the Woods*, or even *Tomcat in Love*. This may reflect or represent emotional constriction, as we shall see, but it may also derive from the apparently successful extrication of all American soldiers from the war after 1972, the phony withdrawal with honor that lulled many Americans, and perhaps O'Brien himself, into thinking that Vietnam was over. The rewriting and intensification of trauma in the later books is thus not a product of O'Brien's immediate experiences in Viet Nam, which are more directly represented in *Combat Zone*, but of subsequent reflection and refabrication.

The writing is much closer in time to O'Brien's direct battlefield experiences, and it is transparently autobiographical. "Step Lightly," a descriptive catalog of enemy booby traps, was published in the July 1970 *Playboy*, but the publications in which the other early pieces appeared nominally rule out even the possibility of fiction: the *Washington Post*, the *Minneapolis Tribune*, and the *Worthington Daily Globe*, O'Brien's hometown newspaper.[2] At times, these earliest portions appear as contemporaneous chronicles of the war produced by O'Brien's ongoing experiences. Thus, two-thirds of the way through "Step Lightly," the writer interrupts his sardonic inventory of enemy mines and their effects on GI bodies to look about him in the combat center at Landing Zone Gator: "In the three days I spent writing this, mines and men came together three more times. Seven more legs, one more arm. The immediacy of the last explosion—

three legs, ten minutes ago—made me ready to burn the midsection of this report, the flippant itemization of these killer devices" (129). The use of present tense here and elsewhere makes descriptions seem to be situation reports and O'Brien a combat journalist with a gift for sarcasm and simile: "The troops are going home, and the war has not been won, even with a quarter of the United States Army fighting it. We slay one of them, hit a mine, kill another, hit another mine. It is funny. We walk through the mines, trying to catch the Viet Cong Forty-eighth Battalion like inexperienced hunters after a hummingbird" (129). Even formally retrospective chapters, like O'Brien's description of basic training, refer to the war as an event that is still going on: "To understand what happens among the mine fields of My Lai, you must know something about what happens in America. You must understand Fort Lewis, Washington" (40).

In early chapters of *Combat Zone*, O'Brien describes his personal history before the war, and we may draw upon this sketch to outline his life before and during his year in Viet Nam. Born in southern Minnesota one year after the end of World War II, William Timothy O'Brien, Jr., grew up in Worthington, Minnesota, and graduated summa cum laude from Macalester College in St. Paul as a political science major in May 1968. Drafted into the army in August, he went through basic and advanced infantry training at Fort Lewis and ended up in March 1969 in Viet Nam, Quang Ngai Province, where he was an infantryman and radio carrier for Alpha Company, 198th Infantry Brigade, Americal Division. One year before O'Brien had arrived in-country, and in the aftermath of the Tet Offensive, an Americal Division platoon commanded by Lieutenant William Calley massacred two hundred to five hundred Vietnamese civilians in Thuan Yen, a subhamlet of Son My village that was labeled My Lai 4 on American military maps. Among other operations, O'Brien's company patrolled the My Lai area, still enemy-controlled one year after the atrocity. He was wounded there and received the Purple Heart, but he never mentions the award and barely mentions the wounding ("Nothing hurt much"—120) in Chapter XIII ("My Lai in May"). During his last six months, he worked as a clerk in battalion headquarters at Landing Zone Bravo and returned to Minnesota in March 1970.

O'Brien's dual army career as battlefield grunt and battalion clerk initiates and anticipates the roles of soldier and writer that were to produce the work of the next thirty years. "Step Lightly," which O'Brien regards as his first published piece of serious writing (Schroeder 1984: 148), was evidently written within the time for meditation provided by his rear echelon position. If the writing of other portions of *Combat Zone* began here as well, it means that the entire memoir is a product of fictive reshaping after the fact, a deliberate refashioning of direct experiences recollected in relative tranquility. As Kali Tal has noted, most posttraumatic memoirs are written ten years or more after the primal event, but they present themselves as reproductions of the soldier's direct experiences and feelings. Even in his first piece of published work, however, O'Brien appears not as a soldier but as a writer who has been in the combat zone, a survivor of the minefields of Quang Ngai. Since we are made aware of the act of writing as well as the facts of this soldier's transit through the Vietnam War, *Combat Zone* looks forward to the more self-advertising metafictionality of O'Brien's later work. As we have seen, such brief glimpses of the author at work are multiplied in his most recent war memoir, "The Vietnam in Me."

Fictionalized Testimony

When he focuses on himself in his combat memoir, O'Brien often leaves the war altogether; the subject of such self-revelations becomes his own thinking rather than combat operations, and there is a separation between the imposed, external role of soldier and a more authentic identity, which is internalized. For example, Chapter XI is titled "Ambush," but much of it represents O'Brien's personal reflections in a night ambush position as he alternates sleeping and watching with Reno, a squad leader younger than the writer. His "memories and fantasies" include reflections on wanting to write about war, like Hemingway or Ernie Pyle, and recalling a serious but friendly conversation about Vietnam with an economics graduate student named Li who was also a lieutenant in the North Vietnamese Army and, like O'Brien, studied in Prague in the summer of 1967. What is imagined and remembered is more real and significant than the ambush, which anticlimactically and typically ends with no action at all. A later ambush in May, recounted at the end of the chapter, results in O'Brien's only possible kill in *Combat Zone* but leaves him reflecting again rather than celebrating: "I would not look. I wondered what the other two men, the lucky two, had done after our volley. I wondered if they'd stopped to help the dead man, if they had been angry at his death, or only frightened that *they* might die. I wondered if the dead man were a relative of the others and, if so, what it must have been to leave him lying in the rice. I hoped the dead man was not named Li" (101). And the chapter ends with a postscript to O'Brien's trial by fire that renders it even more meaningless: "The platoons had registered other kills. They were talking these matters over, the officers pleased with their success and the rest of us relieved it was over, when my friend Chip and a squad leader named Tom were blown to pieces as they swept the village with the Third Platoon. That was Alpha Company's most successful ambush" (101). "Ambush," which sounds like a conventional episode in a conventional Vietnam combat memoir, is thus a multiply ironic title: One ambush doesn't occur, the one that succeeds brings American deaths and anguish, and the real subject of the chapter is O'Brien's reflections, which continually remove him from the action itself. He actually feels closer to his Vietnamese counterpart than to the boorish and negligent GI with whom he's been forced to share a foxhole, who "liked his job too well" (93) but keeps falling asleep when he should be keeping watch. And even Chip's death is most important as a psychic event, since it eases O'Brien's conscience when he later participates in subsequent small atrocities. The abandonment of a soldierly for an authorial role is conveyed by various writerly references and gestures; the first citation above reads like the inspiration for a short story. Moreover, as the narrative of *Combat Zone* becomes a collective or typical account and the narrator an observer rather than an actor, the memoir begins to assume the form and rhetorical mode of fiction. Personal feelings and judgments are muted, and scenes are left up to the reader to interpret. This invitation to read literarily rather than simply following one soldier's testimony is furthered by O'Brien's naturalistic, precise descriptions of the ordinary details of situations encountered in Viet Nam, a characteristic of all his war writing that superficially places him among the realist stylists of the war. But O'Brien's work is marked by deliberate understatement into seeming to say *less* than it means, so that the reader's imagination is engaged and left to consider the implications of what has been registered.

O'Brien's first extended description of combat, which appears in Chapter VIII ("Alpha Company"), provides a good example of this summons to read beyond the details without authoritative interpretation. "It was not a bad war until we sent a night patrol into a village called Tri Binh 4," O'Brien introduces his account. "Mad Mark [their platoon commander] led

it, taking only his shotgun and five other men" (86). O'Brien and the others
wait, hear the infiltrators' weapons fire, and, ten minutes later, the men return with news of their success in surprising a squad of Viet Cong, bringing back the ear of one of the enemy, cut off his corpse by their leader.
"What you gonna do with it? Why don't you *eat* it, Mad Mark?" one of the
soldiers asks, and O'Brien continues with the lieutenant's response, and
then closes the chapter with straight narrative:

> "Bullshit, who's gonna eat a goddamn dink? I eat women, not dead dinks."
> Kid laughed. "We got some money off the gook, too. A whole shitload."
>
> One of the men pulled out a roll of greasy piasters. The members of the
> patrol split it up and pocketed it; then they passed the ear around for ev-
> eryone to fondle.
>
> Mad Mark called in gunships. For an hour the helicopters strafed and
> rocketed Tri Binh 4. The sky and the trees and the hillsides were lighted up
> by spotlights and tracers and fires. From our position we could smell smoke
> coming from the village. We heard cattle and chickens and dogs dying. At
> two in the morning we started to sleep, one man at a time. Tri Binh 4 turned
> curiously quiet. Smoke continued to billow over to our position all night,
> and when I awakened every hour, it was the first thing to sense and to re-
> mind me of the ear. In the morning another patrol was sent into the village.
> The dead VC soldier was still there, stretched out on his back with his eyes
> closed and his arms folded and his head cocked to one side so that you
> could not see where the ear was gone. Little fires burned in some of the
> huts. Dead animals lay about. There were no people. We searched Tri Binh 4,
> then burned most of it down. (87–88)

Although simply a recording of actions and impressions, this matter-of-
fact episode subverts our usual expectations of realistic war literature,
alienating us from the soldiers and their shared enterprise. The casually
brutal adolescent humor, racism, and macho posturing of the squad is typical of representations of GIs in other Vietnam narratives; but it's given an
additional twist by its context within a chapter titled "Alpha Company," in
that camaraderie, the only redeeming feature of war as represented even
in the antiwar tradition that stems from *All Quiet on the Western Front*, is
unsettling here, a ghoulish sharing among thieves. And O'Brien's psychic
alienation from his victorious brothers in arms, conveyed by the deadpan
understatement, invites us to see what has happened as more than just a

battlefield description. The mutilated ear becomes a badge of solidarity
that O'Brien is invited to touch, not just a melodramatic example of the
horrors of war, and he connects it with both the burning village and his
own sleeplessness. At the end of the episode, the invisibility of the dead
enemy's mutilation and the eradication of Tri Binh 4 curiously parallel
each other, so that we don't know whether what has been described is a
military operation or an atrocity or an atrocity that is being covered up as
a military operation. The outcome is typical of thousands of combat patrols through hamlets that were enemy strongholds—the residents have
left because they know what happens after Viet Cong are found to be
overnight guests—but the cut-off ear is palpable evidence of evil, and it infects the rest of the operation with a stain that goes beyond the violence.
By the end, the timid abstraction "bad war" has been given a local habitation without a single word of moral evaluation. The final irony is that
this is the most successful operation of Alpha Company recorded in *Combat Zone*, the destruction of what would be recorded as an enemy base,
and yet the good results make its moral implications all the worse.

The placement of this episode within O'Brien's sequential war narrative
is also thematically purposeful. The first two-thirds of Chapter VIII rather
casually describe his first month in-country, presenting the mundane details that we might expect in a mimetically directed memoir about the initial experience of being a soldier in Viet Nam: "It was mostly a vacation.
We wandered up and down the beaches outside Chu Lai, pulling security
patrols and a very few night ambushes. It was an infantryman's dream.
There were no VC, no mines, sunny days, warm seas to swim in, daily re-
supplies of milk and beer. We were a traveling circus. A caravan of local
children and women followed us from one stretch of sand to the next, ped-
dling Coke and dirty pictures, cleaning our weapons for a can of C rations"
(83). O'Brien goes on to describe a little Vietnamese boy who tagged along
as his personal servant; provides a brief glossary of GI lingo that he began
to pick up as an FNG ("fuckin' new guy"); explains how soldiers named
each other; and offers a character portrait of Mad Mark, the Green Beret
who was his platoon's commanding officer and would have been "the perfect guardian for the Platonic Republic" (85). The turning point of the
chapter is the clause "It was not a bad war until . . . ," cited above. "Not a
bad war" looks back colloquially to everything that has preceded it in the
chapter—O'Brien was in the combat zone, the caravan of soldiers and

camp followers was peculiar, GIs were profanely sardonic, Mad Mark was just this side of being a mercenary—but things could have been much worse. O'Brien's casual litotes metamorphoses into another sort of irony, however, through his representation of the successful search-and-destroy mission at Tri Binh 4. "Bad war" understates the intimations of evil that are conveyed by that account. And "not a bad war until" thus becomes virtually a thematic marker of the chapter as a whole, defining everything that preceded Tri Binh 4 while replacing it with everything that follows. Since O'Brien chooses not to describe the night ambushes and other earlier operations referred to in the first two-thirds of the chapter, Mad Mark's reconnaissance of the hamlet is O'Brien's first real description of combat in Viet Nam and thus identifies not only this operation but the entire war as a "bad" one.

That episodes like this one can be treated as fictional texts rather than just recollected events is reflected in some of the early printings of *Combat Zone*, which identified it on the book spine as fiction rather than nonfiction. Although O'Brien has conceded refashioning scenes, re-creating dialogues, and changing names ([Mad] Mark is the only actual name used), he has also insisted that the work is completely autobiographical and represents his actual experiences in Viet Nam, as noted in Chapter 1. While this characterization of *Combat Zone* insists on the fictionality of the six novels that have followed it, it underplays the reshaping of his year in Viet Nam into the depersonalized commentary that allows this memoir to be (mis)taken for fiction. At the heart of O'Brien's transformation of personal memories into paradigm is his own self-representation, which we will now examine more closely to see how the internal sequence in *Combat Zone*— the growth of or changes in O'Brien himself—cooperates with the external sequence of actions and episodes in its signifying enterprise. We will begin by reexamining the last third of "Alpha Company," part of which has been already cited above.

O'Brien's Self-Representation: Soldier Versus Writer

In the assault on Tri Binh 4, O'Brien is largely a bystander or witness of the actions of others. "I" becomes an explicit agent only in one clause within the entire episode: the account of O'Brien's waking up every hour in the platoon's night position, smelling the burning village and connecting it with the mutilated ear. In two other instances, the platoon becomes observer of the destruction ("From our position we could smell smoke coming from the village. We heard cattle and chickens and dogs dying"). But only in the last sentence of the chapter does O'Brien actually do something, and even this is depersonalized as a collective action: "We searched Tri Binh 4, then burned most of it down." Even omitting the pronoun in the final phrase seems to be evasive, as if the narrator wanted to leave us uncertain about whether he had "burned" as well as "searched." But the most significant evasion occurs in the middle of the episode, as a soldier called The Kid shows off the booty stolen from the Viet Cong corpse ("One of the men pulled out a roll of greasy piasters. The members of the patrol split it up and pocketed it; then they passed the ear around for everyone to fondle"). The transition from "The Kid" to "one of the men" to "they" to "everyone" records a widening circle of shared atrocity among these young GIs, momentarily transformed from soldiers to hoodlums, one that comes closer and closer to including O'Brien himself. But we can't be sure that "everyone" is used inclusively or exclusively. If the former, O'Brien, the FNG, touched the bloody badge in a gesture of initiation with his new comrades; but then the narrator's voice, moving from intimate to omniscient point of view, detaches itself from his own action, as if moving away from the scene of the soldier's symbolic crime. If "everyone" is used exclusively, however, O'Brien simply observed all the others touch the bloody token but did not do so himself. In either case, we are aware of his subject position as witness, observer, and recorder rather than initiator of or participant in actions, the position that may be associated with the activity of a writer rather than a soldier, although O'Brien is both, of course. Moreover, the episode is narrated both as a series of external actions and as the internal reaction to them, with O'Brien's consciousness becoming the theater within which the significance of this otherwise unremarkable incident resonates. It is only within that private, subjective field that the severed ear takes on its symbolic and moral countersignificance as a badge of shame rather than of solidarity.

Within the conventional battlefield narrative of Vietnam, "Alpha Company" functions as introduction to the war, introducing the protagonist to his fellow GIs and to combat. But O'Brien's roles as bystander, self-conscious observer, and moral reflector effect a separation between him and the men with whom he is titularly integrated in Chapter VIII. Furthermore, insofar as he participates in touching the ear and burning down the hamlet, this section of the book presents a moral breakdown within the silent protagonist, who participates in evil, like the rest of the soldiers, and knows he is doing so. (For severed ears as symbols in other Vietnam writers, see Constance Brown.)

The details of the Tri Binh 4 operation and the resultant dual alienation are handled as if O'Brien were describing traumatization, including the representation of his sleeplessness. Traumatic constriction is suggested as well by the understatement, lack of personal affect, and absence of evaluation or judgment. No Americans are killed or even wounded in this episode, nor do we see O'Brien acting directly. But he deliberately summons our own moral imaginations to engage with what has been left unspoken. The bloody ear is not simply the private symbol or fetish of an unspeakable trauma, because its significance within O'Brien's representation of this experience is clear to all of us. In fact, the lack of evaluation or interpretation forces us to make judgments, avoiding what *would* be merely idiosyncratic—as well as presumptuous coming from a member of Alpha Company—if he had presented his own moral evaluation. His positions as bystander/observer and register of shame that separate the FNG from more experienced yet younger comrades in Chapter VIII suggest dual roles of writer and moral reflector. Indeed, the internal narrative of *Combat Zone* depends crucially on O'Brien's taking on these dual roles. Within the memoir, both functions complicate and ultimately displace the ostensible and conventional memoir identity as soldier. Thus, self-representation in *Combat Zone* already anticipates the literary career that would incorporate but go beyond Vietnam. Moreover, because both writing and moral reflection are the subjects of early chapters of the memoir that precede the extended Viet Nam combat narration, we might even say that these concerns both preexist the war and outlast it.

Although its ordering of events is largely chronological, *Combat Zone* is a deliberately discontinuous narrative. An ambush in May 1969 recounted at the end of Chapter IX actually took place after the April 12 letter from a friend that begins Chapter XI and the mid-April operations that follow in that chapter; but otherwise, beginning with his account of basic training at Fort Lewis, Washington, in Chapter V ("Under the Mountain"), O'Brien presents a conventionally linear account of his life as a soldier. By violating chronology, however, the first four chapters implicitly serve as an intro-

duction to the combat chronicle that follows them. The first chapter begins in the middle of a sniper attack early in his year in Viet Nam, with
O'Brien and a younger soldier named Barney exchanging remarks while
spread out alongside a trail under protective cover: "We lay next to each
other until the volley of fire stopped. We didn't bother to raise our rifles.
We didn't know which way to shoot, and it was all over anyway" (11). The
next two chapters flash back to present details of O'Brien's hometown life
before he went away to college ("Pro Patria") and then describe the
summer when he was drafted and inducted into the army ("Beginning")
before we return to the battlefield in Chapter IV. Then, as we have noted,
a second retrospective takes us back to Fort Lewis and the experiences in
Viet Nam that follow in serial order.

Within what I would label a four-chapter "introduction" to the combat
memoir proper, the two Minnesota chapters are thus bracketed by battlefield scenes in Viet Nam, which are *not* presented simply as particular episodes within an ongoing personal narrative but as paradigmatic scenes.
The titles of these chapters, "Days" (Chapter I) and "Nights" (Chapter IV),
suggest an endless round of operations as ultimately mundane and purposeless, despite the threat of violence, as the ones that are described.
Chapter I begins with O'Brien's representing himself as a character already
rewritten into a dramatic scene; typically detached and observant, responding to the words and actions of others, he comments on the repeti-
tiveness of combat:

> "It's incredible, it really is, isn't it? Ever think you'd be humping along
> some crazy-ass trail like this, jumping up and down like a goddamn bull-
> frog, dodging bullets all day? Back in Cleveland, man, I'd still be asleep."
> Barney smiled. "You ever see anything like this? *Ever?*"
>
> "Yesterday," I said.
>
> "Yesterday? Shit, yesterday wasn't nothing like this."
>
> "Snipers yesterday, snipers today. What's the difference?"
>
> "Guess so." Barney shrugged. "Holes in your ass either way, right? But, I
> swear, yesterday wasn't *nothing* like this."
>
> "Snipers yesterday, snipers today," I said again. (11)

Despite traumatic experiences in the subsequent combat narrative, this
opening emphasizes the aimless and futile repetition that characterized
O'Brien's combat tour, the tactic of search and destroy generally, and ulti-

mately the entire American enterprise in Viet Nam. Combat is presented here without heroism or even conclusive violence; indeed, the soldiers don't want to encounter anything exceptional: "Johansen gave the order to move in. And slowly, carefully, we tiptoed into the little hamlet, nudging over jugs of rice, watching where we walked, alert to booby traps, brains foggy, numb, hoping to find nothing" (15). The image of tiptoeing soldiers is unexpected and macabre, one of many references in "Days" and "Nights" to the simple tedium and terror of walking through the countryside of Viet Nam, as in this excerpt from the latter: "We walked along. Forward with the left leg, plant the foot, lock the knee, arch the ankle. Push the leg into the paddy, stiffen the spine. Let the war rest there atop the left leg: the rucksack, the radio, the hand grenades, the magazines of golden ammo, . . . the body's own fat and water and meat, the whole contingent of warring artifacts and flesh. Let it all perch there, rocking on top of the left leg, fastened and tied and anchored by latches and zippers and snaps and nylon cord" (34–35). The infantry, the Queen of Battle, are reduced to automata or beasts of burden, dependent on the left leg, "[p]ackhorse for the soul" (35), the flesh nearly seeming to war against its own artifacts or what it is being forced to endure.

Within these paradigmatic scenes we learn nothing about Tim O'Brien except for the unheroic humping about that he shares with the other soldiers. Only the two pre-Vietnam chapters between "Days" and "Nights" provide specific and sequential autobiographical details, as if O'Brien's particular identity had been effaced once he became a warrior. Thus, although *Combat Zone* begins in the middle of battle, it presents this veteran's story as part of a collective drudgery that has *reduced* all of the protagonists to combat soldiers. Whatever the capabilities of the young man who had just graduated from college, took Plato's *Dialogues* seriously, and worked for Eugene McCarthy, they are being wasted in the role of soldier, which diminishes his truer self.

O'Brien's first four chapters deal with priorities quite literally as well as figuratively. We might say that we have already read two false starts— O'Brien as combat soldier and O'Brien as patriotic son of Worthington, Minnesota (Chapter II)—by the time we reach Chapter III, "Beginning." Only here does O'Brien become his ultimate identity, the narrator who is offering us his Vietnam memoir. The chapter begins with his draft notice in the summer of 1968, and it ends with his induction into the army. But the external events are merely the starting and ending points of a more authentic internal drama. An antiwar moderate as a student who re-searched Viet Nam and the war more fully after being drafted, O'Brien had reached a judgment that summer that has remained unchanged since: "I was persuaded then, and I remain persuaded now, that the war was wrong. And since it was wrong and since people were dying as a result of it, it was evil" (26). Years later, rewriting his moral struggle that summer in *The Things They Carried* (1990), O'Brien rephrased his opposition to the war by characterizing the lack of national consensus: "Certain blood was being shed for uncertain reasons. I saw no unity of purpose, no consensus on matters of philosophy or history or law. . . . The only certainty that summer was moral confusion. It was my view then, and still is, that you don't make war without knowing why. . . . You can't fix your mistakes. Once people are dead, you can't make them undead" ("On the Rainy River" 44). Such argu-ments, derived from O'Brien's reading of political and moral philosophy as much as from his knowledge of Vietnam, are the substance of "Beginning," which largely revisits O'Brien's meditations and reflections about whether he should have participated in a bad war before he had ever joined the army. Acknowledging both factual and moral uncertainties about Vietnam and rejecting pacifist arguments against war in general, the writer views his own agony as he languished about Worthington in July and August of 1968 and considered running away from his hometown, family, and coun-try. On the one hand, civic debts and obligations made him recall Socra-tes's refusal in the *Crito* to escape from Athens in order to save himself from an unjust execution: "He had not chosen Sparta or Crete. And, I re-minded myself, I hadn't thought much about Canada until that summer" (27). On the other hand, moral outrage and self-pity led to a futile protest against authority that is communicated publicly only in *Combat Zone*:

> The war and my person seemed like twins as I went around the town's lake. Twins grafted together and forever together, as if a separation would kill them both.
>
> The thought made me angry.
>
> In the basement of my house I found some scraps of cardboard. I printed obscene words on them. I declared my intention to have no part of Vietnam. With delightful viciousness, a secret will, I declared the war evil, the draft board evil, the town evil in its lethargic acceptance of it all. For many min-

utes, making up the signs, making up my mind, I was outside the town. I was outside the law. . . .

Later in the evening I tore the signs into pieces and put the shreds in the garbage can outside. I went back into the basement. I slipped the crayons into their box, the same stubs of color I'd used a long time before to chalk in reds and greens on Roy Rogers' cowboy boots. (28–29)

The self-deflating portrait of himself as vainly and even childishly polemical deliberately characterizes O'Brien as a buffoon rather than hero, an unwilling soldier without the courage of his antiwar convictions. Ultimately, he notes, "I submitted. All the soul searchings and midnight conversations and books and beliefs were voided by abstention, extinguished by forfeiture, for lack of oxygen, by a sort of sleepwalking default. It was no decision, no chain of ideas or reasons, that steered me into the war" (30–31).

But the chapter has a postscript following O'Brien's account of his induction. Suddenly moving from past events to present reflections, O'Brien offers an envoy to the book that we are only beginning to read. Addressing us directly as author, he wishes that

this book could take the form of a plea for everlasting peace, a plea from one who knows, from one who's been there and come back, an old soldier looking back at a dying war.

That would be good. It would be fine to integrate it all to persuade my younger brother and perhaps some others to say no to wrong wars.

Or it would be fine to confirm the old beliefs about war: It's horrible, but it's a crucible of men and events and, in the end, it makes more of a man out of you.

But, still, none of this seems right. (31)

The optative mood makes this reflection seem an author's honest confession of inadequacy. The two conventional purposes of combat narratives—denouncing war or validating its formative effect on personal identity—have not been achieved in *Combat Zone*, O'Brien appears to concede. The latter, the combat bildungsroman, is of course an older and more conventional handling of war that appears only fitfully in Vietnam narratives; the former, the Vietnam veteran's authoritative protest, is more conventional in Vietnam memoirs, including the well-regarded works of Ehrhart, Kovic, and Caputo. But for Tim O'Brien, the reluctant soldier, the silent protester who went to the war against his will, either scenario would be dishonest to his own experience.

In the end, O'Brien has chosen another way out of the war that turns his personal confusion into something more meaningful. He ends Chapter III by turning its pervasive irony against himself in a new direction: "Now, war ended, all I am left with are simple, unprofound scraps of truth. Men die. Fear hurts and humiliates. It is hard to be brave. It is hard to know what bravery *is*. Dead human beings are heavy and awkward to carry, things smell different in Viet Nam, soldiers are dreamers, drill sergeants are boors, some men thought the war was proper and others didn't and most didn't care. Is that the stuff for a morality lesson, even for a theme?" (31) The "lessons of Vietnam" are of little value in themselves: a mixture of personal experiences and reactions on the one hand and, on the other, revelations that do not require participation in a bad war to be realized. Whether as material for homiletics or for literature, combat has no intrinsic human value. Pushing its skepticism further with additional rhetorical questions, the chapter concludes on a grace note: "Do dreams offer lessons? Do nightmares have themes, do we awaken and analyze them and live our lives and advise others as a result? Can the foot soldier teach anything important about war, merely for having been there? I think not. He can tell war stories" (31–32). As noted in Chapter 1, O'Brien's narrator was to comment on the value and nature of war stories in *The Things They Carried*. Combining the extremes of what may be only imagined and what has been merely experienced, they can transform Vietnam into a meaningful fiction that may be shared by writer and reader. O'Brien's tone remains self-deprecating—only the possibility of simply telling stories constitutes his claim—but the entire passage is an implicit critique of privileging combat and of simply providing information, moral polemics, or therapy as substitutes for literature.

By the end of the chapter, O'Brien has brought together past and present, his career as a soldier and his career as a writer, his army induction and his author's introduction. In one sense, he has changed identities; in another, the self-absorbed reluctant draftee and callow political philosopher have been re-created by the author. The final self-representation anticipates the entire career to come: O'Brien's insistence on the greater significance of stories over the experiences that they transform has been fundamental to his fictional purposes and practice, beginning with *Combat Zone*. Indeed, this coda to Chapter III anticipates the writing that follows, the refabricated sequential narrative that both follows and fractures our conventional expectations of a combat chronicle or memoir. We have noted that O'Brien's self-representation metamorphoses throughout these early chapters of the book—from Vietnam grunt to son of Minnesota and finally to feebly antiwar college graduate and apathetic draftee in Chapter III. But the final identity, combat soldier turned writer, both follows and precedes all the rest. At the end of this third chapter, "Beginning," constituting himself as a storyteller defines the final origin of all the selves that are represented in O'Brien's postwar memoir.

Chapter IV, "Nights," which completes the sequence of paradigmatic scenes that began with "Days," largely follows its predecessor's technique of providing actual details of the combat zone without commentary or personal feelings. It ends with the men of Alpha Company bedding down in their night position, looking out fearfully as the landscape of Quang Ngai loses its color and form to darkness and becomes a mysterious and threatening template upon which they inscribe the presence of the enemy. Barney pulls out a starlight scope, the latest miracle of American military technology, which uses the light of the heavens to bathe the darkness with illumination, and they take turns looking through it: "[T]hrough the scope, nothing moved. The colors were green. Bright, translucent green like the instrument panel in a jet plane at night. 'It's not right,' Bates murmured. 'Seeing at night—there's something evil about it.'" O'Brien continues to be obsessed by the instrument as the night watch continues:

Chip went off to sleep. Soon Barney joined him, and together Bates and I used the scope.

I watched the green dancing night.

"I wish for peace," Bates said.

A green fire. The countryside burned green at night, and I saw it. I saw the clouds move. I saw the vast, deep sleep of the paddies. I saw how the land was just the land.

I laughed, and Bates laughed, and soon the lieutenant came over and told us to quiet down.

We put the scope back in its case.

"Who needs it?" Bates said.

For a time we just sat there. We watched the dark grow on itself, and we let our imaginations do the rest. (39)

Finally crawling into their ponchos, the two soldiers bid each other good night, Bates clinging to his rifle and looking out into the darkness as "Nights" comes to an end.

Placed just after O'Brien's miniessay on telling war stories in the previous chapter, this exquisite episode both illustrates and symbolizes his fictionalizing practice. The "green fire" recalls Wilfred Owen's "green sea" of poisoned landscape seen through the speaker's gas mask in "Dulce et Decorum Est" (a poem ironically fragmented within *Combat Zone*, as we will see) and alludes as well to the actual burning of the landscape that was one of the accompaniments of combat patrols. The "evil" scope recalls the preinductee's rage against the war in "Beginning" and tropically calls to mind the technologically advanced havoc that America brought to Viet Nam as we fought the war our way. But the scene is also genuinely pastoral, the scope also a plaything that contents even Bates and allows him to think of peace.

Symbolically, the scope and its star-generated illumination remind us of the instrument of fiction itself, imaginatively transforming the real landscape and, more generally, the darkness of Viet Nam for American observers into something that is less obscure. Its potential for abuse and distortion is acknowledged—there can be something "evil" about it—and we may not need it, if we don't care to understand Vietnam. If we do, however, a clarifying, ordering vehicle is needed to comprehend the darkness. O'Brien enacts the role of reader as well as writer here, since the scope both registers what's there and transforms it into something satisfyingly meaningful. And although the vision may seem temporary, it can change our perception of what has been illuminated. Since O'Brien goes to sleep as the chapter ends, we might even entertain another fiction: that the chronological narrative of the next nineteen chapters is the writer's dream, re-created with clarifying and magnifying power through the imagination's starlight scope.

Moral Combat

O'Brien's futile opposition to the war, which is recounted in "Beginning,"
underlies the representation of Vietnam and self in all the works that follow *Combat Zone.* The account in Chapter III is not only the "beginning" of
this moral trauma but persists throughout the narrative. He returns to it
even more decisively in Chapter VI, the ironically titled "Escape." Back at
Fort Lewis, Washington, for advanced infantry training, O'Brien found himself assigned to Viet Nam as a combat soldier. No pacifist and not even radically antimilitary, he was now forced to choose directly whether or not he
would participate in a bad war. "Escape" details his attempts to be reas-
signed, beginning with fruitless interviews with the unit chaplain and battalion commander. In the end, he was forced to devise a careful plan to desert across the Canadian border and then fly to Sweden. "Escape" details
the painstaking preparations for flight, which led him to write self-justifying letters to family and friends and take a weekend leave in preparation
for a final bus ride into British Columbia and exile. But at the last moment,
ill with fever and fear in a Seattle hotel, he could not go through with it: "I
burned the letters to my family. I read the others and burned them, too. It
was over. I simply couldn't bring myself to flee. Family, the home town,
friends, history, tradition, fear, confusion, exile: I could not run. I went into
the hallway and bought a Coke. When I finished it I felt better, clearer-
headed, and burned the plans. I was a coward. I was sick" (73).

The implied paradox of being a coward by remaining a soldier, which
sees running away as a test of courage ("I could not run"), has been at the
heart of O'Brien's self-representations in all his works. Twenty-five years
after the decision, it is the conclusion of a "Cambridge, June 1994" section
of "The Vietnam in Me": "I have written some of this before, but I must
write it again. I was a coward. I went to Vietnam" (52). Defining his decision
to fight in Viet Nam as both moral and intellectual cowardice *and* loyalty
to family and friends' expectations characterizes his combat career as an
unheroic choice between two shames, complicating not only conventional
notions of courage but also of what constitutes right and wrong. As a result, both the memoir and all the subsequent war fiction take as a given
that the war was unjust and immoral, but dramatize what that meant for
the men who had to fight it, including the author. O'Brien's Vietnam writ-

ing thus originates from a conflicted moral position that antedated his arrival in Viet Nam, has never been personally or politically resolved, and
has been subsequently rewritten in various ways throughout his career.
Within the battlefield narrative of *Combat Zone*, it helps to account for the
protagonist's relative silence, his unheroic self-representation, and the lack
of political or polemical judgments. Deprived of the ideological certainty
and moral self-righteousness of many of the literary critics of the war, unable or unwilling simply to condemn it like Kovic, Ehrhart, or Caputo—
eager volunteers who only later became antiwar critics—O'Brien has variously refabricated the moral complexity and ambiguity of his own
experience in his writing. The epigraph of *Combat Zone* is an excerpt from
Dante's *Paradiso*, Canto V: "[T]he greatest gift that God in his bounty /
made in creation . . . / . . . was the freedom of the will" (Sinclair translation).[3] The freedom to make moral choices is dramatized in O'Brien's decision to go to Viet Nam, but the choice leaves him feeling dishonored and
unsatisfied.

The quotation from Dante is one of numerous literary and philosophi-
cal citations in *Combat Zone*. For example, an excerpted Socratic dialogue
from the *Laches* is quoted directly in the middle of Chapter XVI, whose title, "Wise Endurance," is itself a definition of courage within Plato's work.
The chapter is organized as a personal exercise in moral philosophy by
O'Brien, who combines his own reflections on courage with descriptions of
actual operations and a character study of the company commander, Captain Johansen. As a platoon radio carrier, O'Brien was both physically and
operationally close to the captain, but in this chapter he is also spiritually
close, recounting two brief conversations between himself and Johansen
about bravery. By the end of the chapter, Johansen has become the only
real hero presented in O'Brien's memoir, joining the fictive figures mentioned in this anatomy of courage: Hemingway's Frederic Henry, Melville's
Captain Vere, Bogart in *Casablanca*, and Alan Ladd in *Shane*. Replaced by a
new commander, Captain Smith, whose self-destructive incompetence is
recounted in "July," the following chapter, Johansen enters O'Brien's exclu-
sive pantheon:

On the outside, things did not change much after Captain Johansen. . . .

But losing him was like the Trojans losing Hector. He gave some amount
of reason to fight. Certainly there were never any political reasons. The war,

like Hector's own war, was silly and stupid. . . . Captain Johansen helped to
mitigate and melt the silliness, showing the grace and poise a man can have
under the worst of circumstances, a wrong war. We clung to him. (145)

The operations recounted in "Wise Endurance" are used to illustrate what
courage is and isn't, so that the chapter becomes a moral investigation
with examples, with O'Brien himself the investigator. Here as elsewhere,
the details of the war gain significance only from their reshaping by the
author, which is much more explicit than in the quasi-fictive "Alpha Company." As in the rest of the combat narrative from Chapters V through
XXII, the memoir is most meaningful where most internalized, and
O'Brien's identity is most fully developed in passages of reflection or meditation and most effaced when he is acting as a soldier.

O'Brien presents an actual Platonic interlocutor in these chapters, a
friend in basic training named Erik with whom he shares friendship, literature, and philosophy while contemning the "boors and bullies," including
their fellow trainees, with whom they share the "cattle pen" of military life
(52). Later in Viet Nam, the spiritual comrades continue to exchange letters.
But O'Brien's earlier assumptions of moral and intellectual superiority are
treated ironically, as when he celebrates the two friends' contempt for the
protocols of basic training as a secret operation against the army:

> The idea, loosely, was to preserve ourselves. It was a two-man war of sur-
> vival, and we fought like guerrillas, jabbing in the lance, drawing a trickle of
> army blood, running like rabbits. We hid in the masses. Right under their
> bloodshot eyes. We exposed them, even if they were blind and deaf to it.
> We'd let them die of anemia, a little blood at a time. It was a war of resist-
> ance; the objective was to save our souls. . . . Our private conversations were
> the cornerstone of the resistance. . . . Simply to think and talk and try to un-
> derstand was evidence that we were not cattle or machines. (42–43)

Nearly all of the cattle who endured basic training with O'Brien in 1968
would have despised it as much as he did, but few would have been able
to label their dissatisfaction spiritual salvation. When faced with an actual
opportunity to reject not only the army but an evil war, however, O'Brien
failed to escape, so that the private, philosophic rebellion detailed in
"Under the Mountain" seems only a posture of real resistance. Once he becomes a combat soldier, O'Brien continues to be truest to himself when

most private or reflective, but the most important ethical issue is no longer the morality of the army or the justness of Vietnam but, as we have seen, courage—What is bravery once you have submitted yourself to a bad war? Instead of clothing personal outrage in the guise of categorical statements, O'Brien uses irony, understatement, and quasi-fictional scenes to register the war's moral darkness imaginatively, as in "Alpha Company."

O'Brien's use of allusions and his representations of the Vietnamese also anatomize the war morally, while providing a counterstructure to the combat memoir's overall chronological sequence. The conventional Horatian dictum *dulce et decorum est pro patria mori* ("it is sweet and fitting to die for the fatherland") is alluded to several times within *Combat Zone*: Erik recites Pound's mockery of its relevance to the horrors of the Great War in *Hugh Selwyn Mauberley* ("Died some, pro patria / non 'dulce' non 'et décor'"—45), and O'Brien is similarly contemptuous with reference to the American war in Viet Nam: "Horace's old do-or-die aphorism—'Dulce et decorum est pro patria mori'—was just an epitaph for the insane" (174). More significantly, he uses the expression as a title, like Wilfred Owen, but fragments its parts into three separate chapter headings in *Combat Zone*. Its applicability to Vietnam is thus obviously called into question, yet the bitter condemnation of patriotic gore found in Owen's great World War I antiwar poem is also undercut by O'Brien. Horace's words (and Owen's title) are parceled out among chapters that present different stages of O'Brien's combat biography: boyhood, service as a combat soldier in Viet Nam, and service as an army clerk in Viet Nam. "Pro Patria" ("for one's country"), Chapter II, presents O'Brien as a typical product of the American century—"I was fed by the spoils of 1945 victory" (20)—and of a small prairie town in Minnesota that billed itself as the Turkey Capital of the World, where patriotism, baseball, and wage-earning were as inevitable as small-minded conformity. The land had originally been taken from the Indians, we are reminded, and when O'Brien leaves for college, disturbed and uncertain about the latest American war, town and native son seem to be connected only by mutual indifference.

"Dulce et Decorum" ("sweet and fitting"), Chapter XIX, describes O'Brien's ultimately successful attempt to be transferred to a relatively safe desk job back at Chu Lai during a month (August) when the only company casualty is an unpopular staff sergeant fragged by some discontented black GIs. This death is neither sweet nor fitting, nor is it for any country, but it serves as a brief reminder of the continuing civil conflicts between whites and blacks in Vietnam-era America and the internal breakdown of the American army as it withdrew for four years under Nixon's morale-eroding Vietnamization program. What is sweet, if not fitting, is any assignment that would turn a combat infantryman like O'Brien into anything else: "If foot soldiers in Vietnam have a single obsession, it's the gnawing, tantalizing hope of being assigned to a job in the rear. Anything to yank a man out of the field—loading helicopters or burning trash or washing the colonel's laundry" (170).

Chapter XII, "Mori" ("to die"), dramatizes the lingering, painful death of a Viet Cong female soldier, watched over by GIs who give her water and try vainly to save her life, sardonically regretting that they have shot her: "'Damn, she is pretty. It's a crime. We could have shot an ugly old man instead'" (117). There is little that is literally sweet about this death, yet the young GIs' wonder at, admiration of, and growing tenderness for their dying female counterpart ironically disputes the irony of Owen's poem. The war *is* a senseless waste for O'Brien and his comrades, but the girl's death reminds us that patriotism is not always a meaningless lie. Although she is vainly airlifted out by an American chopper pilot soon disgusted that he has risked his life for a dead woman, the GIs' concern for her validates her tragic heroism.

"Mori" is one of the many episodes, like the final part of "Alpha Company," in which O'Brien is merely a silent observer, mimicking or suggesting the authorial detachment that has revised this personal experience so effectively. The chapter is also the second of five in which O'Brien focuses on Vietnamese protagonists. Besides Chapter XII, the others include "The Man at the Well" (Chapter X), "Centurion" (Chapter XV), "The Lagoon" (Chapter XVIII), and "Hearts and Minds" (Chapter XXI). As critics from Timothy Lomperis in 1987 (63) to Renny Christopher in 1995 (165–66) have noted, American Vietnam literature has largely ignored the Vietnamese. One of O'Brien's purposes in his "war" books is to register such ignorance. In *Combat Zone*, he takes on the bystander function in these Vietnamese-focused chapters, literally reflecting his alienation from the strangeness of Viet Nam. But because all the episodes involve violence or contempt visited by his comrades upon Vietnamese—whether Viet Cong or South Vietnamese civilians—O'Brien's detachment also suggests moral alienation and shame. As with other chapters in which his own identity recedes into mute observation, these episodes become fablelike exempla, a fictional mode reinforced by their undated titles and lack of narrative connection with adjoining chapters. Their American participants seem to be aliens within a much larger social environment that is perplexing to them; and within the chronological narrative of O'Brien's memoir, the encounters seem repetitive, inevitable violations of the political morality that attempted to justify Vietnam.

In "The Man at the Well," a blind old farmer helps shower GIs until one of them throws a milk carton in his face, cutting it open. In "The Lagoon" (also the title of a novella by Joseph Conrad), Alpha Company sets up camp to protect a village of friendly South Vietnamese until an American mortar barrage mistakenly targets them, wounding thirty-three villagers and killing thirteen, including eight children from two to ten years old whose names are identified by O'Brien. The alien presence of the Americans is emphasized by O'Brien's imagining the village before the war, creating an idealized pastoral scenario that even includes local legends of a lagoon monster, but the fable dissolves with the unintended atrocity and the payment of blood money: "[T]wenty dollars for each wounded villager; thirty-three dollars and ninety cents for each death. Certain blood for uncertain reasons. No lagoon monster ever terrorized like this" (167). "Hearts and Minds," the last episode in O'Brien's sequence of Vietnamese-focused scenes, provides an ironic final word about the ideological campaign to win the Vietnamese over to democracy by defeating Communist aggression. The chapter records the conversation between a U.S. captain and a former Viet Cong U.S. Army guide who abandons the American war when he is prohibited from returning to his wife and sick child in his own village—and his own country. In "Centurion," the only one of these episodes in which O'Brien himself is an actor, literary resonance is suggested by the title, as in "Mori" and "The Lagoon." O'Brien and Bates guard three old men from a VC village who have been tied to trees and beaten by interrogators. Here, in this Asian Golgotha, the imperial sentry is an American, O'Brien himself. As soldier, he offers his canteen to the oldest of the peasants, but can do little more; as author, he records his own guilty connivance with the bad war that he has chosen as his fate.

Other chapters besides the Vietnamese fables also contribute to O'Brien's moral anatomy of the war and his own part in it. "July" casually records the standard procedure of taking civilians captive to guard against night attacks by their VC relatives, and ends its series of bloody fiascoes under Captain Smith, Johansen's replacement, with the accidental destruction of a statue of the Buddha after a Claymore mine is triggered outside a monastery where Alpha Company has been graciously hosted. But most important structurally is O'Brien's treatment of My Lai, which anticipates its later use in subsequent books as a touchstone for the evil of the war. The first sentence of the combat narrative that begins with basic training implicitly alludes to the massacre: "To understand what happens among the mine fields of My Lai, you must know something about what happens in America" (40). Chapter XXII, the final chapter before O'Brien's departure from Viet Nam, recalls the revelation of the war crime a year and a half after it had occurred, when O'Brien was a clerk for the battalion that had taken over Calley's area of operations and served under an executive officer responsible for escorting reporters and investigators out to the scene of the murders. O'Brien's combat memoir is therefore bracketed by an allusion to the massacre, already a symbol for American war crimes, and its revelation in January 1970. Moreover, as an area of Alpha Company's patrols, the My Lai district was familiar to O'Brien, and although he and his comrades were innocent of genocide, the effects of fear, frustration, and the loss of friends there could ignite murderous reactions:

> Captain Johansen would ask, nicely enough, "Where are all the men? Where is Poppa-san?" No answers, not from the villagers. Not until we ducked poppa's bullet or stepped on his land mine.
>
> Alpha Company was fatigued and angry leaving My Lai 5. . . .
>
> In the next few days it took little provocation for us to flick the flint of our Zippo lighters. Thatched roofs take the flame quickly, and on bad days the hamlets of Pinkville[4] burned, taking our revenge in fire. It was good to walk from Pinkville and to see fire behind Alpha Company. It was good, just as pure hate is good. (120–21)

The collective pronoun includes O'Brien's actions here (his own friend Chip had been recently obliterated by a mine), as well as the satisfaction of revenge. My Lai thus accompanies the battle memoir from basic training through combat to battalion headquarters, naming the conditions under which a bad war was traumatizing for the men who fought it.

In Chapter XXII, "Courage Is a Certain Kind of Preserving," O'Brien once more becomes a combat philosopher, debating justice in warfare with Major Callicles, the executive officer. The chapter's title epigraph is taken from Plato's *Republic,* and the pseudonym is taken from the *Gorgias,* where Kallikles is a proponent of the will to power who is eventually reduced to silence by Socrates. Major Callicles's argument is that war is hell, that civilians are always victims, and, most disturbingly, that the Americal Division was simply caught doing what was done everywhere in Viet Nam: "There's a billion stinking My Lai 4's, and they put the finger on us" (190). O'Brien argues the classical position from Thomas Aquinas to the Geneva Conventions: "But, sir, the law says killing civilians is wrong. We're taught that, even by the army, for God's sake!"(193). Despite the bewildering military and moral landscape of Viet Nam, battlefield trauma including the loss of comrades, and his own participation in operations that approach deliberate murder, O'Brien has retained his pre-Vietnam principles. Major Callicles taunts him with his own combat experiences: "Damn it, they're all VC, you should know that. You might own a diploma, for Christ's sake, but does that mean you can't trust your own eyes and not some lousy book? You've been there, for Christ's sake!" (193). If anything, however, being there has confirmed in the blood and on the body what O'Brien had known only as ethical principle.

These arguments are the last of the book's casual Platonic dialogues, a series of exchanges with Erik, the basic training chaplain Captain Edwards, Captain Johansen in the field, and finally Major Callicles at LZ Gator. Like Chapter XVI, which centered on Johansen, this final Viet Nam chapter functions as an indirect moral commentary on everything that has preceded it and all that it contains, the military operations that desolated O'Brien's soul and achieved a significance beyond violence only by being reconsidered and revised. Major Callicles also completes O'Brien's anatomy of heroism, his bullying braggadocio and Captain Smith's cowardly and incompetent destructiveness the extremes that highlight Johansen's "wise endurance." In the second half of the chapter, Callicles suddenly drags O'Brien back into combat, a three-man ambush in the dead of night outside Tri Binh 4—*still* a VC-controlled village—to teach him what real courage is. Like virtually every operation recounted in *Combat Zone,* it ends in anticlimax, and this time in comedy: The drunken Callicles falls into a stupor after planting a Claymore mine uselessly, as "if he were hunting eagles" (200), and the night passes peacefully until the commanding

officer picks himself and the Claymore up and boastfully leads O'Brien
and a Delta Company scout out of Indian Country.

Combat Zone as Source for a Career

Combat Zone is significantly productive of O'Brien's subsequent fiction.
Its representation of the author as bystander or observer may reflect his
actual experience of the war, but it also creates a quasi-authorial subject
position and tendency toward detachment, avoidance, or evasion that will
characterize protagonists in all the later books. The internalization of the
narrative and its elaborately repetitive formal structure—particularly striking for an autobiographical account—anticipates the self-conscious writerliness that marks all of the later Vietnam writing. O'Brien's rewriting of
facts as fictions and the refashioning of himself in various guises are
also characteristic. Finally, the use of war writing to address important human issues—justice, courage, good and evil, shame and guilt—initiates
O'Brien's ongoing career as a morally engaged writer who trusts in literature as transpersonal, transhistorical discourse.

By emphasizing how actual experience is converted into quasi-fictional
scenarios and paradigmatic significance in Combat Zone, I have down-
played O'Brien's insistence that the work is nonfictional. Whether we call
it memoir or fabulated experience, however, Combat Zone is raw material
from which the author has drawn in representing Vietnam. One striking
example will illustrate how the memoir is a quarry for fictive recyclings. In
"Wise Endurance," O'Brien recalls how Alpha Company opened up one
day on some boys guilty of "herding cows in a free-fire zone": "We fired at
them, cows and boys together, the whole company, or nearly all of it, like
target practice at Fort Lewis. The boys escaped, but one cow stood its
ground. Bullets struck its flanks, exploding globs of flesh, boring into its
belly. The cow stood parallel to the soldiers, a wonderful profile. It looked
away, in a single direction, and it did not move. I did not shoot, but I did
endure, without protest, except to ask the man in front of me why he was
shooting and smiling" (139). The cows and boys are later cited in the chapter's suggestion that courage must involve wisdom: "Was the cow, standing immobile and passive, more courageous than the Vietnamese boys
who ran like rabbits from Alpha Company's barrage? Hardly. Cows are

very stupid" (141). But we also see O'Brien "endure," fixed in his frequent
position of moral shame, only half-wise, the bystander who knows better.
Here, as at Tri Binh 4, in the Vietnamese fragments, and in the torching of
villages that succeeded Chip's death, the tone of the writing suggests an
emotional constriction of traumatic experiences that will continue to
haunt the observer.

This personal experience used as ethical illustration reappears in *Going
After Cacciato, The Nuclear Age,* and *The Things They Carried* ("How to Tell
a True War Story"), where the narrator identifies it as a tale he has told earlier (85). In the first revision, Stink Harris begins firing manically at two
water buffalo that suddenly appear in the road before Paul Berlin's infantry squad: "Someone was screaming for a cease-fire but Stink was on full
automatic. He was smiling. Gobs of flesh jumped off the beast's flanks"
(71). In the last, Rat Kiley obliterates a "baby VC water buffalo" (85) that he
has tried unsuccessfully to feed just after his friend Curt Lemon has been
evaporated by a booby-trapped howitzer shell. Both these scenes involve
shocking violence, but while one simply describes adolescent brutality on
the edge of gleeful criminality, the other emphasizes the overwhelming effects of grief and shame on a young man who has lost his friend. The *Cacciato* episode is crucial in the narrative of that novel, for the carabao's
owners are subsequently picked up by the squad; the Rat Kiley episode is
exemplary, showing us how a "true war story . . . makes the stomach believe" (84).

Most surprisingly, O'Brien rewrites the scene in *The Nuclear Age,* nominally a non-Vietnam narrative. But here its paradigmatic significance is explicit. Indoctrinating a group of antiwar protesters, Ebenezer Keezer, a
former Marine turned domestic guerrilla, recalls how his platoon burned
down a village and then wiped out all its water buffalo with their rifles,
machine guns, and grenade launchers, as if they were latter-day U.S. Cav-
alry exterminating bison. The graphic details reappear apocalyptically, followed by the message: "'That's the Nam,' he said softly, 'and it's unbecoming. I've seen my share of buffalo,' . . . The war, he told us, was a buffalo
hunt, and we would be wise to disabuse ourselves of romantic notions regarding the propriety of peaceful protest and petitions of grievance. We
were soldiers, he said. Volunteers one and all. It was an army" (203). The ge-
nocidal intimations of the original experience—water buffalo are virtually
symbols of rural Vietnamese life, the most important possession of every

family and village—run through its retellings and may be one reason the domestic terrorist uses it to represent "the Nam." But whether or not Keezer has made it up is as irrelevant as which of O'Brien's versions actually happened, including the initial version in *Combat Zone*, which is simply one of four different revisions. None simply replicates what O'Brien experienced, and all are true within the various literary re-creations that give shooting water buffalo its imaginative meaning as a variously traumatic experience.

By the end of *Combat Zone*, O'Brien's moral rejection of the war has become fully informed by experience but more complex because he has become a participant. In the final chapter, "Don't I Know You?", addressing himself as if the soldier and the sensitive young man who had entered the war need to become better acquainted, O'Brien describes his flight back to America at the end of the year in Viet Nam. As the plane taxis to the gate in Minneapolis, he strips his uniform off, changing into sweater and blue jeans in the bathroom, only to find upon emerging that he is still wearing army footwear. "Much as you hate it, you don't have civilian shoes, but no one will notice. It's impossible to go home barefoot," *Combat Zone* ends (205), suggesting that the infantry grunt cannot simply walk out of the war and leave it all behind—his experiences will go with him to his next destination, for better or worse.

As his Freedom Bird approaches its destination, however, O'Brien leaves us with little sense of fulfillment or joy, while also suggesting that the young man who has gone to Viet Nam *has* been changed by the experience, or at least has a new perspective on America from having gone there:

> The flight to Minnesota in March takes you over disappearing snow. The rivers you see below are partly frozen over. Black chunks of corn fields peer out of the old snow. The sky you fly in is gray and dead. Over Montana and North Dakota, looking down, you can't see a sign of life.
>
> And over Minnesota you fly into an empty, unknowing, uncaring, purified, permanent stillness. Down below, the snow is heavy, there are patterns of old corn fields, there are some roads. In return for all your terror, the prairies stretch out, arrogantly unchanged. (205)

From jungles and rice paddies to frozen rivers and snow-covered cornfields, the transition from the combat zone to the World is anticlimactic, even grim. At Fort Lewis, before the dread flight to Cam Ranh Bay, the great snowy expanse of Mount Rainier "stood for freedom" (40). Here the wintry scene seems sterile, denuded of its cover, ugly. O'Brien's next work begins with the return of a veteran damaged by the war to his hometown in Minnesota. At the end of *Combat Zone*, as the soldier who will be a writer descends into Minneapolis, we seem already to be entering the landscape of *Northern Lights*.

CHAPTER 3

THE OLD MAN AND THE POND

Self-Displacement in *Northern Lights*

At the beginning of *Northern Lights*, Paul Milton Perry is anxiously considering the imminent homecoming of his younger brother Harvey to Sawmill Landing, a rural hamlet in the Arrowhead, that desolate spike of northern Minnesota that cuts into Lake Superior. It is a predawn Sunday in July 1970, hot and uncomfortable, and Paul cannot sleep: He is bothered by the heat and mosquitoes, by thoughts about the wilderness outside, by memories of his brother and their deceased father, and by reflections about his wife Grace, sleeping peacefully at his side; but one thought has disturbed all the others into consciousness: "Harvey was coming home. . . . He sat on the bed. Harvey was coming home, and he was dizzy" (4). After emptying a can of insecticide on the mosquitoes, awakening his wife, Paul leaves the bedroom and walks out to Pliney's Pond, a swampy pool on the Perrys' property where he sits and reflects further before returning inside and fixing breakfast for Grace as the first section of the novel ends. As the mundane details accumulate, we come to realize that the younger Perry is returning home from Viet Nam, where he has been wounded in the war and lost his sight in one eye. And we share the suspense of Paul, who "[tries] to imagine what great changes the war might have made in his kid brother" (6).

Northern Lights thus begins where *If I Die in a Combat Zone* ended, with a combat soldier's return to Minnesota. Since the Vietnam veteran in the memoir was the writer, we might expect additional parallels between

O'Brien and Harvey and assume that in narrating Harvey's war story and its aftermath O'Brien will be continuing his own as a postwar narrative that extends the trauma of Vietnam. Paul's recollection of the day that Harvey "[boarded] the bus that would take him to a fort in California and from there to Saigon or Chu Lai or wherever" (7) ends by naming the head-quarters of the Americal Division, O'Brien's own first destination in Viet Nam. When the two brothers endure a Minnesota blizzard later in the novel, Harvey starts to sing *"if I die in a combat zone, box me up and ship me home"* (196), deliberately marking *Northern Lights* with a trace of the earlier war memoir.

Once Harvey arrives in the second section of the novel, however, his characterization denies autobiographical implications. Except for having suffered a combat wound in Viet Nam, Harvey is nearly a contrary of his creator: silent or inarticulate about the war, but manically fixated on pur-suing fantasies of adventure elsewhere; physically rather than intellec-tually impressive; and unreflective in general. The protagonist turns out to be the older brother who stayed home rather than the former soldier, an exact reversal of O'Brien's situation—his younger brother (who was only fourteen in 1969) was never in Viet Nam. Not only do Paul's activities con-stitute the plot of *Northern Lights*, but the story is told exclusively through his point of view, and many of the scenes take place within his imagina-tion or memory as he reflects upon his relationship with his dead father ("the old man"), living family members and acquaintances, and the town in general. Nonetheless, although Paul Perry resembles the soldier/writer of *Combat Zone* in his relatively passive reflectiveness, he is otherwise just as different from his creator as Harvey is. Not only was he never in Viet Nam, but he also has no apparent interest in the war at all. Bored with his use-less job as a federal farm agent in a dying community, his marriage, and himself, he continually embitters the present by reviving memories of an authoritarian preacher father who favored the younger son.

Just as characterization initially suggests personal identification only to refuse it, the novel's plot appears to bring the war home but then deliber-ately undercuts its apparent extension of Vietnam. While providing a por-trait of the numbing boredom of rural hamlet life, seen from the point of view of the older brother, most of Part One of *Northern Lights* simply dramatizes the problematic relationships that tie together the four main characters: Paul and Harvey Perry, Paul's wife Grace, and Harvey's girlfriend Addie, a mildly exotic beauty, thought to be an Indian, who attracts Paul toward flirtation. The middle of the book, which links Part One with Part Two and takes up about half its length, brings the four characters to a cross-country ski tournament in Grand Marais, a neighboring town about sixty miles from Sawmill Landing, from which Harvey and Paul plan to ski home after their races. But the overland trek turns catastrophic when they lose their way in a blizzard and Harvey contracts pneumonia, so that Paul is forced to save himself and his brother through enduring the elements. The last chapter of Part Two resumes Paul's aimless existence in Sawmill Landing after the winter ordeal with Harvey; resolves, terminates, or complicates his relationships with the other three characters; and ends the novel with his self-liberating decision to leave Sawmill Landing and begin a new life.

Thus, O'Brien's first novel initially raises the subject of Vietnam only to focus on Paul Perry's relationships to others and his interior turmoil. What seems one of the earliest examples of an important subgenre of American Vietnam literature, the veteran's return from the war to the United States (detailed in Bonn and Searle), deliberately scuttles that classification. In doing so, *Northern Lights* diminishes both the war and conventional masculine heroism as it pursues its domestic agenda. Not only does Paul save Harvey's life in the wilderness, but he proves to be the stronger man as son, brother, and husband. As the novel proceeds from Part One to Part Two and Paul's fortitude surpasses Harvey's, references to the war decrease sharply, and reflections on the brothers' relationship with their father markedly increase. Descriptions of Harvey's wound, the "bad eye" constantly gazing out at Paul and the world around him, decrease also.[1] A reminder of Vietnam and Harvey's status as a hero in Part One, it becomes an image of his sad failure as a man in Part Two. The few desultory attempts to question the younger brother about his battlefield experiences, including his wounding, are met with unresponsive vagueness; two ceremonies to honor his service actually diminish it; and otherwise, as far as Sawmill Landing is concerned, the war might as well be taking place on another planet. Paul's own lack of interest in Vietnam after his initial anxieties about Harvey's return virtually eliminates the subject thereafter. Moreover, insofar as it is mentioned at all, there is almost no reference to its political or cultural contexts and implications. In its progressive effacement of Vietnam, *Northern Lights* is unique among O'Brien's seven books.

The author has denied intending even the "muted presence" of Vietnam in the novel. According to him, Harvey's going off to fight is simply meant to illustrate his machismo, his wound to symbolize a weakness in his character (McCaffery 141). Reprinted in 1999 by Flamingo (United Kingdom), *Northern Lights* has most recently been characterized by Christopher Tayler as "an early attempt by O'Brien to avoid being pigeonholed as a Vietnam writer." Nonetheless, critical treatment of the novel has connected it with O'Brien's representation of the interplay between Vietnam and America in all his work (Beidler 1991); seen it as part of a "Vietnam trilogy" including *If I Die in a Combat Zone* and *Going After Cacciato* (Nelson); and considered it as the key text, along with the other two books, in a tripartite "myth of courage" fashioned by O'Brien (Bates 1987). Even Steven Kaplan (1995), who treats the novel's anatomy of courage with little reference to the two war-sited narratives, points out parallels between Paul's struggle to establish his own identity and O'Brien's guilty submission to going to the war in *Combat Zone*. The author's disclaimers of handling Vietnam at all are thus extreme, perhaps a defense against having his first novel reduced to war writing or autobiography. O'Brien's abandonment of his war experiences in this book must be acknowledged; but because it is so deliberate and so carefully wrought, it is worth further consideration.

In *Combat Zone*, O'Brien had found himself as an author by rewriting his Vietnam experiences, but he had not transformed them fully into fiction. In fact, he has deprecated the artistry of his first work and claimed to be surprised that readers and even publishers have identified it as fiction (Schroeder 1984: 136, 148). In an important review of *Northern Lights*, Michael Harris even referred to the Vietnam memoir as a "novel." But *Northern Lights* is O'Brien's first novel, and one that calls attention to its own fictiveness through significant allusions to other books and stories. Whatever the relationship between *Northern Lights* and Vietnam, nearly every reviewer or interpreter of the book has noted its close relationship to earlier modernist literature. In particular, the novel contains numerous stylistic, thematic, and even narrative echoes of Hemingway, especially of *The Sun Also Rises* (noted once more by Tayler in his recent review). If *Combat Zone* must be formally categorized as nonfictional, autobiographical war literature, then O'Brien seems to deliberately break with those categories by deliberately marking *Northern Lights* as modernist fiction. Concern that his post-Vietnam novel might be mistaken for fact colors his dedication of the book to the residents of Minnesota's northeastern border, the setting of the novel: "With gratitude to the Arrowhead people, who will know perfectly well that there is no such town as Sawmill Landing, that Grand Marais doesn't sponsor ski races, that these characters are purely fictitious and that this is just a story." This clever blend of facts and fabrications allows O'Brien to ground his narrative in authenticity (he knows northern Minnesota as well as anyone who lives there), to acknowledge his deliberate alteration of facts, and to transcend mere circumstantiality, since "this is [just] a story."[2] A dedication to his wife Ann follows this first dedication, so that even the prefatory material of *Northern Lights* looks back to Hemingway. *In Our Time*, one of O'Brien's sources in *Northern Lights*, combines a dedication to the author's wife, Hadley, with a half-snarling dismissal of autobiographical interpretations: "In view of a recent tendency to identify characters in fiction with real people, it seems proper to state that there are no real people in this volume: both the characters and their names are fictitious. If the name of any living person has been used, the use was purely accidental." O'Brien's more graceful claim to fictional refabrication denies personal references by never suggesting them. As we have seen, characterization and plot initially hint at autobiography only to deny it.

Although personal references are even more muted than the subject of Vietnam in the novel, *Northern Lights* begins the refashioning of self that accompanies O'Brien's refabrications of Vietnam in all of his subsequent works. The Perry brothers' ordeal in the blizzard radically reimagines a terrifying childhood experience for O'Brien when he became lost for several hours and felt abandoned during a summer excursion in the Minnesota forests with his father (telephone interview, November 3, 1998). This primal trauma was to be revised again in *Going After Cacciato* (59–60 and 218, the version closest to the original experience), at the end of *In the Lake of the Woods* (in Minnesota), and in Chapter 7 ("Jungle") of *Tomcat in Love* (in Viet Nam). Moreover, the fraternal struggle between the two Perrys not only traumatizes O'Brien's relationship with his younger brother but may also displace a crisis within O'Brien himself. As Marie Nelson has suggested, the conflict between being a soldier and being opposed to the war (internalized by O'Brien's self-characterization in *Combat Zone*) seems to split into the separate characters of Harvey and Paul Perry in *Northern Lights* (272). Finally, *Northern Lights* not only incorporates and practices the mode of modernist realistic fiction, it also represents and mimics traumatization. Harvey's inability to say or remember anything significant about the war in which he has lost an eye exemplifies the emotional constriction of a trauma survivor. But Paul's taciturn unwillingness or inability to express his feelings to others exemplifies constriction as well, and the recurrent, self-contemning memories that make up so much of his reflection mimic traumatic intrusion. Both brothers need to overcome past trauma, but since *Northern Lights* presents the psychic turmoil of the older brother, not the Vietnam veteran, Harvey's war is increasingly subordinated to Paul's anomie, whose sources, domestic and private rather than public or political, ultimately center upon a traumatic experience in childhood with the "old man."

The protagonist's name, Paul Milton Perry, portentously combines references to the blind poet (noted by Kaplan 1995: 66) and the apostle who was reborn after being struck blind on the way to Damascus, but the family name is most important. Although other characters call him "Paul," O'Brien exclusively uses the name "Perry," rather than Paul's given name, to refer to his protagonist throughout *Northern Lights*.[3] As readers, we initially read "Perry" as the equivalent of "Harvey," mistaking a patriarchal for a given name and the integral self-identity that the latter normally implies. But in the first part of the novel, this paternal naming weakens and diminishes Paul's individual identity in contrast to Harvey's. It also reflects Paul's haunting by the old man, who is dead but whose name has effaced his own within the novel's narrative voice (which cohabits his own). Jacques Lacan's nom du père, the "name"/"no" of the father (see Kurzweil 271–72 and Bowie 13), thus literally evacuates the identity of his older son, who is bound to the old man by ties of guilt and resentment. By the end of the novel, however, this distinctive use of the patronymic has come to reinforce and ultimately signify Paul's assumption of paternal authority. Paradoxically, by rejecting the old man's will, he not only begins to establish and accept his own identity but also proves to be the stronger and more responsible son. The mundane enlightenment of "Paul" allows him to become "Perry" by putting childish things behind him, including the old man's apocalyptic gospel.

Its literary allusiveness, progressive effacement of Vietnam, and focus on domestic rather than combat trauma are the marks by which O'Brien puts the war, mere experience, and autobiography behind him in his first nominal work of fiction. Yet the author regards this attempt to move his career and his life beyond the war as his least successful book. Whatever its weaknesses, *Northern Lights* extends O'Brien's refabrications of Vietnam and his own life in ways that will be characteristic. The trauma of the war is subordinated but also symptomatized in Harvey's refusal to address it, a silence or covering-up that is shared by O'Brien and the work itself. By contrast, Paul's achievement of manhood, which involves breaking with paternal expectations, leaving his hometown, and beginning a new vocation, parallels O'Brien's post-Vietnam choice of fiction, realized in *Northern Lights*, as his calling. Paul's life has been largely shaped by traumatic childhood experiences and his relationship with his father, motifs that reappear in all the non–Vietnam-sited works. He will ultimately choose his wife's values over his father's, a feminization of virtue and an implicit critique of conventional manliness whose ultimate source in O'Brien's life is the trauma of Vietnam. In his dependence on a female Grace to heal him, however, Paul Perry also anticipates later protagonists who will be traumatized by their desperate need for such love.

Viewed without reference to the celebrated memoir that preceded it or the award-winning book that followed, *Northern Lights* is an ambitious first novel, and even critical reviewers mixed their blame with praise for O'Brien's skills of observation and description, just as Vietnam-oriented critics have been impressed by the novel's authentically and effectively domesticated anatomy of courage. But the author of *Combat Zone* is self-consciously, deliberately trying to go beyond both Vietnam and autobiography in this peculiar "coming home" book that leaves the war behind by turning toward family trauma. What Tayler calls its "qualified success" depends on its writerly referentiality, symbolism, and structure; its ironic treatment of Vietnam—Harvey's story; and its rejection of Sawmill Landing—Paul's story.

Literary Mimicry: Realism, Symbolism, Allegory

As noted above, discussions of *Northern Lights* have often called attention to its derivativeness. Original reviewers of the novel had mixed responses: Most were impressed by O'Brien's strength as a naturalistic writer and found the nearly fatal ski trip powerfully convincing writing; on the other hand, the echoes of other writers seemed labored and secondhand if not second rate. Such criticisms resemble some of O'Brien's own. *Northern Lights* is the only one of his novels with which he is fundamentally dissatisfied—with "more echoes of Hemingway than any of [his] other books," it is "maybe eighty pages too long," with "a lot of interior monologue material that's too set up, and there's a lot of unnecessary repetition" (McCaffery 138–39). His own judgment that the novel needs cutting was shared by several reviewers, and his self-critique was strongly reiterated most recently in his April 1999 interview with Lynn Warton. In fact, among O'Brien's works only *Going After Cacciato* is longer, and *Northern Lights* is longer than *In Our Time* or *The Sun Also Rises* and nearly twice the length of *If I Die in a Combat Zone*, its predecessor. Two British reviewers mindful of its intimations of Hemingway and critical of its length felt that O'Brien was trying to write the "great American novel" but that the book's pretensions to significance fell short of its accomplishment (Fallowell 22, Maclean 498).

Whatever its pretensions, however, the novel is rigorously limited in its subject and focus. *Northern Lights* is exceptional among O'Brien's works in its attention to mundane details and simple plot. Confining its action to small-town life in rural Minnesota during the year after Harvey Perry's return from Viet Nam, it is the most conventionally realistic of O'Brien's works, employing a consistent third-person intimate viewpoint and fashioning a seamless narrative that is insistently domestic in its attentiveness. Because the entire novel is told through Paul Perry's point of view, it assumes and utilizes a coherent subject position that is actually more stable and explicit than O'Brien's own self-representation in the earlier combat memoir. The novel is also unique among O'Brien's works for being nearly devoid of any historical or political context: Only one post–World War II event is mentioned in the book, the Cuban Missile Crisis of 1962, and only on the basis of that reference (8) can we derive the fictional time frame of the story, which runs from July 1970 to July 1971 but seems almost irrelevant to the concerns of characters in the novel.[4] In sum, *Northern Lights* is anomalous among O'Brien's works, the least focused on Vietnam and the most externally derived. Although the former may help account for its relative neglect by both reviewers and later critics,[5] the latter lies behind some of the author's own dissatisfaction. Its strengths and limitations are those of a first novel, a trying out of the trauma artist's powers, so well-realized in the memoir, before he more fully realized them in the fiction that would follow. Just as Paul Perry keeps recalling the old man, O'Brien's writing is haunted by dead fathers, modernist masters whom he both emulates and parodies.

The analogies and echoes of Hemingway and other writers are one of many deliberate marks of literary self-consciousness in *Northern Lights*, which somewhat anxiously identifies itself as O'Brien's first true novel. Whether viewed as successful rewriting, unsuccessful imitation, or intentional or unintentional parody of his literary mentors, O'Brien's most conventional novel reminds us of its roots in literature throughout. In *Combat Zone*, O'Brien had identified Frederic Henry as one of his personal heroes, but *The Sun Also Rises* is the Hemingway text most obviously rewritten in *Northern Lights*. Roger Sale parallels the four main characters—Paul and Grace, Harvey and his girlfriend Addie—with Jake Barnes, Hadley Hemingway, Bill Gorton, and Brett Ashley. And others besides him have seen the ski tournament at Grand Marais as deliberate analogue to the bull fights at Pamplona.

Besides its resemblance to one classic American postwar novel, *Northern Lights* also recalls *In Our Time*, Hemingway's modernist pastiche of intrusive World War I and bullfighting scenes, first-person reminiscences, and postwar stories. Beidler (1991: 19) notes connections between Harvey's return to Minnesota and "Soldier's Home," the seventh piece in Hemingway's book and the prototype of all subsequent stories of an American veteran's readjustment to civilian life after overseas warfare. But there are other parallels to *In Our Time*. The title subjects of Hemingway's chapters "Cross Country Snow" (xii) and "My Old Man" (xiii) suggest two of the most important elements of *Northern Lights*: the winter episodes that make up the middle of O'Brien's novel and the father whose posthumous presence as "the old man" continues to haunt the Perry brothers throughout the work. Like Nick Adams, the brothers try to reconstitute themselves through nature, with their cross-country skiing trip analogous to his camping and fishing experiences in Hemingway's final story, the two parts of "Big Two-Hearted River." And specific details from "River" are recalled in O'Brien's work. *Northern Lights* opens with Paul's awakening to "mosquitoes at the screen windows . . . crazy for blood" before he assaults them with insecticide (3–4); Part I of Hemingway's tale ends with Nick unable to sleep because "a mosquito hummed close to his ear" (192) before he incinerates it with a match. Paul's fascination with Pliney's Pond, which both attracts and repels him and to which he returns throughout the book, resembles Nick's attitude toward the swamp that he comes upon at the end of Part II after he has caught two trout along the river. Both represent symbolic challenges, reflectors of trauma and barriers to posttraumatic development for the protagonists. For Nick, "swamp fishing was a tragic adventure. [He] did not want it. He did not want to go down the stream any further today"; and Hemingway's final story ends with Nick cleaning the trout and going back to camp, with one last glimpse backward: "The river showed through the trees. There were plenty of days coming when he could fish the swamp" (212). By contrast, Paul ultimately immerses himself in his swamp at the end of *Northern Lights*, a quasi-baptismal act that involves releasing his bowels and being coated with the fecund, malodorous deposits of Pliney's Pond but also anticipates beginning a new life.

In addition to the almost palpable presence of Hemingway in *Northern Lights*, O'Brien has noted the influence of other modernist masters who strongly influenced his early work through *Cacciato*, including Faulkner and Joyce (Naparsteck 2, Coffey 60). Extensive symbolism and internal monologue, as employed by Faulkner and Joyce, are distinctive features of *Northern Lights*, although O'Brien is much less experimental, avoiding their use of idiosyncratic free association and syntactic incoherence in rendering consciousness. In one instance, O'Brien explicitly mimics Joyce, ending his third chapter ("Shelter") with a four-page monologue by Grace as she fondles Paul in bed. This abridged echo of Molly Bloom's extravagant rhapsody to herself at the end of *Ulysses* calls attention to O'Brien's rewriting of Joyce, but it concludes anticlimactically. Paul apparently falls asleep, or pretends to, rather than being aroused or responding to his wife's testing out the idea of their having children, and she is left talking to herself but wishing she had an audience. As with its use of the symbolic swamp of "Big Two-Hearted River," *Northern Lights* ironizes the earlier conclusion, employing Joyce's monologue within a more conventionally domestic narrative: After returning from his fecal purification in Pliney's Pond, Paul and his wife finally have intercourse and anticipate having a child—"A son, of course," hopes Grace (346).

Beyond such echoes of scenes and symbolic associations, O'Brien's style in *Northern Lights* often reflects the influence of Faulkner and Hemingway, both the former's use of overstatement and eloquent, accretive hypotaxis, and the latter's use of short, unemphatic statements, parataxis, and repetition. At times, the effects seem awkwardly parodic, as when O'Brien describes Paul's attempts to remain alert in a state of hunger-induced fatigue by counting numbers, as he skis through the wilderness to find help for Harvey:

> . . . he counted to a thousand and kept going, counting on, perfectly in control, his wits intact, beginning to believe he could reach the very end of the numbers, the last number, 1201, 1202, 1203, 1204, 1205, 1205, 1205, 1206, 1207, 1208, 1209, 1210, 1211, 1212, 1212, 1212, 1212, 1213, some of the numbers having a symmetry that made them stick in his brain, and he counted in the growing conviction that one of the numbers would pop before him as the final number, beyond which there would be no further numbers, the red limit, the very edge of the universe beyond which the past started . . . (249)

Such imitations of Faulkner are relatively rare in the text, which more typically recalls Hemingway at his best and worst. Mundane details and repetition are often used effectively to suggest rather than identify powerful feelings, as when Paul Perry begins to realize fearfully that the two brothers' ski excursion has become a struggle for survival:

> Harvey was moving fast, getting too far ahead. Perry pushed hard with the poles, brushing through the pines, hearing them ripple behind him, hearing the skis cut the snow. Harvey's orange rucksack bobbed and dropped down an incline and disappeared. The wind was whipping the snow. He tried to think of a friendly song. It was cold. A nice cheerful skiing song. He pushed in and skied hard, the sting growing behind his eyes. A nice friendly yodeling song. He tried to think and ski and follow Harvey's orange flaming rucksack. The wind came from behind him and pushed him along, and he felt his skis slipping downward, down the incline, and Harvey's orange rucksack darted behind a rill and Perry followed. (180–81)

Sometimes, however, repetition is merely banal, as when Paul observes of a waitress with whom Harvey is flirting, "She was very young. She had no expression. She was somebody's daughter" (39); and mundane descriptions meant to suggest a state of mind do not always rise above the details: "It was dead winter. Two men in overalls came in. They sat at the bar. The younger of them turned to stare at Addie. In her felt hat and dark skin she looked good. Perry stared at her, too. Under the table, Grace had his hand. The booths were hardwood. The tabletops were formica" (106). O'Brien has claimed that writing *Northern Lights* provided important lessons in what to avoid as he developed his later style but wishes he had cut some of the material in Part One that precedes the Grand Marais ski tournament (McCaffery 138).

The use of Ecclesiastes in its title headnotes the sense of world-weariness and idle tedium that pervades *The Sun Also Rises*. O'Brien also uses a Biblical text to introduce his novel, a prefatory epigraph from "Revelations" [*sic*]: "[A]nd, lo, there was a great earthquake; and the sun became black as sackcloth of hair, and the moon became as blood. And the stars of heaven fell unto the earth even as a fig tree casteth her untimely figs, when she is shaken of a mighty wind. And the heaven departed as a scroll when it is rolled together; and every mountain and island were moved out of their places . . . For the day of his wrath is come. And who shall be able to stand?" The epigraph is the most important of numerous portentous references, symbols, and quasi-allegorical figures that O'Brien uses to deepen the significance of what would otherwise be an extended naturalistic novella. Just as it seeks to go beyond autobiography and Vietnam war literature, *Northern Lights* intends to be more than simply regional literature, a realistic tale of Vietnam-era Minnesota.[6]

While it might claim too much to suggest that the Perrys' family saga recalls the patriarchal legends of Genesis with their repetitive struggles between older and younger sons for a father's/God's favor, other Biblical references are quite explicit. The end of the world and the eventual destruction of Sawmill Landing by fire or ice are constant themes of the old man's sermons and conversations as recollected by Paul, and the Cuban Missile Crisis of 1962 becomes the fulfillment of his apocalyptic prophecies as well a traumatic crisis for the two sons: While Harvey obediently builds his dying father a bomb shelter, Paul guiltily observes the deathwatch, unwilling to help but incapable of intervening to stop it. Phrases from Revelation serve as titles for two of the nine chapters of the book—"Black Sun" and "Blood Moon"—and their connection with natural disasters recurs in three of the others, "Blizzard" and the two chapters titled "Heat Storm." The two other repeated titles—"Elements" and "Shelter"—invest O'Brien's story with archetypal as well as Biblical significance and allude to the dead father's survivalist philosophy as a prophet of the bleak northern wilderness. Other explicit references are more prodigious and more labored. Paul, who will finally see the northern lights at the end of the book, is eventually saved by Grace and abandons the Damascus Lutheran Church, founded by his grandfather, where his father was preacher. The grandfather's devotion to the Kalevala and the legendary "Bull of Karelia, a moose with antlers gone and head down in the dead of winter" (70), adds the national epic poem of Finland to O'Brien's miscellany of myths. On the index page of the original Delacorte edition, the chapter titles are grouped around the figure of an arrowhead that is reproduced on the title pages of Parts One and Two of the novel, suggesting Native American contexts as well as the Indian-derived artifact that is the name of the novel's setting.

O'Brien has insisted on the reality of the bomb shelter and the reality of imminent apocalypse in the nuclear age, and recent revelations by Carl Anthony that John F. Kennedy urged Jackie to take their children from the White House to a nearby bomb shelter during the Cuban Missile Crisis make the old man's apparent lunacy seem less idiosyncratic. Symbols are always real things, of course, and much of the reality of *Northern Lights* is palpably symbolic and obviously intended to extend the significance of O'Brien's small-town, domestic scenario. The shelter, a product of the Cold War and apocalyptic mania, is less a refuge than a tomb, completed just before the old man's death, that suggests, along with other allusions, the death impulse that characterizes the Perry family as a whole. It contrasts stereotypically with Pliney's Pond, the other notable feature of the family's property: manmade versus natural, concrete versus water and mud, ideology versus biology, Harvey's place versus Paul's, the old man versus Grace, masculine versus feminine, tomb versus womb, death versus life. Many other frequently repeated references also take on complementary symbolic suggestions. The Arrowhead is associated with the harsh survivalism and quest for adventure of the all-male Perry clan; Iowa, where Grace would like to take a vacation with Paul and visit her own family, with dullness, domesticity, and fertility. Harvey's blind eye and Paul's glasses are symbols of the brothers' complementary weaknesses of vision.

Northern Lights also initiates the almost obsessive concern for significant formal structure that characterizes all of O'Brien's novels and is evident even in the memoir's violations of strict chronology and arrangement of chapters. Such deliberate arrangement of material in works that imply or invite identification of traumatized protagonist with author elaborates the difference between the fictional subject and the artist who has fabricated him and his story. The binary formal organization of *Northern Lights* is schematically appropriate to a struggle between two brothers.

Each of the novel's two parts is made up of separately titled sections that
we may define as chapters, although they are not so labeled. Part One includes "Heat Storm," "Elements," "Shelter," and "Black Sun"; Part Two contains "Blizzard," "Heat Storm," "Elements," "Shelter," and "Blood Moon."
Each chapter in Part One traces Harvey's apparent superiority to Paul up to
the ski tournament at Grand Marais. As a returning war hero, Harvey wins
the admiration and passion of Addie and plans an overland excursion after
winning his cross-country skiing trophy at the Grand Marais winter festi-
val, whereas Paul, whose government job has just been eliminated,
scratches from his race. Part Two, however, details Paul's superiority over
Harvey, who comes in last in his own heat after all and then leads the
brothers to near destruction on the way home by getting them lost in the
wilderness and caught in the blizzard. Paul, who has built himself up
physically in response to the implicit challenge of his brother's return,
must save them both after Harvey falls ill. At the end of the novel, Paul
overrules Harvey's childish desire to hold on to the old man's house (and
the bomb shelter) and prepares to leave the town and start a family with
Grace, while Harvey has been abandoned by Addie. The fulcrum for the
transfer of patriarchal authority is the nearly fatal snowstorm that the
brothers encounter in "Blizzard," the middle section of the novel and the
only one that does not have a titular counterpart. Parts One and Two end
with literal apocalyptic chapter headings, and the other chapter titles of
Part One are repeated in Part Two. The entire narrative thus is both bipar-
tite, reflecting the complementary narratives of the two brothers, and circular, suggesting their being trapped by debilitating paternal influences
and natural circumstances that only Paul can understand and try to overcome.[7] Furthermore, the entire plot transpires within a precise seasonal
cycle, beginning in July and ending almost exactly one year later. Deliberately repeated plot elements call attention to the changing relationship between the two brothers and give otherwise mundane details cumulative
significance. For example, Harvey rescues Paul from drowning in Part One
but is rescued by him from freezing to death in Part Two; Harvey has a parade to himself in Part One but is simply one among many veterans in Part
Two; the first chapter ends with a public birthday party for Harvey, whereas in the last Paul and Grace celebrate her birthday alone; Harvey greets
visitors in his bomb shelter in "Heat Storm" Part One, whereas in "Heat
Storm" Part Two Paul prepares shelter for himself and the desperately ill

Harvey in the ruins of an old homesteader's house; Paul is humiliated by his failure to kill a junkyard rat in "Shelter" (Part One) but kills and cooks a woodchuck to keep himself and Harvey alive in "Elements" (Part Two); Paul simply touches the surface of Pliney's Pond at the beginning of "Heat Storm" (Part One) but immerses himself in it in "Blood Moon" (Part Two); Grace masturbates him at the end of the first chapter, but they finally achieve intercourse at the end of the novel.

Other significant parallels pervade the two parts of the novel, which is both a naturalistic adventure story and a schematic examination of male virtue. O'Brien's stylistic, symbolic, and structural patterns, however officious, are among the elements that attempt to make *Northern Lights* more than just a realistic family saga. More vital, perhaps, are its ironic treatment of Vietnam and Paul's development from death to life as he both satisfies and rejects a bleakly heroic masculine code of virtue. In his view of male fortitude, O'Brien parts company with Hemingway, his own literary father. Reviewing *Northern Lights*, Michael Harris shrewdly cautioned critics who might see the author as a Hemingway would-be that "O'Brien knows a cliché when he uses one, bending [familiar motifs] into his own offbeat patterns. He almost talks us out of an adventure story." O'Brien has both criticized his overuse of other writers in the book and claimed that he was self-consciously parodying them (Kaplan 1991: 100). The line between intentional and unintentional verbal excess is an uncertain one in *Northern Lights*, but Paul's antiheroism constitutes more than just a stylistic counterecho and subversion of the ethic of grace under pressure.

Harvey's Story: Vietnam as Tragicomedy

Treating *Northern Lights* in relation to *Combat Zone* and *Cacciato*, Milton Bates (1987) sees the novel as the middle movement in a three-part anatomy of courage that culminates with its successor. Handling the same three books in relation to the work of Eric Fromm, Marie Nelson finds it the solution of an ethical conflict in these works, representing through Paul Perry's final self-awareness a choice of humanistic over authoritarian moral principles.[8] The apocalyptic vision that is the novel's epigraph authorizes a bleak and repressive message of ultimate doom promulgated by the Perry brothers' grandfather, a Finnish immigrant who became Sawmill Landing's town preacher after being crippled in a logging accident:

"[P]reaching a mixture of folklore and Christianity and Finnish mythology, relying as much on his native Kalevala as on Matthew, Mark, Luke, or John, [Pehr Peri] called for no acts of repentance, offered no hope of salvation, anointed nobody, elected nobody, promised nothing to the choppers and swarmers and barkers, ignored heaven and delineated only hell. His promise was that things would get worse, and his theme was apocalypse: forest fire, death in the snow, a new Ice Age. He was a preacher of the elements, more pagan than Christian, appealing to the only true emotion of his frontier congregations, which was fear" (69–70). His son, the "old man" remembered with awe and fear by his own sons Harvey and Paul, anglicized the family name to "Perry" but otherwise continued his father's profession and message, preaching "that Sawmill Landing was a dying town, that there was no sense trying to escape it because the next town may already be dead and the next on the verge of death, that the Ice Age was returning, ice a mile thick, a glacier that would level the forest and fill the lakes, the sun would turn black and the moon red as blood" (71).

Raised under this testament of despair, the two brothers are unable to exorcise the dead father's presence and remain locked within a rivalry for his approval. They both emulate and resist his bleakly heroic legacy in contrasting ways, each of them self-defeating: Harvey, the outdoors survivalist, gifted with physical strength and an artisan's skills, imagines abandoning Sawmill Landing to pursue romantic adventure but gets no farther than Viet Nam; Paul, the village intellectual who would follow his father as preacher, rejects his message openly but sinks into a torpor of self-pity whose horizons extend no farther than Sawmill Landing, where he processes Department of Agriculture forms for farmers who can't grow anything in an area that has lost its lumber industry. Locked within Paul's self-absorbed memories of the old man and meditations upon his present ennui, the novel traces the brothers' struggle against family history as they renew their fraternal conflict in the present. Paternity and brotherhood underlie the novel's emphasis on courage as an important theme. Ultimately, O'Brien is exploring what it means to be a man in the wisest sense, and Paul comes closer to the ideal. As aimless in his passive reflectiveness as Harvey is in his schemes of great adventure, Paul at least understands the deadening hand of the past upon both brothers: "Like twin oxen struggling in different directions against the same old yoke, they could not talk, for there was only the long history: the town, the place, the forest and religion, partly a combination of human beings and events, partly a genetic fix, an alchemy of circumstance" (315). Paul's reflection here, just after he has survived the cross-country ski trek and saved Harvey's life, precedes his climactic surmounting of the past—the decision to sell his father's house, leave Sawmill Landing, and begin a family of his own with Grace.

As *Combat Zone* makes clear, of course, courage requires moral choice for O'Brien, and his own self-representation as a coward for going to Viet Nam and for passively enduring the evil that he found there complicates conventional notions of bravery here as elsewhere. Unlike O'Brien, neither brother seems to have seriously reflected on the war. Harvey, like his creator, is a draftee, not a volunteer, and although his authoritarian upbringing and macho posturing might tempt us to see him as a spiritual brother of Mad Mark, his resentment toward the town that sent him to Viet Nam and his lack of satisfaction about serving complicate such an easy judgment. Whatever the symbolic meaning of his crippled vision, after all, Harvey's wound—his blinded eye—makes him a literal victim of the war. In any case, Paul's moral position on Vietnam is not obviously superior to his brother's. While Harvey is half-blind, Paul is nearsighted, spending most of the first half of the novel "in myopic wonder" (7) about how an unhappy childhood has led to his unsatisfying adulthood. The more reflective Perry brother regards the war with indifference, insofar as he considers anything beyond melancholic dissatisfaction with his own life. Harvey's going off as a soldier highlights the vacuousness of Paul's undistinguished life, and his return as a wounded veteran refreshes Paul's sullen self-contempt, an attitude that Grace tries unsuccessfully to heal as they drive off to pick up the returning veteran at the beginning of *Northern Lights*:

> "What's the matter?"
>
> "Nothing. I'm happy. Can't you see how happy I am? Watch out or I'll drive into the ditch . . ."
>
> "If you're happy, then, let's see a nice smile," Grace was saying, snuggling closer. . . .
>
> "I am nice. I'm priceless. Don't you think I'm priceless? Harvey's a soldier and I'm priceless. That's the way it always seems to go. Perfectly priceless."
> (11–12)

Since he was never drafted, Paul never had to make a political or moral decision about the war; but Grace's subsequent attempt to cheer him with his avoidance of Vietnam prompts more self-disgust rather than pride or satisfaction (13). The older brother's only extended reflection on the war simply registers his resentment at his father's favoring Harvey: "Perry stayed out of it. Nothing he could do, and the war wasn't real anyway, and, besides, it seemed somehow natural that a rascal and a bull like Harvey was the one to go off to the war. . . . In the tangled density of it all, Perry sometimes wondered if the whole show were a masquerade for Harvey to dress in khaki and display his bigballed outdoorsmanship, proving all over again how well he'd followed the old man into the woods, how much he'd learned, to show forever that he was the Bull" (21). For Paul, Vietnam is only an episode within the more important sibling rivalry that Harvey's return home reignites.

But Paul's indifference to Vietnam is shared by the town in general: "[N]o one knew a damn about it. Vietnam was outside the town orbit. 'A mess,' was what people would say if forced to comment, but a mess was still not a war, and it did not become a war until Harvey went to fight in it" (20–21). Although two Indian boys go with him, and one is killed in Viet Nam, "even then it wasn't really a war . . . until Harvey got himself wounded and the paper carried another front-page story" recalling his earlier heroics as a football player and his family history. The war in Viet Nam thus provides a touchstone of Sawmill Landing's provincial narrow-mindedness, recalling O'Brien's representation in *Combat Zone* of his own southern Minnesota hometown—"a place for wage earners . . . not very spirited people, not very thoughtful people" (21). And he sardonically suggests, in old man Perry's account of the village's mustering of patriots for the Civil War, that such moral indifference does not make Vietnam a unique case: "In 1863 a meeting was convened to choose the village's soldiers for the war against slavery. No one understood the war, but everyone wanted to fight it. They hadn't heard how many were dying" (66). Conflicts between Swedish and German settlers reduced the number of volunteers to a single Swede, who fought at Gettysburg and "was buried in the Swedish half of the cemetery, solidifying the Scandinavians' grasp on the land, another root sunk deep in. For reprisal, the Germans convened a secret meeting and voted to change the name of the place from Rabisholm to New Köln" (67). The undercutting of American cultural myths—the antislavery crusade, the melting pot, the winning of the West (the brothers stalked "Indians" as children, Addie is misnamed "Geronimo" by the town's mayor, Indian Vietnam War veterans are neglected)—extends the questioning of conventional American heroism and moral ideals that had been initiated in *Combat Zone.*

The embarrassing irrelevance of Vietnam in *Northern Lights* undercuts the heroism represented by Harvey. The town fathers feel obligated to honor his service because they were responsible for drafting the younger Perry and sending him away to lose his eye, but the welcome home is forced, covering up half-guilty indifference on their part and contempt toward them on his. Herb Wolff, the town druggist who helped send him off to Viet Nam, nervously assures Sawmill Landing's hero that he would have arranged a grand welcome if he had known of his return, and is reassured, falsely, that he is forgiven.

> Harvey shook hands with Wolff, then stood with his hands on his hips and looked up and down Mainstreet. The bells were ringing loud.
>
> "Let's get you home."
>
> "So long, Wolffie," Harvey said. "You're a helluva man. Good man. War's over, baby."
>
> Wolff grinned.
>
> Perry started the engine and backed up and drove up Mainstreet.
>
> "That weasel," Harvey said. (24)

The bells are not ringing for Harvey, who has come home on a Sunday and finds the center of town deserted because everyone is in church.

The scene is one of several heavily ironic allusions to the war suggesting that whatever Harvey did there is of little interest to Sawmill Landing. When Jud Harmor, the half-senile mayor, insists to Paul that Harvey will have his parade, his words are not reassuring:

> "Take care, son. Tell that brother Harvey I'll get his blasted parade for him, hear?"
>
> "Okay." . . .
>
> "Tell him that losing one eye never hurt a blind man. You tell him that for me. Perk him up."
>
> "Okay, Jud."
>
> "Tell him the town thinks he's a hero. Tell him we're all proud." Jud was

grinning, waving his hat. "Tell him anything you want. A pack of lies, anyway. Okay? Hell, tell him he's lucky to be alive, that's what. Tell him I
thought he was dead or something." (30)

Not even Paul's wife can feign enthusiasm for the lavishly hollow local
newspaper tribute to Harvey's heroism: "It says you were badly wounded
and that you served your community and country and everything" (34).
Later, at a birthday party for Harvey, O'Brien casually notes that "Jud Harmor came in his pickup and straw hat and talked about the war and garbage" (52).

Harvey is finally given his public celebration in "Shelter" (Part One),
months after his return to Sawmill Landing and after winter has settled in.
Instead of being the honoree of a parade down Main Street, however, he is
part of the half-time show at a high school football game played in bliz-
zardlike conditions. Because of the snowstorm, he can barely be seen, and
his speech is drowned out by the wind. Jud's introduction is a collection of
barely audible phrases (e.g., "honor and service . . . a hero in a war without
. . . Sawmill Landing, where he . . ." 101 [ellipses in the original]) that mix together Harvey with Paul and their father, an incoherent babble of sounds
competing unsuccessfully against the fury of the storm. To Addie, who has
encouraged Harvey's ostentation, the event is "silly"; to Grace, it is "awful"
(102); and Paul simply observes without comment or apparent interest.
This snowing out of Vietnam has its counterpart in Part Two when Harvey
marches in the Sawmill Landing Memorial Day parade. Despite an unsea-
sonable chill, nearly the whole town attends what is the closest approx-
imation to a positive communal ritual in *Northern Lights*. But Harvey is
simply part of a larger procession in which he is rather insignificant,
marching by after the veterans of earlier wars have passed and directly behind a "troop of green Girl Scouts" who sing campfire songs while he
counts cadence for no one but himself: "He marched erect, the only veteran of Vietnam. He did not seem much different from all the others, except that he fit his uniform and he was alone" (317). He doesn't even have
the honor of being at the end of the parade, which goes to Jud Harmor, following Harvey in his World War I helmet. The day ends with rain and a
desultory trip to the cemetery for the final ceremony, where a local dentist
"gave a speech of some sort, and the veterans stood in groups according to
their war" (319)—all except Harvey, who has dropped out of the procession

to berate it: "Some miserable parade. I still haven't gotten a decent parade out of all this. Some miserable town, not giving me a decent warm sunny parade" (318–19). In the end, his self-pitying disgust echoes more plangently Paul's alienation from the civic commemoration: "It was a dreary, nothing kind of day. [He] wished he were sleeping" (316).

By undercutting public acknowledgment of Vietnam, *Northern Lights* suggests its insignificance for a society that would prefer not to be bothered by it. Indeed, the novel is remarkably honest and accurate in reflecting the viewpoint of not only small-town Minnesota but the great silent majority of American citizens, the "crowd of ordinary decent folk," to cite Auden, regarding the tragic war. Outside of media and academic centers, Vietnam increasingly became peripheral to the concerns of most Americans, a "mess" left to politicians and the Pentagon to make worse. Public Vietnam trauma is even more understated in *Northern Lights* than it was in *Combat Zone*, and as with that work, the date of writing and publication may be partly responsible. Indifference about Vietnam would have been widespread during the years of composition, 1972–74, the limbo between America's withdrawal and its ultimate defeat, but less likely in 1970, when Harvey comes home.

Even more striking than the public undercutting of the war's significance is its private meaninglessness for Harvey. By the end of the novel, we know little more about the circumstances of his wounding than we did at the beginning. Except for a reference to My Khe (36) and a commonplace observation to Paul that worried soldiers were bad soldiers (189), we know nothing at all about where he fought and what he experienced. When he does volunteer information to Paul, O'Brien's narration either covers it up, or Harvey is inarticulate, or both: "[Paul's] mouth was dry from a night of drinking beer and laughing and listening to Harvey tell about the bus ride from Minneapolis, the hospital, a few things about the war" (25).

> "War hero. I'm a bloody war hero. You know that?"
>
> "I know it."
>
> "Scary. Did you know I lost an eye over there? Do you know how it happened?"
>
> "No."
>
> "Me either. Turn the bloody light off. Can't even remember. Everything was so dark, cow shit and mildew." (141)

"Came home from . . . [ellipsis in the original] feeling like a bum. War and all. Wasn't so good, you know. I told you something about it last night, didn't I?"

"Just a little. You were drunk. I forget." (144)

Only once does Paul care to ask him about the war, so that only the two women seem concerned about Harvey's experiences. Addie insists on dragging out "the whole gruesome story" (47), but nothing is ever revealed. During her monologue at the end of the third chapter, Grace more humanely worries about Harvey's silence: "Yesterday he was talking about his training but he never talked about the war. I think it would be good for him to just talk about it. Don't you ever wonder if he *killed* anyone? . . . I wonder about that. But I'm sure if he did kill somebody then he just had to do it" (131). Near the end of the novel, after Harvey's nearly catastrophic failure on the cross-country ski trek, Paul reflects on his brother's continuing avoidance of war stories: "He did not talk about the long days of being lost. The same way he never talked about the war, or how he lost his eye, or other bad things. He would not talk about it. 'Yes, we'll go to Nassau,' he would say instead. 'Where it's warm. By god, we'll have us a lovely time, won't we? Buy a sailboat and sail the islands, see the sights, sleep at night on the beaches. Doesn't it sound great?'" (312).

"Bad things" echoes the "bad war" O'Brien revisited in *Combat Zone*; ultimately, of course, Harvey's near-silence about Vietnam is symptomatic of traumatic constriction. The downplaying of his wound recalls O'Brien's dismissal of his own wounding near My Lai, which is barely mentioned in *Combat Zone*, and his resultant Purple Heart (which is not mentioned): "As any Vietnam veteran will tell you in loud and no uncertain terms, many medals were awarded for deeds of stupidity, negligence, and outright evil. Others were awarded for no reason at all. . . . Decorations had little currency among common grunts" (Baughman 214). Harvey's mixed attitude—resentment at not being lavishly and publicly honored and his inability to communicate what he should be honored for—reflects the ethical ambiguity of fighting in a bad war.

Within both the public and domestic contexts of *Northern Lights*, Harvey is diminished psychically as well as physically by his Vietnam experiences, which seem to have made a boy out of him. His manic insistence that the four protagonists should pursue Adventure with a big "A"—"Asia,

Africa, Australia, Alaska, . . . the Arrowhead, . . . Afghanistan, . . . Algiers and Atlantis and Allentown. Aruba and Athens" (37) is the obverse of his avoidance of Vietnam, and both suggest denial of his repressed trauma. The war can be assimilated only within the illusions of escapist fantasy: "While he never talked much about the war or losing his eye, he didn't seem bitter and even sometimes appeared to treat it all as a great adventure that, if opportunity came, he wouldn't mind repeating" (33). His psychic underdevelopment eventually drives away Addie, and although it is Harvey who first suggests leaving Sawmill Landing, he is later unable to accept going away, a prisoner of his father's influence and the bomb shelter that represents his proudest accomplishment. Harvey's characterization as a Bull reflects his strikingly mesomorphic character, his father's inculcation of frontier fortitude, and the mythic Bull of Karelia celebrated as a symbol of stoic endurance in the old man's sermons, but it also reminds us of Hemingway's cult of bullfighting, whether in the chapter prefaces of *In Our Time*, the ironic narrative of *The Sun Also Rises*, or elsewhere. Admiring Addie's control of his brother's bluster about pursuing heroic adventures, Paul notes that "she was free and clear of his influence, able to ride him with ease, effortlessly swaying with him, guiding him like a matador, stopping him short, turning his plunges into wasted energy" (95). During the Pamplona-like episode of the ski races at Grand Marais, she deserts him for Daniel, a young pre-Olympic ski champion and the counterpart of Pedro Romero in *The Sun Also Rises*. When Paul proves the stronger of the two brothers during their subsequent cross-country trek, he takes over the bullfighter's role, awakening the broken down Harvey with a parody of the Bull's own manly heartiness: "'Harvey! Gotta get up! Buddy! Old buddy buddy! Up and at 'em as they say! Get that old blood circulating, up, up, up! Come on, Harv! Toro! Toro! Up and at 'em, Toro! Hi ya, hi ya!' It was spectacular boiling white daylight. 'Up, up, Toro!' he called, getting Harvey out of his bag and walking him round and round the homesteader's tombstone chimney" (201–2).

Although Harvey breaks down physically and replaces thoughtfulness about the past with recurrent fantasies of the future, Paul thinks too much: Most of the novel takes place within his memory, insistently recalling the past and poisoning the present. Although his self-awareness may be a necessary condition for beginning a new life, it is also debilitating. Paul tries to calculate the source of his malaise as he sits on the edge of

Pliney's Pond the morning before Harvey's return from Vietnam: "It was partly the town. Partly the place. Partly the forest and the old man's Finnish religion, partly being a preacher's kid, partly the old man's northern obsessions, partly a combination of human beings and events, partly a genetic fix, an alchemy of circumstance" (9). The same phrases appear in subsequent recollections as he accompanies Harvey into the wilderness in summer (72) and winter (191) and even after he has survived the blizzard and saved his brother (315—quoted above). Such recurrent self-reflections symptomatize a traumatization that persists nearly to the end of the novel. Only after his climactic immersion in Pliney's Pond, site of a primal humiliation before his father, will the old man's elder son be able to give him decent burial.

Paul's Story: The Feminization of Virtue

At the beginning of *Northern Lights*, Paul Milton Perry, flabby and anemic, is a nearly inert U.S. farm official in the Minnesota Arrowhead, out of love with his wife Grace, futilely attracted to a younger Native American woman, jealous of a younger and more adventuresome brother, still living in the house of a father, dead ten years, from whom he had alienated himself but whose presence continues to haunt him. Unable to sleep, "his fists closing and clenching like a pulse" (3), he anticipates Harvey's return from Vietnam with dread and reviews anxiously the paternal and natural inheritance that has left him feeling sorry for himself. By the end of the novel, Paul has finally buried his father's ghost, saved his brother's life, sold his patrimony, and decided to begin a family and a new life with Grace elsewhere. By making its protagonist the overly passive and reflective older brother rather than the returning Vietnam veteran, *Northern Lights* ironically redefines male fortitude within an American cultural tradition that has exalted the rugged individualist and his various metamorphoses into frontiersman, Indian fighter, Cold War warrior, CEO, and Silicon Valley/dot.com magnate. Although Paul comes to appreciate and take on much of Harvey's strength and endurance, he is ultimately a hero of the mundane, beginning the unglamorous struggle to become a loving husband, son, brother, and father by the end of the novel. Taunted by Harvey early in *Northern Lights* for his uninterest in lighting out for the great northern woods in summer ("You know how I hate mosquitoes"—35) or winter

("Snow, cold, freeze. They go together. They give me the creeps"—36), Paul proposes an alternative:

> "Why don't we go down to Iowa for a nice vacation? That sounds better. We can visit Grace's folks and have a fine time."
>
> "Iowa," Harvey said with scorn. "Some adventure. What we need is a good adventure."
>
> "I have an adventure," Perry said. "I'm a pioneer in this town. Scratching for a living, married, trying to help a bunch of crazy farmers grow corn in the woods, living in my father's house. That's an adventure." (36)

Even though Paul will lose his government sinecure and leave his "father's house" to find his own, the domestic and communal virtues commended ironically here will be validated by the end of the novel once he has recognized and accepted their worth: Being a good man may not be conventionally heroic, but unlike the war that has wounded Harvey, it is "not so bad," he comes to realize (345). His growth to maturity will include the winter expedition into the wilderness where he proves stronger than Harvey as well as the culminating individual trial at Pliney's Pond in summer, but Paul's most valuable transformation is a private, psychic experience registered by such commonplace details as buying Grace a birthday present, selling their house, and putting his arm around Harvey at the end of the novel. Months after his heroic adventure in the north woods, he is becoming as flabby as ever, but *Northern Lights* repudiates conventional expectations of courageous endurance. Paul does not need to struggle against nature, he needs to allow himself to love. In doing so, he must overcome the alienation that separates him from both a dead father who is still psychically present and a wife from whom he is psychically absent.

As noted above, O'Brien uses symbolic actions and objects and parallel scenes to define and develop Paul's character. His apocalyptic use of insecticide against mosquitoes at the beginning of the book ("Killed a billion of them" he ironically boasts to Grace—5) establishes him initially as a parody of Harvey, a would-be hero aware of his own ridiculousness. The mosquitoes soon reappear, so he flees outside, where O'Brien introduces several important symbolic counters: "Standing on the porch, he urinated into Grace's green ferns, then he laced up his shoes, hurried across the lawn, passed the bomb shelter without looking, followed the path by memory to Pliney's Pond" (7–8). Paul's watering the plants (which will be rewritten tragically in *In the Lake of the Woods*) is an act of macho self-assertion that will later be recalled in a scene at the local tavern, where "it was a ritual that the men peed outside and the women peed in the women's room" (46). But like the poisoning of the bedroom, Paul's assault against the ferns miniaturizes his uneasy relationship with nature and his suppressed hostility toward Grace, whose desire for children and maternal care for her husband are suffocating and threatening to his already attenuated masculinity. Although she brings him to ejaculation at the end of the first chapter, his masturbation simply reinforces the self-pity and self-absorption that characterize this most solipsistic of O'Brien's reflective protagonists. Paul's official position in the town mirrors his sterility as well: As the local agent for the Department of Agriculture in a forested area of northern Minnesota, he spends most of his time processing claim checks for farmers who can't grow corn. The U.S. government's decision to close down his office turns out to be a blessing in disguise, but the initial news in "Shelter" (Part One) as winter sets in seems to put an official signature on Paul's failure as a man.

Although O'Brien's two female characters are both well-realized figures, their characterization is a parabolic supplement to that of the two brothers. Addie and Grace are employed so symmetrically to mark contrast and conflict between the two Perry brothers that one reviewer referred mistakenly to the "two wives" as "stick figures" (Gold). But Addie is unmarriageable, abandoning Sawmill Landing when Harvey begins to get serious, in accordance with her role as the mildly exotic small-town femme fatale. On the other hand, the constant references to Grace's large breasts (Harvey has called her "Boob" in the past) and her nurturing and nuzzling instincts threaten to turn her into a symbolic earth mother as well as a theologically resonant figure. Paul's nearly pathological passivity is highlighted by Grace's phlegmatic domesticity; Harvey's aimless quest for adventure, underlined by Addie's carnivalesque hedonism. Paul's weakness in Part One is intensified by Addie's abandoning his futile gaze for Harvey's lovemaking; and his growth in Part Two, by his full acceptance of Grace's love, while Harvey is abandoned by Addie as an ineffectual "pirate." Paul's relationships with both women are symptomatic of his obsessive self-regard, and his lack of openness and intimacy will be characteristic of other protagonists in O'Brien's work who are unable to love fully or satisfactorily. He likes to touch Addie's legs but will go no further, and his

sterile voyeurism, dramatized early in the book as he watches her swimming but will not join her, prompts her uneasily jocular label for him:
"peeping Paul." On the other hand, like a boy who both craves and resents
mothering, he takes Grace's love for granted, while regarding her with indifference. At the beginning of the novel, he finds her "gazing at him
placid and soft-eyed, featureless as warm milk" (14) as they wait for Harvey's bus to arrive, and even his more positive reflections are patronizing:
"He liked her bigness. It was nothing erotic, no Addie, but the big bones
had flesh that seemed to sink to the touch, down and down. He wondered
what the hell she thought about" (97). Although she teaches school and
conducts Sunday School classes, Grace's own thoughts and ideas are
nearly ignored by Paul, who is irritated by her whispering in bed, a reflection of her frustrated desire to communicate beyond the body. And while
we are exhaustively aware of Paul's thoughts and reflections throughout
the novel, he does not share them with others, a suppression of intimacy
that was part of the brothers' paternal inheritance: "No one ever talked,
not in the rugged house" (206). While Grace nakedly confides everything
to her husband, as in the bedroom monologue that he ignores at the end
of "Shelter" (Part One), Paul's inability or unwillingness to open himself to
her, even after he has decided to sell the ancestral house at the end of the
book, is baffling and hurtful:

> ". . . what do you think about selling? Are you . . . [ellipsis in the origi-
> nal]? You never tell me anything of what you're thinking."
> "I never know what I'm thinking." He was thinking of his father.
> She sighed. "I can't read minds, you know. If you don't think you want to
> sell, if you changed your mind, well then just tell me. I won't mind, really.
> Really. I can't read minds."
> "We'll sell," he said softly. "I never said we wouldn't." (341)

Throughout *Northern Lights*, what Paul never says is more important than
what he does, and much of his monologue with himself revolves around
his father.

As noted above, Paul's imagination is almost pathologically retrospective, endlessly concerned with the sources of his own melancholy. Sunk in
a morass of self-pity, he sometimes attributes his misery to bad luck and
sometimes to physiology, the element of "black bile" that seems to domi-
nate his temperament. But most important are unsatisfying experiences

centered about his father that reappear in the novel as intrusive scenes of past trauma. His oldest recollection is of his father waiting out a storm in the house, his second and third of sobbing sounds connected with a snow-storm, the birth of Harvey, and the death of his mother (71–72). And three recurrent memories involve self-diminishing contrasts with his younger brother: a traumatic immersion in Pliney's Pond as a child, intended by his father as a survival test, which left him bawling and unwilling afterward to accompany the other two on hunting excursions into the wilderness; a re-fusal by the adolescent Paul to attend any more church services after be-ing punished by the old man for "playacting," emulating the father by dressing in his preacher's robes; and, most recent and most recurrent, his climactic refusal to help Harvey build the bomb shelter ordered by their dying father during the Cuban Missile Crisis in 1962. The first two involve the dual paternal inheritance of physical fortitude and religious ideology, the first pursued successfully by Harvey, the second abandoned by Paul. The climactic trauma had put the obedient and disobedient sons in direct conflict as their old man waited for the end of the world: Harvey built him a bomb shelter while the older son simply prepared meals. In posttrau-matic desolation, Paul spends summer evenings looking into Pliney's Pond, the original site of his subsequent alienation from brother and father; "Heat Storm" (Part One) begins and ends with such scenes, as does the conclusion of O'Brien's second chapter, "Elements" (Part One). And Paul's self-reflections culminate and are purged by his immersion in the pond at the end of the novel.

During his reflections there in "Elements" (Part One), Paul is joined by the eccentric Jud Harmor, an avatar of the old man in his less-forbidding guises. Indeed, Paul jumbles them together during one of his reveries in "Blizzard" and is more fond of Jud, who functions as a trace of the dead father, than of anyone else in Sawmill Landing. In turn, the old mayor knows where to find Paul in the summer, assures him that it is Harvey who is crazy, and even advises Paul, "Don't let your old man shove you around, you hear me?" (29). Jud's seeming confusion over whether Paul's father is dead or alive clairvoyantly recognizes the old man's continued haunting of both sons, and his tendency to identify Harvey, Paul, and their father indiscriminately reflects the tormented self-identifications that still bind all three Perrys together. Even before it has entered Paul's mind, Jud accuses him of wanting to sell the ancestral house and leave Sawmill

Landing, an ultimate abandonment of his patrimony and his father's doctrine of blind endurance, and the old mayor's death not only anticipates the selling of the house but seems its prerequisite: "He wanted to talk to Jud Harmor, but Jud Harmor was dead" (333), Paul thinks as he considers the implications of going through with the transaction. As an uncanny alter ego of Paul's father, Jud indirectly gives voice to the old man's unexpressed concern, love, and admiration for Paul. His final words at Pliney's Pond foreshadow Paul's displacement of Harvey in the second part of the novel: "[H]ey! Tell Harvey I got him his parade. You hear? Tell him I got his parade for him. Tell your pa, too. You hear? We're all heroes, you hear? Hee, hee. So long, now. We're all of us heroes, you hear, even you, down to the last man, hee, hee" (91).

Jud's nearly incoherent prophecy is realized in the adventure story that takes up the middle of *Northern Lights* and in its aftermath. The cross-country ski trek home from Grand Marais begins with Harvey leading the way for his inexperienced older brother, now finally testing himself in the great wilderness that he had never dared to enter with the old man, but it ends with Paul's rescuing both of them. Paul takes over his father's map from Harvey, who has misread it; finds shelter and builds the fires that keep them alive after Harvey gives up the task; goes hunting successfully, and roasts what he has killed for them; brings his brother back from death twice by reviving him after he has nearly frozen and suffocated; and finally strikes out on his own to find the nearest farmhouse and then the nearest town, before directing the police to find Harvey. O'Brien anticipates their reversal of roles through Paul's losing weight and building himself up physically in Part One once Harvey has come back from Viet Nam; and through Harvey's ignominious failure at the end of Part One, where he comes in last in his ski race and loses Addie for a night to a younger champion.

Despite its detailed authenticity, Paul's survivalist heroism, which might have made the old man proud, is qualified or undercut by O'Brien. As conventional narrative, the four-chapter ski trek (in Part Two: "Blizzard," "Heat Storm," "Elements," and "Shelter") is the heart of *Northern Lights*, taking up about half the book and revising Paul's fecklessness in the first three chapters of Part One ("Heat Storm," "Elements," and "Shelter"). But the physical journey across the wilderness is accompanied by an imaginative journey back to the scenes of family trauma, and although external nature is ultimately overcome, there is no resolution to Paul's conflict with his father, although he tries to imagine what might have been if he had told the old man that he loved him. At the end of "Blizzard," Paul recalls in vivid detail the miniapocalypse of October 1962, when he refused to help Harvey build his bomb shelter and watched his father die. "Heat Storm" (Part Two) begins by recalling his rejection of the old man's religion after he had been "defrocked by the mockery of child's play, pretending, practicing, playacting" by his angry father (217). And as Harvey declines in the blizzard, he begins to share his own ghosts with Paul, including his first rifle, a father's Christmas gift to his child that the boy had obediently accepted with joy although it also made him sick with fear and dread. Paul cannot even remember the episode, just as Harvey has no memory of his brother's breakdown in Pliney's Pond, a complementary initiation into a manhood that one has self-destructively embraced, the other self-destructively rejected. But being told by Harvey that the old man had actually admired his resistance to him provides Paul no satisfaction, for it is now too late for either reconciliation or an end to regret: "He'd never really paid attention, always hoping the old man would change when instead he ought to have paid better attention to why he hadn't changed and wouldn't and didn't" (200).

Not only is Paul's physical heroism unable to heal his psychic wounds, but his fortitude is also ironically undercut by O'Brien. Led to an isolated farmhouse by a little girl and restored to health by her young mother, Paul later finds that he and Harvey have been the objects of a countywide search that has the locals mocking their stupidity for getting lost and failing to provide a signal visible from the air. Paul's hunting consists of battering to death a woodchuck trapped in the snow ("a fucking big *rat*" according to the amused and appalled Harvey [272]) by using an eleven-foot tree branch because he is afraid to use his knife. Satisfied with their feast, Paul imagines himself to sleep with endless repetitions of "how much wood would a woodchuck chuck . . ." (273). After losing his glasses and one of his ski poles, he blunders through to survival but belies his earlier heroic scenario: "He skied erect, thinking he might be watched, photographed for some epic motion picture spinning on sparse themes of survival and manhood" (226). Looking forward to regaling Sawmill Landing with his tales of adventure, the myopic, careless adventurer skies into Tofte at the end of his ordeal only to find himself unappreciated: "He was depressed. There ought to have been crowds. The highway should have been jammed with well-wishers. He took up the branch that he had used as a pole, gripped it hard and flung it across the highway and into the woods" (307). The scene recalls Harvey's disillusioning arrival in Sawmill Landing at the beginning of the novel. Paul has successfully followed and overgone Harvey's fortitude in conventional terms, but O'Brien deflates his triumph. Like his younger brother, Paul returns half-blind, determined to go without glasses as well as to keep the beard that he has grown during his month in the wilderness, another symbolic gesture of manliness. But in May he buys new glasses, by June he is back out of shape and re-visiting Pliney's Pond to feel sorry for himself, and in July he has the beard shaved off.

The lack of change in Paul's life *after* his experience in the wilderness signifies the adventure's ultimate insignificance. "In the winter, in the blizzard," he realizes, "there had been no sudden revelation, and things were the same, no epiphany or sudden shining of light to awaken and comfort and make happy, and things were the same, the old man was still down there alive in his grave, frozen and not dead, and in the house the cold was always there, except for patience and Grace and the pond, which were the same, everything the same" (314–15). Paul's physical heroism has brought no positive change, because his anomic melancholy is a product of unresolved guilt and grief connected with the will of the father. Nominally, Harvey is the obedient son who followed the old man's precepts, while Paul refused. In continually replaying traumatic scenes of conflict with his father, however, it is actually the apparently rejected son who is more profoundly tied to the old man. The ski trek itself is an unconscious attempt to meet paternal standards of endurance exemplified by Harvey, and the father's ghost still haunts Paul after the blizzard. One of the resolutions to change his life after the winter ordeal would even undo the earlier rejection of his father's church: "A job, though. A preacher, perhaps. Like the old man. Return to Damascus Lutheran, filled with new religion, sparkling ice insight seen on the road to Damascus Lutheran, delayed and detoured by years of mawkish melancholy. Wear the old man's vestments. Put on the garb in the attic, and be a man. And preach neither salvation nor love, preach only endurance to be ended by the end" (313).

At the end of the novel, it is this desolating paternal credo that drives Paul back to the site of his earliest failure to satisfy the old man:

He did not notice the northern lights. He did not look up. He did not see the rocketing, wavering, plummeting red in the sky. The mosquito rattled in his ear and he plunged toward Pliney's Pond. . . . It was sullen and hot, and he listened, his fists clenching and closing, and he was thinking suicide. He did not see the northern lights, but he heard the mosquito shrieking in his ear. "So, at last, here we are," he said.

He shed his clothes and at last went in.

At last.

He glided inch by inch into Pliney's Pond. (343)

The images of pond, mosquitoes, and anxious fists return us to the first episode in *Northern Lights* as well as to the primal scene of childhood trauma that initiated the separation between father and first son. Unable to recover from that initial breakdown, Paul feels suicidal, a resolution that would be only a more extreme form of the apocalyptic nihilism that is the paternal legacy. Indeed, the first patriarch of the clan surrendered his own life to the implications of his bitter gospel: "In 1919, when Pehr Peri hanged himself from the rafters of Damascus Lutheran, his son was ready to endure, having listened" (71).

Instead of being his tomb, however, the muddy pond becomes both a secular font within which Paul's pathological obsession with the past is finally washed away and a womb out of which he is reborn:

Coming out, emerging, he saw the great lights.

He waded to the rocks and sat still. He smelled the pond in his lungs. The old man's crazy illusions seemed dull and threadbare, as though their vitality and old importance had somehow flowed with the black bile into Pliney's Pond. (344–45)

Paul goes into the woods without his glasses, but his blindness is psychic rather than physical, an inability to "look up" and beyond rather than merely down, into, and behind himself. He is still physically half-blind upon coming out, but his vision of the northern lights portends a new perspective now that he has been reborn:

There were mosquitoes but they were not hungry, and everything was very quiet and peaceful and things were not really so bad or so urgent as the old man had preached. . . . The old man *was* crazy. That was the terrible hell of it. And there was still Grace. Warm deepdown Grace, the ripe deep pond. He

would tell her that he loved her and mean it, mean it at precisely the moment he said it, rather than not saying it or saying it and not meaning it,
meaning it later when he did not say it. Someday he would say it and mean
it at precisely the same time. Not so bad, he thought. He smelled the pond
inside him. Not so bad, at all. (345)

Neither O'Brien's irony nor Paul's unfamiliarity with happiness allows this
epiphany to be ostentatious, but "not bad" is a characterization appropriate to Paul's small blessings. The phrases also echo and repudiate the operational and moral futility of the "bad war" that O'Brien had revisited in
Combat Zone.

This characterization of Grace redefines Paul's fascination and anxiety
concerning Pliney's Pond with his relationship to what is female. The Perrys' paternal inheritance is relentlessly masculine, from Harvey's childhood
rifle to their grandfather's and father's embrace of apocalyptic closure, and
neither Pehr Peri's wife nor the brothers' own mother survived the birth of
their sons: "'I didn't have a mother,' Perry's father once explained, 'because
I didn't need one'" (69). Paul frequently recalls his father's dismissive attitude toward Grace: "'Looks like somebody's mother,' the motherless old
man had once said" (9). His contempt targets Paul as much as Grace, suggesting that the son who seems to have rejected him is childishly dependent on maternal care. But its resentment is also profoundly thanatotic, a rejection of the source of human life itself. Harvey sarcastically refers to
Paul's "Sucking the Federal Titty" (19), displacing misogyny as it also extends Paul's infantilism to his job as a petty federal bureaucrat.

In the end, however, it is Paul's attraction to the feminine that frees him
from the traumatic past. After his epiphany at Pliney's Pond, he comes to
the marriage bed coated with its residue, and the lovemaking that follows
validates and duplicates his immersion in its "blood and motherwarmth"
(344): "'Don't stop,' she said in a loud voice that was not a whisper, but still
like the pond which was always so rich-smelling and muddeep and unconscious, scaring him away and still attracting as if to a natural element,
attracting until in calm desperation, with nothing to lose, he relented and
went in" (346). Here, sexual intercourse replaces the masturbation that had
followed his trip to the pond one year earlier.

Paul's attraction to and his own capacity for nurturing love, a virtue associated with the female throughout *Northern Lights*, is fully realized only

at the end of the novel, but it is anticipated throughout. Lying in bed with
Grace in "Shelter" (Part One), he had imagined the mother who died giving
birth to Harvey: "He listened to the house, brittle timbers, a man's house.
He listened to the outside wind. It had been that way forever. He tried to
reconstruct his mother's face. Imagination played its tricks. He did not
know her but he still imagined a face, like Grace, a certain feel and sensation that was entirely separate from the old man's house. No notion . . . of
his father or the squatting bomb shelter in the backyard" (97). At the end
of his monthlong ordeal in the wilderness, he follows a little girl to her
mother's house and regains the strength and guidance he needs to complete Harvey's rescue. The young woman allows him to stay the night (her
husband, who would have objected, is absent), feeds him, and directs him
toward the nearest town and county police. And even before the epiphany
at Pliney's Pond, but after he has decided to sell his father's house, Paul
has begun to explore the forest with his wife, as if her guidance through it
had replaced both the old man's bitter endurance and Harvey's blind ad-
venturism: "She showed him the underbelly of the forest, the quiet and
safe spots. Much of the forest, she noted, was neither pine nor birch, but
rather soft tangles of weed and fern and moss and simple things. She
showed him a delicate fern which she called maidenhair, plucking it from
the soil" (335). While the old man had led Harvey through the wilderness,
and Paul had initially followed Harvey's lead, the younger brother ultimately needed Paul's guidance to survive. As he recuperates from the
trauma of the blizzard and the loss of his job, however, Paul finds his own
guide in Grace:

> Perry followed her through the waiting days.
>
> He helped her with the gardening and shopping. Near the end of the
> month they drove down to Two Harbors for the county fair, and he followed
> her through the pavilions of women's work, quilts and mason jars filled
> with preserves and stewed tomatoes, needlepoint and aprons and apple
> pies. (335–36)

Earlier in O'Brien's concluding "Heat Storm," Paul had closely observed his
wife's instinctive ministrations at his father's grave the morning after Memorial Day: "She was absorbed in her work. Placid and quiet, she was digging out weeds along his father's headstone. She was on her knees in the
rain, her face set in its sane and perfect way, her hands deep in the mud.

She'd dug three holes for the plants, and when the weeds were gone, she set the plants in and covered the roots and packed the mud down. 'There,' she said. 'That should do it.' She stood beside him. The plants had dark red flowers growing. 'That should do it,' she said" (321). Her ritual of care contrasts with Paul's stony indifference and hidden trauma as well as with Harvey's inability to let go of the father when he stops before the gravestone following the dismal town Memorial Day parade: "The old man's pretty dead by now, . . . I don't know. He was a bastard, wasn't he?" (320). Ironically, it is Grace, derided by the old man for her palpable maternity, who most appropriately acknowledges that the old man is dead yet honors his presence in the imaginations of the living. Paul can only witness the gestures of a reverence that the two brothers are unable to articulate.

Even his ordeal in the blizzard makes a man out of Paul by summoning nurturing instincts that his father's house has denied. He saves Harvey not just by skiing his way through the frozen wilderness but by providing fire and food in a makeshift shelter where his activities are strikingly maternal:

Smoothing his brother's hair, clucking, he washed the red face and beard, got him into the bunk, laid a warm cloth on his brow.

With the last of the coffee grounds, he brewed coffee and held Harvey's head and helped him drink. "Harvey, Harvey," he murmured. "Love you, Harvey. I do. You know?" He wiped brown spittle from his brother's mouth. "You bull, I do love you, you know. There, there." (279)

Earlier, he wishes that he could also "at last huddle with the old man and eat with him and hold him and warm him beside a waxing fire. . . . [h]old him and warm him and not speak, knowing without language the way the old man knew everything without language" (267). Paul's love for Harvey and the awareness of his love and pity for his father are psychic outcomes of the ski trek more valuable than his physical heroism. Paul's endurance has little value in itself; it is in saving his brother's life that he is both most courageous *and* most maternal, overcoming Harvey's death-directed stoicism and cowardly apocalypticism: "You don't even know the end. This is the end, brother. I'm not going on, I'm sick. . . . You don't even . . . [ellipsis in the original] don't understand, . . . This is, just look into it. For Christ sake, this is the whole purpose of it, don't you see that?" (235–36).

Just as he had proposed the ski trip but proved weaker than Paul in its outcome, so it is Harvey who first proposes selling his father's house and leaving Sawmill Landing. Here too, Paul initially follows Harvey's lead but proves the stronger Perry. Harvey's decision to leave is typically impulsive, a direct response to having his marriage proposal rejected by Addie, who has moved to a Minneapolis suburb (it also follows his disgust with the Memorial Day parade). Paul's first response is typically indecisive ("Let's both of us think about it. I'm not saying yes or no"), and Harvey's rejoinder is sarcastic: "That's your style, isn't it?" (332). But Paul's thinking leads to the final crisis at Pliney's Pond and his movement toward Grace. O'Brien punctuates this movement toward self-transformation with significant details: Just before Harvey's abrupt decision, Paul has spent an afternoon razoring his name off the window of his now-abandoned office; afterward, he consults with his wife (she is eager to move), has his ski-trek beard cut off, and accompanies his wife in her rounds of ordinary intercourse with the forest and provisioning cited above just before he looks up to see the northern lights that guide him from Pliney's Pond to the bed of Grace.

Following his immersion in the pond and his lovemaking, Paul's passage to manhood culminates with abandoning his hometown and accompanying Grace to Iowa. By contrast, Harvey sulks and eventually resists the sale when it becomes a reality. The bomb shelter—the sign of Harvey's fidelity to the old man's craziness—is going to be turned into an artist's studio by the young professional couple that have also purchased house and pond. For the Bull, leaving the old man's house and community is a traumatic act of betrayal with apocalyptic overtones. His refusal to sell leads to a final confrontation between the two brothers. Harvey accuses his brother of a sterile selfishness that Paul has actually transcended: "It's all falling apart, isn't it? The whole thing blowing up into pieces . . . I'll just watch . . . some good cartoons to cheer things up as the world comes to an end . . . You never loved the old man, did you? . . . You're a coward" (350, 352).

In the end, Harvey's will is overborne by Paul, who has them sell the house. He recognizes the need to decently bury their patrimony if the brothers' own lives are to emerge, a closure that was publicly effected by Grace's memorial rites at the old man's grave. But the mundane final scene of *Northern Lights* captures the provisionality of Paul's new manhood as the brothers walk together through Sawmill Landing for the last time. Harvey moves from agitated protest to remorseful self-pity to final schemes of manly adventure with his brother that are punctuated by Paul's noncommittal, laconic responses. At the end of the book, the brothers are closer than ever before, but it is Harvey who will have to be guided by Paul's strength, since he is less capable of revising the delusions of manliness prompted by the old man's code: "Too bad, Perry thought. He caught up with his brother and put his arm around him" (356). And Harvey has the last word in the novel, proposing a purely masculine ideal of brotherhood that Paul can only pity:

> "How does it sound? Doesn't it sound great? Addie . . . [ellipsis in original] Who needs her? Always running around barefoot. Who needs that? We'll have us a great time. The Big A, right?"
>
> Perry shut his eyes.
>
> "Doesn't it sound great?" Harvey kept saying. "Doesn't it?" (356)

O'Brien provides no easy resolution, since Paul cannot simply reject manhood but must revise it into an ethos less harsh and more nurturing than his father's, less escapist and more responsible than his brother's. He cannot abandon Harvey but must he be his brother's keeper? Any resolution must be found somewhere between Harvey's "great" schemes and his own "not bad" role as a husband and future father.

Novel Revisions

Paul Perry is the first of the ironic heroes that O'Brien will create in the novels that follow. All are survivors of domestic or public trauma that leave them reflective, detached, and anxiously self-conscious figures, wise and foolish. These sympathetic but flawed and unheroic personae all reflect the Tim O'Brien of *Combat Zone*, the moral observer of an evil that he is powerless to prevent. Although *Northern Lights* largely eschews the larger political and historical contexts considered in the other books, the partial vision and limited effectualness of Paul Berlin, William Cowling, "Tim O'Brien," John Wade, and Thomas Chippering are anticipated by Paul Perry in the portentous but much smaller world of O'Brien's first novel.

Despite its derivativeness and overloaded symbolism, *Northern Lights* is a provocatively original reconsideration of male virtue, locating heroism in the everyday blessing of love that Paul comes to find through Grace. The Vietnam veteran turns out to be pitiable at best, his domesticated brother the hero. Within the straightforward naturalism of the novel, the old man and Grace are also resonantly parabolic figures, and in no other work does O'Brien so fully vindicate stereotypically feminine values and so strikingly reject masculine. Subsequently, major female figures will be invested with Grace's redemptive powers, but they will also be sources of trauma for O'Brien's protagonists, who will be less able than Paul Perry to be healed. Relationships between sons and fathers will also be a major concern of O'Brien's subsequent fiction, reflecting, as in *Combat Zone*, the more general transition between World War II and Vietnam generations. While it was the pull of community and paternal expectations that overcame O'Brien's own resistance to fighting in Viet Nam, Paul Perry can become a man only by repudiating his father's house and his hometown. But none of O'Brien's subsequent fathers will be as quasi-allegorical as the old man, whose insubstantiality makes such repudiation more possible. Although O'Brien would abandon or radically alter style, point of view, and narrative mode in later works, other important elements of *Northern Lights* are also reconceived and rewritten in them. Paul Perry will be metamorphosed into Paul Berlin in *Going After Cacciato*; the household bomb shelter, an important adjunct to the family history of *Northern Lights*, will become the primal site of significance in *The Nuclear Age*; Harvey's ironically anticlimactic return from Viet Nam will be darkened into the stories involving Norman Bowker in *The Things They Carried*; *In the Lake of the Woods* will rewrite the domestic trauma of *Northern Lights* as tragedy; and *Tomcat in Love* will revise it as ironic comedy.

Although its representation of Paul Perry as an actual small-town preacher was rejected in the novel, an early character sketch, "A Man of Melancholy Disposition," appeared in a "special 'realism' issue" of *Ploughshares* (1974).[9] O'Brien's own later criticism of his first novel calls attention to his dissatisfaction with writing realistic fiction in the neomodernist tradition, however, as does his occasional undercutting of that mode in the novel. *Northern Lights* is O'Brien's only book whose text was initially published in toto; one or more parts of *Combat Zone* and all the later works appeared in print before each was completed. His first novel is thus anomalous not only in its uninterrupted chronological narrative but in its appearance as a coherent fictive world that has effaced evidence of composition or construction by the author. Here too, the book follows a modernist model of internal coherence that O'Brien was to abandon in the more postmodern, metafictional narratives that would follow. Not only would the final publication of *Going After Cacciato* be preceded by eight excerpts of the work in progress, but the novel itself is literally generated out of the memory and imagination of its traumatized protagonist as he produces a discontinuous narrative combining "facts" and fantasies. After *Northern Lights*, O'Brien would abandon conventional realism to find narrative structures and literary modes more appropriate to his exploration of survivorhood. But the fabrications of *Going After Cacciato* also suggest dissatisfaction with the subject matter of *Northern Lights*: Having tried to write himself beyond Vietnam in his first novel, O'Brien chose to recover its trauma in his second and produced a masterpiece.

CHAPTER 4

A SOLDIER'S DREAM

The Re-covering of Trauma: Paul Berlin as Tim O'Brien

Whether it is the finest American novel of the Vietnam War, as many readers and critics would argue, *Going After Cacciato* is a great and lasting work of American literature as well as a brilliantly organized posttraumatic narrative. The recipient of the 1979 National Book Award for fiction, *Cacciato* has provoked more critical articles and studies than any other literary representation of Vietnam and has probably been more widely read and more frequently taught in schools and universities. O'Brien has denied that the book's subject is Vietnam, but whether its main concern is the imagination or peace or any of the other themes that he would prefer to emphasize, its writing constitutes a return to the trauma of Vietnam, a psychic journey that is at the heart of its elaborate structure. O'Brien's own refabulating of the war is mimicked—or epitomized—by his fictional double, Paul Berlin, who tries to deal with the traumatic facts of his war by dreaming of a scenario that will allow him to escape it. In the end, the dream cannot escape or change reality, but its creation is at least imaginatively redemptive for him. The same might be said for the book as a whole, a fictional revisiting of the site of O'Brien's own traumatization that validated forever his authority as a writer, whatever else he may publish.

Just as Paul's first name recalls the protagonist of *Northern Lights*, "Berlin" and "O'Brien" are nearly anagrams of each other, and O'Brien has claimed that one motivation for writing *Cacciato* was to imagine what might have happened if he *had* tried to desert from a "bad" war (McCaffery

133). He has also noted, without simply dismissing connections between himself and his protagonist, that Paul is a more frightened yet more sensitive soldier than he was (Schroeder 1984: 142). Differences in background, experience, and attitudes rule out narrowly autobiographical readings, but both O'Brien and Berlin are engaged in a reimagining that attempts to transcend the trauma of Vietnam. One source of anxiety shared by Paul Berlin and his creator is a feeling of shame about their actions. *Cacciato* refashions the ironies of courage implied by O'Brien's claim in *Combat Zone* that in going to Viet Nam he had been a moral coward. The more naïve and more obviously traumatized Berlin only dimly understands and can barely articulate the sources of shame that motivate his actions and his meditations, and O'Brien leaves it up to the reader to uncover what has been repressed—a web of fear, self-preservation, escapism, and moral revulsion.

Cacciato: From Short Stories to Trauma Narrative

In *Cacciato* O'Brien abandoned forever the straightforward, seamless narrative and mundane realism that he had used in *Northern Lights*. Virtually all of the novel is a fantasy that takes place within the mind of its protagonist, whose acts of imagination intertwine three separate narratives, with three different time frames. But Paul Berlin's interwoven meditations are the direct product of and an indirect compensation for a mysterious breakdown. Just as his squad began mounting a hill to capture Cacciato, a deserter, Paul lost control of his weapon and his body, fouling himself and firing his M-16 on full automatic while Cacciato (i.e., "the hunted one" in Italian) either escaped or was killed—the outcome is uncertain for Berlin, who blanked out during the assault on the hill. Several weeks later,[1] while absorbed in thinking about Cacciato, he forces himself to stand guard all night in an observation tower on the edge of the South China Sea. As he does more than his duty, Berlin imagines what might have happened if the squad had pursued the deserter all the way to Paris, his final destination, from October 1968 through the following April. But as he works out the details of the odyssey across Asia and Western Europe, Paul also recalls the deaths of other platoon members that he has witnessed during the six months of his service in Viet Nam. The three strands of narrative are intertwined throughout the novel, chapter by chapter, as

Paul Berlin extends his watch long enough to recuperate all the dead and to reach Paris, along with the rest of the squad and Cacciato himself, where the originating trauma is reexperienced in fantasy inside a Parisian flat. In *Cacciato*, then, a series of guard tower chapters (each of them titled "The Observation Post") occurs in a fictional present that alternates a hypothetical fantasy of the future with past facts. While the fantasy chapters represent a flight away from the past and the war toward Paris and the future, and the chapters that recall others' deaths revive past trauma in order to ultimately bury it, the observation post chapters mediate between escaping and facing facts as Berlin puzzles over the shape that his double narrative is taking. As if entering the workshop of the imagination, we experience Berlin's own reactions to the narrative as he tries to understand and control its development. Since he imagines everything else in the novel between midnight and 6:00 A.M., however, it is appropriate to label the whole book Paul Berlin's dream. *Cacciato* thus embodies its epigraph, Siegfried Sassoon's aphorism that "soldiers are dreamers"—just like writers.

Early reviewers and critics associated the novel with *Catch-22* because both works blend fantasy and factuality in a convoluted yet carefully constructed plot (e.g., Pochoda 344; Bates 1987: 274; Couser 9; Slabey 206). Joseph Heller's rational coward literally escapes from the war, however, whereas O'Brien's frightened young GI, whose entire story is merely a product of his own imagination and memory, never physically abandons his post and resumes his place within the war once he has investigated other possibilities. Paradoxically, because so much of it is literally one soldier's fantasy, *Cacciato* is a less escapist work than *Catch-22*. As a deliberate dream, the work is shaped by O'Brien to reflect Paul Berlin's attempt to understand the circumstances of his traumatization and to surmount them. Suggestions that O'Brien was influenced by Latin American magical realism have been denied by the author (Schroeder 1984: 139), and the violations of probability typically reflect motifs and references to American popular culture that a young soldier like Berlin might reimagine. Explanations of the book's structure as a deliberate analogue to the absurdity and meaninglessness of the Vietnam War have also been questioned by O'Brien, for whom the direct experience of all wars is surreal (McCaffery 135–36). In any case, as other critical analyses of *Cacciato*'s structure have demonstrated (Herzog 1983, McWilliams, Raymond, Vannatta), O'Brien's representation of the war is almost preternaturally well-ordered, whatever the grotesqueness or anomalies of individual incidents. Indeed, early reviewers who found themselves less than fully satisfied with the novel complained that it was too transparently well-controlled. But what Don Ringnalda has called the novel's "understood confusion" (90) can best be understood as a narrative constructed by both O'Brien and Berlin to revise traumatic circumstances.

In writing *Cacciato* O'Brien returned to the chapter-by-chapter mode of composition that ultimately produced *If I Die in a Combat Zone* but that he abandoned in constructing the continuous narrative of *Northern Lights*. Altogether, O'Brien published eight pre-*Cacciato* stories, six of which appear as separate chapters in the completed novel.[2] The changes between the earlier and later versions of these *Cacciato* fragments have been studied by O'Brien's bibliographer, Catherine Calloway. She has shown that the stories are largely reproduced in their original form in *Cacciato* and argues that any changes reflect a major theme of the completed novel, the ambiguity of real experiences. For our purposes, however, particular changes are less significant than the role of the stories in both generating and organizing *Cacciato* as a whole and in the relationship they suggest between O'Brien and Berlin as trauma survivors and as trauma writers.

"Fire in the Hole" appeared as a tentative title for *Combat Zone* as early as 1972 in the *Washington Post*, but it is also the title of Chapter 11 of *Cacciato*, which therefore may be considered along with the other stories from which the novel was composed. It describes the willful destruction of a Vietnamese village, Hoi An, after one of Alpha Company's most respected members has been killed in the deserted paddy fields nearby. As their lieutenant calls in white phosphorus and high explosive shells, the GIs join the carnage, firing their M-16s into the holocaust "until they were exhausted." By then, "the village was a hole" (100). The fragment/chapter ends with their making night camp along the Song [river] Tra Bong, where "they bathed in the river and made camp and ate supper. When it was night they began talking about Jim Pederson. It was always better to talk about it" (100). An understated description of a war crime, "Fire in the Hole" could have appeared in *Combat Zone*; it closely resembles O'Brien's description there of the destruction of Tri Binh 4 in Chapter VIII. In fact, it might even be a refabrication of that disturbing experience, with an ironically cathartic coda that made it more appropriate for use in *Cacciato*. The early appearance of its title in the *Washington Post* also marks "Fire in the

Hole" as something of a transitional piece between the memoirist mode of *Combat Zone* and the more complex fictionalizing of the later novel.[3] The narrative centers on two traumatic experiences for the soldiers of Berlin's platoon, both of them involving destructive violence: the grisly death of an intimate and the brutalizing of civilians. "Fire in the Hole" begins with graphic details of their comrade's mutilation: "Pederson was a mess. They wrapped him in his own poncho. Doc Peret found the broken dog tags and slipped them into Pederson's mouth and taped it shut" (98). It ends with the eradication of the village, which is already empty of its evidently hostile or frightened inhabitants. Talking about what has happened is better than repressing feelings of shame, guilt, hatred, and grief, but it is unlikely to fully cleanse the soldiers' traumatic staining any more effectively than washing themselves in the river will.

Like "Fire in the Hole," all but two of the six earlier published portions of *Cacciato* focus on moments within the war when Paul Berlin or other squad members are traumatized while undergoing the experiences of combat, abusive violence, deprivation, or disorientation. In each of the four, one or more of Berlin's comrades has just been killed or is about to be. And even the two stories that do not directly involve trauma focus on Paul Berlin's psychic desolation. In "Calling Home," the last one published, Paul telephones his parents in Iowa (the symbolic site of domestic happiness in *Northern Lights*) from Chu Lai and imagines his family, their typical activities, and his hometown while the phone rings, but no one answers. "The Way It Mostly Was" describes the numbing boredom and physical strain of a full-pack infantry march, juxtaposing his lieutenant's admiration for Paul's stoic endurance with Berlin's mindless exhaustion. O'Brien's commanding officer eloquently satisfies himself with the epigraph from Dante that ironically introduced *Combat Zone*: "The greatest gift of God, thought the lieutenant in admiration of Private First Class Paul Berlin's climb, is freedom of will" (*Cacciato* 203). For him, the "boy represented so much good—fortitude, discipline, loyalty, self-control, courage, toughness." But Paul himself feels only a loss of self that alienates him from his own body: "He marched up the road with no exercise of will, no desire and no determination, no pride, just legs and lungs, climbing without thought and without will and without purpose. . . . He was dull of mind, blunt of spirit, numb of history, and struck with wonder that he could not stop climbing the red road toward the mountains" (202–3, 204). By contrast, neither of the

Cacciato-related stories left out of the novel focuses on the direct experience of combat trauma: "Keeping Watch by Night" involves a conversation among Paul's squad members, and "Speaking of Courage" takes place in the United States after Berlin has returned from the war.

The genesis of *Cacciato*, therefore, is a group of stories that portrays the war as a site of trauma and psychic alienation; and the novel so generated incorporates them into a more comprehensive narrative that tries to use them cathartically. Within *Cacciato*, the five traumatic fragments help to fill out Paul's recovery of past facts that have been too terrible to recall until he begins his observation post meditations. Here the parallel between O'Brien as the author of *Cacciato* and Berlin as the protagonist who is trying to dream his way out of the war becomes very close: Beginning with significant traumatic incidents, both Paul and his creator construct a larger narrative in which each fragment will become more meaningful. Whether O'Brien simply imagined these shocking episodes, refabricated them from the accounts of American GIs or other writers, or rewrote his own personal experiences merely specifies the exact terms of the parallel. *Cacciato* is a novel grounded on the trauma of American combat soldiers in Viet Nam that attempts to imagine beyond it.

Some reviewers (e.g., Updike) found O'Brien's vignettes of battlefield trauma extremely powerful writing but complained that the book lost focus and force by continually shifting to the fantasy quest after Cacciato, which seemed by comparison an adventure story altogether less serious in subject and tone. Structurally, however, the pursuit is the primary narrative of the novel (as well as its title), and its interruption by traumatic circumstances and recollections provokes, in turn, Paul Berlin's observation post reflections on the progress of his dream. Indeed, without Berlin's attempt to sustain the fantasy, the earlier stories would simply be a collection of grim sketches, like the chapters of *Combat Zone*. Moreover, the imagined odyssey to Paris incorporates the trauma of Vietnam within itself, so that only by following it all the way can Paul Berlin try to overcome his breakdown.

While going after Cacciato is the most important element of Paul Berlin's dream, his attempt to remember trauma in order to transcend it, the fantasy narrative is not only an afterthought of its protagonist but also a later addition to the originally published material out of which O'Brien developed the novel. None of the eight early stories describes the journey to

Paris, although it takes up nineteen of the novel's forty-six chapters; by contrast, there are only ten chapters each of combat deaths and of observation post meditations. Thus, just as Paul Berlin has been traumatized at the beginning of the novel and imagines the pursuit of Cacciato as a supplement, substitute, or imaginary compensation for what he has experienced, O'Brien's pre-*Cacciato* stories—three of which won national prizes for short fiction even before the novel was published ("Going After Cacciato," "Night March," and "Speaking of Courage")—were transformed into a more comprehensive fiction by the invention of a journey to Paris.

This fantasy is first contemplated by Paul Berlin near the beginning of Chapter 2, the first of the "Observation Post" chapters, where it is defined as countertherapy:

> Yes, he thought, a fine idea. Cacciato leading them west through peaceful country . . . toward Paris.
>
> It was a splendid idea.
>
> Paul Berlin, whose only goal was to live long enough to establish goals worth living for still longer, stood high in the tower by the sea, the night soft all around him, and wondered, not for the first time, about the immense powers of his own imagination. A truly awesome notion. Not a dream, an idea. An idea to develop, to tinker with and build and sustain, to draw out as an artist draws out his visions. (43)

The final simile makes explicit the analogy between Berlin's meditations and O'Brien's creation of the novel. While the immediate context of Paul's need to imagine a redemptive scenario is his breakdown during the search for Cacciato, *Cacciato* as a whole is also O'Brien's attempt to turn the trauma of Viet Nam into something more meaningful.

"Going After Cacciato": From Catalog to Breakdown

Although the fantasy narrative is not described in any of the early stories, the idea of an escape from the war motivates the longest of them, the prize-winning "Going After Cacciato." Besides giving its name to the novel, this earlier masterpiece lays its groundwork. With minor revisions, it serves as Chapter 1 and defines Viet Nam as a site of trauma that must be escaped. It also shows us why Paul Berlin's dream is necessary and how it becomes possible.

Cacciato opens with O'Brien's most distinctive stylistic device, the mundane catalog or list that evokes significance through deliberate understatement. He has described this beginning as a "threnody" (McCaffery 144), but it also initiates a cumulative sequence of details and references that mark the soldiers' experience as unbearable, and it records ways of enduring or rejecting it: "It was a bad time. Billy Boy Watkins was dead, and so was Frenchie Tucker. Billy Boy had died of fright, scared to death on the field of battle, and Frenchie Tucker had been shot through the nose. Bernie Lynn and Lieutenant Sidney Martin had died in tunnels. Pederson was dead and Rudy Chassler was dead. Buff was dead. Ready Mix was dead. They were all among the dead" (13). "Bad time" understates the terrible circumstances described and carries with it the weight of psychic and moral hopelessness that the term "bad" had carried in *Combat Zone.* "The dead" that round out this catalog of names remind us of all the victims of the war, however, so that the sense of loss goes beyond this particular platoon of American soldiers. But "they" has double reference in the sentence, referring not simply to the dead soldiers but also to their living comrades, who must deal with the fates of Billy Boy Watkins and the others, and who may be haunted by their continued presence in memory or imagination. Indeed, the very presence of the catalog supposes an audience for its details, and the rest of the paragraph makes clear that the roll call of the dead continues to engage the minds of the survivors, including Paul Berlin. Billy Boy's death seems to require explanation, the sort of thing that would stick in the memory—and it also suggests that trauma itself can kill; Frenchie's death is grotesque, but the tunnel casualties are reported matter-of-factly, and the roll call ends by simply ticking off names, as if remembering all the details would become so unbearable that it would be better to bury them quickly.

The list of the dead is the source of Paul's narrative of past facts, a series of war stories that recall, as fully as he had been able to witness them, the circumstances of his former comrades' deaths. Each records what had been a traumatizing event, and their cumulative effect is overwhelming— hence the progressive suppression of details in the list. But because the dead are already absent at the beginning of *Cacciato*, the retelling becomes elegiac rather than merely disturbing. Paul's subsequent memories have a therapeutic effect for himself, since being able to reimagine the terror of those earlier moments helps to put it behind him. Moreover, insofar as O'Brien's protagonist is ashamed of his fear, fully rewitnessing these terrible episodes constitutes an imaginative act of courage. But Paul's fleshing out of the catalog has a more communally therapeutic purpose as well, particularly for someone who feels alienated from his comrades, as we shall see. While each episode finally puts the dead behind him, it also allows them to live again in Paul's imagination. Thus, the retrospective episodes constitute an extended burial service, mimicking the memorializing role of literature itself.

Many of Paul's recollected scenes end just before the subject dies. This truncation has the antitraumatic, self-protective function of stopping just short of physical atrocity, but it also resurrects the individual while he is still alive. Thus, Pederson is last seen shooting at the army helicopter that has brought him to his death and "accidentally" killed him (Chapter 20, "Landing Zone Bravo"); Bernie Lynn is last seen being fed M&Ms by the medic Doc Peret, a placebo that indicates imminent death (Chapter 9: "How Bernie Lynn Died After Frenchie Tucker"); Rudy Chassler is last seen just as he triggers a mine (Chapter 16: "Pickup Games"); and Lieutenant Sidney Martin's death cannot be described at all. In two cases, those of Frenchie Tucker and Buff, Paul had arrived only after the death had occurred, so he must describe the corpse in recalling his experience. And Ready Mix dies unobserved and virtually anonymous, like his name. Whatever the circumstances, however, remembering transforms the catalog into stories that memorialize the dead so that the survivor's life can go on.

The names of the dead are followed by the circumstances of the living, who are themselves being reduced to the state of nature, one of O'Brien's few attempts at suggesting the effects of physical deprivation, a clinically defined source of traumatization (Shay 121–23):

> The rain fed fungus that grew in the men's boots and socks, and their socks rotted, and their feet turned white and soft so that the skin could be scraped off with a fingernail, and Stink Harris woke up screaming one night with a leech on his tongue. When it was not raining, a low mist moved across the paddies, blending the elements into a single gray element, and the war was cold and pasty and rotten. Lieutenant Corson, who came to replace Lieutenant Sidney Martin, contracted the dysentery. The tripflares were useless. The ammunition corroded and the foxholes filled with mud and water during the nights, and in the mornings there was always the next village and

the war was always the same. The monsoons were part of the war. In early September Vaught caught an infection. (13)

Casualties include the wounded and are not limited to combat operations: Vaught scrapes his arm with his bayonet to show how well he has sharpened it—"Like a Gillette Blue Blade," he proudly tells Oscar Johnson, "but in two days the bacteria soaked in and the arm turned yellow, so they bundled him up and called in a dustoff, and Vaught left the war. He never came back" (14). But he loses the arm in a hospital in Japan from which he sends a breezily racist letter (Japan was "smoky and full of slopes") and comically obscene poses of himself, and his example in turn encourages more direct self-mutilation: "Soon afterward Ben Nystrom shot himself through the foot, but he did not die, and he wrote no letters" (14).

Following the catalog of the dead and the misery of field conditions, these self-inflicted injuries seem like desperate responses to traumatic circumstances, means of removing oneself from an intolerable situation. Vaught's million-dollar wound may be accidental; but Nystrom's, a response to his comrade's escape from the war zone, is not. For the rest of the platoon, however, another means of dealing with trauma is to reimagine it sarcastically:

> These were all things to joke about. The rain, too. And the cold. Oscar Johnson said it made him think of Detroit in the month of May. "Lootin' weather," he liked to say. "The dark an' gloom, just right for rape an' lootin.'" Then someone would say that Oscar had a swell imagination for a darkie.
>
> That was one of the jokes. There was a joke about Oscar. There were many jokes about Billy Boy Watkins, the way he'd collapsed of fright on the field of battle. Another joke was about the lieutenant's dysentery, and another was about Paul Berlin's purple biles. There were jokes about the postcard pictures of Christ that Jim Pederson used to carry, and Stink's ringworm, and the way Buff's helmet filled with life after death. Some of the jokes were about Cacciato. Dumb as a bullet, Stink said. Dumb as a month-old oyster fart, said Harold Murphy. (14)

Oscar's joke operates by making Viet Nam absurdly familiar, but it also locates the soldiers in an environment where rape and looting go on. Jokes about the dead function to dismiss trauma through clowning about death rather than worrying about it—rough humor and slightly heretical, like the mockery of the postcard Christ, and perhaps distasteful to Paul Berlin, who is himself a subject of mockery.

Since jokes about the lieutenant would probably not be told in his presence, we might wonder about those that caricature Paul and Cacciato. If told behind their backs, they suggest that neither soldier is on easy terms with the rest of the platoon—unlike Oscar, for instance, who can be playfully addressed as a "darkie." Certainly Berlin never seems at ease within the platoon, distancing himself physically and emotionally from the others. He always walks last in file when his squad is on patrol, and when brought to Lieutenant Corson at the beginning of the search for Cacciato, he has to be introduced by Doc Peret and is then mistaken for Vaught by the lieutenant, who doesn't know what squad he is in. Paul's "purple biles" are Doc Peret's euphemism for Berlin's hyperanxiety: He suffers a series of traumatic breakdowns in *Cacciato* and is frequently ashamed that he is so afraid to endure combat. Cacciato, on the other hand, seems almost witlessly fearless, but while Paul tends to shun the rest of the platoon, the childish and maladroit future deserter is shunned by the others. Labeled "the gremlin" by Stink Harris—an epithet that combines eeriness with fouling things up—he seems to be tolerated as an oddball. (According to O'Brien, he was modeled after a clumsy, incompetent basic trainee who is named Kline in *Combat Zone* [Schroeder 1984: 150].)

Paul and Cacciato, as subjects of disparaging jokes by other members of the platoon, are thus casually associated together from the beginning of the novel: Paul is emotionally unstable, Cacciato mentally empty. The fantasy narrative will try to bring the squad together as intimate comrades, since in reality Paul feels distanced from everyone in the squad except the medic, Doc Peret. Don Ringnalda has associated Peret with O'Brien's fictional enterprise itself (99), and the medic's vaguely French name might even be echoed in Berlin's fantasy of the peace of Paris. But Paul's relationship to Peret throughout the novel most obviously parallels that of a therapist and his client, as if Berlin were in need of detraumatization. Paul's uneasiness with the rest of his comrades begins from his first day in the war, just after he has witnessed a combat fatality for the first time: "He would begin to smell like the others, even look like them, but, by God, he would not join them. He would adjust. He would play the part. But he would not join them. . . . When they joked about Billy Boy, he would laugh, pretending it was funny, and he would not let on. . . . The trick was not to take it personally. Stay aloof. Follow the herd but don't join it. That would be the real trick. The trick would be to keep himself separate. To watch things" (253). Staying aloof from the "herd" of GIs verbally echoes O'Brien's ironic self-characterization in *Combat Zone* and suggests that Berlin, like his creator, is embarrassed to be a soldier. When Paul does join in with other squad members, the circumstances are traumatically shameful: the obliteration of Hoi An (Chapter 11), the brutal frisking of civilians along the Song Tra Bong (recalled in Chapter 21 as he fantasizes a "rail road toward Paris"), the murder of the squad's commanding officer (Chapter 36). Ultimately, Berlin's uneasiness toward the rest of the squad is a product of traumatization and self-contempt: He fears revealing his own terror of combat to those whose apparent inurement to the war he both envies and despises. His father has encouraged him to "be calm . . . ignore the bad stuff, look for the good" (250), but since everything about the war is bad, the only way he can follow such counsel is to imagine another scenario. "To watch things" marks him as an observer, like Sergeant O'Brien, registering details for later refabrication.

According to Paul, the idea of walking to Paris is Cacciato's, not his own. While Berlin rejects others, locked in a posttraumatic survivorhood that seems to have started after his first experience of combat, Cacciato seems oblivious to hardship and trauma and eager to please but is shunned by his companions as a "ding-dong" (19). When the squad finally passes him the ball in a pickup basketball game, he misses the open shot; when he persistently practices dribbling afterward, he gets on everyone's nerves during an ominously uneventful search-and-destroy mission (e.g., "Jesus! Somebody tell Cacciato to stop bouncin' that fuckin *ball"*—129). Berlin has difficulty even visualizing Cacciato's appearance, which is "curiously unfinished" and childlike, but he is most frequently characterized as stupid, perhaps because he seems so ignorantly fearless. He keeps a childish scrapbook, VUES OF VIETNAM, which treats the war as a tourist spectacle; it includes shots of himself posing with everyone in the squad but also with "the corpse of a shot-dead VC in green pajamas . . . holding up the dead boy's head by a shock of brilliant black hair, . . . smiling" (147). He is happy to crawl down into a VC tunnel to retrieve Frenchie Tucker, who has just been killed, but his self-endangerment is rejected. And when Buff is decapitated, only Cacciato is willing to retrieve his helmet and toss the head inside it into the rice paddies.

Yet it is Cacciato who literally brings the squad together to follow him. Just after the list of Cacciato jokes ends, so does O'Brien's catalog:

> In October, near the end of the month, Cacciato left the war.
>
> "He's gone away," said Doc Peret. "Split, departed."
>
> Lieutenant Corson did not seem to hear. He was too old to be a lieutenant. The veins in his nose and cheeks were broken. His back was weak. Once he had been a captain on his way to becoming a major, but whiskey and the fourteen dull years between Korea and Vietnam had ended all that, and now he was just an old lieutenant with the dysentery. . . .
>
> "Paris," Doc Peret repeated. "That's what he tells Paul Berlin, and that's what Berlin tells me, and that's what I'm telling you." (14–15)

By this point in Chapter 1, O'Brien has introduced virtually his entire cast of characters, and the cumulative force of his ironic description of lost souls, the living repressing their fear by making jokes about the dead, makes Cacciato's resolution to walk to Paris understandable. The roll call of the dead makes an escape from the war seem necessary, and the examples of Vaught and Nystrom make it seem possible. Walking to Paris is evidently lunatic, but is it more crazy than remaining in the war?

Corson is stoned at the beginning of the novel and only gradually realizes what has happened. Initially, he sees Cacciato's flight as not just crazy but also symptomatic:

> "I mean, why? What sort of silly crap is this—walking to gay Paree? What's happening? Just tell me, what's wrong with you people? All of you, what's wrong?" . . .
>
> "Answer me. What for? What's wrong with you shits? Walking to gay Paree, what's *wrong*?" (18–19)

His befuddled questions register a lack of purpose within the platoon; although "the men loved him" because he does not risk their lives for the sake of military mission (175–76), he is aware that the mission itself is hollow. In attributing Cacciato's motives for desertion to the rest of the platoon, he acknowledges their legitimacy. The question "What's wrong?" has so many disturbing answers—political, military, moral, psychological— that it can't be resolved, certainly not by the lieutenant. If the platoon's secret desire to desert is one symptom of demoralization, Corson's pot smoking is another.

O'Brien's initial allusion to jokes about the commanding officer, Paul Berlin, and Cacciato curiously connects the two openly alienated GIs and their physically decrepit commander, who suffers the embarrassments of dysentery (just as Paul befouls himself during his traumatic breakdowns). Indeed, the lieutenant and the deserter will be Berlin's closest psychic companions, impelling the creation of Paul's quest fantasy and subsequently motivating and sustaining its content and form. It is Corson, after all, who first validates going after Cacciato when he orders the Third Squad to follow him. The lieutenant's quest after the gremlin lasts a full seven days, punctuated by discussions about continuing or breaking it off, and ends just at the Laotian border, beyond which the deserter would have escaped the war. Its motivations are as ambiguous as those of Cacciato's flight, however, and both provide Berlin with the redemptive possibilities of his own fabulous journey. On the second day, Corson reports to headquarters that he is in pursuit of the enemy in order to justify an otherwise dubious operation. Indeed, he becomes more and more ill as it continues, as if there were something deeply troubling about the mission. While Stink Harris later insists on continuing the pursuit and gleefully anticipates bringing Cacciato to justice—"Dummy's got to be taught you can't hump your way home" (24)—Doc Peret and Harold Murphy advise giving up because the deserter will return anyway once he realizes the impossibility of his situation. Meanwhile, Cacciato leaves Berlin with a detailed map of his route and makes no attempt to hide himself from his pursuers. And when they reach the Laotian border, the possibility of desertion is now available to everyone in the squad, as if Cacciato has provided an escape route from the trauma of Vietnam. The night before he orders the assault on Cacciato's final hill, Corson is deathly ill: Does the lieutenant really want the deserter to escape? Would he secretly wish to follow him farther? Paul's own attitude toward Cacciato's flight also changes as the squad follows the route of escape. At first, the idea of "humping to Paris . . . was silly. It had always been silly, even during the good times, but now the silliness was sad. It couldn't be done. It just wasn't possible, and it was silly and sad" (21). But on the night before the squad prepares to surround and capture Cacciato, Paul realizes that

the odds were poison, but it could be done.

He might even have tried himself. With courage, he thought, he might even have joined in, and that was the one sorry thing about it, the sad thing: He might have. (39)

That deserting would have been an act of bravery returns us to the moral anxiety that pervades *Combat Zone*, of course. But when Third Squad advances on Cacciato's hill in the morning, O'Brien reshapes the paradox of courageous fear as traumatic breakdown.

Paul Berlin: From Breakdown to Trauma Writing

While Paul Berlin mimics O'Brien's own fictional sense-making, he does so as a trauma survivor, and his dream is an attempt to cope with his own psychic collapse. O'Brien breaks off the first chapter of the novel at the point when Cacciato has been surrounded by the squad on his hill and Paul fires off a green flare to signal his advance with Stink Harris. The outcome remains uncertain until the final chapter, which is also titled "Going After Cacciato" and is physically divided into two sections. In the first, Paul has imagined himself and the squad all the way to Paris, where they have finally cornered Cacciato in a rundown tenement apartment and are about to burst through its green door. Paul is forced by Oscar Johnson to lead the way, but when he opens the door, he finds an empty room and breaks down physically and psychically, hysterically firing his weapon on full automatic and losing control of his bowels. Bewildered, he wonders "what had gone wrong" (389) and then—after an explicit break in the text—he finds himself back with the rest of the squad at the base of Cacciato's hill, being variously comforted and despised for his mad minute, changing his soiled trousers, ashamed of his breakdown and trying to comprehend it:

> How did it start? A kind of trembling, maybe. He remembered the fear coming, but he did not remember why. Then the shaking feeling. The enormous noise, shaken by his own weapon, the way he'd squeezed to keep it from jerking away from him. Simple folly, that was all.
>
> He picked up the rifle.
>
> Gold cartridges sparkled where they had fallen, strewn in the grass like spilt pennies. (392)

Here at the end of the novel, then, Berlin's fantasy of a future pursuit to Paris wraps back into the end of the actual assault on Cacciato's hill, and

"Going After Cacciato," Chapter 1, is concluded in Paul's memory by "Going After Cacciato," Chapter 46. His actual breakdown is thus doubly displaced and doubly re-covered up, first intruding into the fantasy pursuit of Cacciato and breaking it off inconclusively, then yielding to direct memory of what happened *after* his collapse on Cacciato's hill. The break in O'Brien's text marks a transition from fantasy to fact, from an imagined future to the past, from Cacciato's vanishing in Paris to his vanishing in Viet Nam, but it also represents an experience of traumatization so intense that Paul cannot understand, articulate, or even clearly remember what has happened. The fantasy, which had been devised as a means of considering what might have happened to Cacciato, ultimately leads back to the same blank place in Paul's consciousness that it had attempted to satisfy: Because of his blackout below Cacciato's hill, Paul does not know what has become of the deserter, and thus his green flare leads to a green door with no one on the other side. In one sense, then, *Cacciato* is an immense working out of the ineffability of trauma.

The working out, therefore, must be its own reward. By the end of the novel, Paul Berlin's dream has at least brought him to discover its own origins as he confronts his posttraumatic humiliation. His spent cartridges are displaced images of both shame and possible redemption, "spilt" like a premature ejaculation, yet pieces of "gold" to be gathered up. As he re-collects in his own imagination his rifle and the empty cartridges, he recalls the reactions to his folly by other squad members, enduring the mockery of Stink Harris, the anger of Harold Murphy, the contempt of Oscar Johnson. But he also accepts again the good-humored therapy of Doc Peret ("It's okay, . . . all over. Fine now. . . . Just the tinkle of the biles, no sweat"—389) and some vintage Kool-Aid ("one last magnum of 1914 Goofy Grape"—391), posttraumatic medicine. Doc dismisses his anxious questions about the fate of Cacciato—"It's over. Tell me if that isn't the sweetest stuff you ever swallowed"—for Cacciato's fate is at the heart of Paul's trauma.

Most important is the reaction of the lieutenant, who comforts Berlin just after his breakdown and blanking out and later keeps guard with him on the night following his collapse. Neither Paul nor we can know just what happened to Cacciato—was he killed, possibly by Paul's barrage, or has he escaped, alerted by its noise? If he has escaped, an outcome that Paul needs to believe in, no one in the squad will ever know the outcome of Cacciato's flight, for Corson has called off continuing the pursuit. As the old lieutenant and the twenty-year-old PFC survey the darkness before them, however, Corson allows some reasons for hope:

> They watched the immense stillness of the paddies, the serenity of things, the moon climbing beyond the mountains. Sometimes it was hard to believe it was a war.
>
> "I guess it's better this way," the old man finally said. "There's worse things can happen. There's plenty of worse things."
>
> "True enough, sir."
>
> "And who knows? He might make it. He might do all right." The lieutenant's voice was flat like the land. "Miserable odds, but—"
>
> "But maybe."
>
> "Yes," the lieutenant said. "Maybe so." (394–95)

This final scene of the book generates everything between the unresolved conclusion of the first "Going After Cacciato" chapter and this moment, which ends the second and the novel itself. In between the assault on Cacciato's hill and its aftermath, Paul has broken down, so that Cacciato's fate has become a mystery to him. But Corson's final words encourage him to replace the blank at the heart of his personal collapse with an imagined continuation of Cacciato's flight that will transform traumatization into redemption for himself, for the lieutenant, and for the squad as a whole. An escape from Viet Nam can be imagined because of the lieutenant's willingness to consider Cacciato's reaching Paris a possibility. Just as important, it validates an escape ethically—"worse things" are the norm in this bad war, as O'Brien's introduction grimly records, and Corson is both blessing Cacciato's possible escape and approving Berlin's desire to believe in it.

Since Paul Berlin's breakdown has ended the search for Cacciato, the lieutenant's approval of the attempt to reach Paris not only relieves Paul's guilt but also inspires the compensating fiction of escape for the entire squad. The conversation with Corson thus has directly prompted the beginning of Paul's fantasy narrative, which begins to take shape at the beginning of Chapter 2:

> Cacciato's round face became the moon. The valleys and ridges and fast-flowing plains dissolved, and now the moon was just the moon.
>
> Paul Berlin sat up. A fine idea. . . .

Yes, he thought, a fine idea. Cacciato leading them west through peaceful country, deep country perfumed by lilacs and burning hemp, a boy coaxing them step by step through rich and fertile country toward Paris. (43)

Standing guard alone now, Paul embraces the suggestion that Corson had validated when they had kept watch together after his breakdown, an inspiration fathered by the lieutenant's suggestion that Cacciato "might make it." The moon was present then, as it was when Berlin first encountered Cacciato just after the death of Billy Boy Watkins (261), and it will summon Cacciato's presence throughout the journey to Paris as well, like some symbolic talisman of the imagination.

The dream of pursuit that follows Paul's initial meditations in the observation post attempts to transform his shameful interference with the capture of Cacciato into something positive. Because his own revulsion with the war seems to be shared by his commanding officer, because the most hapless of his comrades has had the courage to leave the war and has had his flight implicitly commended by Corson, Paul can dare to dream of desertion himself. Since Corson can only hope that an escape is possible, however, because Cacciato's fate is unclear, and since both his flight and his pursuit are morally problematic, Paul's imagined escape from the war becomes an exploration of specific questions that he cannot answer and that, in turn, raise larger issues that he cannot, or dares not, articulate.

Cacciato has been commonly interpreted as a novel primarily concerned with the ambiguity of reality or the thin line—if any exists—between fact and fiction, or what has been experienced and what can be imagined. Certainly, these issues occupy its protagonist as he considers the uncertain fate of Cacciato and imagines pursuing him to Paris. Such traditional, even clichéd themes, have been validated by O'Brien's own comments on the novel, but Paul's uncertainties have a simpler and more direct explanation. Paul doesn't know what happened to Cacciato because he suffered a nervous breakdown at the moment when he and the rest of his squad were about to capture or kill the deserter. But Berlin's personal collapse is a product of all his experiences in Viet Nam, experiences shared by his comrades and variously displaced, repressed, or ignored. In particular, they have been shared by Cacciato, whose flight reflects their own fears and their deepest desires. Paul thus imagines a collective narrative of desertion—a continued pursuit of Cacciato—that might incorporate and ultimately heal his own trauma by freeing all his fellow soldiers from Vietnam. Although incorporating what has happened helps to generate the soldier's dream, however, it also threatens to terminate it, leaving Berlin continually surprised and uncertain about the course of his fantasy but all the more determined to carry it on, although it leads in the end to an empty room in Paris. Ultimately, what happened to Cacciato remains a mystery—even in fantasy—reflecting a traumatic breakdown that the survivor can never fully recuperate or understand.

Berlin never explicitly addresses the mystery of his collapse on Cacciato's hill. It had been anticipated by an earlier incident during the squad's pursuit of Cacciato, when Stink Harris triggered a smoke grenade planted by the deserter on the trail behind him. For the squad, however, reacting to the familiar and horrifying sounds of its detonation, Cacciato's grisly joke is traumatizing:

> Stink knew it as it happened. In one fuzzed motion he flung himself down and away, rolling, covering his skull, mouth open, yelping a trivial little yelp. . . .
>
> Eddie and Oscar and Doc Peret dropped flat. Harold Murphy did an oddly graceful jackknife for a man of his size. The lieutenant collapsed. And Paul Berlin brought his knees to his belly, coiling and falling, closing his eyes and his fists and his mouth. (34)

Paul tries to count numbers as a means of controlling himself psychologically and physically, but fear paralyzes his mind and he fouls himself anyway: "First the belly, the bowels, and next the lungs. He was steeled, ready. There was no explosion. Count, he thought. But he couldn't get a grip on the numbers. His teeth had points in his brain, his lungs hurt, but there was no explosion. Smoke, he thought without thinking, smoke" (34–35). Even after Doc has noted that it is harmless—"'Smoke,' [he] whispered softly. 'A booby's booby trap'"—the squad remains traumatized:

> Stink Harris was bawling. He was on his hands and knees, chin against his throat. Oscar and Eddie hadn't moved.
>
> "Had us," the lieutenant was chanting to himself. Senile-sounding. "Could've had us all, he could've." (35)

And Paul remains frozen in his shame and paralysis even as the others begin to recover:

The numbers kept running through his head, and he counted them, but he could not move. Dumb, he thought as he counted, a struck-dumb little yo-yo who can't move. . . .

He was vaguely aware of being watched. Then keenly aware. . . . He wanted to apologize to whoever was watching, but his lungs ached and his mouth wouldn't work. He wasn't breathing. Inhale? Exhale? He'd lost track.

You asshole, he thought. You ridiculous little yo-yo. (36)

This minutely described traumatic breakdown anticipates what happens shortly afterward when Paul empties his bowels and his M-16 as the squad begins to mount Cacciato's hill, and it helps to account for his blackout. At the heart of each collapse is a paralyzing, literally overwhelming fear. But its motivation, complex and self-contradictory, repels self-awareness.

Most simply, of course, Paul is afraid of losing his life, a primal, animal fear that has already similarly disabled him during an earlier large-scale operation: "Twitching in his hidden little depression, hiding out during the one big battle of the war, he could only lie there, twitching . . . as the bombers came to bomb the mountains" (214). But to Paul, fear itself is a threat. Another breakdown occurs on his first combat operation, when Billy Boy Watkins literally dies of fear, lethally traumatized by having his foot blown off. Then, too, fear is a sign of cowardice and a reproach to his own dignity, threatening him with a humiliating loss of self-control. "He knew he would not fight well" in the battle in the mountains (202), well-aware that his fear would certainly shame him even if it didn't kill him.

The assault on Cacciato's hill provokes more complex anxieties, however, which are buried in the series of traumata that Paul will be able to re-visit only when he begins to imagine his dream. The smoke grenade that might have killed Stink Harris and other squad members is a startling re-minder of the grenade that the squad did use earlier to kill its previous commander, Lieutenant Sidney Martin. Martin in turn had been partly re-sponsible for the deaths of Frenchie Tucker and Bernie Lynn by forcing them to search VC tunnels instead of just dropping explosives in them, so that by fragging him Paul and his comrades have saved themselves from carrying out his orders. Everyone in the squad except Cacciato had as-sented to his death by touching the fatal grenade, which Paul had been forced to press against the lone holdout. Cacciato's grenade thus rein-vokes and condemns a traumatic buried history of indirect but deliberate fratricide and calls attention to the moral implications of his recapture. If he is protecting his life by fleeing, the squad is threatening it by bringing him back. Paul can even imagine the mission's outcome as an execution, a displaced version of the murder of Lieutenant Sidney Martin: "Where was it going, where would it end? Paul Berlin was suddenly struck between the eyes by a vision of murder. Butchery, no less: Cacciato's right temple caving inward, silence, then an enormous explosion of outward-going brains. It scared him" (28–29). After all, Cacciato has traumatized his comrades but spared their lives, tried to escape but led them toward freedom.

The ambiguity of the mission—are they prosecuting the war or fleeing from it themselves?—adds to Berlin's moral confusion and makes him fearful of capturing the deserter. The night before the assault Berlin cannot sleep: "He tried to imagine a proper ending. The possibilities were closing themselves out, and, though he tried, it was hard to see a happy end to it" (38). In the morning, waiting as the rest of the squad cuts off routes of escape for Cacciato, still "trying to imagine a rightful but still happy ending," he wishes for "a point at which he could stop being afraid. Where all the bad things, the painful and grotesque and ugly things, would give way to something better. He pretended he had crossed that threshold" (41). But as he follows Stink Harris and the green flare that signals their advance to the others, his final thoughts turn from meditation to ambiguous encouragement: "'Go,' whispered Paul Berlin. It did not seem enough. 'Go,' he said, and then he shouted, 'Go'" (42).

"Go" is the last word Berlin utters before his breakdown on Cacciato's hill. In the last of his observation post meditations, with the sun about to rise and the fantasy pursuit of Cacciato about to reach its inconclusive climax in Paris, he has at last recovered everything that led to the pretraumatic moment. As the dream of escape yields to one more day of aimless patrolling in Quang Ngai Province, Paul has awakened to the fact that

> [t]he war was still a war, and he was still a soldier. He hadn't run. The issue was courage, and courage was will power, and this was his failing.
>
> . . . the facts were simple: They went after Cacciato, they chased him into the mountains, they tried hard. They cornered him on a small grassy hill. They surrounded the hill. They waited through the night. And at dawn they shot the sky full of flares and then they moved in. "Go," Paul Berlin said. He shouted it—"Go!"

That was the end of it. The last known fact.

What remained were possibilities. With courage it might have been done. (379–80)

The breakdown is thus an extreme reaction to an unbearable moral crisis. Since it is associated with lack of courage, the last known fact is a self-directed exhortation to confront a terrible situation of potential fratricide and betrayal: Even if Cacciato is not killed, even if he does not kill to protect himself, he will be punished for leading his comrades to the edge of freedom. More generally, capturing Cacciato would deny the moral force of desertion, the courage that would reject a bad war rather than participate in it. But, of course, Paul's exhortation to himself is also an exhortation to Cacciato, punctuated by the hysterical barrage from his M-16 that both ends Paul's participation in the operation and warns Cacciato that he is being assaulted. Ultimately, Paul's traumatized reaction to the agony of capturing Cacciato culminates a series of breakdowns prompted by abusive violence and his own fear of death. Yet it is even more unbearable than the actual deaths of others. He is able to recall those terrible moments in full over the course of his dream, but the assault on Cacciato's hill has been almost obliterated—he remains sentient of only the final "go" and an experience of losing control over his weapon and his body. As noted above, the assault is closest in its significance and circumstances to the murder of Lieutenant Sidney Martin, and its psychic repression is also similar. In both instances Paul joins in violence against another American soldier, and in each instance exactly what happened is unclear. As Dean McWilliams notes (248), the fragging is the only certain platoon member's death that is never detailed, as if the very fact were too difficult to remember. Unlike the execution of Martin, however, his breakdown over Cacciato has some redemptive moral and psychological value for Berlin.

Paul never tries to analyze his collapse on Cacciato's hill, which is too shameful and too ethically problematic to be confronted. But one of its outcomes—his ignorance of Cacciato's fate—enables him to entertain the possibility of escaping from war to peace through the fantasy narrative. His own breakdown can be morally validated as long as going after Cacciato can replace capturing Cacciato; and as long as what happened to Cacciato remains an open question, he can be pursued to Paris. Paul tries to imagine what might have happened by posing such questions and then imagining the entire narrative between "Going After Cacciato," Chapter 1, and "Going After Cacciato," Chapter 46, in order to investigate them: "Had it ended there on Cacciato's grassy hill, flares coloring the morning sky? Had it ended in tragedy? Had it ended with a jerking, shaking feeling—noise and confusion? Or had it ended farther along the trail west? Had it ever ended? What, in fact, had become of Cacciato? More precisely—as Doc Peret would insist it be phrased—more precisely, what part was fact and what part was the extension of fact? And how were facts separated from possibilities? What had really happened and what merely might have happened? How did it end?" (44). The initial questions, which fearfully return to the scene of the breakdown and pose the worst possible outcome, are gradually replaced by more satisfying uncertainties that leave what has simply happened in fact behind them. Unable to bear affirmative answers to the first three questions, Paul abandons the circumstances of his own traumatization for questions that cannot be answered "yes" or "no." What happened to Cacciato "in fact" gives way to more important questions: "Why had Cacciato left the war? Was it courage or ignorance, or both? Was it even possible to combine courage and ignorance? . . . What became of Cacciato? Where did he go, and why? What were his motives, or did he have motives, and did motives matter? What tricks had he used to keep going? How had he eluded them? How did he slip away into deep jungle, and how, through jungle, had they continued the chase? What happened, and what might have happened?" (45–47). These questions, which focus on motivation, character, and a sequence of actions, come to assume the form of invention in both the literal and rhetorical sense: Paul is searching for material with which to make up an account that will replace the traumatic blank spot. By the end of his meditation, Cacciato and his pursuers are becoming figures in a plot that has displaced the original anxieties about what really happened. And by the beginning of Chapter 3, they are characters within it: "Yes, they were in jungle now. Thick dripping jungle. Club moss fuzzing on bent branches, hard green bananas dangling from trees that canopied in lush sweeps of green, vaulted forest light in yellow-green and blue-green and olive-green and silver-green. It was jungle. Growth and decay and the smell of chlorophyll and jungle sounds and jungle depth. Soft, humming jungle. Everywhere, greenery deep in greenery. Itching jungle, lost jungle" (48). The final green flare over Cacciato's hill is almost frantically metamorphosed into the riot of greenery that will lead to the green door in Paris. This seems a parody of the literary, as if Paul Berlin were trying out his descriptive powers a bit uncertainly, although the paragraph is almost rescued by his first attempt at characterization: "'A botanist's madhouse,' Doc said." But once past this deliberately awkward transition from merely thinking about what might have happened to creating a narrative in which it does, Berlin is also able to recreate himself as both dreamer and protagonist: "Single file, they followed the narrow trail through banks of fern and brush and vine. . . . They moved slowly. The heavy grind of the march: Stink still at point, then Eddie, then Oscar and the lieutenant, then Harold Murphy toting the big gun, then Doc, then, at the rear, Spec Four Paul Berlin, whose each step was an event of imagination" (48). The title of the chapter, "The Road to Paris," literally turns the subsequent narrative away from the circumstances of trauma to pursue a comprehensive therapeutic fantasy. The mission allows Paul to be doubly courageous, leaving behind a bad war yet pursuing a deserter. The pursuit also allows him to overcome his alienation from the others. Having embarrassed himself by breaking down in front of the squad, he can incorporate them all into a dream that transforms duty into desire. And by releasing everyone from the murderous circumstances that have brutalized them all, he can satisfy his need for comradeship.

The Quest for Cacciato: Fantasy and the Burial of the Dead

Going after Cacciato takes Paul and his fellow soldiers from Viet Nam through Laos, Mandalay, Delhi, Afghanistan, Tehran, Turkey, Athens, and Germany from November 1968 to spring 1969, until they arrive in Paris, with each stopover comprising at least one chapter. In imagining places he has never been, Paul creates an exotic, Americanized tour of the world that reflects popular stereotypes and Hollywood adventure films, leavened by his awareness of current events and foreign social circumstances. The titles of twelve of the nineteen quest chapters include the phrase "the road to Paris," echoing Hope-Crosby musical comedies. Their hostess in Delhi loves America and Americans, leaving Lieutenant Corson smitten and Berlin reminded of his own mother as she serves elegant dinners with French wine and Hunt's tomato ketchup. In Mandalay, which reminds Oscar Johnson of Detroit, they take up rooms in the Hotel Minneapolis—a personal joke by the Minnesota-born author—and in Tehran they visit a discotheque. The squad's final destination allows full scope to Midwestern fantasies about higher civilization and culture and romantic love—they spend "April in Paris"—but the French capital also inspires conscious and subconscious historical and political associations and dreams for Paul Berlin. Their arrival at the site of the American-Vietnamese peace talks that have just opened at the time of O'Brien's fictional narrative suggests a vain hope that the common soldier's voice might be heard at the desultory negotiations that would be stretched out for four more years. The pursuit to Paris embodies other allusions significant to the war that the GIs are trying to escape: Eisenhower's recent death reminds old Lieutenant Corson of Paris as the city liberated by the Americans near the end of a "good" war; Paris was the administrative capital of an earlier colonial war in Viet Nam that eventually ended; but it was also the place where the United States was officially recognized as a nation in 1783. The westward movement of the pursuit parodies the subsequent mythic direction of American civilization that pushed the frontier farther into Indian Country until at last it came to grief in Viet Nam, as John Hellmann and Richard Slotkin (and Michael Herr) have noted.

As Paul's imagination invests his odyssey with traces of America, it also attempts to reshape the bad war more redemptively. In "Detours on the Road to Paris" (Chapter 6), after Stink Harris has slaughtered the family water buffalo (the episode revised from *Combat Zone* that will be rewritten in *The Nuclear Age* and *The Things They Carried*), the squad picks up some civilian refugees and leads them out of the war, reversing and compensating for the usual brutalizations in which Paul has been a witness and participant. Sarkin Aung Wan, the lovely young girl accompanying them, initially fulfills Berlin's naïve humanitarian instincts, frustrated and baffled in his few encounters with civilians, such as an earlier war victim: "A little girl with gold hoops in her ears and ugly scabs on her brow—did she feel, as he did, goodness and warmth and poignancy when he helped Doc dab iodine on her sores? Beyond that, though, did the girl *like* him. Lord knows, he had no villainy in his heart, no motive but kindness. He wanted health for her, and happiness. Did she know this? Did she sense his compassion? When she smiled, was it more than a token? And . . . [ellipsis in the original] and what *did* she want? Any of them, what did they long for? Did they have secret hopes? His hopes?" (311). An older, eroticized transformation of that earlier figure, Paul's female companion shares his hopes of reaching Paris, and rescuing her from the war becomes a mission that further validates going after Cacciato: "He liked her smell, her smile, the way she seemed to be holding things back. She was pretty. That was part of it. In Quang Ngai, where poverty abused beauty, women aged like dogs. So, yes, it was curious to watch this girl, to imagine how it might have happened" (77). Paul and the girl become partners and "almost made love" (143), in accordance with his own innocence and the limits of what can be imagined. Since she is not only willing to be rescued by the Americans but also willing to lead them when they become trapped in an enemy tunnel complex, Sarkin Aung Wan also enacts the policy of "winning hearts and minds" that assumed an eagerness among the Vietnamese to welcome and assist the American presence in their country. Here, Berlin's dream reverses his actual experience of abusive combat patrols among a fearful, sullen, unhelpful, or hostile populace. And with the squad hopelessly trapped underground, she provides the enlightenment needed to escape the war, eloquently glossing desertion through pseudo-Confucian aphorisms: "The way in is the way out"; . . . "To go home one must become a refugee"; . . . "We have fallen into a hole. Now we must fall out" (122).

By "Falling Through a Hole in the Road to Paris" (Chapter 13) just before they leave the Southeast Asia war zone, Berlin's dream allows a positive revision of the Vietnamese enemy just as his girlfriend redefines the civilian population. For the first time, Corson and his squad actually meet an NVA soldier and talk with him after a phantasmagoric earthquake has tumbled them into his underground command bunker. Greeted with courtesy and refreshments, they engage in an illuminating discussion of enemy strategy, literally see the war from the other side's point of view, and sympathetically come to realize that the combatants on both sides are POWs. Even though Corson has to tie up their host and captor with shoelaces as they follow Sarkin Aung Wan's directions to crawl out, the enemy is treated with respect and neither abused nor killed.

Although the beautiful and grateful refugee and the friendly and informative NVA officer are as tangible as any of the American characters in the book, they both enter Paul Berlin's dream unexpectedly, "detours" on the road to Paris. Their intrusion into Paul's itinerary marks them as fantasy figures, sublimations of the fear, shame, and ignorance that mark his attitude toward the Vietnamese. Indeed, their implausible names bear the mark of his merely imaginary relationship to Viet Nam and its inhabitants.

His girlfriend's first name may recall "Sarkan," the fictional equivalent of Viet Nam in *The Ugly American*, Lederer and Burdick's early Cold War roman à clef. In any case, as Renny Christopher notes (231), the name "Sarkin Aung Wan" is not Vietnamese, nor is it Chinese, although her family is from Cholon, the Chinese district of the capital city. Major Li Van Hgoc bears a name that may look Vietnamese, but Hgoc is unpronounceable in any language. The fantasy descent into his headquarters is a particularly striking instance of refashioning trauma because it allows the squad to courageously endure the terror of descending an enemy tunnel complex and winning a bloodless victory over an obliging adversary. But the sudden appearance of Major Li's hole in Chapter 10 is generated as countertherapy to an actual traumatic intrusion: Paul's memory, in Chapter 9, of the deaths of Bernie Lynn and Frenchie Tucker after they were ordered to search a lethal VC tunnel.

This is Paul's first recovered memory of actual combat trauma, and it is followed by eight more episodes recalling the deaths of those squad members cataloged at the beginning of *Cacciato*. As noted above, being able to revisit rather than repress these terrible scenes is itself an act of courage for Berlin. And although they disrupt the quest for Paris, they also make it more necessary and thus help to generate the dream, which alternates these traumatic war memories with pursuit-of-Cacciato fantasies. Thus, Paul is both fleeing and recapitulating Bernie Lynn's trauma when the entire squad falls into the fantasized enemy tunnel (Chapter 10); in turn, his ambiguous psychic escape recalls the complexly traumatic aftermath of Pederson's death, the obliteration of Hoi An, in the following chapter, "Fire in the Hole" (the expression used to warn GIs away when a tunnel was being detonated); then after an observation post meditation on his shameful fear of retrieving Frenchie Tucker's body, Paul enters the fantasized NVA underground bunker, where he is enlightened about enemy tactics and invited to look through the tunnel periscope by Major Li at the end of Chapter 13. What he sees, in the next chapter, "Upon Almost Winning the Silver Star," is his own cowardice in turning away from Lieutenant Sidney Martin's order to enter the tunnel and Bernie Lynn's subsequent fatal wound. The return to fantasy in Chapter 15 ("Tunneling Toward Paris") allows him to participate with the rest of the squad in getting out of the imagined VC tunnel successfully without anyone being killed. In turn, however, their ominous mazelike progress through the underground network, led by Sarkin Aung Wan, brings back the memory of an increasingly tense monthlong combat patrol without casualties that was finally broken when Rudy Chassler was blown to pieces by a mine (Chapter 16). Finally, in "Light at the End of the Tunnel to Paris" (Chapter 17), the squad emerges from the fantasy tunnel, and from the previously repressed series of traumatic deaths, into the streets of Mandalay, continuing the quest of Cacciato, Paris, and peace.

While bringing back the dead has a memorializing and cathartic function for Paul, their deaths actually reappear as traumatic intrusions within his dream and so resist and interrupt the more self-conscious plotting of the quest to Paris, which follows Cacciato's map sequentially, populating each destination with Paul, his girlfriend, and the rest of the squad and contriving yet another tour scenario. The bad memories, on the other hand, are recovered nonsequentially and in fragmentary fashion, a sign of their traumatic nature and origin. Only the deaths of Rudy Chassler and Ready Mix are fully contained within a single chapter: The former steps on a mine at the end of "Pickup Games," cited above, and the latter's death is casually mentioned at the end of a catalog that briefly describes the squad members ("Who They Were, or Claimed to Be"—Chapter 22). The relatively brief and unproblematic recall may indicate that neither death was particularly traumatizing for Paul. By contrast, the tunnel deaths of Bernie Lynn and Frenchie Tucker, which shamed him with his own cowardice, are recalled in two separate chapters interwoven amid the fantasy tunnel narrative, as noted above, and in reverse chronological order: Although Bernie Lynn is killed in Chapter 9 while trying to recover Frenchie Tucker's body because no one else dares to enter a deadly VC tunnel, his friend is mortally wounded in Chapter 14, which ends with Bernie just entering the tunnel. Pederson's death is brutally avenged in Chapter 11, but it is not recalled until Chapter 20. The death of Billy Boy Watkins occurs on Paul's first combat patrol, which is briefly recalled but broken off at the end of Chapter 4, just before the traumatic moment itself. Billy Boy's fate then reappears intrusively in the fantasy narrative as one of the "war stories" that the squad tells a Savak officer in the Tehran disco at the end of Chapter 29, but Paul walks outside to avoid hearing it; finally, two chapters later, he is at last able to reimagine the death and his reaction to it in detail. A brief reference to Buff, floating "with life after death in his big helmet" resurfaces during the fantasy train trip from Mandalay to Chittagong (Chapter

21), but the incident is fully recalled only in Chapter 41 ("Getting Shot") as
the last of the squad casualties that Paul imaginatively revisits.

Such fragmentation reflects Paul's repression of particularly deep traumatic experiences. By contrast with these terrible memories, Ready Mix,
"whose true name no one knew," expires within a half sentence as a casualty of the great battle in Lake Country. Rudy Chassler's death can also be
fully recovered in a single chapter because it was experienced as a psychic
release. It put an end to a preternaturally peaceful combat operation that
built to unbearable tension as each individual anticipated his own sudden
and unexpected death, so that "when [Chassler] hit the mine, the noise
was muffled, almost fragile, but it was a relief for all of them" (137). Rudy's
misfortune ironically relaxes his comrades from the anxiety of hyperarousal (see Shay 91) and allows them the posttraumatic blessing of their own
good luck, the factor most often cited as the cause of their survival by
trauma survivors (Herman 60).

By contrast, the details of Lieutenant Sidney Martin's fragging are never
recalled. As noted above, this is the worst trauma of all for Paul because it
brands the squad members as deliberate murderers and perhaps cowards
as well, afraid to follow Martin's recklessly rigorous orders to search enemy
tunnels rather than simply blowing them with grenades. Brief and ominous references to the plot to remove their commanding officer as a threat
to their own lives pervade *Cacciato* before Berlin can fully recall, in Tehran,
the squad's symbolic agreement to support the fragging by touching Oscar
Johnson's grenade. The mountainous landscape of Iran recalls the great
battle in the Vietnamese highlands where Frenchie, Bernie, and Martin
died in tunnels, the latter killed by his own men, and allusions to the traumatic fragging in "Lake Country" intrude throughout the Tehran narrative, climaxed by two full chapters that detail the squad's solidarity in sup-
porting Oscar's plot. Remembering his individual culpability for Martin's
death is as far as Paul Berlin can go, however: The actual circumstances
have been repressed beyond recovery, perhaps because they would
threaten the fantasy narrative and his self-control with another breakdown. Satisfaction at Martin's death and his personal survival could not
easily be integrated with the accompanying guilt and shame.

Instead, Paul has contented himself with the deserter's euphemism for
what happened in Lake Country: "'A sad thing,' Cacciato had said on the
day afterward. 'Accidents happen,' said Paul Berlin" (294). Berlin's fullest re-

flection on the incident follows the squad's cartoonlike escape from im-
prisonment as deserters in Tehran, where Cacciato has actually appeared
outside their cell and passed them his M-16: "A very sad thing. Cacciato
was dumb but he was right. What happened to Lieutenant Sidney Martin
was a very sad thing" (294). "The gremlin" is in fact the only innocent
among them: In Berlin's recollection of Lake Country, Cacciato fantasti-
cally insists on fishing in flooded bomb craters while Paul presses the grenade against him, and it is after this invitation to murder that Cacciato
leaves for Paris. The deserter is thus intimately connected with the most
traumatic of the GI deaths that Paul recalls. Although his reaction to it
differs radically from Paul's, it represents a response that Berlin could have
chosen if he had been morally courageous enough to have resisted the
squad's act against Lieutenant Martin—or to have run away from the war
altogether.

Moreover, Berlin's dream reflects how Cacciato has been intimately related to the most traumatizing deaths witnessed by Berlin: those of Martin,
Billy Boy Watkins, and Buff. As noted above, Cacciato was the only squad
member stupid, insensitive, or brave enough to dispose of Buff's remains.
The death of Billy Boy on Paul's first day in the war also produced his first
traumatic breakdown, a self-protective, hysterical fit of giggling in response to the terrible joke that fear can not only be shameful but lethal.
And the boyish GI who wonders at Doc Peret's diagnosis—"a heart attack
on the field of battle" (258)—and eventually pacifies Paul by holding him
down and then offering a stick of Black Jack gum also turns out to be Cacciato. In all three instances, then, Cacciato's behavior contrasts with Paul's
own and throws into relief Berlin's fear and shame. In going after him,
then, the protagonist is not simply fleeing from the trauma of Viet Nam
but also pursuing a figure whom he associates with a more proper response to it.

Since these repressed memories of others' deaths continually intrude
upon Paul's quest after Cacciato, appearing in brief associations and fragments and out of sequence, he has difficulty integrating them with the
rest of his dream. This apparent narrative confusion derives from unresolved trauma, and accordingly it becomes psychically important for Paul
to give the traumatic fragments formal closure and meaningful arrangement. This authorlike function is evident in the observation post meditation of Chapter 30: "He tried again to order the known facts. Billy Boy

was first. And then . . . [ellipsis in the original] then who? Then a long
blank time along the Song Tra Bong, yes, and then Rudy Chassler, who
broke the quiet. And then later Frenchie Tucker, followed in minutes by
Bernie Lynn. . . . Then Cacciato" (248). Remembering all the dead and fig-
uring out the sequence in which they perished are the narrative equivalent of Paul's attempts to count numbers whenever he is terrorized in
combat. They fulfill much the same function, allowing him to regain self-
control in the presence of terrible circumstances. Not until the dead have
been fully accounted for can the quest for peace be pursued without
interruption. After Buff's decapitation has been finally reexperienced in
Chapter 41, the subsequent observation post reflection registers full
closure:

> That was all of them. Frenchie, Pederson, Rudy Chassler, Billy Boy Watkins,
> Bernie Lynn, Ready Mix, Sidney Martin, and Buff. Six months. A few half-re-
> membered faces. That was the curious thing about it. Out of all that time,
> time aching itself away, his memory sputtered around those scant hours of
> horror. The real war was forgotten. The dullness and the heat and the end-
> less tracts of time and the tired villages and petty conversations and
> warmed-over jokes and rivalries and rumors and hole-digging and hole-fill-
> ing and the long marches without incident or foul play—all this was blurred
> and fuzzy like a faroff summer day. (338)

Ultimately, only by confronting the traumatic and emptying it of significance can Berlin finally go forward: "[W]hat he remembered was so trivial,
so obvious and corny, that to speak of it was embarrassing. War stories.
That was what remained: a few stupid war stories, hackneyed and unprofound. . . . Stories that began and ended without transition. No developing
drama or tension or direction. No order" (338). Having put the dead behind
him, therefore, he prepares to resume the peace story and enter Paris before another day in the war begins: "He checked his wristwatch. Five
o'clock. Barely half an hour before dawn. . . . Five o'clock sharp—he had to
hurry" (339).

Ultimately, however, the quest for Cacciato cannot transcend trauma
any more than reducing combat deaths to war stories can either make
them humanly acceptable or make them go away. Fabulating but also incorporating the trauma that has inspired it, the fantasy narrative cannot
be freed from the war, which both generates its scenarios and is sum-

moned by them. Thus, Sarkin Aung Wan joins the quest for Paris because Stink Harris has massacred the family water buffalo. Thus, in looking for Cacciato on the train between Burma and India, the squad conducts a brutal search mission, frightening, abusing, and alienating the passengers and reintruding "the one truly shameful memory" (168), Paul's participation in a degrading and destructive "flame frisking" of a Vietnamese village along the Song Tra Bong. Thus, when Lieutenant Corson insists on settling down in Delhi, the squad argues that they desperately need him to lead the pursuit and then kidnap him onto the train to Afghanistan. This coercion comically revises their relationship with his predecessor but also intrudes that "sad thing" into the fantasy, for in Delhi, mocking their tribute to his leadership, Corson exposes a terrible secret that he would not have been aware of in Viet Nam: "You need me? The way you needed Sidney Martin?" (211). In turn, the question immediately provokes Paul's memory of Lake Country, which will intrusively alternate with the fantasy narrative in Tehran over the next several chapters.

Many of the traumatic incidents within the journey to Paris are generated by the ambiguous nature of the fantasy quest itself: Is Third Squad pursuing a deserter or deserting? leaving the war or extending it from Viet Nam to Paris? The pursuit of Cacciato frequently parodies the typical World War II GI prison escape film, but here, Third Squad is rejecting the war, not trying to rejoin it. Cacciato's reappearances—in Laos, in Mandalay, in Delhi, and in Tehran—allow his pursuers to continue their flight from Viet Nam while enforcing military obligations. But the narrative of escape and peace always carries with it the potential goal of bringing Cacciato and themselves back into the war, an imaginative outcome that is morally and psychologically unsatisfying for Paul. Ultimately, the fantasy quest's dual motivations—pursuing desire or following duty—are irreconcilable, at least in war, and their conflict becomes traumatizing in Tehran and then in Paris itself.

Once they have reached the former, they are forced to observe the gruesome beheading of an Iranian Army deserter and are later imprisoned by the Shah's secret police as U.S. Army deserters until Cacciato appears to help them escape so that they can continue pursuing him. The legal fiction of their status as "touring soldiers," comically rationalized by Doc Peret, falls apart, and they are broken down by a Savak interrogator, their heads and necks shaved for the executioner. The shame of desertion generates this nightmare scenario, which even more profoundly reawakens the plot against Lieutenant Sidney Martin in Lake Country: Whether or not they are guilty of going after Cacciato, they *are* guilty of murdering their commanding officer.

Once the squad reaches Paris and Cacciato resurfaces for the last time, the contradiction within the two motives for going after him has to be resolved: They must either follow his example—desert—and disband, or they must pursue him to his final hideout and apprehend him to prove that they are not deserters themselves. In Chapter 44 (372), Berlin finally tracks down Cacciato to an apartment where he discovers that "the truth was simple," that whatever drove the "dummy" to desert, what has motivated the odyssey to Paris has been Paul's own desire to flee from the war. By revealing Cacciato's hiding place to Oscar Johnson, Berlin is bringing to an end the fantasy fueled by his own breakdown on Cacciato's hill, when he urged the deserter—and himself—to "Go."

Resolving the hunt for Cacciato also leads to a crisis for Paul and Sarkin Aung Wan, who have by now separated themselves from the squad, setting up housekeeping in their own Parisian flat and looking forward to marriage. The argument between them, a scene that Paul imagines within the larger fantasy of settling down in Paris, is carried on in the conference room of the Majestic Hotel, the site of the peace talks, where the lovers appear as political adversaries who can come to no agreement. Paul's refugee girlfriend is transformed into a spokeswoman for the [North] Vietnamese side, and her words now have to be translated into English. She urges him to see the quest as a courageous rejection of the war in favor of peace, love, and, indeed, the pursuit of happiness. "[D]o not fear the scorn of others," she concludes her formal statement: "You have come far. The journey to this table has been dangerous. You have taken many risks. You have been brave beyond your wildest expectations. And now it is time for a final act of courage. I urge you: March proudly into your own dream" (375). Berlin's response to her eloquent plea for desertion recapitulates O'Brien's own rueful explanation for his decision not to flee to Canada and Sweden in *Combat Zone*: "I am afraid of running away. I am afraid of exile. I fear what might be thought of me by those I love. I fear the loss of their respect. I fear the loss of my own reputation. . . . The real issue is how to find felicity within limits. Within the context of our obligations to other people" (377–78).

In the fantasized peace talks, which conclude Chapter 44, Berlin thus recapitulates O'Brien's decision to risk his life and his integrity in a bad war. Paul rejects his own dream, which can have no happy ending, by terminating it in the name of duty and by rejecting desire. "Even in imagination," he concludes, "we must be true to our obligations, for, even in imagination, obligation cannot be outrun. Imagination, like reality, has its limits." After Paul has finished, the former lovers pick up their statements and separate; there is, the narrator continues, "no true negotiation. There is only the statement of positions," much like the historical peace talks themselves (378). Sarkin Aung Wan's final metamorphosis also recognizes the alienation between Americans and Vietnamese that Paul's dream had tried to deny; and by identifying her with the enemy, O'Brien boldly reminds us that the United States ultimately fought and lost a war against Viet Nam, not against the spectre of expansionist Asian Communism, and, abandoning the defeated South Vietnamese, lost the peace as well. By the beginning of the final chapter, Sarkin Aung Wan leaves with Lieutenant Corson, who had already dropped out of the pursuit for Cacciato in India. As he brings his own dream to an end, Berlin revises theirs: "Heading east," Corson's final note to the squad proclaims boldly, "A long walk but we'll make it" (382). Although their return to Viet Nam and military service anticipates his own, it combines duty and desire in a way that has broken down for Berlin, as the retraumatizing conclusion of *Cacciato* indicates.

The Observation Post: Retraumatization and Endless Fantasy

The observation post meditations, which alternate with the chapters of war memories and the pursuit of Cacciato, provide a formal grid for the novel as Paul reflects upon memories and fantasies and counts down the hours before sunset. But they also have a psychologically therapeutic function for Paul in dealing with his traumatization by the war and dissolving his fantasies. Early in his watch (Chapter 8), Berlin leaves his guard tower to take a swim in the South China Sea and idly imagines swimming east to California. From one point of view, his dereliction of duty involves an extreme fantasy of desertion that never even takes imaginative form, unlike the quest for Cacciato; but it is also an act of reckless courage, since he risks being caught in the dark without his weapon by any enemy infiltrators. By returning to the tower and deciding to stay up all night, taking everyone's watch, he overcomes fear while protecting his comrades. This responsible courage cannot efface but helps to supplement earlier moments of shameful fear. Moreover, the nightlong vigil allows him to recall and acknowledge his previous breakdowns and to endure all previous terrors of the war. Finally, it also provides him imaginative room for daring to dream of peace by pursuing Cacciato.

By the time the sun begins to rise at six o'clock in the final observation post chapter, therefore, Berlin is prepared to resume his place in the war. The dead have been memorialized and reburied, his personal terrors have been confronted, and the dream of escape has been rejected in his own private peace talks. Yet *Cacciato* ends not by validating the soldier's growth beyond trauma and compensatory dreams—it evokes their necessary persistence. Paul has fully revisited his own traumatization and the deaths of others, yet he remains unresolved to them: "Those were all facts, and he could face them squarely. The order of facts—which facts came first and which came last, the relations among facts—here he had trouble, but it was not the trouble of facing facts. It was the trouble of understanding them, keeping them straight" (379–80). The facts of Cacciato's flight have also been separated from his own dream; but here, too, "[t]he last known fact" (380)—the ambiguous "Go!" that preceded his breakdown—leaves him unsatisfied. Even his endurance and self-awareness are cause for regret: "The war was still a war, and he was still a soldier. He hadn't run. The issue was courage, and courage was will power, and this was his failing" (379).

The novel ends not in the observation post, nor with the beginning of another day in the war, nor with psychic maturity or manly endurance or doing one's duty or any of the other lies that must be used to normalize the experience of combat, but with a final chapter of "Going After Cacciato." The dreamer abandons the daylight of present reality and returns imaginatively to past facts and his fantasy of the future. This is the only chapter in which the pursuit of Cacciato to Paris is combined with the pursuit of Cacciato to the Laotian border, but the narrative comprehensively resists closure. As noted above, Paul finds an empty room when he leads the squad into the deserter's hiding place in Paris, where he simply reexperiences his original breakdown on Cacciato's hill. And he is left only with Corson's hopeful uncertainty—"Maybe so"—when they try to imagine Cacciato's reaching Paris at the end of the novel. This final dream is symptomatic of unresolved trauma—intrusion of the original breakdown, blanking out, narrative fragmentation and reversal (first Paris, then Cacciato's hill)—and it ends not with the resolution of Paul Berlin's questions about Cacciato but with their starting point. "Going After Cacciato," Chapter 46, is a coda to Berlin's painful self-awareness, at the end of the long night, that he has not been able to "run," even in imagination. Unable finally to either capture or follow Cacciato, he can only dream of someone else's escape—like O'Brien himself. Since the novel ends with Corson's hope that Cacciato "might just make it," the suggestion that inspires Paul's fantasy, its conclusion cycles us back to the beginning of the dream, not only denying closure but suggesting that what happened in Viet Nam is less important than what can be made out of it. Cacciato is O'Brien's first work published after the end of the war in 1975, but its ceaseless, seamless, and recursive trauma narrative indirectly registers an historical tragedy that was to haunt the conscience of America for decades.

The end of *Cacciato* returns us to the analogy between dreamer and author, but with an important difference. Paul Berlin's dream has no audience but his own imagination; he is left trapped within the war, aware of his traumatization but unable to share his enlightenment with others. As the author of *Going After Cacciato*, however, O'Brien has been able to refashion his own in a form that has been validated by his readers. A National Book Award and O'Brien's subsequent literary career can never erase for the soldier the terrible facts that *Cacciato* has so masterfully transformed, but they have generated a community of readers whose moral engagement with O'Brien's work satisfies what Jonathan Shay identifies as the ultimate goal of all trauma narratives (194). Because it deliberately recasts the war as one soldier's dream, of course, *Cacciato* denies authoritative representation of Vietnam, let alone Viet Nam. By the end of the novel, little has been resolved about either Cacciato's ultimate fate or what constitutes true courage, but O'Brien's imaginative circuit from Viet Nam to Paris has skillfully and beautifully asked the right questions.

CHAPTER 5

THE BOMBS ARE REAL

An Ambitious Failure?

Born of "a desire to treat apocalypse as a startling fact of modern life" and presented as the personal history of its peculiar protagonist, William Cowling, *The Nuclear Age* has been characterized by its author as a partly humorous book about two serious issues: "[H]ow and why we become politicized and depoliticized" and "the safety of our species, our survival. We *won't* survive if we can't stop thinking of nuclear weapons as mere metaphors" (McCaffery 141). Cowling's involvement in politics begins in college, where he stands mutely outside the dining hall every day with a cryptic hand-lettered reminder to his fellow students that "THE BOMBS ARE REAL" (85). O'Brien evidently intended the entire novel to carry the same message. As a comic novel about catastrophic violence, *The Nuclear Age* works the vein of dark humor mined by Cold War satires such as *Doctor Strangelove, Catch-22*, and *Gravity's Rainbow*. Like these earlier masterpieces, O'Brien's novel overstates extravagantly. He has described it himself as "a big cartoon of the nuclear age, with everything heightened and exaggerated . . . blown way out of proportion, the way Trudeau does it in *Doonesbury*" (Kaplan 1991: 100). The novel's deliberately broad comic tone is something new in O'Brien, and so are its explicitly political subject matter and polemical message. The first excerpt from the novel-in-progress was a short story, "The Nuclear Age," which appeared in the June 1979 *Atlantic Monthly*, a year after the publication of *Cacciato*, and the whole book came out in 1985, although its action ends in 1995. At its appearance, therefore, *The Nuclear Age* projected the balance of terror ten years further into a potentially catastrophic future, adopting the implicitly prophetic mode of such modern classics as *1984* or *Brave New World*. And its epigraph, from the Second Book of Esdras ("And the dead will be thrown out like dung, and there will be no one to offer comfort. For the earth will be left empty and its cities will be torn down . . .") combines prophetic and apocalyptic modes, like the novel itself: Cowling is periodically visited by graphic visions of thermonuclear warfare that threaten annihilation at the end of the millennium. Although Biblical apocalypse and bomb shelter were important elements in *Northern Lights*, there they were relics of the past that its protagonist rejected; here, however, they are not only fixations for Cowling but denounce a catastrophe that might threaten all of us.

After finishing it, O'Brien evaluated *The Nuclear Age* as "my strongest book by far" (Myers 1995: 152). Combining personal memoir and cultural history, politics and domesticity, comedy and tragedy, fiction and polemics, it may well be his most ambitious work. Coming in the wake of the kudos bestowed upon *Cacciato*, however, the novel was a disappointment for many reviewers. For those who were unsatisfied, its characters seemed to be lifeless caricatures, its protagonist voluble but unaffecting, its political engagement shallow, its polemics monotonously shrill. Nor has the novel attracted either the critical admiration or even the interest accorded O'Brien's Vietnam War books.[1] The author's inventiveness has been reduced to plot summaries or brief descriptions by commentators on the novel, and even they disagree on the book's characteristics. Whereas Philip Beidler (1991: 24) identifies its mode as "essentially realistic," contrasting it with the fantasy of *Cacciato*, Steven Kaplan (1995) praises the comic book nature of O'Brien's characterizations as appropriate to a "cartoon age" of political irresponsibility (130). Seeing it as an explicit attempt by O'Brien to fictionalize trauma allows a better understanding of its anomalies. Whatever its critical or popular success, *The Nuclear Age* introduces subjects that are central to O'Brien's later fiction: the crucial effect of traumatic childhood experiences on the life history of the adult (a theme that O'Brien had handled earlier in *Northern Lights*); the need for love and marriage and their breakdown as a traumatic, identity-destroying effect of previous traumatization; and the symbiotic relationship between public policy and events and private trauma. Crucial to O'Brien's expanded representation of trauma in *The Nuclear Age* are the character-

ization of Cowling, its protagonist; the mode and structure of the narrative
that O'Brien and his protagonist put together; the relationship between
The Nuclear Age and Vietnam; and parallels that link O'Brien's fourth book
to the previous three and its protagonist to its author.

The Traumatization of William Cowling

"Am I crazy?" asks William Cowling as *The Nuclear Age* begins, inviting
us to follow his preparations to build a nuclear bomb shelter in April 1995:

> It's after midnight, and I kiss my wife's cheek and quietly slide out of bed.
> No lights, no alarm. Blue jeans and work boots and a flannel shirt, then out
> to the backyard. I pick a spot near the tool shed. A crackpot? Maybe, maybe
> not, but listen. The sound of physics. The soft, breathless whir of Now.
>   Just listen. (3)

And listen we must, as Cowling, certain that the end of the world and the
end of his marriage are near, interweaves an account of the widening hole
with a narrative of his life from 1946 to the present. As he digs deeper into
the earth, he excavates his memory to show how his identity has been
shaped by post–World War II America.

Cowling's inescapable voice—variously sardonic/sentimental, cynical/
idealistic, matter-of-fact/manic, self-confident/self-pitying—is the most
distinctive feature of the book. Its rhetorical instability, which contrasts
markedly with the understated eloquence of O'Brien's previous works, deliberately reflects the narrator's traumatized reaction to the terrors of the
nuclear age. Cowling's entire life is marked by recurrent, intrusive fears of
annihilation, beginning as a child in Fort Derry, Montana, where he converts the family Ping-Pong table into a bomb shelter in 1958. During the
Cuban Missile Crisis in 1962, he suffers physical and psychological symptoms, faints in school, and has to be taken by his parents to see Charles
Adamson, a psychiatric counselor in Helena. Growing up preternaturally
frightened by the threat of nuclear annihilation, O'Brien's narrator becomes a Vietnam War protester, a draft dodger, and a courier for an antiwar guerrilla movement based in Key West and trained in Cuba before he
ultimately turns himself in to the U.S. government. Resuming his interrupted life in 1977, Cowling pursues his future wife, a former airline stewardess, from New York to Bonn to Minnesota before finally settling down

with her in his native Montana after making a fortune through uranium prospecting, only to end up still obsessed by the nuclear terror that has troubled him since childhood. Threatened by a world careening toward destruction, O'Brien's protagonist either tries to flee or to create circumstances he can securely control, beginning with his childhood shelter and ending with the hole into which he intends to place himself and his family. Cowling's endless monologue—manic, paranoid, expressionistic, rhetorically coercive—contrasts markedly with the largely affectless narrative voices of *Combat Zone* and *Northern Lights* as well as the imaginatively open, emotionally interrogative register of Paul Berlin's dream in *Cacciato*. His story is a nightmare, and the figure who constructs it seems hyperaroused, unable to sleep until his shelter has been completed. Like the protagonists of *Northern Lights* and *Going After Cacciato*, Cowling suffers from traumatic intrusions, but rather than constricting his feelings or repressing what is haunting him, he self-destructively unearths everything.

By the time the digging stops, his project has become a nineteen-foot crater into which he has deposited his wife Bobbi and daughter Melinda against their wills after drugging them. Apparently prepared to turn the family shelter into the family tomb by dynamiting it, Cowling is dissuaded from obliteration by his twelve-year-old, who wakes up prematurely and clutches the firing device, now terribly aware "that there is no mercy between fathers and daughters" (354). As the novel nears its end, Cowling brings his family safely back inside their home and then blows up the empty hole after providing a final paradoxical answer to his initial question:

> Am I crazy?
>
> I am not.
>
> To live is to lose everything, which is crazy, but I choose it anyway, which is sane. (357)

As the narrative of William Cowling, then, *The Nuclear Age* dramatizes the appearance, persistence, and eventual closure of personal trauma that has been generated by public events, and recurrent symptoms of traumatization pervade the book. Cowling is haunted by visions of nuclear apocalypse, beginning with his childhood nightmares in Montana:

> Kansas was burning. Hot lava flowed down the streets of Chicago. It was all there, each detail: Manhattan sank into the sea, New Mexico flared up and

vanished.... Oddly, I felt no fear. Not at first. It was a kind of paralysis, the
curiosity of a tourist. There were dinosaurs. The graveyards opened....

Clutching my pillow, I watched the moon float away.

And then the flashes came . . . all colors, the melted elements of nature
coursing into a single molten stream that roared outward into the very
center of the universe—everything—man and animal—*everything*—the
great genetic pool, everything, all swallowed up by a huge black hole.

The world wasn't safe. (34–35)

Over the rest of Cowling's life, these childhood nightmares reappear as a
series of visions, periodically set off by Cold War conflicts and taking the
ultimate form of nuclear warfare. Besides nightmares and hallucinations,
Cowling's traumatic symptoms include cutting himself off from other
people. In high school, he conducts imaginary telephone conversations as
a substitute for a social life; in college, he is more interested in studying
rocks than talking with fellow students at Peverson State College ("a student body without student brains"), an undistinguished mythical state in-
stitution in Montana where "football was still king and booze was queen
and raw physicality was the final standard of human excellence" (77); although he generates a campus antiwar movement, he soon drifts away
from active involvement and finds himself profoundly alienated from the
would-be antiwar guerrillas that he joins after fleeing the draft. Trying to
save his family by excavation, his traumatized state even isolates him from
those he loves: "Dig, it [the hole] whispers. Two weeks on the job, and my
hole is nearly four feet deep, ten feet square. It's a beauty—I'm proud—but
I've paid a terrible price. My daughter says I'm nutto. My wife won't speak
to me, won't sleep with me. She thinks I'm crazy. And dangerous. She refuses to discuss the matter. All day long, while I'm busy saving her life,
Bobbi hides in the bedroom . . . " (66). By the end of the book, Cowling has
indeed become dangerous to himself and his family as well, preparing to
bury them all in his shelter ("Folded in forever like the fossils" [347])—until his preparations to dynamite are interrupted by his daughter. As if he
were a traumatized survivor of extreme violence, Cowling becomes both
suicidal and homicidal, and his attempts to "save" his family become increasingly oppressive as they resist his mania to avoid the catastrophe that
has overwhelmed his imagination. As a college sophomore, he had responded suicidally to earlier visions of nuclear war and the reality of the

war in Viet Nam: "No question. I was depressed. Scared, too. One evening I picked up a scissors and held it to my throat. It was a ticklish sensation, not unpleasant. I drew the blade upward. No blood, just testing" (83). And suicide also attracts him briefly while he is recovering from a nervous breakdown after going through antiwar guerrilla training in Cuba (221).

Cowling's traumatization may be influenced by guilt as well as overwhelming fear. By 1995 he has become rich, along with the rest of the antiwar guerrillas, after finding uranium deposits in the Montana mountains above his home and then selling the land to Texaco. His childhood obsession with geology, itself a response to the instability of human life under the threat of nuclear terror ("Rocks lasted. Rocks could be trusted" [79]), has led him to a Ph.D. in the field and the discovery of bomb-making resources that have been sold to big business and the government.

Like other survivors of trauma, Cowling is also haunted by visions of the dead, including his father, who used to "die" every summer during his hometown's annual Custer Days celebration while impersonating the doomed general: "I see my father dying under yellow spotlights. He won't stop, he's a professional, he keeps dying" (347). He has imaginary conversations with his former girlfriend, Sarah Strouch, who took over leadership of Cowling's tiny antiwar Committee and later gained national notoriety as an armed antiwar radical, only to die horribly of viral encephalitis while hiding out in his Montana home after the war. And his imagination also keeps replaying the holocaust, broadcast on national television, that engulfed the rest of the Committee: "And now it's late in the century, it's 1995, and I'm digging, and I see sharpshooters and a burning safe house and the grotesque reality of the human carcass. The dead won't stop dying. Ned and Ollie and Tina, all of them, they die in multiples, they can't call it quits" (113–14).

Finally, as he completes his preparations for sealing himself and his family in their ultimate shelter, Cowling reflects the anomie and nihilism of a survivor so psychically scarred that life itself no longer has meaning:

> The safe house burns. In the attic, a warhead no doubt burns. Everything is combustible. Faith burns. Trust burns. Everything burns to nothing and even nothing burns. . . . The state of Kansas, the forests, the Great Lakes, the certificates of birth and death, every written word, every sonnet, every love letter. . . . Memory burns, and with it the past, all that ever was. The reasons

for burning burn. Flags burn. Liberty and sovereignty and the Bill of Rights and the American way. It just burns. And when there is nothing, there is nothing worth dying for, and when there is nothing worth dying for, there is only nothing.

The hole makes a sound of assent.

Nothing. (348–49)

This vision of universal holocaust replicates the accelerating catastrophe of his early childhood dream but carries it further by incorporating the actual losses of his life in the nuclear age, including faith and hope. As the shelter turns into a grave that speaks Cowling's darkest impulses, his indecision parodies Hamlet's, pausing on the edge of death's quietus: "The question is simple. In this age, at this late hour, how do I make a happy ending?" (341). Finally preparing to seal himself in forever with those he loves, Cowling reaches a final point of indecision even as he recognizes his own breakdown:

I smell daylight coming.

The hole says, *Now and never.*

I lift the firing device. . . . All it takes is a touch. Not even courage, bare volition. It occurs to me that I'm not immune to curiosity—so easy. I think about Ned and Ollie and Tina, my father, my mother, and it's the simple desire to discover if the dead are ever truly dead.

In the absence of hope, what can we hope for?

Does love last forever?

Are there any absolutes?

I want to know what the hole knows. The hole is where faith should be. The hole is what we have when imagination fails. (351)

Whether directly disturbed by her father's monologue or not, Cowling's daughter awakens at this point, and her reaction helps him to recognize his own madness:

I feel unsteady.

There's a sudden compression when she says, "Daddy?" Enormous pressure, it's too much for me. I place the firing device at my feet and get down on my hands and knees and practice deep breathing. The hole, it seems, is in my heart. (352)[2]

As Melinda becomes aware of the absurd horror of her situation, she childishly seizes control of it by grabbing the detonator. Confronted with his daughter's bewilderment, fear, and revulsion, forced to protect her from his own atrocity rather than from the nuclear apocalypse that he has only imagined, Cowling risks both of their lives while trusting the intimate ties that he has nearly betrayed: "When I get to my feet, Melinda whimpers and says, 'Stay *away* from me.' But I'm willing to risk it. I'm a believer. The first step is absolute. 'Daddy,' she says, 'you better not!' But I have to. I cross the hole and kneel down and lift the firing device from her lap and hold her tight while she cries. I touch her skin. It's only love, I know, but it's a kind of miracle" (357). Cowling's first shelter had been dismantled by a father who loved him; as a father, he does away with his final shelter, and perhaps the disabling and destructive nuclear traumatization that has plagued his entire life, through the love of his child.

Cowling's guide and protector throughout the novel is Charles Adamson, his childhood therapist but also a curious alter ego. Taken by his parents to see the psychiatrist after breaking down during the Cuban Missile Crisis, the sixteen-year-old William initially regards the officious "Chuck" with contempt but finds that they are kindred spirits: Like his patient, Adamson hated high school, felt isolated from his disgusting classmates— "snobs and bullies" to Adamson (53), "turds and jocks" for William (54)— and turned to science rather than socializing, although he took up astronomy rather than geology. Furthermore, although Adamson tries to "treat" the teenaged Cowling's fears of nuclear war, William finds him the most depressing personality he has ever met and ends up counseling his therapist. Like Cowling, Adamson knows that human civilization will ultimately be wiped out, but his scenario depends on cosmology and foresees an absolutely inescapable, inevitable end to the solar system that would both incorporate and transcend Cowling's nuclear apocalypticism, but which also parodies it. For although he knows that human life is meaningless in some ultimate sense—"Nothing lasts. Doom, it means no children. No genetic pool. No memory. When the lights go out, Edison goes out. And what significance did his life have? Erased. Shakespeare and Einstein. You and me" (62)—it does not stop him from being happily married, with two well-adjusted children, a loving wife, and a career in politics as mayor of Helena. Cowling discovers Adamson's "secret" life when his friend arranges William's return from draft-dodging exile in 1971 and his surrender to the government in 1976. As his name suggests, Cowling's therapist and mentor represents a straightforward acceptance of mortality as the human condition, a psychic maturity that O'Brien's protagonist comes to realize only through the eyes of his own child.

At the end of his narrative, then, William Cowling is trying to overcome a fear of nuclear destruction so nearly psychotic that the only remedy seems to be suicide and the murder of his family. His final resolution is wisely paradoxical, refusing to ignore the nuclear menace even while embracing human life: "[W]hen we hear that midnight whine, when Kansas burns, when what is done is undone, when fail-safe fails, when deterrence no longer deters, when the jig is at last up—yes, even then I will hold to a steadfast orthodoxy, confident to the end that E will somehow not quite equal mc^2, that it's a cunning metaphor, that the terminal equation will somehow not quite balance" (359). The 359-page monologue that is *The Nuclear Age* comes to an end with these words of tentative hopefulness. It has outlined Cowling's life up to the point when he begins digging the bomb shelter while giving us a blow-by-blow description of the struggle between himself and his family to accept what has become increasingly lunatic. But what is its fictional provenance and purpose? If we see the narrative as the product of a traumatized persona, then everything that precedes Cowling's ultimate rejection of the bomb shelter is a final testament intended to justify it. Only when the hole falls silent and is abandoned does Cowling's nightmare end, so that his testimony is both a product and symptom of traumatization as well as the narrative means by which he is able to recover from it. Cowling's derangement, marked both literally and figuratively by hyperarousal, is reflected not only by the rhetorical instability of his account but also by the wildly miscellaneous character of its narrative materials, which flip-flop from historical events to cataclysmic visions, from past recollections to present imaginings, from comedy to tragedy. Because the manic narrative is also Cowling's apologia for his apparent breakdown, it gathers together everything that has contributed to it, including arguments with others, imaginary conversations, hallucinations, news reports, his wife's poetry, warnings to the reader, dialogues with himself. As a result, the novel resembles the confessional form of a work such as Dostoevsky's *Notes from Underground* rather than the omniscient political fables of Orwell, Huxley, Heller, and Pynchon.

O'Brien's most important literary analogue is figured by Cowling himself while defending his apparent neurosis as a rational response to
dangers that must be escaped because they cannot be controlled: "I did
have problems, obviously, but they weren't the kind a shrink can solve.
That's the key point. They were *real* problems" (40). During his first session
with Adamson, young William denounces the "charade" of psychological
counseling as "worthless": "I stared him in the eyes. I meant every word of
it. 'Take an example. Edgar Allan Poe: a disturbed guy. All those weird visions running through his head, fruitcake stuff. But I'll tell you something,
he didn't go crying to some stupid counselor. He *used* his nuttiness. He
made something out of it—those disturbed poems of his, those disturbed
stories. He had willpower, like me. . . . And there's plenty to be disturbed
about. Real stuff, I mean. Realities. They don't shrink'" (52). Years later,
stringing Christmas lights about his hole to allow him to dig on through
the night without having to sleep, Cowling continues to assure himself
(and us) of his sanity:

> I skip supper. I keep at it, whistling work songs.
>   It isn't obsession. It's commitment. It's me against the realities.
>   *Dig*, the hole says, and I spit on my hands. Pry out a boulder. Lift and
> growl and heave. Obsession? Edgar Allan Poe was obsessed. (71)

A hole that can speak undercuts Cowling's claim to rational enterprise
here, and the (w)hole episode is reminiscent of passages in Poe in which
an obsessed storyteller alienates us even as he takes us into his confidence. Cowling's reference here assumes that Poe and his often disturbed
and haunted narrators share the same identity, an assumption shared by
reviewers who scorned O'Brien's political fecklessness—rather than Cowling's—in *The Nuclear Age*. There has been no repetition of Hiroshima and
Nagasaki, and the balance of terror has held for more than fifty years; nor
is nuclear war unleashed or represented in O'Brien's fiction outside of
Cowling's imagination. Like his protagonist, O'Brien is appalled by our indifference toward mass destruction, but he is not pathologically obsessed
by it. *The Nuclear Age* critiques the subject of its title not by presenting a
solution to the nightmare—Cowling ultimately rejects his own—but by
showing how the very state of nuclear preparedness produces lethal lunacy of various kinds. As our hero notes when a portion of the shelter wall

caves in accidentally: "You can die saving yourself" (228). Leaving the outright condemnation of the Bomb to Cowling, O'Brien uses parabolic characterization and structure in *The Nuclear Age* to represent a more insidious moral catastrophe in which the distinctions between war and peace, hate and love, and public policy and private relationships come to be dissolved.

Parabolic Fiction: Mutual Assured Destruction and Civil Defense

Cowling has been dismissed as tiresomely repetitive by readers and critics who have left unconsidered the significance of his traumatization and accelerating insanity. But his breakdown is also one of the ways by which O'Brien dramatizes the disruption of domestic tranquility in the nuclear age. Cowling becomes something of a picaresque hero moving through a geopolitical landscape, his odyssey a fable about American life under the shadow of the Bomb. Moreover, because the trajectory of his life history is crucially influenced by the history of the Cold War, his traumatization becomes a parablelike commentary on postthermonuclear America. Because the retrospective narrative alternates with chapters that enact Cowling's ongoing three-month struggle to dig his shelter while pacifying wife and daughter, what he has gone through in the past implicitly explains or justifies what he is doing in the present.

As noted above, his lunacy is reflected by the generic fluctuations of the narrative, a frenzied monologue that combines the autobiographical registers of memoir, confession, apology, and self-analysis with more public modes: historical chronicle, political commentary, jeremiad. Employing apparent logic to explain his apparent craziness ("If you're sane, you're scared; if you're scared, you dig; if you dig, you deviate" [230]) and certifying his extreme behavior as simple necessity ("The world has been sanitized. Passion is a metaphor. All we can do is dig" [152]; "A radical age requires radical remedies" [229]), Cowling often comes to take on the manic certitude of a nuclear age prophet as well as a hyperaroused crank:

> Nuclear war—is it embarrassing? Too prosaic? Too blunt? *Listen*—nuclear war—those stiff, brash, trite, everyday syllables. I want to scream it: Nuclear war! Where's the terror in this world? Scream it: Nuclear war! Take a stance and keep screaming: Nuclear war! Nuclear war! (143)
>   . . . don't call me crazy. I'm digging. You're diddling. You, I mean. The

heavy sleepers. The mealy-mouthed pols and hard-ass strategists who talk
so reasonably about containment and deterrence. Idiots! Because when
there's nothing, there's nothing to deter, it's uncontained. (229)

Cowling's inability to moderate his pitch is a mark of traumatization, but
its sources are no less true than the visions of proto-Isaiah, Jeremiah, Eze-
kiel, John of Patmos, or Esdras, whose apocalyptic message is the epigraph
of *The Nuclear Age*. There is something of the ridiculous about this late-
twentieth-century fanatic, but the bombs *are* real in a way that the Seventh Seal is not.

Cowling's fixation upon paradoxes of sanity and madness becomes a
vehicle for O'Brien's satiric perspective, variously recapitulated in the
novel, upon the destructive folly of nuclear age America in general. Cowling's attempt to build a nuclear shelter for his family seems crazed and futile, yet the missiles of deterrence themselves have been a lunatic shield
for American society at large, as signified even in the doctrine of Mutual
Assured Destruction (MAD). Only if the ICBMs failed to fulfill their function would they actually be used; the entire nation dug itself in after 1945,
but its weapons of "defense" have been instruments of mass destruction
and mass traumatization that anticipate their inability to defend. As a boy,
Cowling fears an attack on his hometown because its name—Fort Derry—
might be mistaken for a military target. Indeed, the seeding of the American Midwest and Great Plains with ICBM complexes militarized even un-
derpopulated farmlands, turning them into strategic targets. "Kansas is on
fire!" Cowling recurrently proclaims, apocalyptic visions obliterating Dorothy's realm of the everyday far beyond what any late summer tornado
might do. Cowling's shelter digging is crazy only if deterrence (or missile
defense) could be 100 percent effective or if no shelter would ever be safe
from a nuclear bomb. The emergence of the nuclear shelter industry in
the 1950s and 1960s undercuts any claim that deterrence provides security,
of course. Although he is digging his shelter in 1995 (or the date of publication, 1985), Cowling seems a throwback to those happy days when governmental support and encouragement for family shelters revealed most
nakedly the nation's doubts about nuclear war strategy. Even the U.S.
government's faith in deterrence has not kept it from trusting in its own
bomb shelters to rescue officials from the failure of their own policy.[3]

Nonetheless, while Cowling's counterexample is parabolically used to denounce the lunacy of American nuclear war assumptions, those assumptions also pervade his own mania. Cowling's digging rejects the illusory security of MAD, guarding against its breakdown. If "the bombs are real," however, the only effective defense against them would be their removal; using bomb shelters could not save American society any more effectively than using the missiles. The fantasies of self-protection through building shelters, whether in the 1950s or in Cowling's own retrograde digging, are belied by the vision of survivorhood articulated in the epigraph to the novel: "None will be left to till the ground and sow it. The trees will bear fruit, but who will gather it? The grapes will ripen, but who will tread them? There will be vast desolation everywhere" (Second Esdras 16:24–27).

Moreover, beyond the pragmatics of survival, Cowling shares with the nuclear strategists a profound moral blindness that becomes more pronounced as his digging continues. To use the bomb one must be willing to engage in the murder of millions; but to be obsessed with merely finding shelter is to accept millions of other deaths, including those of fellow citizens. O'Brien darkly implies the death-directed equivalency of building missiles and building bomb shelters by having Cowling gradually move toward burying himself, his wife, and his daughter within the hole in order to save his family. Here, "civil defense" parodies and undercuts the misleading euphemism "national defense" under which Americans have justified killing themselves and considerably more foreigners in wars far from U.S. borders since World War II. Finally, Cowling's increasingly mad self-justifications throughout the book force O'Brien's readers, situated in their normalcy somewhere between the bomb builders and the shelter digger, to examine their own connivance with nuclear deterrence, the most heinous network of civilized violence ever contrived or contemplated.

Besides such parabolic analogies, the formal structure of the book also reflects parallels between Cowling's breakdown and thermonuclear apocalypse. O'Brien has divided the narrative into thirteen titled chapters that are distributed into three larger sections, "Fission," "Fusion," and "Critical Mass." The titles of the three parts had been used five years earlier in the short story "The Nuclear Age," the first excerpt from the novel-in-progress to be published; revised in a shorter form, it is the twelfth chapter of the completed book. In the story, the three section titles provide an ironic commentary on the activities of the onetime anti–Vietnam War Committee founded by Cowling as he directs them in a search for uranium deposits that are later sold to Texaco for $25 million. During the war, by reminding his fellow students that "the bombs [were] real," he had helped to generate an antiwar movement; after the war, he enables his old friends to make their fortunes by discovering resources for generating nuclear explosives. In the novel, however, "Fission," "Fusion," and "Critical Mass" define Cowling's whole life as a series of explosive reactions to the circumstances of the times: In the first, he decides to flee the draft and leave nuclear age America behind him; in the second, he joins an antiwar guerrilla movement whose activities are also traumatizing for Cowling and finally prompt him to turn himself in and then spurn any political involvement; in the final section of the book, having become wealthy through servicing the bombmakers and then marrying the woman of his dreams, he moves toward blowing up himself and his family in the shelter he has constructed to outlive the apocalypse. Individual chapters also link Cowling's past life to the nuclear age that he is trying to escape: "Civil Defense" and "Chain Reactions" reprise his trauma-prompted childhood shelter building and his responses to the Cuban Missile Crisis as a teenager; "First Strikes" and "Escalations," his response to the Vietnam War as a student, from initial antiwar sentiments to draft dodging; "Underground Tests" and "Fallout" trace Cowling's failure to complete terrorist training successfully with the rest of the Committee and his subsequent dropping out. And the narrative of his digging a nuclear shelter in 1995, interwoven with the retrospective memoir, comprises five separate chapters with the same title that trace the movement of Cowling's mind between past and present during its progressive implosion as the potential shelter becomes a potential grave and protecting his family moves toward suicide and murder. These "Quantum Jumps" reflect Cowling's own leap from traumatization to near-madness, but they also present an ironic parallel between "protecting" the family and "protecting" the nation, the ostensible purpose of nuclear deterrence.

Responding to some reviewers' negative reactions to the novel, O'Brien was disappointed that its careful structuring had gone unnoted, and pointed out for example that the varying length of the nuclear shelter–building chapters replicated the progression of a release of nuclear energy, an effect that was physically mimicked in the original printing of the novel (Baughman 212–13). Perhaps such a pattern is overly mechanical, but as the "quanta" chapters get progressively longer in a quasi-mathematical series, so Cowling's own meltdown increases accordingly, becoming more self-evident and more deadly. The entire narrative speeds up after 1971, and in "Fallout" Cowling comments on the experience of his life's acceleration: "I have a theory. As you get older, as the years pile up, time takes on a curious Doppler effect, an alteration in the relative velocity of human events and human consciousness. The frequencies tighten up. The wavelengths shorten—sound and light and history—it's all compressed." He notes that for a twelve-year-old, hiding underneath a Ping-Pong table, "a single hour seems to unwind toward infinity, dense and slow; at twenty-five, or thirty-five, or forty, approaching half-life, the divisions of remaining time are fractionally reduced, like Zeno's arrow, and the world comes rushing at you, and away from you, faster and faster. It confounds computation. You lose your life as you live it, accelerating" (297). Escalation and acceleration seem to Cowling the spirit of the age, but we can also see his life as a chain reaction derived from his initial nuclear traumatization and about to explode at the end of the book. As O'Brien's protagonist digs deeper and his life is uncovered by him and for us, its accumulation gathers a momentum that threatens to blow him apart. The novel careens from offbeat comedy to grotesque tragedy as Cowling's nuclear reactions proliferate. His responses to real and imagined threats are typically hyperbolic and frequently comic, as when he faints in high school during the Cuban Missile Crisis:

> A fun-house experience—topsy-turvy, no traction. In a way I felt very loose and relaxed, letting things spin; lying there on the floor while everybody yelled, "Give him air."
>   I almost laughed.
>   I didn't *need* air. I needed peace. (47)

But as he recounts his experiences after college and the hole nears completion, the narrative becomes increasingly dark and its humor strained, although Cowling insists to himself that everything is under control:

> Down the ladder, grab my spade, go to work. A hot day, but the earth smells cool and moist. I'm at home here. This is where it ends. *Hey man*, the hole whispers. *Here's a riddle: What is here but not here, there but not there?* Then a pause. "You," I say, and the hole chuckles: *Oh, yeah! I am the absence of presence. I am the presence of absence. I am peace everlasting.*

There's a giggling sound, high and crazy, but I don't give it credence.

Discipline, I think. Mind and body. I work steadily, pacing myself. The key to progress, I now realize, is gradual accretion, routine and rhythm; that's how monuments get built. (227–28)

The chronologically organized testament of his past life includes brief references to important events in American political and military history after World War II, so that Cowling's family crisis is connected with governmental foreign policy during the Cold War. Accordingly, O'Brien's representation of his mania from 1958 to 1995—the "nuclear age" of the title—is bracketed by two complementary chapters of personal shelter building that literally disrupt domestic tranquility. In the novel's second chapter ("Civil Defense"), which may have been intended as Chapter 1 at an earlier stage of O'Brien's work on the novel,[4] Cowling recounts his earliest fears of nuclear catastrophe and his earliest attempt to protect himself from annihilation in his Ping-Pong table shelter. The twelve-year-old boy eventually loads his hideout with "lead" pencils to guard against radiation, convinced that his parents are indifferent to the end of the world that he can imagine from news reports, elementary school air-raid exercises, and the rest of the anticipations of nuclear war that characterized the Eisenhower years. Initially amused but increasingly concerned about his son's apocalyptic anxieties, his father ultimately pacifies William by challenging the boy in a Ping-Pong match after taking apart the would-be refuge. At the end of the novel, another twelve-year-old confronts her father concerning nuclear war, but it is now 1995 and Cowling himself who is the father, trying to remove himself, his drugged wife, and the bewildered Melinda from nuclear war by burying them in his culminating shelter. Between one father's dismantling of the Ping-Pong table shelter and Cowling's own demolition of his final refuge, O'Brien uses his role as child, father, and husband to sardonically magnify the insecurity of American family life under the shadow of the Bomb.

As Lee Schweninger has noted (180), the term "nuclear family" was coined in 1947. It defined an American postwar ideal of upwardly mobile middle-class parents and children living in detached single-family houses. O'Brien's nightmarish representation of Cowling's attempt to hold on to this part of the American dream provides some of the book's funniest episodes, but also its most disturbing, culminating in his final confrontation with Melinda. Although the ostensible purpose of both deterrence and bomb shelters is to protect nuclear families, Cowling's near-destruction of his own grimly suggests the near-psychosis that underlies such deadly forms of self-protection.

Cowling's relationship with his wife is intimately linked to his nuclear paranoia and nearly destroyed by it. He first meets Bobbi, then a flight attendant, when he flies from New York to Miami, trying to escape the draft by joining Sarah Strouch and the rest of the Committee, which is now planning direct action to stop the war in Viet Nam. The double anxiety of Vietnam and his own exile reawakens in Cowling, for the first time in a decade, visions of nuclear annihilation: "criss-crossing threads of color in the great North American dark, bright flashes zigzagging from sea to sea. It was not a dream. One by one, all along the length of the eastern seaboard, the great cities twinkled and burned and vanished" (172). When Bobbi appears and comforts him, she seems to promise refuge from a lifetime of nuclear age traumatization:

> The jet dipped, bounced, and woke me up.
>
> I pushed the call button.
>
> Just a nightmare, the stewardess said, and I nodded, and she brought me a martini and wiped my brow and then held my hand for a while.
>
> Over Miami we went into a holding pattern. I was sick, but I fell in love.
>
> When I told her so, the stewardess smiled and said it was the martini or altitude sickness.
>
> We circled over the Everglades at ten thousand feet.
>
> She said my skin was green—pale green, she said, like a Martian. Then she gave my hand a squeeze. She asked if I was feeling better. I said I felt fine, I was in love. (172)

By the time they have landed, Cowling is not only feeling well again but has already asked her where they will elope and how many children they should have. Although Bobbi calls him "crazy" (she does not yet know the real source of his illness), she recites poems to him and leaves one of her own, "Martian Travel," pinned to his suit coat and autographed. This comic encounter initiates a relationship that has become pathological by the end of the book as Cowling's attempt to fashion his wife into an antidote against the nuclear age ends up nearly destroying her. Retraumatized in 1970 both by the war in Viet Nam and by his attempts to fight against it,

Cowling begins a decade-long search for happiness and stability: "In May I began looking for Bobbi. Madness, I realized, had now become viable. Fantasy was all I had. Something to hang on to—that one-in-a-million possibility—so I went after it" (259). Following her traces—including several affairs and a short-lived marriage—from TWA to graduate school to the United Nations (where she is working as a guide), he finally makes her his wife in 1981 with a desperate proclamation of love that is also a warning: "I love you with all my heart, and I swear to God—I swear it—I'll never let you go. That means *never*" (325).

Cowling tries to make his marriage a stable refuge from any further public or political involvement, falling comfortably at first into the prosperity of the 1980s while managing a Montana motel that he has bought: "I was more determined than ever to hold the line against dissolution. When the newspapers warned of calamity, I simply stopped reading: I was a family man" (325). But isolating his private life from the deadly momentum of the nuclear age proves impossible. His prosperity is based on selling uranium to the government, after all; indeed, his first step to secure Bobbi after giving up all political involvement had been to make a fortune through that transaction. His nightmares return in the mid-1980s, reinforced by the catastrophe of Beirut and the race by both the United States and USSR to MIRV their nuclear missiles: "At night I would often wake up and squeeze Bobbi for all she was worth, which was everything. The flashes were killing me" (329). But vacation trips around the world provide no escape from trauma, nor does the attempt to protect himself and his family within an American dream home at the base of the Sweetheart Mountains in Montana, where he and the Committee had staked their uranium claim: "It was a large, expensive house, with decks and fine woods, not a neighbor for miles. To be safe, though, I bought up the surrounding land and spent a summer fencing it in. I installed a burglar alarm and dead-bolt locks on all doors. It was a lovely sort of life, Bobbi said, horses and hiking, our daughter, but even so I could sometimes feel an ominous density in the world" (328–29). Cowling's breakdown is furthered by the reappearance of Sarah Strouch and an atomic warhead stolen by what remains of the Committee in their continuing attempt to combat the continuing nuclear threat in the 1980s. He and Bobbi temporarily shelter Sarah, the missile, and Cowling's former comrades, but in vain: Sarah dies of an old blister that has turned malignant, and the wealthy subversives are later annihilated in the conflagration of their tropic hideout during a police assault. Public and private trauma thus converge in the destruction of his old friends, and, in turn, Cowling's own gathering collapse threatens to overwhelm his refuge from the world: Bobbi has a brief affair and, after the deaths of Sarah and the others, she proposes a separation in the winter of 1994: "[She] said she needed space" (339).

Cowling, however, provides a space she does not need. The shelter building that follows in the spring is a final crazed attempt by her husband to hold on to his only remaining hope in a world gone mad. His nuclear family is thus a double victim of the nuclear age. Cowling's retraumatization, a product of the terrors of deterrence, initiates its disintegration by alienating his wife from her increasingly unstable husband; but, as noted above, his own behavior grotesquely replicates the murderousness of the system that he fears. Cowling's five "Quantum Jumps" detonate an initially absurd domestic quarrel that escalates to near-suicide and homicide. At the beginning of the second, Bobbi is no longer speaking to William, registering her dismay and distress through poems whose titles figuratively lament his obsessive attempt to build a family shelter and reflect the implosion of the family itself (e.g., "Fission," "The Balance of Power," "Relativity," "Backflash"). By the beginning of the third of these chapters, she has locked herself and Melinda in her bedroom and has called a taxi to leave home altogether. In turn, Bobbi's progressive alienation from her husband prompts more desperate and coercive measures to preserve his family by Cowling, who regards her metaphorical warnings as "horseshit of the worst kind" (75), "bad poetics compounded by bad logic" (229). To keep them together, he nails wooden slats across the bedroom door and window to prevent the planned escape and constructs a tiny "service" door to pass in the meals he prepares for them and to take out dirty dishes and the chamber pot. In the fourth "Quantum Jump," Cowling drugs their dinners with barbiturates so that he can carry Bobbi and Melinda unconscious into the bomb shelter that they would never have entered willingly. Like the great fenced-in house itself and the barricaded bedroom, it has become a prison rather than a refuge.

Originally planned as an underground home built to outlast the age, with "a family room, a pine-paneled den, two bedrooms, lots of closet space, maybe a greenhouse bathed in artificial sunlight, maybe a Ping-

Pong table and a piano" (7), this unfinished apotheosis of the nuclear family ideal has become its bare tomb by the final chapter of the book as Cowling, following the voice of the hole that is within him, prepares to dynamite its inhabitants into eternity. Cowling's faith in the family has been his substitute for deterrence; having lost his wife's trust, he is left unprotected from his despair. So, as if the missiles were already on their way, he is about to launch a suicidal counter strike when his daughter's terror pulls his hands from the detonator and his mind from the fear of death to the risks of love. At the end, he saves his family by leaving trauma and shelter behind to accept life in the nuclear age. Cowling's final acceptance of mortality, uncertainty, and lack of control releases him from both the public and private nuclear apocalypses that have imprisoned him in his own terror:

> I know the ending.
> One day it will happen.
> One day we will see flashes, all of us.
> One day my daughter will die. One day, I know, my wife will leave me. It will be autumn, perhaps, and the trees will be in color, and she will kiss me in my sleep and tuck a poem in my pocket, and the world will surely end.
> I know this, but I believe otherwise.
> Because there is also this day, which will be hot and bright. We will spend the afternoon in bed. I'll install the air conditioner and we'll undress and lie on the cotton sheets and talk quietly and feel the coolness. The day will pass. And when night comes I will sleep the dense narcotic sleep of my species. I will dream the dreams that suppose awakening. (359)

The balanced repetition, calm tone, and quiet eloquence of this resolution, unprecedented in the rest of Cowling's narrative, registers stylistically a dissolving of traumatization and a willing submission to the uncertainties of the nuclear age.

The Nuclear Age and Vietnam

The counterlunacies of deterrence and civil defense self-destructively and murderously exemplify attempts to provide security in *The Nuclear Age*. But so does Vietnam, since the domino theory was the doctrine of deterrence applied to conventional warfare: By fighting in Viet Nam, Americans would avoid having to fight in Thailand or Australia or California. Moreover, intervention would prevent having to use nuclear weapons and thus disturb the uncertainties of nuclear deterrence itself. Although the war is subordinated to a more comprehensive terror in *The Nuclear Age*, it provides the most important and the most convincing source of trauma in the book.

The Nuclear Age represents reactions to the war in Viet Nam within America rather than the war itself. For the first time, therefore, O'Brien handles explicitly the larger cultural context of Vietnam as Cowling becomes, in succession, a campus war protester, an antiwar activist, a draft dodger, a member of an antiwar guerrilla group, and finally an antiwar dropout who leaves the movement in 1971, returns home, and turns himself in—without legal penalty—in 1976. Like Cowling's reaction to nuclear war, the antiwar movement is handled parabolically by O'Brien: Characters and their actions are represented through grotesque exaggeration or fablelike typicality. Thus, Cowling's antiwar Committee, a product of deliberate revision between the 1979 story "The Nuclear Age" and the completed novel,[5] is a symmetrically configured foursome that joins two short, ugly malcontents with low self-esteem—Ollie Winkler and his eventual girlfriend Tina Roebuck—and two campus heroes, the glamorous cheerleader Sarah Strouch and Ned Rafferty, a star football player and her future boyfriend. Cowling, the unlikely founder of the campus antiwar movement, is in the middle, an antisocial nerd attracted to Sarah's charisma and jealous of Ned's grace. Sarah, who has been an object of fantasy and imaginary phone calls for William since middle school, refashions herself from cheerleader and campus beauty queen to antiwar guerrilla cover girl for *Newsweek* as Vietnam accelerates (and there are periodic references by Cowling to Jane Fonda's analogous metamorphosis). A blister on her lip, an attractive beauty mark before Vietnam, grows larger over her years of fighting for peace, eventually becomes infected, and swells hideously just before it kills her. A blatant symbol of the self-consuming violence of the age, the lethal blister anticipates the terrible destruction of the rest of the Committee a few months later, a television extravaganza that occurs in 1994 but replicates the end of the Symbionese Liberation Army exactly two decades earlier.[6] Cowling's two lovers are themselves contrary ideals, figural objects of his desire as much as they are independent characters: In abandoning Sarah and pursuing his manic search for Bobbi, Cowling rejects political activism for nuclear domesticity.

O'Brien's parodic or emblematic treatment of the domestic war against Vietnam is less well-realized than his representation of Cowling's traumatization. The war first intrudes upon his mental space in 1964 at college, where he has tried to cut himself off from fatuous classmates and the world at large ("The geology lab was my true home on campus" [78]). The trauma of Vietnam nearly drives him crazy again, however, reawakening his nuclear dread, refertilizing his visions of destruction, and, finally, driving him toward political involvement:

> I recovered. I spent the next six months seeking traction. Finally, though, what does one *do?*
>
> By the autumn of my junior year, October 1966, the American troop level in Vietnam exceeded 325,000. Operation Rolling Thunder closed in on Hanoi. The dead were hopelessly dead. . . .
>
> In a time of emergency, the question will not be begged: What does one do?
>
> I made my decision on a Sunday evening.
>
> Politics, I thought.
>
> On Monday morning I purchased some poster paper and black ink. The language came easily. In simple block letters I wrote: THE BOMBS ARE REAL.
>
> Trite, I realized, but true. . . .
>
> I was in control. Over the next two months, every Monday, I stationed myself at the same spot in front of the cafeteria. It was a feeble exercise, I realized that, but in conscience what does one do? Take a stance—what else?
> (84–87)

Although Cowling's individual protest against the war temporarily heals his moral neurosis and anxiety, the literal echo of Lenin here anticipates the transformation of opposition into imitation as symbolic protest against the war becomes direct action: "I was alone until early December. A frigid Monday, another noon vigil, then Ollie Winkler tapped me on the elbow and said, 'Bombs . . . a catchy tune. Who do we assassinate?'" (87). As those who join him increasingly take over the planning and implementation of protests, symbolic actions, and break-ins, Cowling begins to drop out emotionally and spiritually, disturbed by the accelerating illegality and threats of counterviolence that mirror the escalating devastation of the war itself. For one whose watchword is "safety first" (140), both Vietnam and the fight against it are retraumatizing: Fleeing the draft reawakens nightmares of nuclear apocalypse during his flight to Florida, as noted above; in Cuba, he literally breaks down during antiwar military training; his subsequent relatively passive role as a movement courier is ultimately abandoned for tracking down Bobbi and fulfilling his dream of withdrawing from the world altogether into love and domestic security; but he is subsequently haunted and traumatized by the memories of his former comrades' lives— and deaths.

Although just part of the traumatizing age that includes it, Cowling's involvement with Vietnam actually takes up the bulk of the book, and in many ways it is more substantial than his nuclear terror. The war enters Cowling's consciousness at the beginning of Chapter 5 and doesn't leave it, nominally, until the end of Chapter 11, when he returns home to Montana from Key West: "For me, at least, the war was over" (299). By then it is June 1971, but the final few pages of "Fallout" briefly record events in the final four years before Jimmy Carter's blanket pardon for draft evaders on January 21, 1977. Thus, nearly 80 percent of Cowling's retrospective narrative focuses on his activities as an opponent of the war in Viet Nam. The American war itself is registered through a series of chronologically marked references that trace its futilely destructive expansion from 1964 until the final explosion of strategy and policy in 1975. Within Cowling's apologia, these Vietnam references function to increase his anxiety over the escalations of violence, but they are more numerous and more insistent than all the other nuclear age graffiti. Moreover, they ironically complement the Committee's own evolution into increasing militance and symbolic or potential violence.

Cowling's sense of being trapped by the war is particularly striking during the two years he spends underground. When he finally flees conscription and accompanies his friends to Cuba, the fugitive finds that he has actually been drafted into a simulacrum of the U.S. Army itself, complete with two sardonic and merciless African American instructors, Ebenezer Keezer and Nethro, who had fought in Viet Nam before becoming domestic antiwar terrorists. The Cuban episodes ludicrously mimic the little brutalities and absurdities of military regimentation that Cowling thought he was fleeing:

We assembled in the courtyard.

A single rank, stiff at attention. All around us were khakied soldiers with heavy boots and bad tempers. "Freeze!" someone shouted, and we froze. . . .

We stood with our backs to a tile wall.

At noon we were still there.

Near midnight Tina said, "Wow," then smiled and collapsed. . . . (198)

Over the morning hours we engaged in supervised waving practice. "Hi, there!" we yelled, and we waved with both hands, vigorously. The courtesy was painful. I could feel it in my throat and shoulders. Nethro counted cadence, Ebenezer Keezer smiled and offered instruction in matters of form and posture. . . . It was a kind of basic training, clearly, but with numerous innovations. Standing there, waving, I recognized the diverse and intricate plenitude of a world on tilt. (201)

He comes to see both the war and the fight against it as elements of a more comprehensive violence: "Here, I thought, was everything I'd run from. But you couldn't run far enough or fast enough. You couldn't dodge the global dragnet. The killing zone kept expanding. Reaction or revolution, no matter, it was a hazard to health either way" (206). Once the Committee members return to Key West and begin their struggle against the warmakers, this mimicry of legal violence accelerates: A consignment of M-16s is hijacked, as well as, eventually, a nuclear warhead. In trying to bring an end to war, the Committee acquires the only bomb that appears physically in *The Nuclear Age*.

Cowling and Rafferty eventually get drunk enough to dump the M-16s in a lake, prohibiting their use by either GIs or the Committee, the protagonist's only effective direct action against war in the novel. Moreover, unlike his visions of nuclear apocalypse, Cowling's involvement with Vietnam confronts actual rather than imagined or potential violence. His lone political message—"the bombs are real"—refers not just to inert warheads in their hardened silos but to the ongoing destruction of Viet Nam by the American war and to its hundreds of daily victims. And his traumatic visions and nightmares of Vietnam are not just imaginary, like those of nuclear apocalypse, but incorporate what is actually happening in the world around him:

In February I watched thirteen marines die along a paddy dike near Chu Lai.

I recall an encounter with napalm.

Voices, too—people shouting. In the hours before dawn I was awakened by Phantom jets. I saw burning villages. I saw the dead and maimed. I saw it. I was not out of my mind. I was *in* my mind; I was a mind's eyewitness to atrocity by airmail. There were barricades before public buildings. There were cops in riot masks, and clubs and bullhorns, and high rhetoric, and Kansas burning, and a black bomb pinwheeling against a silver sky, and 50,000 citizens marching with candles down Pennsylvania Avenue. (82)

It is this tangible presence of violence that drives Cowling to political action but also to the personal and political withdrawal that will end just before suicide and murder.

The nihilism that nearly consumes the nuclear family has its origins in Cowling's mimicry of combat in Viet Nam. His terrible epiphany occurs during the "final exam" at the terrorist training camp in Cuba, a mock commando raid on a guard tower under live machine gun fire behind him and with a field of barbed wire ahead. Earlier, during weapons firing at the rifle range, O'Brien had replicated Paul Berlin's initial breakdown in *Cacciato* by having Cowling lose control of his M-16 and his body, spraying the ground wildly on full automatic while fouling himself in front of his comrades and instructor: "This development . . . gives scared shitless a whole new meaning," Ebenezer Keezer smirked loudly at the time (213). Now, determined like Berlin to overcome his earlier shame, Cowling slowly crawls through the night firing range toward the tower: "two hundred meters up the beach. No panic, I thought. Just this once, I would perform with dignity. I would not wail or freeze or befoul myself . . . I was a commando now. Anything was possible. Push-glide, no thinking. Off to my right I could make out the peaceful wash of waves where the sea touched land [an echo of the observation post scenario in *Cacciato*]. Dignity, I thought, then I said it aloud, 'Dignity'" (214–15). But as he becomes bloodily entangled in concertina wire, fearfully transfixed by flares and tracer bullets whizzing overhead and paralyzed by Ebenezer's grotesquely comic ultimatums over the loudspeaker, panic gives way to defeat, but also to a primitive enlightenment:

I surprised myself by crawling forward.

It was a crabbing kind of movement, without dignity. I heard myself saying "Sorry," then saying "Stop it!" Squirrel chatter. I was thinking squirrel

thoughts: There is nothing worth dying for. Nothing. Not dignity, not politics. Nothing. There is nothing worth dying for. . . .

A tracer round corkscrewed over my head. I was twitching, but the
twitches were strictly amoral. I was lucid. I understood the physics: If there
is nothing, there is nothing worth dying for.

I blinked and looked up and swallowed sand. There were no ethical patterns. (216–17)

Ultimately, as his friends reach the target and demolish it with explosives,
Cowling stops moving forward entirely and begins to dig himself a refuge:

I scooped out a shallow hole at the edge of the sea and slipped in and
carefully packed wet sand against my legs and hips and chest. I apologized
to my father . . . and he was there beside me, with me, watching me dig. I
told him the truth. "There's nothing to die for," I said, and my father
thought about it for a time, then nodded and said, "No, nothing." His eyes
were bright blue. He smiled and tucked me in.

"Am I crazy?" I asked.

"That's a hard one."

"Am I?"

There was a pause, a moment of incompletion, but he finished it by saying, "I love you, cowboy," then he bent down and kissed my lips. (220)

Thus, the digging-in that will mark Cowling's ultimate defense against the
nuclear age has its origins in this refabricated facsimile of the trauma of
Vietnam. It is further motivated by Cowling's dismissing any value other
than self-preservation. The final vision, with its reversion to infantilism, reflects an early fantasy after the first day of guerrilla training: "I imagined
myself in repose beneath a plywood Ping-Pong table. I imagined my
father's arms around me. I imagined, also, a world in which men would not
do to men the things men so often do to men. It was a world without armies, without cannibalism or treachery or greed, a world safe and undi-
vided" (205). In turn, this childish dream of a world free of male violence
evokes the stewardess who had held his hand on the flight into exile: "I
imagined embarking on a long pursuit. Pick up the airborne scent and
track her down and carry her away. A desert island, maybe, or the planet
Mars, where there would be quiet and civility and poetry recitals late at
night. Peace, that's all, just a fantasy" (205–6). In the end, the fantasy will

provoke the subsequent quest for domestic security that effaces Cowling's political involvement. But the nihilism implicit in his self-absorbed pursuit of happiness will work out its reductio ad absurdum in Cowling's quantum jumps: When Bobbi threatens to leave, Cowling's final shelter threatens to become their grave.

The Failure of William Cowling

The parallels between Cowling and Paul Berlin as reluctant warriors point to a larger structural similarity between *The Nuclear Age* and its predecessor, which otherwise seem so different in subject and protagonist. Cowling's nuclear trauma may seem more comprehensive, but each work is constructed as a posttraumatic meditation that puts together a series of retrospective narratives in order to allow the protagonists to understand and recover from an initial crisis. Both Paul and William are traumatized by Vietnam and seek to find a peace that will remove them from the circumstances of violence. While Paul tries to imagine a peaceful future in Paris, however, William can only anticipate the end of the world, whether as nuclear apocalypse or as the end of his marriage. *Cacciato* demonstrates the limits of the imagination; *The Nuclear Age* warns of its dangers. As Adamson reminds his teenaged patient at the end of their week of mutual therapy: "Imagination . . . that's what you and I have in common. A wonderful faculty, but sometimes it gets out of control, starts rolling downhill, no brakes, and all you can do is hang on for dear life and hope you don't—" "Crack up," adds William (62).

The grotesque reprise of basic training in *The Nuclear Age* also rewrites *If I Die in a Combat Zone*. Moreover, because it is told in the first person, with no formal gap between protagonist and narrator, the later novel replicates the memoirist mode of O'Brien's first book. Just as that narrative had opened with the future author under fire in Viet Nam in order to explain how he got there, *The Nuclear Age* introduces Cowling digging away in 1995 and then recalls the events from 1946 that have led to his present crisis. If anything, Cowling's is a more voluble, more intimately confessional self-expression than O'Brien's detached, ironic, and constricted voice in the memoir, and *The Nuclear Age* more seamlessly autobiographical than *Combat Zone* itself.

More than narrative form links the antiwar protester and the reluctant GI. If *Cacciato* allowed O'Brien to imagine the possibility of desertion, *The Nuclear Age* enables him to consider another alternative that he was unable to choose—rejecting the army altogether. As *Combat Zone* presents it, by fulfilling the draft laws and following overseas orders, he became a soldier, but both choices are represented as cowardly failures to act decisively against the war. The protagonist of *The Nuclear Age* dares to choose the extreme alternative of exile that had proved too difficult for O'Brien, who characterized Cowling as "courageous . . . the only hero I've written" in a 1991 interview (Naparsteck 5). But O'Brien represents William's decision as no more satisfying than it would have been for himself: "I could've backed out with honor," Cowling reflects as he considers alternatives that might have been easier: "I could've pursued my studies and graduated with distinction and spent the next decade lying low. . . . No armies, no social milieu, no drafts to dodge, no underground strife . . . I could've avoided some funerals. A choice, and I chose, but I could've avoided the rest of my life" (97). Rather than realizing his desire for peace, security, and doing what's right, Cowling's antiwar involvement leaves him psychically and morally traumatized. And in two brief episodes, unusual for their poignancy within O'Brien's nuclear age fable, his exiled alter ego suffers the consequences of that abandonment of hometown and family that O'Brien could not endure. When the draft dodger and domestic guerrilla calls his mother from exile, Cowling can reassure her only with silence because he fears her phone is tapped; and when his beloved father dies, he can watch the funeral only distantly from a nearby hill.

Cowling's childhood fear of nuclear war and his public opposition to Vietnam as a college student are drawn more directly from O'Brien's own experiences and suggest also that he is an alternative version of the author. Cowling objects to the war as an expenditure of "certain blood for uncertain reasons" (160), a phrase that he has picked up in college and attributes to Sarah; its real source is O'Brien himself, however, who has used the phrase in public readings of his work to explain his opposition to the war and employed it definitively in *The Things They Carried* ("On the Rainy River" 44). Cowling's anguish about the threat of service in Viet Nam mirrors O'Brien's own:

I did not want to die, and my father understood that.

It wasn't cowardice exactly, and he understood that, too, and it wasn't courage.

It wasn't politics.

Not even the war itself, not the coffins or justice or a citizen's obligation to his state. It was gravity. Something physical, that force that keeps pressing toward the end. (160)

No choice emerging from such mixed and ambiguous motives could be clear-cut or satisfying, of course, and Cowling proves to be as unhappy in fighting against the war as his creator was while fighting in it. Like all of O'Brien's previous protagonists—including the author in *Combat Zone*—Cowling is torn between obligations to others and the desire to save himself. Furthermore, doing the right thing, whatever that might be, depends crucially on satisfying the expectations of a father whose values are challenged by the son's critical situation. Ultimately, Cowling rejects the draft and the war, but, like O'Brien in Viet Nam, he is never comfortable with the choice he has made. Like his fictive predecessors, the protagonist of *The Nuclear Age*, alienated almost immediately from the goals and tactics of his comrades in Key West and Cuba, ends up passively observing the actions of others.

Two intimate details further identify Cowling as an alter ego, a figure O'Brien uses to imagine what might have happened if he had evaded the draft. Like his protagonist, O'Brien was born on October 1, 1946, and he calls attention to the date by having William describe his own birthday celebrations on three occasions. The first occurs on October 1, 1968, at Key West, where he has just fled conscription and is about to join the antiwar underground; the second occurs in Cuba one year later, after Cowling has washed out as a terrorist but begun to serve the movement as a courier. On his own birthdays during those years, Cowling's fabricator was at Fort Lewis, undergoing advanced infantry training (1968), and then in Chu Lai, working as an army clerk after half a year of combat (1969). Finally, on his thirtieth birthday, October 1, 1976, Cowling surrenders himself to the U.S. government as a fugitive from justice. By then, of course, the war is over, America has celebrated its two hundredth anniversary, and O'Brien's protagonist seems a refugee from another era: "There were fireworks and tall ships. Amnesia was epidemic. Gerald Ford: My life was like his presidency; it happened, I'm almost certain" (300). In the same year, the thirty-year-old

O'Brien, the author of *Combat Zone* and *Northern Lights*, published several excerpts from a new novel in progress, including "Going After Cacciato." Cowling shares his name as well as date of birth with the author, who was christened William Timothy O'Brien. While the name William represents an O'Brien who would have had the courage to flee from the war, it also reminds us that the authorial identity itself—"Tim O'Brien," the trauma artist who has reconceived himself—is a product of the choice that Cowling rejected.

William Cowling thus represents what O'Brien would have lost by evading the war, his subsequent career as an imaginative writer, as well as what he suffered—the trauma of participating in Vietnam. Cowling prides himself on his extravagant imagination and can be seen as a perceptive and even heroic visionary able to apprehend that accepting the nuclear balance of power is not realism but madness. But Cowling's imagination is too narrowly self-absorbed to be productive, and ultimately it becomes destructive, fixated upon digging a hole in the ground from which to flee the nuclear age. Although like Paul Berlin he mimics O'Brien's own storytelling function, Cowling comes to realize that his project in *The Nuclear Age* is as anticreative as the nihilism of nuclear deterrence, that the hole is within. Cowling's failure of imagination is as important in O'Brien's novel as his prescient fear of annihilation or the imaginary dialogues that he creates as a substitute for real conversations, and all have the same origin: a radical solipsism that measures and evaluates everything according to its own desires. When he courts and marries Bobbi, Cowling finds the poems that she gives him beautiful. When she threatens to leave him, resisting his shelter building and registering her own incarceration through poems that express her anguish, her verses are either incomprehensible or trite and poetry itself a worthless discourse: "I don't get it. Meanings, I mean. What's the point? Why this preference for metaphor over the real thing?" (67). Of course, the same question might be asked of O'Brien, whose career has been dedicated to the proposition that "metaphor" is what makes "reality" meaningful.

Although he shares his first name with O'Brien, Cowling's patronymic figures his ineffectualness and ethical near-meltdown. The echo of "coward" in the name is reinforced by its being a diminutive of "cowl," reflecting the protagonist's accelerating drive to barricade himself from the world in monastic seclusion, a dead end whose futility is suggested by the final verses of *The Nuclear Age*'s epigraph: "For one man will long to see another, or to hear his voice. For ten will be left, out of a city, and two, out of a field, who have hidden in the thick woods or in holes in the rocks." The word "cowling," originally a term for the hood covering an airplane's engine, was extended in the nuclear age to refer to the outer canopy of a rocket engine. Even more literally than Pynchon's Tyrone Slothrop, Cowling is a "rocket man," willing to assist the construction of ICBM warheads by finding and then selling uranium to the nuclear industry for a million-dollar payout that has made possible his family retreat in the Montana wilderness. As Sarah Strouch tartly chides her former radical comrade: "You've changed. . . . Ban the bomb to boom the bomb. Denim to shark-skin, plowshares to swords" (313). When he and Sarah tour the University of Minnesota in 1980, searching for Bobbi, Cowling looks askance at the apathetic campus around him without reflecting on his own retreat from politics: "Freshman season, kickoff, the rush, and the campus was clean with Swedes and maroon and gold and Big Ten fever. We'd won the peace for them. Hair was out, health food was in. And it was our labor of a decade ago that made all this possible" (322–23). But although Sarah and the rest of the Committee remain outside the law, they too have shared in the profits of Cowling's sellout, and her deepest desires are for marriage, a honeymoon in Rio, and having children. By 1995, all her hopes have been cruelly obliterated, while Cowling's radicalism has receded into a merely destructive mania for domestic security. If Cowling's flight from the draft exaggerates O'Brien's hatred of the war, transforming it into moral courage, his apolitical self-absorption exaggerates his creator's compromise with the complacent postwar consensus. "Where's Gene McCarthy in this hour of final trial?" asks Cowling to himself at the beginning of the book, "No heroes, no heavies. And who cares? That's the stunner: Who among us really cares? A nation of microchips. At dinner parties we eat mushroom salad and blow snow and talk computer lingo" (9). Here as elsewhere, Cowling frequently mimics the sentiments of O'Brien, the former McCarthy volunteer, who confessed to Maria Lenhart in 1985: "I'm a total drop-out compared to how I was ten years ago when there were issues we all cared so much about—peace, poverty, civil rights. This book is confronting my own apathy" (cited in Graham 443).

By the end of *The Nuclear Age*, Cowling is a posttraumatic survivor, like O'Brien. Having stopped his own chain reaction in order to save his daughter, he can now begin to believe, against darker expectations, that the rest of us will not self-destruct either. Otherwise, however, his traumatization has been almost completely disabling, for even his pursuit of Bobbi and his marriage have been self-protective and futile barriers against his own nightmares. O'Brien, too, went to graduate school after the war but abandoned political science for a more productive use of his imagination. By converting his personal trauma into fictions of our age and sharing them with the rest of us, he has avoided Cowling's ultimate retreat into his own terrors. His hero, who ultimately dismisses his wife's poems contemptuously and even swallows one at the breakfast table, produces only one text himself in *The Nuclear Age*, a mute signboard that contrasts with the hyperaroused volubility in the rest of his monologue.[7] Nonetheless, the transformation of lives that it produced, despite the resultant casualties, is more valuable than building shelters. "The bombs are real" is not just a fact—it summons the reader's moral imagination, like the book that incorporates Cowling's perspective but transcends it.

Ultimately, *The Nuclear Age*, like many fictions grounded on a polemic, may end up being evaluated on the basis of its political and social analysis, a precarious situation for a novelist. Even with the end of the Cold War, however, O'Brien's concern about warheads, physical and human, remains prescient. The balance of terror that he projected into an indefinite, millennial catastrophe has not yet been safely escaped: Unaccountably yet inevitably, the thermonuclear hardware continues to outlast the ideologies that produced it, reemerging only when it produces catastrophes such as the August 2000 sinking of the Russian nuclear supersubmarine *Kursk*. And just as shelter building ironically cooperates with military preparedness, nuclear traumatization continues to be a valuable resource for the national defense state, whether in the form of Star Wars research, fabricating missile threats from "rogue regimes," or encouraging fear of China. Whether a future national missile defense system will protect any American city is almost irrelevant because its primary purpose is to shield and protect funding for the American military-industrial complex in the twenty-first century. Perhaps even more prophetic are other ramifications of civil defense, including the growth of the barricade mentality within a society where insecurity increases with private wealth and the only freedom now sacrosanct is free enterprise. Impressive as fable or parable of our civic stultification, the novel seems less successful as a *comic* attempt to treat serious issues. Cowling's growing madness and his reflections on the world about him often achieve a nice balance between pathos and bathos, comedy and tragedy. But the other cartoon characters are not as successfully conceived, partly because of Cowling's solipsism: Bobbi has virtually no identity beyond his own desires and anxieties, for example. Much of the dialogue is both clever and wooden, a series of brief phrases and clichés playing off each other. Finally, Cowling's periodic surveys of political events are necessary to the book's subject but too brief to be involving. His survey of the nuclear age after 1971, when he returns from exile, is particularly threadbare.

While this telescoping of public events exemplifies Cowling's theories about the relativity of human consciousness and reflects his accelerating breakdown and withdrawal from politics, it has another explanation. Cowling's relative uninterest in events from the 1970s onward coincides with the winding down of the war in Southeast Asia as well as the end of O'Brien's own service there. As we have argued, Vietnam is actually the crucial historical event in Cowling's life, as it was in O'Brien's, even though *The Nuclear Age* treats it as merely part of a larger social and political madness. In his next book, O'Brien will return to the war more directly through another first-person narrator traumatized by Vietnam. But instead of rewriting himself as someone who tried to flee from the war physically and psychologically, he will reappear as "Tim O'Brien," a writer who has carried Vietnam with him and continues to refashion its trauma for his readers.

CHAPTER 6

TRUE WAR STORIES

Recirculated Trauma, Endless Fiction

After publishing his fable of nuclear age trauma in 1985, O'Brien's next novel was to have been *The People We Marry*, a work that eventually appeared as *In the Lake of the Woods* in 1994 (Kaplan 1995: 218). In the interim, however, he published several short stories, some set in Viet Nam and others in the United States but all related to the war. The shorter stories took on a life of their own and eventually a comprehensive form that became *The Things They Carried*, published by Houghton Mifflin in 1990, four years before the novel that was to have followed *The Nuclear Age*. Its award-winning title story, which appeared in 1986, was the first part of the larger work to be published. In 1989, just before its publication, O'Brien called *Things* the best thing he had yet written (Naparsteck 8), and he has noted how much he enjoyed putting together the book as a whole. Indeed, reviewers greeted *The Things They Carried* as O'Brien's triumphant return to form after the relatively disappointing achievement of *The Nuclear Age*. The work has received admiring academic critical attention as well. Calling it a "remarkable text" (28), Philip Beidler used a citation from the title story as an epigraph to his 1991 study of Vietnam authors, and Don Ringnalda referred to *Things* as O'Brien's "ultimate Vietnam War fiction" (105). Even Lorrie Smith, a critic who finds much of the work "pernicious" in its masculinist discourse, concedes that *Things* "contributes significantly to the canon of Vietnam War fiction" and is "remarkable" in its treatment of writing and soldiering (38).

O'Brien has told one interviewer that the genesis of the book was the image of the war as something to be carried, a weight of things that derived from his own experiences: "remembering all this crap I had on me and inside me, the physical and spiritual burdens" (Lee 200). As a work derived from painful memories that must be borne again, *The Things They Carried* has also been admired by mental health professionals for its insightful representation of combat trauma. *Things* is the only work of Vietnam War fiction quoted in Jonathan Shay's comparative study of the *Iliad* and PTSD or in Judith Herman's *Trauma and Recovery*. (And among the jacket blurbs for each book appear commendations by O'Brien.) Shay cites the narrator's insistence in "How to Tell a True War Story" that "a true war story is never moral" to argue more generally that trauma can never be easily resolved through writing (183), a point also emphasized by Kali Tal in discussing Lawrence Langer's study of Holocaust literature (Tal 1996: 49–50). Herman, as noted in Chapter 1, cites passages from *Things* to exemplify Vietnam War trauma generally.

As O'Brien's satisfaction with the writing of the book suggests, however, *Things* is a work of recovery as well as trauma. Although "you can tell a true war story by its absolute and uncompromising allegiance to obscenity and evil" ("How to Tell a True War Story" 76), yet "this too is true: stories can save us" ("The Lives of the Dead" 255). *The Things They Carried* negotiates between these two truths by making storytelling itself the most important subject of the book. Throughout the work, stories are produced through a wide variety of discursive gestures, including recollection, confession, and explanation, as well as explicit storytelling; and many tales are repeated, elaborated by further details, or supplemented by additional explanation or commentary. This ceaseless replication of the fictive process witnesses to the mutual dependence of trauma and narrative as O'Brien reinvents himself as a soldier and as a writer. In the end, the work exemplifies both the need to write one's way beyond trauma and the impossibility of ever doing so.

The Things They Carried as Self-Revision

Composed of twenty-two pieces, beginning with "The Things They Carried" and ending with "The Lives of the Dead," O'Brien's fifth book has been characterized both as a collection of short stories and as a novel, but

neither classification exhausts its generic range. Among the "things" carried in the volume are apparent fiction and apparent nonfiction, including
straightforward realism, fantasy, memoir, author's notes, and literary commentary. In content and form, *Things* revises O'Brien's two previous war-
sited works. Like *If I Die in a Combat Zone*, the book originated in a few independently published pieces that prompted a larger structure that would
come to incorporate them; as with *Going After Cacciato*, those earliest elements were a series of prize-winning stories.[1] Although closely resembling
Combat Zone in form and mode, *Things* is not a memoir; and although it
includes many interconnected stories, it is not a continuous narrative
work like *Cacciato*. O'Brien has called it simply a "fiction," and it is more
appropriate to identify its twenty-two "fictions" as "pieces" or "sections"
rather than as chapters or stories. For example, "Spin," the third section,
merely narrates or recalls a number of short, unconnected sketches, some
of them identified as memories, others as stories; the seventh piece, "How
to Tell a True War Story," and the last, "The Lives of the Dead," are similarly
miscellaneous. Whatever its genre, most of *Things* follows a group of about
a dozen GIs who experience the mixed trauma and boredom of combat in
Viet Nam and reappear in the various episodes that make up the book.
These protagonists are a rewriting of *Cacciato*'s Third Squad, and both
groups are fictional versions of the men of Alpha Company with whom
O'Brien served in Viet Nam during his year in-country; indeed, the soldiers
in *Things* belong to an Alpha Company themselves. As in *Combat Zone*,
Tim O'Brien is one of its members, and a great deal of first-person narra-
tive and commentary in the book presents his own point of view.

   Revisiting the war through the experiences and point of view of a rep-
resentative group of GIs is a cliché in American representations of Vietnam (Leland 740), but *Things* is also a self-conscious refashioning of the
structure of *Cacciato*. The novel had begun with a list of the dead, followed by a description of the living. The title fiction of *Things* is O'Brien's
supreme use of a list, a masterpiece of literary realism and formal patterning that focuses on everything carried by each soldier in the book, from
jungle boots, 2.1 pounds; to letters from home, 10 ounces; to grief, terror,
love, shameful memories, and "the soldier's greatest fear, which was the
fear of blushing. Men killed, and died, because they were embarrassed not
to" (20–21). Thus, both works open with a catalog of characters, burdened
by personal and collective trauma, who will reappear in the episodes to fol-

low. Like *Cacciato* as well, *Things* goes on to recall the deaths of squad members until all have been recuperated by the end of the book, where they reappear in the oxymoronically titled final piece—it seems that "the lives of the dead" are not over in *The Things They Carried.*

Formally, then, O'Brien's fifth book combines the most obvious features of his two earlier Vietnam narratives: A series of structurally coherent scenarios portray the war through the experiences of a small group of GIs; and the writer represents himself as a protagonist, participant, or commentator in all but three ("The Things They Carried," "Speaking of Courage," and "In the Field"). The site of narration thus varies from piece to piece, moving from the first-person point of view of *Combat Zone* (and *The Nuclear Age*) to the third-person intimate perspective of *Cacciato* (and *Northern Lights*). The title narrative, nearly an epitome of the war as it was represented in both *Combat Zone* and *Cacciato*, sometimes takes on an omniscient perspective that reflects what O'Brien has represented in the earlier books about men in combat.

Throughout *The Things They Carried*, O'Brien refashions traumatic experiences that were first represented in *Combat Zone* and rewritten in the later books. Thus, breakdown in combat was briefly described in Chapter XIII (119–20) of the memoir, but its description in "The Things They Carried" (18–19) explicitly recalls not only Paul Berlin's experience on Cacciato's hill but also William Cowling's embarrassment in guerrilla training:

> For the most part they carried themselves with poise, a kind of dignity. Now and then, however, there were times of panic, when they squealed or wanted to squeal but couldn't, when they twitched and made moaning sounds and covered their heads and said Dear Jesus and flopped around on the earth and fired their weapons blindly and cringed and sobbed and begged for the noise to stop and went wild and made stupid promises to themselves and to God and to their mothers and fathers, hoping not to die. In different ways, it happened to all of them. Afterward, when the firing ended, they would blink and peek up. They would touch their bodies, feeling shame, then quickly hiding it. . . . After a time someone would shake his head and say, No lie, I almost shit my pants, and someone else would laugh, which meant it was bad, yes, but the guy had obviously not shit his pants, it wasn't that bad, and in any case nobody would ever do such a thing and then go ahead and talk about it.

Whether or not O'Brien personally did "such a thing," he wrote about it in both *Cacciato* and *The Nuclear Age*. The destruction of Tri Binh 4 recalled in the memoir ("Alpha Company") and revised in the obliteration of Hoi An in *Cacciato* ("Fire in the Hole") reappears in the wiping out of Than Khe in "The Things They Carried." All three operations are ordered by junior officers during patrols near hostile villages, and the two purely fictional accounts are brutal responses to the death of an American GI, Jim Pederson in *Cacciato* and Ted Lavender in *Things*. Alpha Company's destructive takeover of a Buddhist monastery as a combat base in "July" (*Combat Zone*) is refashioned more positively in "Church," where the monks' gracious courtesy is reciprocated by some of their guests. In the same chapter of the memoir, Captain Smith's incompetence leads to an American soldier's being buried in mud when a half-track runs over him, and his comrades have to find his corpse and pull it out of the mire. The episode is elaborately expanded and altered in several of the later sections of *Things*, which focus on the fate of Kiowa, an American Indian GI who is lethally buried under mud and human waste during a nighttime mortar attack. In "On the Rainy River," O'Brien refashions his failure to flee from military service when he had a chance to do so, concluding his account with the same moral paradox that had haunted his recollection in *Combat Zone* ("Escape"): "I survived, but it's not a happy ending. I was a coward. I went to the war" (63). And as noted in Chapter 1, O'Brien's description of the destruction of a water buffalo, recalled in *Combat Zone* (139) and rewritten in both *Cacciato* and *The Nuclear Age*, reappears in "How to Tell a True War Story."

The Things They Carried rewrites O'Brien's earlier work, but it also revises itself as it proceeds, frequently providing multiple versions of a single episode and commenting on its own origins. The work's continual self-reflection upon its own status and purpose as imaginative writing has prompted Catherine Calloway (1995) to label it a metafiction. Perhaps the most comprehensive subject of *Cacciato* is its own making, as represented in the meditations of Paul Berlin. But *Things* is more explicitly metafictional, as the very titles of "How to Tell a True War Story," "Notes," and "Good Form" indicate. In the last sentence of the book, O'Brien reimagines himself as a ten-year-old boy, "skimming across the surface of my own history, moving fast, riding the melt beneath the blades, doing loops and spins, and when I take a high leap into the dark and come down thirty years later, I realize it is as Tim trying to save Timmy's life with a story" (273). The image is a memory, a story, and a metaphor for the story making that has now come to an end—indeed, "Spin" is the third piece in *The Things They Carried.*

In this final passage, O'Brien is re-membering himself, an act that combines the roles of artist, character, and audience. Such self-representation is the most striking feature of *The Things They Carried* and its most significant means of making storytelling a crucial subject. Except in *Northern Lights,* the protagonists of his previous books were authorial surrogates, and even Paul Perry shares the quasi-authorial role of meditative observer or narrator that characterizes Berlin, Cowling, and O'Brien himself in *Combat Zone.* In *Things,* however, the author is directly refashioned as the figure whom O'Brien has referred to as "the Tim character" (Naparsteck 7) and "the character Tim O'Brien" (Kaplan 1991: 96–97).[2] We will refer to O'Brien's persona as "Tim O'Brien" or as "the narrator" to distinguish him from the author. By employing what we may call the *trope of memory,* suddenly recalling and then elaborating in more detail a past scene from the war, this latest version of O'Brien combines his identities as soldier and author, which had been distinct in the earlier books. For example, "Spin" consists of eighteen short sections, most of them brief scenes from the war introduced by the simple formula "I remember" or an equivalent. Four sections are prefaced by the reflection that "what sticks to memory, often, are those odd little fragments that have no beginning and no end" (39). The final section identifies O'Brien's authorial role by making explicit the relationship between memory and fiction: "Forty-three years old, and the war occurred half a lifetime ago, and yet the remembering makes it now. And sometimes remembering will lead to a story, which makes it forever. That's what stories are for. Stories are for joining the past to the future" (40). In remembering, the author rewitnesses what the soldier had seen, so that the two selves also merge, like Tim the writer and Timmy the ten-year-old. Both are present even in brief sketches such as "Stockings," which describes Henry Dobbins's unwavering faith in a personal talisman: "Even now, twenty years later, I can see him wrapping his girlfriend's pantyhose around his neck before heading out on ambush" (129). By the end of the piece, which describes Dobbins's decision to keep wearing the stockings for good luck even though his girlfriend has dumped him, the narrator has rejoined his platoon imaginatively: "It was a relief for all of us"

(130). As in *Combat Zone,* the use of "we" and "us" incorporates the narrator Tim O'Brien into five other brief war pieces that are not directly presented as memories.

In "The Things They Carried," "Speaking of Courage," and "In the Field," however, the narrator is neither remembering what once happened nor is present when it does. But each of these originally independently published stories is followed by a brief sketch in *The Things They Carried*—"Love," "Notes," and "Field Trip," respectively—that identifies O'Brien's persona as the author of the preceding longer story. Indeed, in these three metafictional appendices and in nine of the other pieces in *Things,* Tim O'Brien is the narrator, remembering, describing, arguing, or explaining things to us in the first person.

Two of the other works, "Sweetheart of the Song Tra Bong" and "Night Life," are represented by O'Brien's persona as stories that were narrated by his comrades Rat Kiley and Mitchell Sanders. In "The Ghost Soldiers," Norman Bowker tells how Morty Phillips suffered a lethal infection after taking a swim, and Kiley and Sanders tell additional stories in "Spin" and "How to Tell a True War Story." Telling stories is thus omnipresent in *Things,* and Tim O'Brien represents himself and his comrades as an eager audience:

> By midnight it was story time.
>
> "Morty Phillips used up his luck," Bowker said.
>
> I smiled and waited. There was a tempo to how stories got told. Bowker peeled open a finger blister and sucked on it.
>
> "Go on," Azar said. "Tell him everything." ("The Ghost Soldiers"—221)

Tim O'Brien's presence in such scenes enacts a *trope of storytelling* to represent his fiction as simply the transmission of episodes overhead and repeated, just as the act of remembering defines his function as merely recovering and fleshing out actual incidents. In the latter case, he is a witness; in the former, an audience for twice-told tales. The notion of sharing the accounts of others is reinforced by the narrator's general references to the war as a source of stories; for example: "Vietnam was full of strange stories, some improbable, some well beyond that, but the stories that will last forever are those that swirl back and forth across the border between trivia and bedlam, the mad and the mundane. This one keeps returning to me. I heard it from Rat Kiley, who swore up and down to its truth, although in the end, I'll admit, that doesn't amount to much of a warranty" (101). This is the introduction to "Sweetheart of the Song Tra Bong," Rat Kiley's account of Mary Anne Bell, a football cheerleader from Ohio who flies to the war zone to join her high school sweetheart but gradually becomes so enamored of counterguerrilla terrorism that she migrates into the jungle and is last seen prowling about in her pink culottes, wearing a necklace of human tongues. O'Brien has claimed that the story is based on an actual incident (Coffey 61, Baughman 205), so it perfectly exemplifies the convincing lunacy of a true war story that lasts forever.

Insofar as *The Things They Carried* presents itself as a miscellany of overheard and remembered episodes from the war, strikingly mundane and authentically bizarre, the book resembles the method and material of Michael Herr's *Dispatches*, a work and a writer O'Brien greatly admires. But its self-conscious use of remembering and storytelling also recalls Proust and Conrad. The work ends, like *Remembrance of Things Past*, by recalling the originating instance of the narrator's identity as a writer—in Tim O'Brien's case, the death of his childhood girlfriend Linda and his dreams of her continuing presence in his life. And "Sweetheart of the Song Tra Bong" is O'Brien's *Heart of Darkness*, Americanized, Vietnamized, and surrealized (and possibly encouraged by Francis Ford Coppola's film version of Conrad, *Apocalypse Now*, for which Herr wrote the screenplay). Like Conrad's tale, "Sweetheart" is filtered through three sets of narrators, since Rat Kiley heard the end of the story from a comrade who talked to the Green Berets, and in their account the high school sweetheart is already turning into a ghostly legend: "[A] couple times they almost saw her sliding through the shadows. Not quite, but almost. She had crossed to the other side" (125). The Ohio cheerleader becomes the Kurtz figure who has "crossed to the other side," while the Green Berets practice the barbarous rites that she first emulates and then goes beyond. And both in this story and in those that the other members of Alpha Company tell, O'Brien makes the circumstances of storytelling itself part of the tales, complete with interruptions by listeners and characterizations of his own narrative by GI storytellers, who thus become additional authorial surrogates.

Overall, Tim O'Brien appears in nineteen of the twenty-two pieces that make up *Things* as a participant, audience/observer, or commentator, and he is identified as the author of the other three. Whether as writer or soldier, he is the book's central figure, and his multiple roles as author and character make *Things* a peculiarly Proustian work, despite its subject. But just as Proust's narrator is not the author of *Remembrance of Things Past* but a young man who is about to write it, the Tim O'Brien who appears in *The Things They Carried* cannot be simply identified with the author who has created him. As noted above, O'Brien's book is identified as "a work of fiction" on the title page and in the brief foreword, which notes that "except for a few details regarding the author's own life, all the incidents, names, and characters are imaginary." Although the autobiographical details virtually identify author and protagonist, O'Brien has given himself an imaginary daughter in "Ambush," "Good Form," and "Field Trip," and the last of these pieces details a trip back to Viet Nam with her in 1990 that, needless to say, never happened. There are also less obvious differences between O'Brien and his persona, including some noted by the author: The vengeful behavior of Tim O'Brien in "The Ghost Soldiers" represents some of his creator's darker impulses, but the episode never occurred; and O'Brien does not share the narrator's mystification of war's violence (e.g., "For all its horror, you can't help but gape at the awful majesty of combat"—87) in "How to Tell a True War Story" (Naparsteck 9). Thus, the Tim O'Brien who appears in the book, a soldier who fought in Viet Nam in Quang Ngai Province and is now a writer and the author of a book called *Going After Cacciato*, is a character created by the Tim O'Brien who wrote *The Things They Carried*.

The narrator provides a confession and a justification for O'Brien's self-fabrication in "Good Form," as if the apparent misrepresentation of the first seventeen sections of *Things* were an act of bad faith with the reader:

> It's time to be blunt.
>
> I'm forty-three years old, true, and I'm a writer now, and a long time ago I walked through Quang Ngai Province as a foot soldier.
>
> Almost everything else is invented.
>
> But it's not a game. It's a form. Right here, now, as I invent myself, I'm thinking of all I want to tell you about why this book is written as it is. (203)

The narrator then proceeds to revise "The Man I Killed," an earlier piece that seems to recall his emotional breakdown after killing an enemy soldier, by revealing what actually happened, only to confess that the second account is also invented. And both versions are finally revealed to be fictive substitutes for what did *not* happen rather than what did:

I want you to feel what I felt. I want you to know why story-truth is truer sometimes than happening-truth.

Here is the happening-truth. I was once a soldier. There were many bodies, real bodies with real faces, but I was young then and I was afraid to look. And now, twenty years later, I'm left with faceless responsibility and faceless grief.

Here is the story-truth. He was a slim, dead, almost dainty young man of about twenty. He lay in the center of a red clay trail near the village of My Khe. His jaw was in his throat. His one eye was shut, the other eye was a star-shaped hole. I killed him. (203–4)

What "really" happened was a failure to feel, an emotional constriction in response to trauma that the narrator associates with moral cowardice. "Responsibility" recalls the narrator's choice to participate in a bad war, represented in *Things* by the account of a traumatic breakdown in "On the Rainy River" when he is unable to flee to Canada; "grief" is felt for all the dead, even the enemy, and all the other wasted casualties. "Good Form" thus represents Tim O'Brien, the narrator of *The Things They Carried*, as a trauma writer and as a trauma survivor and provides a significant explanation for his rewriting of Vietnam. But although traumatization may be an important source of the writing, the source of the narrator's feelings remains both unspecific and endless, as "faceless" but also as all-embracing as all the things he carried out of the war. By refashioning himself so, O'Brien not only gives his personal traumatization a fictional form but also represents its ineffability.

The recycling in *The Things They Carried* of material from O'Brien's experiences and from his earlier books indicates the persistence of significant war memories in the writer's imagination. Some of them may be the unresolved traces of traumatic experiences, but they are also the inspiration for his writing. In *Things* the distinction between trauma and inspiration is frequently blurred in any case: Many of the pieces dramatize traumatization and various reactions to it, whereas others show how trauma is directly converted into a fiction. But the repetition of incidents and experiences in O'Brien's work also raises issues of authenticity and verisimilitude. War literature has commonly been validated on the basis of its truth to actual experience, but O'Brien's multiple rewritings radically question such assumptions. The problem of authenticity is addressed by Tim

O'Brien in "How to Tell a True War Story," which questions the categories of "truth" and "war story" through the communication of unspeakable grief.

"How to Tell a True War Story": Misreading Tim O'Brien

"How to Tell a True War Story" is not only O'Brien's most complex meditation on war literature in general but also a brilliant representation of trauma writing. The work is narrated by the Tim O'Brien who is a fictional persona for the author and who self-reflectively interweaves stories and commentary on his own writing. The longest of its fourteen sections is an actual example of formal storytelling that raises issues that are developed throughout the piece, including, the validity of fiction and its relationship to trauma:

> I remember how peaceful the twilight was. A deep pinkish red spilled out on the river, which moved without sound, and in the morning we would cross the river and march west into the mountains. The occasion was right for a good story.
>
> "God's truth," Mitchell Sanders said. "A six-man patrol goes up into the mountains on a basic listening-post operation. The idea's to spend a week up there, just lie low and listen for enemy movement. . . ."
>
> Sanders glanced at me to make sure I had the scenario. He was playing with his yo-yo, dancing it with short, tight little strokes of the wrist.
>
> His face was blank in the dusk. (79)

The blank-faced narrator goes on to describe how the six soldiers become so hyperaroused by the sounds emanating from the mountains—Vietnamese music, a cocktail party, a "terrific mama-san soprano. . . . gook opera and a glee club and the Haiphong Boys Choir" (81)—that they call in an all-night air strike against the mountains and flee back to base camp in the morning. Asked by a "fatass colonel" what happened, "[t]hey just look at him for a while, sort of funny like, sort of amazed, and the whole war is right there in that stare. It says everything you can't ever say. It says, man, you got *wax* in your ears. . . . Then they salute the fucker and walk away, because certain stories you don't ever tell" (82–83). Sanders then moves off into the dark, his story over. But in the next two sections of "War Story," he returns in the morning to give it a moral ("you got to *listen* to your enemy"

[83]) and then later to revise that to "just listen," while confessing to Tim O'Brien that most of the account was made up. "[B]ut listen," Sanders insists, "it's still true" (84).

Mitchell Sanders's fable resembles some of the strange and true stories of the war reported by Michael Herr in *Dispatches* that stand by themselves as comments on its absurd and incomprehensible violence: for example, "Patrol went up the mountain. One man came back. He died before he could tell us what happened" (Herr 6). Like "Sweetheart of the Song Tra Bong," O'Brien's episode mimics Conrad in its careful attention to the narrative situation, metacommentary by the storyteller, and symbolic details (Kaplan [1995] notes that the narrator Tim O'Brien recalls minutely the almost comic icon of the storyteller's magic: "Even now, at this instant, I remember that yo-yo" [183]). Within its fictional setting, this account of American soldiers who go into the mountains, undergo a traumatic experience, but ultimately return safely addresses the anxieties of its listeners, who anticipate their own dreaded mountain mission in the morning. Whether it happened or not, it is true to their fears and hopes. Finally, the survivors' inability to tell others what they have been through suggests that although storytelling is a necessary outlet for traumatization, the trauma event itself is incommunicable. Sanders's attempt to give the tale a moral and to separate "fact" from "fiction" are unnecessary, therefore, as the narrator Tim O'Brien knows and as much of "War Story" demonstrates.

Sanders's tale exemplifies that a story can be truer than what actually happened, that it can be more valuable than actual experience, and that it can make the survivor's trauma meaningful, but only to the right audience. O'Brien's representation of his authorial persona in "War Story" is concerned with these issues as well, particularly in the account of Rat Kiley's slaughter of a baby water buffalo, the ninth of the fifteen sections that make up "War Story." Tim O'Brien introduces this third revision of the water buffalo incident from *Combat Zone* by noting that "I've told it before—many times—many versions—but here's what actually happened" (85). But at the end of "War Story," the Rat Kiley episode—story? memory of actual occurrence?—has become another example of storytelling, a piece that he often reads in public and that is sometimes mistaken for a personal experience still bothering the storyteller, mistaken usually by "an older woman of kindly temperament and humane politics" (90): "She'll explain that as a rule she hates war stories; she can't understand why people want to wallow in all the blood and gore. But this one she liked. The poor baby buffalo, it made her sad. Sometimes, even, there are little tears. What I should do, she'll say, is put it all behind me. Find new stories to tell" (90). The narrator uses her reaction to denounce two sorts of misreadings of O'Brien's own fiction that derive from the relationship between traumatization and war stories.

On the one hand, a story may be interpreted as an actual experience rather than the fabulation of something that may or may not have happened: "Beginning to end, you tell her, it's all made up. Every goddamn detail—the mountains and the river and especially that poor dumb baby buffalo. None of it happened. *None* of it. And even if it did happen, it didn't happen in the mountains, it happened in this little village on the Batangan Peninsula, and it was raining like crazy, and one night a guy named Stink Harris woke up screaming with a leech on his tongue. You can tell a true war story if you just keep on telling it" (91). The narrator initially uses direct experience to validate the episode, only to deny that it happened; but if it did, he adds, it will be found in *Going After Cacciato*! Even the authenticity of the original account in *Combat Zone* must now be questioned, if what "actually happened" is to be found in "How to Tell a True War Story," or in Chapter Six of O'Brien's second novel. Paradoxically, a "true" story is one that has multiple versions. Ultimately, the greater truth of the revisions depends not on what happened, but on the different ways in which killing a water buffalo is rewritten as a powerfully traumatic experience in *Cacciato, The Nuclear Age,* and *Things.*

Nevertheless, introducing the episode in "War Story" as an actual happening has established its credibility and thus met our need to believe that it is literally "true"—the narrator himself uses the mimetic fallacy before he disabuses his sympathetic listener of trusting in it as anything more than a narrative device. And of course the story's authenticity is validated by the listener's concern for the storyteller: She assumes that he has been traumatized because the terrible details are so real, so vivid. Indeed, her response suggests that the story has fulfilled an important criterion of a "true war story, if truly told": It "makes the stomach believe" (84). Whatever her concern about the narrator's obsession with the war, she has enjoyed the story, after all, despite its "absolute and uncompromising allegiance to obscenity and evil" (76), another of the narrator's criteria. In fact, her response is contradictory: Moved by what has been narrated, she exhorts the author to write about something else.

Forced to correct the mistaken assumption that true war stories represent actual experiences, the narrator is even more upset by the notion that their subject is war. If the mimetic fallacy mistakes fiction for fact in a true war story, a second sort of misreading misses the point of the fiction itself. In the first instance, the well-meaning reader or listener misattributes traumatization to the storyteller; in the second, she fails to locate the true fictional source of trauma and its victim. The water buffalo episode is the last of three sections in "How to Tell a True War Story" that deal with Rat Kiley, and although all of them take place during the war, their subject is something else.

"War Story" begins with a narrative episode followed by a commentary upon it, a pattern repeated throughout. In the first, Rat Kiley writes a letter to the sister of a good friend who has been killed, filling it with a few dubiously eulogistic stories to illustrate "how her brother made the war seem almost fun, always raising hell and lighting up villes and bringing smoke to bear every which way" (75). At the end of the letter, "Rat pours his heart out. He says he loved the guy. He says the guy was his best friend in the world. They were like soul mates, he says, like twins or something, they had a whole lot in common. He tells the guy's sister he'll look her up when the war's over" (76). But at the end of the section, his war stories are ignored: "Rat mails the letter. He waits two months. The dumb cooze never writes back" (76). In the commentary that follows, Rat's disappointment is used to illustrate that "a true war story is never moral":

> You can tell a true war story if it embarrasses you. If you don't care for obscenity, you don't care for the truth; if you don't care for the truth, watch how you vote. Send guys to war, they come home talking dirty.
>
> Listen to Rat: "Jesus Christ, man, I write this beautiful fuckin' letter, I slave over it, and what happens? The dumb cooze never writes back." (77)

After two more sections with commentary, Rat's methodical massacre of the baby buffalo is gruesomely detailed, together with the platoon's reaction: "He shot it twice in the flanks. It wasn't to kill; it was to hurt. He put the rifle muzzle up against the mouth and shot the mouth away. Nobody said much. . . . Curt Lemon was dead. Rat Kiley had lost his best friend in the world. Later in the week he would write a long personal letter to the guy's sister, who would not write back, but for now it was a question of pain. He shot off the tail. He shot away chunks of meat below the ribs. . . ." (85). By the end of the atrocity, "Rat Kiley was crying. He tried to say something, but then cradled his rifle and went off by himself" (86). The narrator and the platoon have become witnesses of "something essential, something brand-new and profound, a piece of the world so startling there was not yet a name for it. Somebody kicked the baby buffalo" and eventually Kiowa and Mitchell Sanders dump what remains of the animal in the village well. The episode ends with Sanders's commentary: "'Well, that's Nam,' he said. 'Garden of Evil. Over here, man, every sin's real fresh and original'" (86).

The platoon reacts as if it were the audience for the kind of fiction that "makes the stomach believe," according to the narrator: "[I]n the end, really, there's nothing much to say about a true war story, except maybe 'Oh'" (84). By contrast, Tim O'Brien's own listener has tried to interpret the story as personal testimony and so missed its point:

> I won't say it but I'll think it.
> I'll picture Rat Kiley's face, his grief, and I'll think, *You dumb cooze.*
> Because she wasn't listening.
> It *wasn't* a war story. It was a *love* story. (90)

Keeping his own brutality to himself, the narrator goes on to explain that a true war story is made-up, as we have noted above. But missing its subject is worse than mistaking its fictionality. The story does not represent Tim O'Brien's trauma, but Rat Kiley's. His love for his best friend is displaced through his behavior toward a Vietnamese water buffalo and Curt Lemon's sister; both the little atrocity and the profanity are reactions to combat death, brutal expressions of loyalty to a lost comrade. The atrocity takes crazed vengeance upon the only available trace of the enemy; the letter tries to make something good come out of the waste of his friend, perhaps even to perpetuate his love through someone intimately connected to Lemon. To Rat, the sister is dismissing his love for her brother, even invalidating the Curt Lemon that Rat admired. We can perfectly understand and support her silence, but to the doubly spurned lover her failure to answer is an act of betrayal that leaves his own wound unhealed.

The sister resembles the narrator's well-meaning but theme-deaf lis-

tener, who weeps for the baby water buffalo while ignoring the point of
the episode: Rat Kiley's pain. But the story does not shrink from exposing
the obscenity of the war, a point reinforced by Mitchell Sanders's commentary. Somebody's (i.e., anybody's) kicking the murdered baby buffalo
and the poisoning of the village well by the GIs epitomize their everyday
brutality toward Viet Nam and the Vietnamese, a destructiveness nakedly
celebrated even in Rat's tribute to Lemon. But they, too, have lost a comrade, and Rat's love needs validation, his vengeance and breakdown need
closure. Trauma cannot be healed by sympathetic atrocity, of course,
which will only make it worse, but destruction seems the only means at
hand for these violence-tempered young men. Violence and love depend
on each other so closely in the Rat Kiley episodes that as in any "true war
story, if there's a moral at all, it's like the thread that makes the cloth. You
can't tease it out. You can't extract the meaning without unraveling the
deeper meaning" (84). In his fourth version of buffalo hunting, O'Brien
nonetheless does produce a love story from the elemental filth of the war,
one that avoids sentimentality or a happy ending.

"How to Tell a True War Story" ends with an emphatic denial of the mimetic and thematic limitations of war literature as popularly understood
(and written):

> You can tell a true war story if you just keep on telling it.
>
> And in the end, of course, a true war story is never about war. It's about
> sunlight. It's about the special way that dawn spreads out on a river when
> you know you must cross the river and march into the mountains and do
> things you are afraid to do. It's about love and memory. It's about sorrow.
> It's about sisters who never write back and people who never listen. (91)

By calling attention to its materials, O'Brien reminds us that "War Story"
has fulfilled its own criteria. People who never listen include Curt Lemon's
sister, Tim O'Brien's audience, and everyone denounced when Mitchell
Sanders tries to define the moral of *his* story: "Nobody listens. Nobody
hears nothin'. Like that fatass colonel. The politicians, all the civilian types.
Your girlfriend. My girlfriend" (83). True war stories are not simply stories
about war but fictions of traumatization that require willing listeners as
well as skillful storytellers. Nor are they solely narratives of past events:
Rat Kiley's breakdown is no more merely a record of some terrible events
in the Vietnam War than *Heart of Darkness* is just an account of a trip

down the Congo River in 1890. The war is a fictional creation that speaks of important human truths every time it brings together a storyteller and an audience, whether in Quang Ngai Province in 1969 or in a lecture hall in 1990, and that is the ultimate point of O'Brien's fictional essay with examples (or vice versa). The conclusion also reminds us that everything in the piece has been made up, including the narrator Tim O'Brien and the kindly listener whom silently he browbeats. His repetition of Rat Kiley's profanity links them as both storytellers and fictional characters; like Mitchell Sanders, the narrator has had an audience for his story, and he has taken his listener aside to comment on it; and the narrator himself has also been a listener—to Rat Kiley, to Sanders, and even to his audience.

Through fictionalizing himself here as elsewhere, O'Brien is able to represent trauma and its consequences without merely representing his personal experiences. Everything in the work speaks of psychic or moral breakdown, from the listening post soldiers who call in air strikes upon the jungle and abandon their post, to Rat Kiley, crying over a dead friend, a slaughtered water buffalo, and the wasting of himself and others that is the war. But although stories can both replicate and relieve trauma by displacing it formally, they cannot give it closure. By presenting a fable derived from their own nightmares, Mitchell Sanders's story temporarily calms men who will be facing combat the next day in the mountains, but his attempts to censor its falsehood and draw out a moral call attention to the limited magic of fictions.

And Rat Kiley is not the only figure who cannot forget the death of Curt Lemon. The narrator of "War Story" is obsessed with this traumatic incident. In the third section of the piece, he identifies Lemon as the friend for whom Rat Kiley wrote his love letter and then describes in detail how he was blown to pieces by a booby-trapped mortar round underneath a giant tree while tossing smoke grenades with Rat. Used to help explicate Kiley's letter writing, the description thus becomes a fragment that chronologically reverses antecedent and consequence, as if it were an afterthought to the letter instead of its cause. While Rat cannot let Lemon's death be the end of the story, the narrator Tim O'Brien cannot introduce it directly. Yet this traumatic incident is the origin of all the storytelling in "War Story." Tim O'Brien refers to Lemon in seven of the fifteen sections that make up the work, and he describes his death in four of them. Its continual intrusion suggests an ineffaceable trauma, so that "War Story" epitomizes in miniature the recurrence of traumatization characteristic of *Things* as a whole. The first of the descriptions is the longest and most detailed; the second, which repeats phrases from the first, is the briefest: "We crossed that river and marched west into the mountains. On the third day, Curt Lemon stepped on a booby-trapped 105 round. He was playing catch with Rat Kiley, laughing, and then he was dead. The trees were thick; it took nearly an hour to cut an LZ for the dustoff" (85). This account is followed immediately by the baby water buffalo incident, which it motivates; but the battle in the mountains also recalls Mitchell Sanders's story, which is told the night before such a battle, and the cross-references suggest a complex of traumatization that has been fragmented throughout "War Story."

The third description of Lemon's death follows the briefest of the fifteen sections in "War Story," a typical combination of metafictional comment with example:

> Often in a true war story there is not even a point, or else the point doesn't hit you until twenty years later, in your sleep, and you wake up and shake your wife and start telling the story to her, except when you get to the end you've forgotten the point again. And then for a long time you lie there watching the story happen in your head. You listen to your wife's breathing. The war's over. You close your eyes. You smile and think, Christ, what's the *point*? (88–89)

The paragraph itself is a "true war story," of course, even though the episode occurs two decades after the war is over in the domestic security of a couple's bedroom. But here it is impossible to distinguish between story and traumatic intrusion: Whatever is being reimagined resists even the narrator's attempt at thematic closure, and it cannot be explained, even to his wife. It has no point at which it can be resolved, but it is also pointless to bother her with it—she probably wouldn't be able to listen. (As Jonathan Shay notes, "normal adults do not want to hear trauma narratives" [193].) The third death of Curt Lemon follows immediately in the next section. The narrator introduces it as another example of a "pointless" story, but does so in a way that suggests an unwelcome traumatic intrusion: "This one wakes me up" (89). In this account, Tim O'Brien is involved directly with Lemon's death, for he has to gather the pieces of body left in the trees after the booby trap has detonated, and he uses the trope of memory so chillingly, so tangibly, that story and continued traumatization are indistinguishable: "I remember pieces of skin and something wet and yellow that must've been the intestines. The gore was horrible, and stays with me. But what wakes me up twenty years later is Dave Jensen singing 'Lemon Tree' as we threw down the parts" (89). The last sentence concludes this particular war story but not the nightmare, which now circles back to the dream that wakes him up "twenty years later" in bed with his wife and thus epitomizes the endless recirculation and ineffability of trauma, as well as its asynchronous fragmentation.

"Twenty years later, I can still see the sunlight on Lemon's face" begins the narrator's last description of the death. The "sunlight" will be among the subjects used to illustrate his final assertion that "a true war story is never about war" (cited above). Here, it recalls the moment when the doomed soldier stepped beyond the shade of the trees where he and Rat Kiley were fooling around and onto the booby trap, so that "when his foot touched down, in that instant, he must've thought it was the sunlight that was killing him." "[I]f I could ever get the story right," the witness/survivor/narrator continues, "how the sun seemed to gather around him and pick him up and lift him high into a tree, . . . then you would believe the last thing Curt Lemon believed, which for him must've been the final truth" (90). Here the "right story" would be literally untrue, yet we would believe in it. It might also efface all visible traces of trauma by eliminating the presence of an observer who would watch Curt Lemon die, and then survive to tell about it, dream about it, write a letter about it, and commit atrocities in its name. But the desire to get the story "right" after four accounts of Lemon's death shows that trauma, however displaced, can never be buried: "You can tell a true war story if you just keep on telling it." As Tobey Herzog notes (1997: 29–30), Lemon's obliteration is based on the death of the author's friend Chip Merricks, who stepped on a mine in Pinkville, a traumatic incident that was casually and ironically recorded in Chapter IX of *Combat Zone*. It is also briefly alluded to in "The Vietnam in Me" as the author revisits the site of the fatal ambush. Thus the actual event, nearly irrecoverable for O'Brien and rendered through the register of emotional constriction in both of the autobiographical memoirs, is here replaced and supplemented by a fiction, rendered from four different perspectives, that is more "true" than what actually happened yet remains without closure—and is thus available for additional posttraumatic refabrication. Whether as author or as narrator of "War Story," Tim O'Brien can't get over whatever it was that happened to Chip Merricks or to Curt Lemon.

Other Refabrications of Trauma

Ultimately, the imagined listener is right about the narrator's obsessiveness, wrong about urging him to put the war behind him. Although everything is made up—including Tim O'Brien and the listener herself—the author of *The Things They Carried* has created a true story that shows how trauma may be recycled but can never be closed. "How to Tell a True War Story" is O'Brien's most elaborate metafiction of traumatization, but other sections of the work handle the subject with comparable artistry. Besides Lemon's death, the narrator Tim O'Brien witnesses the deaths of Ted Lavender, Kiowa, and an enemy soldier, as well as several other Vietnamese. Lavender's death is represented in "The Things They Carried," Kiowa's in "Speaking of Courage" and "In the Field," and the Vietnamese soldier's in "Ambush." Traumatic episodes all, their representations are fittingly marked by fragmentation, violation of chronology, intrusiveness, and repetition.

The award-winning title story is a brilliantly organized epitome of O'Brien's representation of the war in *Combat Zone* and *Cacciato*. Written in thirteen sections, it can be seen as a master catalog of combat trauma that combines and refabricates three lists from the earlier novel: the roll call of the dead and living that introduces *Cacciato*, the seriatim characterization of each of the squad members in Chapter 22 ("Who They Were, or Claimed to Be"), and the itemization of ignorance that made Viet Nam and the Vietnamese bewilderingly alien to the GIs who searched and destroyed them (Chapter 39, "The Things They Didn't Know"). The physical, psychological, and moral burdens and the objects of destruction, survival, pleasure, and hope carried by Alpha Company are categorized, section by section, until the war has been established as a site of obscene violence and almost unbearable trauma.

Within the larger catalog, O'Brien weaves two discrete narratives. The first appears only in the middle section, where Lee Strunk goes down an enemy tunnel for what seems to his waiting comrades an eternity and then emerges "right out of the grave," according to Rat Kiley, "grinning, filthy but alive," to hear his friends make "jokes about rising from the dead." This story rewrites the tragic tunnel narratives of *Cacciato* as rough comedy, but we are told that at the moment when Strunk "made [a] high happy moaning sound," Ted Lavender "was shot in the head on his way back from peeing. . . . There was a swollen black bruise under his left eye. The cheekbone was gone. Oh shit, Rat Kiley said, the guy's dead. The guy's dead, he kept saying, which seemed profound—the guy's dead. I mean really" (13).

Lavender's killing interrupts and completely displaces Strunk's survival, a discrete and coherent episode that is buried and isolated in the middle of the narrative. By contrast, the unexpected death reappears throughout the piece from beginning to end. Within the catalog of things carried by necessity, for example, we are told that "Ted Lavender, who was scared, carried tranquilizers until he was shot in the head outside the village of Than Khe in mid-April" and that "until he was shot, [he] carried six or seven ounces of premium dope, which for him was a necessity" (4). And this catalog ends as a parody of an army field issue description with ironic practical application: "Because the nights were cold, and because the monsoons were wet, each [soldier] carried a green plastic poncho that could be used as a raincoat or groundsheet or makeshift tent. With its quilted liner, the poncho weighed almost two pounds, but it was worth every ounce. In April, for instance, when Ted Lavender was shot, they used his poncho to wrap him up, then to carry him across the paddy, then to lift him into the chopper that took him away" (5). These repeated fragments register the persistence of Lavender's death, while their mechanical assignment to the appropriate list suggests emotional constriction.

But Lavender's death also intrudes more dramatically into *Things*, which combines the omniscient narration of lists with the imaginative meditations of Alpha Company's commanding lieutenant, Jimmy Cross, an ironic Christ figure who survives Vietnam and whose men suffer while following him. Cross carries the burden of responsibility for his men, but he also carries ten ounces of letters, two photographs, and a good luck pebble from his virginal girlfriend Martha as well as memories, hopes, and fears about her love for him. Like Paul Berlin or O'Brien himself, Cross is a reluctant warrior, and he dreams of Martha while trying to carry out his duties. He blames his own negligence for Lavender's death, and his hopeless love for his negligence. Alone in his foxhole the night after Lavender is shot, Cross breaks down and cries: "In part, he was grieving for Ted Lavender, but mostly it was for Martha, and for himself, . . . because he realized she did not love him and never would" (17).

Like *Cacciato*, the piece ends with the sacrifice of dreams for duties, but the lieutenant's ironic immolation of his keepsakes will do nothing to efface his guilt:

> On the morning after Ted Lavender died, First Lieutenant Jimmy Cross crouched at the bottom of his foxhole and burned Martha's letters. Then he burned the two photographs. . . .
>
> He realized it was only a gesture. Stupid, he thought. Sentimental, too, but mostly just stupid.
>
> Lavender was dead. You couldn't burn the blame. (22)

Nor can he efface his love for Martha, since "the letters were in his head," or the realization that "she wasn't involved. She signed the letters Love, but it wasn't love, and all the fine lines and technicalities did not matter" (23). Turning away from both his griefs, he resolves at the end of the story to dedicate the one and sacrifice the other to command responsibility: "He would dispense with love; it was not now a factor. And if anyone quarreled or complained, he would simply tighten his lips and arrange his shoulders in the correct command posture. He might give a curt little nod. Or he might not. He might just shrug and say, Carry on, then they would saddle up and form into a column and move out toward the villages west of Than Khe" (25). But the conclusiveness of this resolution is belied by the play-acting going on inside his imagination, which tries to cover up or replace the death of Lavender and the loss of Martha.

The final reference in *Things* carries us back to other vain attempts to close off the trauma of Lavender's death. Kiowa notes so repetitiously that the dead man went down "like cement" that his fixation irritates Norman Bowker, who makes a crude joke of the death ("A pisser, you know? Still zipping himself up. Zapped while zipping" [17]); waiting for the dustoff, his comrades smoke the rest of the dead man's dope. The most decisive reaction displaces traumatization with futilely murderous devastation: "When the dustoff arrived, they carried Lavender aboard. Afterward they burned Than Khe. They marched until dusk, then dug their holes, and that night Kiowa kept explaining how you had to be there, how fast it was, how the poor guy just dropped like so much concrete. Boom-down, he said. Like cement" (8). The constriction of the atrocity is followed so closely by the reintrusion of Lavender's death that traumatization seems to be feeding on itself. And a more detailed repetition of the sequence reintrudes later, suggesting the recurrence of what has been repressed in the narrative: "After the chopper took Lavender away, Lieutenant Jimmy Cross led his men into the village of Than Khe. They burned everything. They shot chickens and dogs, they trashed the village well, they called in artillery and watched the wreckage, then they marched for several hours through the hot afternoon, and then at dusk, while Kiowa explained how Lavender died, Lieutenant Cross found himself trembling" (16). Cross's trembling initiates the little breakdown noted above; and his tears for Lavender, Martha, and himself show the futility of violence as a remedy for traumatization.

In its original form, "The Things They Carried" appeared as a short story in *Esquire* in 1986, and O'Brien's masterpiece has been frequently reprinted in anthologies. By itself, the piece is not explicitly a posttraumatic narrative, and it lacks the presence of the character Tim O'Brien as participant, observer, storyteller, or audience. In *Things*, however, O'Brien adds a first-person postscript that establishes the relationship between traumatization and storytelling which characterizes the book as a whole. This second piece in the volume tells of Lieutenant Cross's postwar visit to the Massachusetts home of the writer Tim O'Brien. Not only does it introduce the figure who will be the chief character in the rest of *Things*, but it also introduces the subject of unresolved trauma and the trope of memory:

> Spread out across the kitchen table were maybe a hundred old photographs. There were pictures of Rat Kiley and Kiowa and Mitchell Sanders, all of us, the faces incredibly soft and young. At one point, I *remember* [emphasis added], we paused over a snapshot of Ted Lavender, and after a while Jimmy rubbed his eyes and said he'd never forgiven himself for Lavender's death. It was something that would never go away, he said quietly, and I nodded and told him I felt the same about certain things. (29)

They reminisce about happier memories, and Cross goes on to reveal that he met Martha in 1979, when he discovered that she was an unmarried Lutheran missionary, and impulsively revealed his undiminished love for her. Gently but decisively rejected, he explains that he now carries a copy of the photo of her that he had burned in Viet Nam, her farewell gift to him at the end of their final meeting. As his former lieutenant's visit ends,

Tim O'Brien gets his approval to write a story about what they have discussed, and Cross jokes about getting Martha back—"Maybe she'll read it
and come begging"—and being portrayed positively—"Make me out to be
a good guy, okay? Brave and handsome, all that stuff. Best platoon leader
ever" (31).

O'Brien's brief narrative, which is titled "Love," thus functions as the inspiration for the longer narrative that precedes it, a truer story than the
heroic melodrama requested by its protagonist. Viewed as a unit, the two
works become a metafiction representing both the persistence of
trauma—Cross is still bothered by Lavender's death and its connection to
his unrequited love for Martha—and the reformulation of trauma into a
fiction that transcends and transforms it: Jimmy Cross's double burden becomes the foundation and groundwork of a fiction masterpiece. "Love" is
also O'Brien's first example in *Things* of a true war story that isn't about
war, as its title indicates. Its title identifies as well the thematic significance
of Jimmy Cross's traumatization in "The Things They Carried": the conflict
between loving his men and loving Martha and the way in which love, like
war, can be unbearable.

Although Lavender's death is recuperated fictionally as Jimmy Cross's
trauma, the deaths of Kiowa and the enemy soldier, which are narrated in
"Speaking of Courage" and "The Man I Killed," respectively, continue to
haunt the narrator. The Native American, who perished during a horren-
dous night mortar attack, was his best friend in the war; the unnamed
North Vietnamese was killed by Tim O'Brien himself. Like Ted Lavender's,
both deaths appear as intrusive fragments that violate chronology. They
persist through several different versions, just as Curt Lemon's death is
narrated four times in "How to Tell a True War Story." Moreover, like Jimmy
Cross's obsession with Lavender and Martha, they are not simply past
events but remain present in the narrator's imagination.

Like Lavender's death, both traumas are also reconfigured metafiction-
ally in *The Things They Carried.* In contrast to the relatively simple sequence of war story followed by its putative origin "many years after the
war" ("Love" 29), however, the traumatic origins of "Speaking of Courage"
and "The Man I Killed" are revealed only indirectly and evasively. Their
complex representation reflects their deeper level of shock: The narrator
cannot get over Kiowa's death or his own killing of the young soldier,
whereas Ted Lavender is Jimmy Cross's burden, and "The Things They

Carried" a finely polished transformation of trauma into a coherent fiction by a former soldier who has become a writer.

The narrator identifies himself also as a trauma survivor in "Love," where he tells Jimmy Cross of his own haunting by unnamed things that cannot be forgotten. Only in the penultimate list of memories in "Spin" does Tim O'Brien's traumatization begin to emerge, however, and only as a disconnected series of fragments that intrudes into and concludes a list of remembered images from the war:

> A red clay trail outside the village of My Khe.
> A hand grenade.
> A slim, dead, dainty young man of about twenty.
> Kiowa saying, "No choice, Tim. What else could you do?"
> Kiowa saying, "Right?"
> Kiowa saying, "Talk to me." (40)

The full story will finally come out ten pieces later, only to be further explained and justified in "Ambush" and "Good Form." While the intrusive memory focuses on the man he killed, Tim O'Brien's fixation on Kiowa's presence as comforter significantly ties together this earlier trauma with his friend's horrible death, as if the latter itself were a terrible memory only beginning to emerge from repression.

Like the stories, therefore, the narrator's traumatization only gradually and fragmentarily defines itself. The reference in "Love" to experiences that will not go away is more fully realized in "The Man I Killed," the twelfth of the twenty-two sections of *Things*. Occupying the center of the book, it begins suddenly as an image of the narrator's victim that goes on for nearly a full page, an anatomy that begins with the head—"His jaw was in his throat, his upper lip and teeth were gone, his one eye was shut, his other eye was a star-shaped hole"—and ends at his feet—"His rubber sandals had been blown off. One lay beside him, the other a few meters up the trail" (139). Gradually the image becomes an obituary as the narrator imagines the background and circumstances that have led the "slim young man" to his death on a trail outside My Khe. And within another page the characterization has become a memory, a narrative, and a scene of trauma as the narrator squats next to the body while Azar exults ("you laid him out like Shredded fuckin' Wheat. . . . Rice Krispies, you know?" [140]) and then Kiowa tries to talk his friend out of his shock: "Nothing *anybody* could do. Come on, Tim, stop staring (141). . . . You feel terrible, I know that (142). . . . Talk to me" (144). These three final words end "The Man I Killed," but not the trauma, which is presented not as an episode in the past but as an intrusive memory haunting the narrator. Talking only to himself, he never responds to Kiowa; therefore, although he is able to recover this traumatic experience (unlike his part in Kiowa's own death, as we shall see), it remains unexpressed to others. As studies of PTSD survivors have revealed (Shay 115–19), destroying the enemy can be as terrible an experience as the death of one's comrades, but ideological and social codes make the public expression of grief in such cases more difficult. O'Brien's narrator tries to resolve his feelings both by re-creating the young Vietnamese soldier in his own image, especially his sense of obligation to others, and by imagining that his victim's death will find some redemption: "He was not a Communist. He was a citizen and a soldier. . . . He was not a fighter. . . . He liked books. . . . Beyond anything else, he was afraid of disgracing himself, and therefore his family and village. . . . He knew he would fall dead and wake up in the stories of his village and people" (140–44 passim). But however much the narrator refigures his own distress, it can neither be laid to rest nor communicated to others.

The persistent cover-up of trauma is also dramatized in "Ambush," right after "The Man I Killed" has dramatically re-created the incident alluded to in the fragments of "Spin." When his daughter was nine years old, the narrator begins, she questioned his obsession with Vietnam: "You keep writing these war stories . . . so I guess you must've killed somebody" (147). "Of course not," he answered her then but now relates for the third time the account of his killing a young enemy soldier with a grenade as the latter passed by his ambush position on a trail near My Khe. This is a matter-of-fact, third-person account that rewrites the fragments of "Spin" and the direct traumatization of "The Man I Killed" as a coherent, cause-and-effect narrative. At the end, however, Tim O'Brien's continued psychic wound is made apparent as he imagines what might have happened if he had simply let his victim pass:

> Even now I haven't finished sorting it out. Sometimes I forgive myself, other times I don't. In the ordinary hours of life I try not to dwell on it, but now and then, when I'm reading a newspaper or just sitting alone in a room, I'll look up and see the young man coming out of the morning fog. I'll watch

him walk toward me, his shoulders slightly stooped, his head cocked to the side, and he'll pass within a few yards of me and suddenly smile at some secret thought and then continue up the trail to where it bends back into the fog. (149–50)

The almost journalistic account of his kill is thus undercut by the persistent trauma that concludes "Ambush," and both seem to make the response to his daughter a lie intended to protect her innocence and his repression of the memory.

As we have noted, however, in "Good Form" Tim O'Brien insists that everything in *Things* has been invented and then presents a fourth version of the incident at My Khe, a confession that he was present but did not kill the young man. "But listen"—he warns us after finishing this account—"even *that* story is made up" (203). Finally, we seem to reach an explanation that would respond both to the kindly listener, who would like the narrator to stop writing war stories, and to his daughter, who wonders why he continues to do so: He writes stories not to recall past experiences but to make them up, to overcome the emotional constriction of the past. Stories, he asserts, can "make things present" so that "I can look at things I never looked at. I can attach faces to grief and love and pity and God. I can be brave. I can make myself feel again" (204). In this account, writing transforms Vietnam into morally meaningful fiction through fictional traumatization; but it also functions as therapy for a still-unidentified guilt connected with things that the narrator couldn't carry at the time they occurred. We might associate his grief with O'Brien's own feelings that if he had been brave enough, he would never have even been in the war. But that would be to mistake Tim O'Brien for the author and to analyze a state of mind that the story deliberately leaves undefinable. Just as the various versions of "The Man I Killed" deny an authoritative account, the narrator's feelings resist the closure of a final resolution. In fiction, he concludes in "Good Form," his daughter Kathleen can ask,

> "Daddy, tell the truth . . . did you ever kill anybody?" And I can say, honestly, "Of course not."
>
> Or I can say, honestly, "Yes." (204)

Storytelling thus becomes a vehicle for the endless reproduction of trauma, revealing *and* covering it up, revising what has happened or inventing what has not. The author of "Good Form" has no daughter, of course; but that everything in the story and in *Things* as a whole is made up means that O'Brien is representing how guilt and grief are endlessly recycled rather than simply recalling his own.

Such recirculation is also fashioned with authentic complexity in the case of Kiowa's death. The narrator's friend is buried alive within a communal privy where the platoon has camped at night when it is heavily mortared during a rainstorm. Kiowa's death is variously described and revised in four of the pieces in *Things*: "Speaking of Courage," a former comrade's reminiscence of the horror as he drives aimlessly about his hometown's lake on the Fourth of July years after his service in Viet Nam; the appended "Notes," in which Tim O'Brien explains how he came to write the story; the following account, "In the Field," which narrates the platoon's recovery of the body from the mud and filth in which it was submerged; and "Field Trip," a description of the narrator's return to the site of Kiowa's death in Viet Nam twenty years after it occurred. Alternately moving, horrifying, and sardonic, O'Brien's sequence of episodes powerfully examines the persistence of trauma and the attempt to put it to rest.

"Speaking of Courage" is a revision of an earlier, prize-winning story of the same title that O'Brien published in 1976. That first version is an appendage to *Cacciato*, for the soldier who drives aimlessly around his hometown's lake, regretting his failure to be a hero by rescuing Frenchie Tucker from a VC tunnel, is Paul Berlin. Details of the setting are taken directly from O'Brien's hometown, Worthington, Minnesota; moreover, Berlin's circuit replicates the description in *Combat Zone* of O'Brien's own desultory drives around town during the summer before his induction into the army (25). Although its counterpart won an O. Henry Prize, its later refabrication in *Things* is an even stronger work, another of O'Brien's masterpieces. Here, the unhappy veteran is Norman Bowker, traumatized by his failure to rescue Kiowa from his terrible fate, alienated from the town and his previous civilian life, unable to talk with his father about almost winning the Silver Star by saving his friend's life. The first sentence sums up Norman's condition with eloquent understatement that could be applied to countless other traumatized veterans: "The war was over and there was no place in particular to go" (157). The narrative bleakly mirrors the trauma survivor's isolation and anomie as he circles the lake twelve times, recalling his failure to pull Kiowa out of the mud and excrement along the Song Tra Bong while distantly observing the minutiae of small-town life. The persistence of the traumatic memory is captured by the meaningless circularity of his drive, briefly interrupted at an A&W Root Beer stand, before he immerses himself in the lake and watches the town's Independence Day fireworks display. Unable either to let go of Kiowa or to feel at home, Bowker narrates his war story as an experience that he would like to tell his father if the latter were not at home watching a baseball game on TV and if his son did not feel so guilty and ashamed: "[H]e would have talked about the medal he did not win and why he did not win it. . . . 'So tell me,' his father would have said" (161). His untold tale becomes for him an epitome of the true story of Vietnam, a revelation that he feels would fall on deaf ears: "The town could not talk, and would not listen. 'How'd you like to hear about the war?' he might have asked, but the place could only blink and shrug. It had no memory, therefore no guilt. . . . It was a brisk, polite town. It did not know shit about shit, and did not care to know" (163). The only willing listener is the voice he hears on the A&W squawk box, his only message an order for a Mama Burger and fries. Just before he stops at Sunset Park and stands in the lake, he finally arrives at a dark enlightenment:

> There was nothing to say.
>
> He could not talk about it and never would. The evening was smooth and warm.
>
> If it had been possible, which it wasn't, he would have explained how his friend Kiowa slipped away that night beneath the dark swampy field. He was folded in with the war; he was part of the waste. (172)

The final personal pronoun is ambiguous, of course, so that the attempt to finally bury Kiowa is not only unredemptive but suggests that Bowker has died in some sense as well.

The "Notes" that follow this haunting portrayal of persistent trauma are the closest O'Brien comes to identifying himself directly with the narrator of *The Things They Carried*, who extends Bowker's guilt to his own. Identifying himself as the author of *Going After Cacciato*, Tim O'Brien tells us that the original version of "Speaking of Courage" was written in 1975 "at the suggestion of Norman Bowker, who three years later hanged himself in the locker room of a YMCA in his hometown in central Iowa" (177). Like "Love," it purports to present the materials from which the preceding story was constructed. Thus, Norman Bowker's long letter to the narrator begins with the confession that "there's no place to go. Not just in this lousy little town. In general. My life, I mean. It's almost like I got killed over in Nam . . . Hard to describe. That night when Kiowa got wasted, I sort of sank down into the sewage with him . . . Feels like I'm still in deep shit" (177–78) [ellipses in the original]. Written originally to give a voice to his former comrade's traumatization, the story disappointed its author as an unfunctional part of the novel—"*Going After Cacciato* was a war story; 'Speaking of Courage' was a postwar story" (181)—and was published as a short story, we are told. But beyond its formal flaws, the substitution of Paul Berlin for Bowker and the elimination of the terrible night in Viet Nam left it morally flawed as well: "[S]omething about the story had frightened me—I was afraid to speak directly, afraid to remember—and in the end the piece had been ruined by a failure to tell the full and exact truth about our night in the shit field," the narrator confesses to us. Upon its publication, Bowker's reaction, too, was a reproach: "'It's not terrible,' he wrote me, 'but you left out Vietnam. Where's Kiowa? Where's the shit?'"—and "eight months later he hanged himself" (181).

Unlike "Love," this account of how a preceding story was written involves the narrator directly in the consequences of traumatization: Unable or unwilling to represent his own experience, he effaces his former comrade's story. "Speaking of Courage" (1976) becomes a "false war story," and Tim O'Brien's failure to refigure the trauma fictionally so that it may be relieved is at least partly responsible for Norman Bowker's final despair. As a result, the narrator is so implicated in Bowker's agony that he identifies the rewritten story as an act of memorialization and deferred obligation: "Now, a decade after his death, I'm hoping that 'Speaking of Courage' makes good on Norman Bowker's silence. And I hope it's a better story" (181).

Noting how strongly he had been moved by Bowker's original letter, Tim O'Brien states that "I did not look on my work as therapy, and still don't" (179). In revising the earlier story, however, the author of *Things* has represented it as a trebly therapeutic fiction. In finally giving voice to Bowker's repressed trauma, the narrator addresses his feelings of guilt for not doing it originally. But in addition, the end of "Notes" reveals that the new story allowed him to give voice to his *own* traumatization: "It was hard stuff to write. Kiowa, after all, had been a close friend, and for years I've avoided thinking about his death and my own complicity in it. Even here it's not easy. In the interests of truth, however, I want to make it clear that Norman Bowker was in no way responsible for what happened to Kiowa. Norman did not experience a failure of nerve that night. He did not freeze up or lose the Silver Star for valor. That part of the story is my own" (182). As Kaplan notes (1995: 192), the final sentence is ambiguous because of the narrator's peculiar fictional role as both writer and participant in his own scenarios: Has he simply made Bowker feel guilty for Kiowa's death, or does he feel guilty for Kiowa's death himself? If the former, Bowker would have revealed in the letter his failure to save his friend; if the latter, the *narrator* failed to pull Kiowa out of the slime. Of course, both Bowker and the narrator Tim O'Brien may feel guilty about Kiowa's death whether or not they could have saved him because soldiers frequently feel guilt and grief if their own survival of a comrade's death seems unfair or incomprehensible (Shay 69). In any case, Tim O'Brien's personal trauma—his "complicity" in Kiowa's fate—has either been refigured through Norman Bowker or remains something that cannot be told.

"In the Field," the piece that follows "Notes," raises the issue of responsibility and guilt again only to leave it unresolved. The story follows the platoon of eighteen soldiers on the morning after the mortar attack as they comb their excrement- and mud-infested night position for Kiowa's body. Formally, this narrative resembles "The Things They Carried" and "Speaking of Courage" in that the Tim O'Brien character is absent and the narration is relatively impersonal. But while those works were followed by metafictional accounts of their traumatic origins, "In the Field" simply extends the trauma of "Speaking of Courage" and "Notes." As with the title story, omniscient narration alternates with an intimate third-person perspective as the point of view alternates from the activities of the platoon as a whole to the private meditations of Lieutenant Jimmy Cross and an unnamed younger soldier who are searching the flooded field by themselves. Both feel responsible for Kiowa's death: Although Cross carried out orders in pitching camp atop the communal waste field, he ignored the villagers' warnings and blames himself for the GI's death. The unnamed soldier feels guilty for switching on his flashlight to show Kiowa his girlfriend's picture just before the lethal mortar rounds hit the platoon. But even the normally sadistic Azar feels chastened. Once Kiowa's body has been pulled out of the slime, Azar sees his own jokes about the death ("[e]ating shit" [187], "one more redskin bites the dirt" [188]) as murderous: "[W]hen I saw the guy, it made me feel . . . sort of guilty almost, like if I'd kept my mouth shut none of it would've ever happened. Like it was my fault" (197).

Norman Bowker's response as he looks "out across the wet field" is closest to the truth, however: "Nobody's fault," he said. "Everybody's" (197). As a result, trauma is at least temporarily relieved, not least because Kiowa's corpse undergoes a strange resurrection. His body, though hideously disfigured, is recovered by his comrades, a communal ritual that leaves them peculiarly satisfied: "For all of them it was a relief to have it finished. . . . They felt bad for Kiowa. But they also felt a kind of giddiness, a secret joy, because they were alive, and because even the rain was preferable to being sucked under a shit field, and because it was all a matter of luck and happenstance" (197).

And for the lieutenant and Kiowa's unnamed friend, too, the story ends with ironic absolution. The young soldier is searching for his girlfriend's picture, not his friend's body; after all, "Kiowa's *dead*" he tells the lieutenant (194), who then watches him continue his search, "as if something might finally be salvaged from all the waste," and "silently wishe[s] the boy luck" (195). And when the young GI finally tries to confess his own culpability, the lieutenant "wasn't listening," floating in the muck and meditating on everything that could be blamed "when a man died," from "the war" to "an old man in Omaha who forgot to vote" (198–99). At the end of the piece, the letter of self-incrimination to Kiowa's father that Jimmy Cross has been revising throughout is replaced by a daydream of going golfing "back home in New Jersey": "When the war was over, he thought, maybe then he would write a letter to Kiowa's father. Or maybe not. Maybe he would just take a couple of practice swings and knock the ball down the middle and pick up his clubs and walk off into the afternoon" (199). Perhaps it is the shit field itself, a symbolic paradigm of the ghastly enterprise of Vietnam, that is the final cause of Kiowa's death. O'Brien's ironic title, "In the Field," modulates from a metonym for a battleground to a sense that everyone in the story is "In the Shit," a morass so all-consuming that staying alive is all that matters.

Yet even after this ironic closure to Kiowa's death, O'Brien's fourth handling of the subject suggests that the narrator's own trauma remains unhealed by his writing. "Field Trip" begins, in fact, by alluding to the earlier episode: "A few months after completing 'In the Field,' I returned with my daughter to Vietnam, where we visited the site of Kiowa's death, and where I looked for signs of forgiveness or personal grace or whatever else the land might offer" (207). Although "Notes" hinted at Tim O'Brien's feeling some responsibility for Kiowa's death, his own role has been left unclear: Did he freeze when his friend was pulled beneath the slime, like Norman Bowker in "Speaking of Courage"? Is the young, unnamed soldier in "In the Field" a version of his guilt, as suggested by Mark Taylor (227–28), distorted beyond being recognized by the reader? In any case, the persistence of trauma is explicit in his meditations as he looks at the field of death:

> This little field, I thought, had swallowed so much. My best friend. My pride. My belief in myself as a man of some small dignity and courage. Still, it was hard to find any real emotion. It simply wasn't there. After that long night in the rain, I'd seemed to grow cold inside, all the illusions gone, all the old ambitions and hopes for myself sucked away into the mud. Over the years that coldness had never entirely disappeared . . . somehow I blamed this place for what I had become, and I blamed it for taking away the person I had once been. For twenty years this field had embodied all the waste that was Vietnam, all the vulgarity and horror. (210)

While a government interpreter waits with his ten-year-old daughter, bemused like Cowling's Melinda by the symptoms of her father's traumatization—"Sometimes you're pretty weird, aren't you?" she has observed earlier (209)—Tim O'Brien wades into the muck of the paddy, squats and then sits down in the slime at the place where "Mitchell Sanders had found Kiowa's rucksack." There, he offers his friend's old hunting hatchet to the land beneath him.[3] As "tiny bubbles broke along the surface" (an image associated with the disappearance of Kiowa's head in "Speaking of Courage" [168] and "In the Field" [193]), his attempt to "think of something decent to say" inevitably settles on the all-purpose GI mantra for the trauma of Vietnam: "'Well,' I finally managed, 'There it is'" (212). This moving scene of expiation and memorialization culminates with the narrator's sense of personal catharsis: "The sun made me squint. Twenty years. A lot like yesterday, a lot like never. In a way, maybe, I'd gone under with Kiowa, and now after two decades I'd finally worked my way out. A hot afternoon, a bright August sun, and the war was over" (212). It also recapitulates but transcends Kiowa's immersion in the field and Norman Bowker's frustrated attempt to cleanse himself—or drown himself—in his hometown lake on the Fourth of July.

This apparent closure of trauma is qualified and decisively undercut by O'Brien, however. The narrator's exact role in Kiowa's death is uncertain, as if that were a story that he can never recount, despite his resolution in "Notes" to tell "the full and exact truth." Within *Things*, "Field Trip" is followed by "The Ghost Soldiers" and "Night Life," two grimly comic accounts of the narrator's wounding and Rat Kiley's self-mutilation in the war, respectively, which is *not* over for his imagination. And "Field Trip" itself includes an unresolved source of guilt and remorse. Tim O'Brien's personal ritual is witnessed not only by his daughter and his official guide but also by a farmer whose land was once taken over by the Americans but has now been restored to its communal purposes. Although Kiowa's hatchet has been buried, the narrator cannot so easily translate his personal peace into a wider redemption: "The man's face was dark and solemn. As we stared at each other, neither of us moving, I felt something go shut in my heart while something else swung open. Briefly, I wondered if the old man might walk over to exchange a few war stories, but instead he picked up a shovel and raised it over his head and held it there for a time, grimly, like a flag, then he brought the shovel down and said something to his friend and began digging into the hard, dry ground" (212). The narrator, an intruder in peace as in war, reacts immediately: "I stood up and waded out of the water" (212). His ten-year-old daughter responds instinctively to what she has seen, and the story ends with questions about its apparent resolution:

> When we reached the jeep, Kathleen turned and glanced out at the field. "That old man," she said, "is he mad at you or something?"
> "I hope not."
> "He *looks* mad."
> "No," I said. "All that's finished." (213)

This reassurance must depend on the farmer's attitude, of course, which the narrator cannot interpret but would prefer not to think about. Like the barely registered destruction of Than Khe after the death of Ted Lavender or Rat Kiley's enthusiasm about how Curt Lemon "liked testing himself, just man against gook" (75), the trauma of Vietnam involves more than the death of American comrades for the narrator—those are simply the stories he can tell best.

As noted above, "Field Trip" is immediately preceded by "Good Form," which reveals that "almost everything" (203) in the book has been invented. This reminder also calls into question the apparent personal recovery dramatized in the subsequent piece. Its soul-baring is so convincing that "Field Trip" seems an authentic personal experience rather than the self-confessed fiction of everything that appears before it; yet we can only believe in its authenticity if we believe in the "happening-truth" of the preceding fictions concerning Kiowa. We are left, therefore, with a series of episodes that represents an attempt to write about an experience that never happened as it is described. Yet by inventing a narrator who makes up traumatic experiences and recoveries, O'Brien paradoxically represents the ineffability of such experiences, what Kali Tal (1996) has called "the impossibility of recreating the event for the reader" (121). Whatever the protagonist of *The Things They Carried* has experienced can never be fully represented through writing—and that is why he can never stop writing about it.

"The Lives of the Dead": Bringing Them Back Alive

The Things They Carried ends with "The Lives of the Dead," an account of how the narrator became a professional writer. Although published as an independent story in the January 1989 issue of *Esquire*, the piece is a deliberate conclusion to the book, incorporating and dramatizing once more what *Things* has exemplified about true war stories and their relationship to traumatic experiences. Beginning with the simple assertion that "stories can save us," this final fiction resurrects Ted Lavender, Kiowa, Curt Lemon, "an old man sprawled beside a pigpen, and several others whose bodies I once lifted and dumped into a truck. They're all dead. But in a story," the narrator's introduction continues, "the dead sometimes smile and sit up and return to the world" (255). Combining the tropes of memory and storytelling, "Lives" brings back the war dead in brief episodes that alternate with the narrator's account of his love for his grade-school classmate Linda, their first and only date, her death from brain cancer at the age of nine, and his dreaming her alive thereafter. By combining Vietnam and a love story, soldiers and nine-year-olds, "The Lives of the Dead" transcends the war and exemplifies the narrator's earlier insistence that "a true war story is never about war" (91).

The paradox of the title identifies its real subject, a central concern of O'Brien's fifth book as a whole: the ways survivors carry the dead with them through the rest of their lives. "The Lives of the Dead" is filled with descriptions of corpses: an old Vietnamese farmer killed by an American air strike on an unfriendly village; Ted Lavender; *The Man Who Never Was*, a dead body dropped along the French coast to deceive the Nazis about the D-Day landings in a movie that Timmy and Linda saw on their one date; Linda's body in her funeral home casket, "bloated," the skin "at her cheeks . . . stretched out tight like the rubber skin on a balloon just before it pops open" (270); twenty-seven "enemy KIAs" [enemy soldiers killed in action] dumped into a truck by Tim O'Brien and Mitchell Sanders after their battle in the mountains—all "badly bloated . . . clothing . . . stretched tight like sausage skins . . . heavy . . . feet . . . bluish green and cold" (271). For Timmy, however, "It didn't seem real. A mistake, I thought. The girl lying in the white casket wasn't Linda. . . . I knew this was Linda, but even so I couldn't find much to recognize. . . . She looked dead. She looked heavy and totally dead" (270). And for Mitchell Sanders, gathering the remains of a great victory that he and the narrator have survived brings a comparably banal enlightenment:

> At one point [he] looked at me and said, "Hey, man, I just realized some-thing."
> "What?"
> He wiped his eyes and spoke very quietly, as if awed by his own wisdom. "Death sucks," he said. (271)

The human imagination is unsatisfied with this trite truth, as Timmy's bewilderment and Sanders's tears for the enemy suggest, and O'Brien dramatizes various attempts to supplement or transmute the dead body throughout the story. "The Lives of the Dead" begins with a traumatic experience for the narrator, who cannot look at the decaying corpse of the old man who is "the only confirmed kill" (255) of Jimmy Cross's punitive air strike. A newcomer to the war, he is further appalled as his comrades shake the corpse's hand and then prop it up as the guest of honor at a macabre get-acquainted party that gradually turns "that awesome act of greeting the dead" into a ceremony: "They proposed toasts. They lifted their canteens and drank to the old man's family and ancestors, his many grandchildren, his newfound life after death. It was more than mockery.

There was a formality to it, like a funeral without the sadness" (256–57). Kiowa comforts him later in the day, praising the courage of the narrator's refusal to participate, wishing that he had done the same but also reassuring him that "you're new here. You'll get used to it," since he assumes that "this was your first look at a real body" (257). The necrology of the scene is not simply repulsive, however, as the narrator realizes. Underneath the GIs' ghoulish humor and postmortem sadism lies an unconscious awareness of the mortality that they share with the Vietnamese farmer and an attempt to imagine beyond it. In "Night Life," the previous piece in *Things*, Rat Kiley has a nervous breakdown when he begins to see himself and his comrades as potential corpses, imagining them as a collection of organic body parts rather than as human beings. By contrast, here the narrator's comrades transform a corpse into a life to be celebrated beyond the "real body." Their grotesquerie contrasts strikingly with the sterile funeral home where Timmy is left bewildered and unsatisfied by the reality of Linda's preserved body.

The resurrection of the dead pervades O'Brien's final work. Kiowa comes back here, after all, as the comforter at the end of this first episode. *Things* began with Ted Lavender's death, and it ends with his corpse waiting for a medevac but miraculously reanimated as Mitchell Sanders and the rest of the platoon conduct a dialogue with their comrade before sending him home: "'There it is, my man, this chopper gonna take you up high and cool. Gonna relax you. Gonna alter your whole perspective on this sorry, sorry shit.' . . . 'Roger that,' somebody said. 'I'm ready to fly'"(261). The last we hear and see of Rat Kiley's dearest friend is not the obliteration of his body but the full account of his trick-or-treating in the Vietnamese countryside on Halloween, "almost stark naked, the story went, just boots and balls and an M-16. . . . To listen to the story, especially as Rat Kiley told it, you'd never know that Curt Lemon was dead. He was still out there in the dark, naked and painted up, trick-or-treating, sliding from hootch to hootch in that crazy white ghost mask" (268).

It is the resurrection of Linda, however, that has made all the others possible. Although Kiowa assumes that the Vietnamese farmer provides Tim O'Brien's first look at a corpse, he is wrong. "It sounds funny," O'Brien's persona tells him, "but that poor old man, he reminds me of . . . [ellipsis in the original] I mean, there's this girl I used to know. I took her to the movies once. My first date" (257). "[T]hat's a bad date," Kiowa understandably responds, ending the first section of "The Lives of the Dead." Most of the rest is taken up with the narrator's memories of his love for Linda, their going off to see *The Man Who Never Was* with his parents as chaperones, the exposure of her fatal illness, her death, and his visit to the funeral home. As he recounts it, his life as a storyteller began when he imagined his love alive the day after Linda died, in "a pink dress and shiny black shoes," all traces of her illness gone, "laughing and running up the empty street, kicking a big aluminum water bucket" (266). Timmy breaks down, knowing that she's dead, but Linda insists that "it doesn't *matter*" (267) and forces him to stop crying. Thereafter, Linda's death and his grief are replaced by dreaming her back to life and his subsequent career as an author: "She was dead. I understood that. After all, I'd seen her body, and yet even as a nine-year-old I had begun to practice the magic of stories. Some I just dreamed up. Others I wrote down—the scenes and dialogue. And at nighttime I'd slide into sleep knowing that Linda would be there waiting for me. Once, I remember, we went ice skating late at night, tracing loops and circles under yellow floodlights" (272). By asking what it's like to be dead, Timmy initially questions the truth of his own imagination, but Linda sets him straight: "'Well, right now,' she said, 'I'm *not* dead. But when I am, it's like . . . [ellipsis in original] I don't know, I guess it's like being inside a book that nobody's reading'" (273).

According to this account, therefore, writing grows directly out of trauma but refashions it beyond the unreality of death. Like the rest of the dead, Linda comes back to life through the narrator's stories, but so does he as he examines a photograph of himself as a nine-year-old:

> [T]here is no doubt that the Timmy smiling at the camera is the Tim I am now. . . . The human life is all one thing, like a blade tracing loops on ice: a little kid, a twenty-three-year-old infantry sergeant, a middle-aged writer knowing guilt and sorrow.
>
> And as a writer now, I want to save Linda's life. Not her body—her life. (265)

In saving her, therefore, he saves himself. Near the end of "The Lives of the Dead," however, we are reminded that while stories can save lives, what is saved is itself a fiction: "I'm forty-three years old, and a writer now, still dreaming Linda alive in exactly the same way. She's not the embodied Linda; she's mostly made up, with a new identity and a new name. . . . Her real name doesn't matter. She was nine years old. I loved her and then she died" (273). The facts are less important than the truth that the story has compelled us to believe. Employing the tropes of memory and storytelling for the last time as the book comes to an end, O'Brien uses them together not to represent the fact of death—even the dead are fictions in a true war story—but to save the lives of Linda and his other characters forever: "And yet right here, in the spell of memory and imagination, I can still see her as if through ice, as if I'm gazing into some other world, a place where there are no brain tumors and no funeral homes, where there are no bodies at all. I can see Kiowa, too, and Ted Lavender and Curt Lemon, and sometimes I can even see Timmy skating with Linda under the yellow floodlights. I'm young and happy. I'll never die" (273). Ultimately, of course, by making us believe in the man who never was, fiction can create people who will never die.

O'Brien's great book has certainly done both, but it is O'Brien's persona, a fictional creation, not necessarily O'Brien himself, who seems to have saved his life through writing by the end of "The Lives of the Dead." A survivor of trauma who has translated what he could not carry into true war stories, Tim O'Brien resembles the author's other protagonists in passing through fear, guilt, and grief to achieve his own separate peace. The narrator's ability to memorialize a terrible war so masterfully makes *The Things They Carried* O'Brien's most accomplished fiction, and his persona's ostensible resolution of his personal trauma also makes it the most redemptive. Yet Tim O'Brien's sense of well-being in *The Things They Carried* is also a function of his narrow characterization. Except for the relationships with his daughter and Linda, he has no life outside of writing; in fact, everything he does, says, or remembers in the book becomes part of its storytelling. Trauma is endlessly recirculated through the tropes of memory and storytelling or explicitly fabricated in multiple versions, never experienced directly by the fictional protagonist as it is in the three previous novels. Like *Things*, O'Brien's next book will be formidably metafictional, but its hero's inescapable, comprehensive, and endless traumatization will cost him his life, not enable him to save it.

CHAPTER 7

THE PEOPLE WE KILL

Trauma, Tragedy, National Disgrace

Near the beginning of *In the Lake of the Woods*, its protagonist awakens briefly to find the sun rising and turns instinctively toward his wife, only to be disappointed:

> For a few seconds he studied the effects of dawn, the pale ripplings and gleamings. He'd been having a curious nightmare. Electric eels. Boiling red water.
>
> John Wade reached out for Kathy, who wasn't there, then hugged his pillow and returned to the bottoms. (52)

Like his main character, Tim O'Brien travels to the bottoms in his harrowing fifth novel, a work of nearly unrelieved desolation and grief. As Steven Kaplan has noted, the original title of the book was to have been *The People We Marry* (1995: 218), but its suggestion of alienation within even the most intimate of human relationships understates the terrible isolation of O'Brien's most self-destroying hero. While *Going After Cacciato*, *The Nuclear Age*, and *The Things They Carried* variously convert trauma into redemptive fictions, *In the Lake of the Woods* introduces and then intensifies a posttraumatic desolation that never ends.

O'Brien's central character is an ambitious young Minnesota politician named John Wade, whose cover-up of his participation in the My Lai Massacre has just been exposed as the novel opens, devastating his promising political career and threatening to destroy his marriage. Having lost the

Democratic U.S. Senate primary election in a landslide, the humiliated and disgraced candidate withdraws with his wife Kathy to an isolated cottage on the shores of Lake of the Woods, where she disappears on their seventh night together, along with a missing boat. After an unsuccessful search is conducted, Wade is suspected of killing his wife, and he is last seen suicidally piloting another boat northward into a blizzard.

The name John Wade sounds like a pinched, adenoidal echo of the American cultural icon "John Wayne." Wade is a gifted amateur magician known by his fellow soldiers as "Sorcerer," but his attempts to fool various audiences ultimately ruin his career, his marriage, and his soul. In presenting the public and personal destruction of his Kennedy-like political star with an official war record as dishonest and as morally disturbing as his country's, O'Brien suggests not only that Vietnam has tainted American myths of heroism but that American politics have become morally rotten and superficial in the wake of national amnesia over the war. The novel thus tackles what he would label "big issues," and its combination of political story, love story, war story, detective story, and, ultimately, mystery is exceptionally ambitious.

Although *In the Lake of the Woods* won *Time's* novel of the year award as well as the American Historians' Cooper Prize for best historical novel (Graham 444), not all reviewers were satisfied with the book. *Newsweek's* Jeff Giles, after praising *Cacciato* and *Things* as "tense, indispensable fictions about Vietnam," damned *Lake* as a "pompous, impersonal book, long on authorial shenanigans and short on sympathetic characters." Even H. Bruce Franklin, who found *Lake* a profound and devastating indictment of American oblivion of its destruction of Viet Nam, found its representation of Wade's political failure "quite unconvincing" (1994: 44). As a conventional fiction, *Lake* seems a work that either needs to be much longer or could have been much shorter, a story or novella rather than a novel. It goes over the same material obsessively, repetitively detailing the Wades' past lives, variously re-representing the My Lai Massacre in fifteen of its thirty-one chapters, periodically sketching possible scenarios of Kathy's disappearance. The minor characters, such as Wade's political adviser Tony Carbo, seem clichéd or underdeveloped, and we never even come to understand the Wades very well. The historical and cultural materials appear as extracts from other texts, seven undigested lumps of "Evidence" scattered throughout the novel in long lists.

Even more than *Cacciato* and *Things,* however, O'Brien's darkest work is not a conventional fiction. Like the former, it alternates a series of imagined narratives and repressed memories of the past with a present reality, the search for Kathy Wade. Like *Things,* the book is narrated by a persona who seems to be O'Brien himself, a former Viet Nam veteran who patrolled Quang Ngai Province one year after Wade did. In addition, certain aspects of Wade's life before and after Viet Nam reflect O'Brien's own. The novel is not simply the story of John Wade; it enacts the process of trying to understand him by reconstructing his life through the broader prism of traumatization. The radically metafictional form and structure of the book mirror that condition, not only in the book's protagonist but also in O'Brien's revision of his earlier fiction in *Lake* as well as the self-representation of the narrative persona. And as the book investigates John Wade's moral and psychic collapse as fully as it can, the "Evidence" chapters invite the reader to consider the relationship between such breakdowns and American political history. The factuality of their material, whether historical or biographical, reminds us that the My Lai Massacre actually happened, that its atrociousness was worse than what we might have imagined in our darkest suspicions or nightmares, and that it was not unique in American history, however much it might be wished away or regarded as exceptional. Similarly, the excerpts from presidential biographies make John Wade's case less exceptional than it might seem because his desire to cover up, ignore, or distort the truth in order to be loved and respected has also motivated the follies and crimes, as well as the accomplishments, of figures from Woodrow Wilson to Lyndon Johnson and Richard Nixon. Citations from works on posttraumatic stress disorder and other texts dealing with abnormal psychology similarly have the effect of making the "abnormal" real, so that the problems that wives face in confronting and trying to help heal in their combat veteran husbands the psychic ruins left by the trauma of Vietnam are similarly grounded in fact, and similarly intractable.

Factual details concerning the Wades are left to the reader to synthesize, a process that will be examined below. Whatever may be postulated or imagined about their ultimate fates, which are left uncertain in the novel, a "happy ending" can be wrung from the material only by ignoring a great deal of bleak circumstantial evidence. While Paul Berlin's "flights of imagination" could at least temporarily satisfy his need to dream his way out of Vietnam, Wade has actually participated in what for him remains an inescapable nightmare but for the reader is historical reality. As Philip Beidler has reminded me, O'Brien's "Evidence" tragically revises the fictive affirmations of another traumatized survivor and witness, the Tim O'Brien who both appears in but also wrote *The Things They Carried*. Indeed, at the end of all of O'Brien's previous works, the protagonist can look forward to beginning over again even though he has been forever damaged by the experiences he has undergone. But John and Kathy Wade are left with little opportunity to escape from or to begin transmuting past trauma into something better. In "fact," their lives are over even before we read the first sentence of O'Brien's obituary.

Metafictional Investigations

In the Lake of the Woods "must be read as a work of fiction," according to O'Brien's foreword. This prescriptive caution arises from the fact that the book "contains material from the world in which we live, including references to actual places, people, and events." But it also points to its paradigmatic discourse, which is biography. The narrator of *Lake* is trying to find out what happened to John and Kathy Wade at Lake of the Woods. In order to do so, he has to reconstruct Wade's entire life and his relationship with Kathy and to re-create their thoughts, motivations, and actions. While "facts" were distinct from "truth" in *Things*, establishing facts—historical as well as biographical—is all-important for the narrator of *In the Lake of the Woods*. As a result, the discourse of O'Brien's novel resembles a nonfictional work such as *A Bright Shining Lie* (1988), Neil Sheehan's Pulitzer Prize–winning biography that uses John Paul Vann's life as an epitome of the American catastrophe in Viet Nam. And Sheehan's title, a haunting phrase that Vann applied both to himself and to the cause for which he died in Viet Nam, might be applied to the life of John Wade as well.

O'Brien's bleak, simple plot is enormously elaborated as a complex search for missing persons. The local authorities, together with Wade, try to find his wife, who seems to have piloted a small boat into the northern Minnesota wilderness. By the end of the book, Wade, who has become the prime murder suspect, has disappeared in another boat. The official search is incorporated into a fuller investigation of what might have happened to the Wades by the narrator of the work, who provides chapters of "Ev-

idence" and 136 footnotes to his text, some of them commenting on the
problems he has found in trying to tell John Wade's story. Although the
book begins by describing the Wades' arrival at Lake of the Woods, they
have already disappeared. An extract from the official Missing Persons Report on Kathy Wade is included within the first collection of evidence in
Chapter 2, and Chapter 6 ends with a footnote to more evidence, acknowledging that "Kathy Wade is forever missing, and if you require solutions,
you will have to look beyond these pages" (30). All the narrator's inter-
viewees refer to Wade in the past tense, and at the end of his third collection of evidence (Chapter 12), the narrator confesses that Wade is "beyond
knowing" (103). His final chapter is titled "Hypothesis," but he concedes the
same about the entire book that he is now completing: "It's all hypothesis,
beginning to end" (303). Because John and Kathy Wade are literally missing
persons, the narrator of *Lake* is in the position of the biographer of dead
subjects, forced to reconstruct them from personal and official documents,
physical remains, interviews, and further research into topics directly relevant to the mystery of the Wades' disappearance: the biographies of politicians and their wives, magic, the My Lai Massacre, and PTSD. But like all
human lives, John Wade's invites a larger context than his own story, so
that further research into American history, human psychology, biography, and literature is also presented as part of the "Evidence" and documented in the footnotes.

The elaborate structure of *In the Lake of the Woods* reflects the narrator's investigation and reconstruction of the Wades. Eight of its thirty-one
chapters describe significant events in Wade's past life and his relationship
with Kathy before her disappearance; the title of each is a formulaic
phrase that gives Wade's story figural significance: for example, "The Nature of Loss," "The Nature of Marriage," "The Nature of Love." Another
eight chapters narrate what happened after John and Kathy withdrew to
Lake of the Woods following the election: their first few days together, the
night she disappeared, the subsequent search for her, and Wade's own disappearance. Their brief titular clauses parody the headings of an official
investigation: "What He Remembered," "How the Night Passed," "What He
Did Next," and so on. Eight additional chapters, each of them titled "Hypothesis," provide possible explanations for Kathy Wade's fate. The first
speculates that she may have gone off with a lover, the last, that she was
murdered by her husband, who sunk her body and the missing boat into

the lake. In between, the narrator dramatizes various scenarios of her getting lost or drowned, including the possibility that she committed suicide to escape a ruined marriage. Finally, there are the seven chapters of "Evidence" upon which the reconstruction of the Wades has been based: physical remains, excerpts from interviews, portions of court testimony concerning the My Lai Massacre, passages from many of the books—fiction and nonfiction—that have been part of the narrator's research, together with footnotes and his own comments about his investigation of the case. These four different kinds of chapters are interwoven throughout the book, which begins with the Wades' arrival ("How Unhappy They Were") and ends with a final "Hypothesis."

Thus, like all of O'Brien's books, *Lake* is meticulously organized; as Kaplan has noted, however (1995: 202), this obsessively systematic arrangement ultimately reflects the incoherence of the narrator's attempts to understand his subject. His final footnote to Chapter 12 refers to Wade's soul as "a nametag drifting willy-nilly on oceans of hapless fact," "[t]welve notebooks' worth, and more to come" (103). We are made aware of the difficulty of reconstructing Wade as well as the activity of reconstruction, dismissed here by the narrator himself as a mere compilation of material with no apparent end.

Such textual self-anatomy is left up to us in the miscellany of "Evidence." Verbally parodying the official investigation narrated within the book, these chapters represent the grounding in physical objects, testimony, psychology and social science, history, and literature upon which John Wade's life has been reconstructed. Thus, on the basis of a discarded tea kettle and the remains of decomposed house plants (Chapter 2), the narrator has created an account of John Wade's waking up in the middle of the night and, in a loud fit of rage and disgust, steaming all the plants in the cottage (Chapter 8); in the "hypothesis" of Chapter 9, Kathy, awakened by her husband's shouting, secretly watches his bizarre activity and then flees into the woods; but in Chapter 27 the narrator has hypothesized Wade's pouring the full kettle of boiling water on his *wife* as she sleeps and then covering up his ghoulish murder by sinking her body into the lake, along with the couple's boat. Such possible scenarios mimic the activity of the official search party, which imagines, on the basis of a missing boat, that Kathy has gotten lost in Lake of the Woods. Their interviews of those who knew her are mimicked as well by the narrator, who has taken testimony from the investigators as well as from anyone who knew John Wade. Quotations from other texts invite multiple application to the narrator's own. For example, the final compilation of "Evidence" quotes Hawthorne's story "Wakefield" as an analogue—or source—or explanation—of John Wade's disappearance: "He had happened to dissever himself from the world—to vanish—to give up his place and privilege with living men, without being admitted among the dead" (297).

Hawthorne's description might be applied to imaginative characters in general, of course, and the relationship between the chapters of "Evidence" and the three other strands of *Lake* mimics the construction of a fiction as well as a biography. Whatever happened to Kathy is pure speculation, an imaginative reconstruction of her character and her relationship with Wade. In fact, the more fully the narrator tries to understand John and Kathy, the more fictive his account necessarily becomes. Only a few biographical details mentioned by witnesses, documents, and physical objects such as Wade's implements of magic remain as traces of these otherwise invented characters. And while portions of the search for Kathy could be based on the "facts" recalled by the official investigators, the words, thoughts, and motivations of the Wades have been made up by the narrator, who has tried to enter their souls.

As a self-described "[b]iographer, historian, medium—call me what you want" (30), the narrator must use the known facts to create a fiction if he is to follow John and Kathy Wade. His multiple attempts to reconstruct character and motivation make *In the Lake of the Woods* an imitation of the activity of representation itself. This focus on the process of writing rather than on its product, identified by Linda Hutcheon as the essence of metafiction (3), has been variously implicit in every previous book by O'Brien except *Northern Lights*, and explicit in *Cacciato* and *Things*, where it appeared in the form of night dreaming and storytelling, respectively. But the imitation of representation is overt in *Lake*, where the narrator provides "Evidence" to support his re-creation of the Wades, footnotes that call attention to his research, and commentary upon his work of representation as it proceeds. Suggestions that *Cacciato* was influenced by magical realism have been denied by O'Brien, who in 1982 expressed his dislike for overly artificial experimentation in modern fiction (McCaffery 138–39) and claimed to be barely "dabbling" with the work of Jorge Luis Borges, for example (142). But postmodernist fictive techniques are more evident in his most recent books, and they pervade *Lake*. O'Brien himself has contrasted his use of documentation in this novel with its absence in *Things*, citing Borges as an exemplar (Bourne 82).

Moreover, *In the Lake of the Woods* overtly uses and carries further two other metafictive practices that are variously present in O'Brien's novels after *Northern Lights*: generic instability and parody and the summoning of the reader to co-create the fictional text he or she is reading (Hutcheon 25–27). The narrative's discursive ambiguity is reflected by the variety of imperfectly realized nonfictional and fictional forms that *Lake* employs: biography, history, psychology, mystery/psychological thriller, detective story/criminal investigation, war story, political novel, romantic tragedy. The multiple discourses transform the passive act of reading into an unstable investigative activity by the reader that mirrors the narrator's; and instead of simply following someone else's narrative, we are forced to construct our own as we move from one hypothetical scene to another and consider the evidence. Our activity is further mirrored by the official investigators and the Wades' survivors, who are also trying to figure out what might have happened. Generic instability and the reader's role as writer culminate in the final two chapters of "Evidence" and "Hypothesis," where a quotation from *Oedipus at Colonus* suggests that *Lake* may be a classical tragedy; an investigator, convinced that Wade has murdered Kathy, sees it as a crime melodrama; John's cynical former campaign manager thinks that the Wades may have pulled off an escape from the law to flee from their debts, a confidence trick; Wade's mother and friends of John and Kathy also half-believe that they planned their disappearances together but see their escape to a new life as a romance. The narrator's final hypotheses are murder or a double escape, but he has to call upon his readers to validate what he would prefer: "Are we so cynical, so sophisticated as to write off even the chance of happy endings? . . . Does happiness strain credibility? . . . Can we not believe that two adults, in love, might resolve to make their own miracle?" (302). A footnote rejects the grisly murder scenario on both moral and aesthetic grounds as "graceless and disgusting," but it is immediately succeeded by another that concedes, "there's no accounting for taste. It's a judgment call. Maybe you hear her screaming. Maybe you see steam rising from the sockets of her eyes" (303). And, indeed, the metafiction has succeeded in provoking varying judgments. H. Bruce Franklin argues that O'Brien wants us to believe that John *did* kill Kathy because traces of only this hypothesis are recalled by Wade in the investigation chapters and because he is capable of covering up this murder just as he has covered up his involvement in My Lai (42–43). But Steven Kaplan believes we are to think that Kathy died accidentally and that Wade ultimately commits suicide to join her, basing his argument on his final recorded words, the narrator's interpretation of them, and a passage added to the preview copy of *Lake* that emphasizes Wade's love for his wife (1995: 215–16, 218).

The Breakdown of John Wade

Whatever its limitations in conventional characterization and narrative, whatever the terrible crimes and psychic desolation of the story it tells, *In the Lake of the Woods* is a brilliant and provocative metafictional mystery that will probably engage critics of postmodernist fiction for years to come. Simply analyzing the relationship between its "Evidence" and the other parts of the novel—a "vertical" rather than sequential reading of the text—would illuminate the simulacrum of his own creation that O'Brien has represented in the narrator persona. Following the references outside the text will open it to more directly political readings or source studies. Underlying all the narrator's hypotheses about Wade, however, is a master theory that has made his reconstruction possible and that is reflected in the representation of his actions, motivations, words, and thoughts as well as in the structure of the narrative itself: John Wade's life is a product of comprehensive traumatization. In re-creating this victim of trauma, the narrator has been able to understand and re-create himself; and in representing both the narrator and Wade, O'Brien has done the same, even as he rewrites much of his earlier fiction as tragedy.

In the reconstruction of John Wade that is *In the Lake of the Woods*, whatever happened to Kathy Wade is the culminating breakdown of a life that has been wounded by traumatic experiences and destroyed by the attempt to make them disappear. As a child, Wade feels unloved by his alcoholic father, who commits suicide when the boy is fourteen. He turns to magic and ultimately politics to gain the approval of others that his father denied him and to control their responses in order to avoid the powerless dependency on another's will that constituted his childhood. He goes to

Viet Nam, hoping to make his dead father proud of him, initially gains his comrades' admiration and the pseudonym "Sorcerer" for feats of violent magic, but has a breakdown during the My Lai Massacre, where he kills a Vietnamese farmer and a fellow GI at the subhamlet of Thuan Yen, and later changes official records to remove himself from Lieutenant Calley's company. Extending his tour for another year in order to punish or purge himself, Wade returns to Minnesota with a distinguished war record and begins a meteoric political career—perhaps another attempt to make up for Thuan Yen—that culminates in his seemingly unstoppable campaign for the U.S. Senate at the age of 41. When political rivals looking for dirt investigate his service in Viet Nam, however, "Sorcerer" is uncovered as a My Lai participant, Wade is crushed in an electoral landslide, and he and his wife withdraw to Lake of the Woods.

Wade loves Kathy passionately but also desperately. He needs her to make up for the rest of his life, and his attitude is marked by the same insecurity and need for control that characterize his childhood, military service, and political career. He spies on her throughout their courtship, trying to anticipate and counter any signs of disaffection or betrayal while keeping his own darker secrets hidden despite hauntings by his father and nightmares about My Lai. In turn, she connives with his needs, ignoring his spying and his bad dreams, participating effectively in his campaigns although she hates politics, ultimately having an abortion when her pregnancy gets in the way of his run for the Senate. As their love becomes hostage to Wade's need for political self-validation, however, she has a brief affair that further wounds her husband, for whom she is "sacred" (305), and they become accustomed to their own unhappiness. The public revelation of his past not only destroys his career but also makes necessary their private retreat to put their lives back together, to save the marriage. Whatever its cause or circumstances, therefore, Kathy's disappearance is the ultimate trauma for Wade, who describes her as "my love. My life. The purpose of all deceit" (287–88) in a final radio broadcast from the boat taking him northward just before he signs off and vanishes.

The above outline of this bleak tragedy distorts the novel's actual account by simplifying, rationalizing, and reordering the nonsequential reconstruction of Wade's life that is presented in the four strands of its investigation. But any reconstruction will reflect that the protagonist's story is generated out of four crucial experiences of psychic breakdown: Wade's relationship with his father and the latter's bewildering suicide, the massacre at Thuan Yen, the election catastrophe, and the loss of Kathy. Sources for this trauma narrative may be found buried in the "Evidence." Sometimes they are brief secondhand hints for larger scenarios: John's mother Eleanor recalls that her son had trouble sleeping, and Kathy told her sister Pat Hood that her husband occasionally had terrible nightmares and "needed help" (149). Sometimes they are extensive: *In the Lake of the Woods* reproduces many excerpts of testimony given by Calley, Paul Meadlo, and others during the official army investigation of the My Lai Massacre. Sometimes they directly record breakdowns: Eleanor Wade reports that John had a tantrum of "awfully loud yelling" at his father's funeral (29). More general sources for both understanding Wade and justifying his trauma-centered characterization include excerpts from Judith Herman's *Trauma and Recovery* (e.g., "The ordinary response to atrocities is to banish them from consciousness"—140); Patience Mason's *Recovering from the War*, a guide for women married to Vietnam Vets (e.g., "You get involved, try to help, put your own needs aside. Then it's twelve years later and you don't know how to have fun anymore"—261); an article by Robert Karen defining "shame" as "a wound in the self . . . frequently instilled at a delicate age, as a result of the internalization of a contemptuous voice, usually parental" (201) that may be repressed or defended against but that remains "like a deformed body part that we organize our lives to keep ourselves and others from seeing" (267).

Wade's traumatization and his attempts to cover it up are represented directly as well as indirectly throughout the book. In the very first chapter, the election defeat becomes a psychic assault that threatens to overwhelm everything Wade has made of his life. Imagining his ruin provokes a near-breakdown: "[I]t was more than a lost election. It was something physical. Humiliation, that was part of it, and the wreckage in his chest and stomach, and then the rage, how it surged up into his throat and how he wanted to scream the most terrible thing he could scream—*Kill Jesus!*—and how he couldn't help himself and couldn't think straight and couldn't stop screaming it inside his head—*Kill Jesus!*—because nothing could be done, and because it was so brutal and disgraceful and final" (5). In turn, the present rage triggers terrible and recurrent symptoms of PTSD that frighten Wade:

He felt crazy sometimes. Real depravity. . . . All those years. Climbing like a son of a bitch, clawing his way up inch by fucking inch, and then it all came crashing down at once. . . .

Forget it, he thought. Don't think.

And then later, when he began thinking again, he took Kathy up against him, holding tight. "Verona," he said firmly, "we'll do it. Deluxe hotels. The whole tour." (5–6)

The wish to escape Vietnam and Minnesota here recalls Harvey's fantasies of postwar adventure in *Northern Lights*, but the dreams of O'Brien's postmodern Romeo and Juliet will not survive Wade's nightmares.

Similar posttraumatic eruptions are marked by psychic disconnections with the world around him and an "anthology of bad dreams" (285). Spying on Kathy outside her college dorm the night after he returns from Viet Nam, Wade feels himself "gliding" and experiences a "dizzy, disconnected sensation" that "stayed with him all night" as he checks into a hotel, where he has a nightmare that merges his father's funeral with the irrigation ditch at Thuan Yen, filled with massacred Vietnamese civilians:

John wanted to kill everybody who was weeping and everybody who wasn't, everybody, the minister and the mourners and the skinny old lady at the organ—he wanted to grab a hammer and scramble down into the ditch and kill his father for dying.

"Hey, I *love* you," he yelled. "I *do.*" (42)

His almost inadvertent killing of a Vietnamese farmer as he tries to make the mass murder going on around him at Thuan Yen disappear ("This could not have happened. Therefore it did not" [111]) is represented as a traumatized response that immediately prompts its own futile repression:

He would both remember and not remember a fleet human movement off to his left.

He would not remember squealing.

He would not remember raising his weapon, nor rolling away from the bamboo fence, but he would remember forever how he turned and shot down an old man with a wispy beard and wire glasses and what looked to be a rifle. It was not a rifle; it was a small wooden hoe.

"The hoe he would always remember," the narrator continues, refabricating it as a recurrent traumatic intrusion: "In the ordinary hours after the war, at the breakfast table or in the babble of some dreary statehouse hearing, John Wade would sometimes look up to see the wooden hoe spinning like a baton in the morning sunlight" (111). Wade even recognizes his condition, as a passage in Chapter 10 ("The Nature of Love") indicates:

> John Wade knew he was sick, and one evening he tried to talk about it with Kathy. He wanted to unload the horror in his stomach.
>
> "It's hard to explain," he said, "but I don't feel real sometimes. Like I'm not *here*." They were in the apartment, making dinner, and the place smelled of onions and frying hamburger.
>
> "You're real to me," Kathy said. "Very real, and very good." (74)

"Something's wrong, I've *done* things," he tries to go on, but as they finish preparing the hamburgers she nervously fends off his abortive confession, "as if she were aware of certain truths but could not bear to know what she knew, which was in the nature of their love" (74). More typically, however, Wade's traumatization is reflected in attempts to hide the past.

The sudden shift from Thuan Yen to the Minnesota State Senate, quoted above, breaks up what had been a grisly but straightforward narrative of Wade's participation in the My Lai Massacre. Here as elsewhere in *Lake*, however, the modal verbs (e.g., "He would not remember squealing") suddenly violate sequentiality and make us realize that we are not just reading an account of past actions as they were witnessed at the time but experiencing an ineffaceable, recurrent traumatic scar that the narrator has imagined Wade repressing or revisiting. More broadly, Wade's life is presented as a series of asynchronous fragments that both re-create traumatic breakdowns in the past and mimic the protagonist's reimagining them forever. Thus, *Lake* does not simply reconstruct Wade's life as a coherent sequence of actions and experiences but as a chaotic interweaving of dreams, reminiscences, and past traumatic events that represents his state of mind. This posttraumatic web is particularly evident in the chapters that detail the Wades' past lives, which juxtapose discrete scenes that are linked only thematically. For example, "The Nature of Love" (Chapter 10) begins with a scene of John and Kathy ducking out of a political fundraiser to make love, immediately followed by an explanation of how Wade's need for love led him to Viet Nam, and how "at times, too, John imagined loving himself. And never risking the loss of love" (60). The chapter draws toward its close with a brief scene of his practicing magic on the afternoon following his father's burial, followed by an account of his bad dreams that begins with the reflection that "it was in the nature of their love that Kathy did not insist that he see a psychiatrist, and that John did not feel the need to seek help" (75–76) and ends with a description of how he would watch Kathy sleep when he couldn't sleep himself. Thus, the chapter juxtaposes the child magician and the Viet Nam soldier, scenes from his political career and scenes from his marriage, the trauma of shooting a fellow GI at Thuan Yen and the trauma of his father's suicide in a melange of episodes and reflections that can be read as a fabrication of Wade's own fragmented state of mind. His killing of PFC Weatherby literally intrudes five times, but because there is no temporal grounding for any of the incidents, reflections, or memories, we can imagine Wade's revisiting them at any time before Kathy's disappearance—or even after. "The Nature of Marriage" (Chapter 7) and "The Nature of Politics" (Chapter 17) are similarly fragmented, and even the chapters that focus more directly on the My Lai Massacre —"The Nature of the Beast" (Chapter 13), "The Nature of the Spirit" (Chapter 21), and "The Nature of the Dark" (Chapter 26)—include pre– and post–Thuan Yen episodes and intrusive recapitulations of what has happened earlier, like the reappearance of the farmer cited above.

Besides this recurrence of traumatic and shameful memories, the narrator of *Lake* also tries to represent Wade's moments of psychic collapse, just as O'Brien had evoked the breakdowns of Paul Berlin and William Cowling. Because such a state involves loss of normal consciousness as well as active repression of the experience as it occurs, it cannot be easily recovered or represented, of course, and the text reflects this. For example, when a GI right next to him is killed by a Vietnamese sniper, Wade runs amok, directly assaulting the enemy soldier and blowing his face off. But his berserk state, identified by Jonathan Shay as the most ineffaceably ruinous effect of traumatization (98), is represented as a dreamlike "gliding" that seems to take him out of his body and represses all other emotions. Later, at Thuan Yen, traumatized by the mass murder of civilians going on around him, Wade tries to flee physically and psychically but ultimately finds himself in an irrigation ditch full of corpses without knowing how he got there. The self-obliterating phenomenon of traumatization is reinforced by Wade's conscious attempts to cover up shameful or horrible events or make them vanish. Thus, he begins his denial of My Lai in the moments just before Charlie Company disembarks from the helicopters to begin an atrocity that will make history:

> Sorcerer felt dazed and half asleep, still dreaming wild dawn dreams. All night he'd been caught up in pink rivers and pink paddies; even now, squatting at the rear of the chopper, he couldn't flush away the pink. All that color—it was wrong[1] . . . PFC Weatherby kept wiping his M-16 with a towel, first the barrel and then his face and then the barrel again. Boyce and Maples and Lieutenant Calley sat side by side in the chopper's open doorway, sharing a cigarette, quietly peering down at the cratered fields and paddies.
>
> Pure wrongness, Sorcerer knew.
>
> He could taste the sunlight. It had a rusty, metallic flavor, like nails on his tongue.
>
> For a few seconds Sorcerer shut his eyes and retreated behind the mirrors in his head, pretending to be elsewhere, but even then the landscapes kept coming at him fast and lurid. (106–7)

As a magician, Wade uses mirrors to practice and produce his illusions, and he uses their psychic equivalents throughout his life to deny or hide shame and trauma or to make them vanish. Paradoxically, however, these two-way mirrors in his head also reflect what they endlessly try to cover up, beginning in childhood:

> In the mirror, where John Wade mostly lived, he could read his father's mind. Simple affection, for instance. "Love you, cowboy," his father would think.
>
> Or his father would think, "Hey, report cards aren't everything."
>
> The mirror made this possible, and so John would sometimes carry it to school with him, or to baseball games, or to bed at night. . . .
>
> The mirror made things better.
>
> The mirror made his father smile all the time. The mirror made the vodka bottles vanish from their hiding place in the garage, and it helped with the hard, angry silences at the dinner table. (65–66)

Just as it did in Viet Nam, Wade's self-protective magic breaks down in the life he creates for himself and Kathy after the war. Thus, waiting as his wife has her politically inconvenient pregnancy terminated, Wade finds himself dissolving:

> Curiously, he felt the beginnings of sorrow, which perplexed him, and it re-
> quired effort to direct his thoughts elsewhere. A few phone calls, maybe.
> Check in with Tony [his campaign manager]. . . . The room wasn't quite
> solid. Very wobbly, it seemed. And suddenly, as though caught in a box of
> mirrors, John looked up to see his own image reflected on the clinic's walls
> and ceiling. Fun-house reflections: deformations and odd angles. He saw a
> little boy doing magic. He saw a college spy, madly in love. He saw a soldier
> and husband and a seeker of public office. He saw himself from inside out
> and upside down—the organic chemistry, the twisted chromosomes—and
> for a second it occurred to him that his own stability was at issue.
>
> At supper that night he tried to describe the experience to Kathy. Except
> it was hopeless. He couldn't find the words. Kathy's eyes went skipping
> across the surfaces of things. (159)

Even this near-breakdown simply reinforces his own self-absorption and produces further cover-ups: Kathy can't talk about the abortion, and he won't.

Wade's loss of his wife is the culminating catastrophe of his self-de-struction, and it provokes the desolate narrative of *In the Lake of the Woods*, whether we view it as Wade's reflection upon a lifetime of covering up shame, guilt, and lovelessness in the wake of Kathy's disappearance or as the narrator's reconstruction of Wade's inner life. The novel begins with a deliberate echo of Hemingway's *A Farewell to Arms*, whose hero was one of O'Brien's models of courage in Chapter XVI of *If I Die in a Combat Zone*: "In September, after the primary, they rented an old yellow cottage in the timber at the edge of Lake of the Woods. There were many trees, mostly pine and birch, and there was the dock and the boathouse and the narrow dirt road that came through the forest and ended in polished gray rocks at the shore below the cottage. Then there were no roads at all. There were no towns and no people."[2] Unlike Frederic Henry, however, Wade cannot establish a separate peace for himself or the woman he loves. He has not withdrawn from his war; he has unsuccessfully tried to make it disappear, and the psychic wilderness of cover-ups and evasions that have led John and Kathy to their crisis is mirrored in Lake of the Woods: "Beyond the dock the big lake opened northward into Canada, where the water was everything, vast and very cold, and where there were secret channels and portages and bays and tangled forests and islands without names" (1). The first chapter's title is its theme—"How Unhappy They Were"—and O'Brien initially presents a posttraumatic scenario in which John and Kathy are unsuccessfully trying to recover from his public humiliation at the polls:[3]

> Everywhere, for many thousand square miles, the wilderness was all one thing, like a great curving mirror, infinitely blue and beautiful, always the same. Which was what they had come for. They needed the solitude. They needed the repetition, the dense hypnotic drone of woods and water, but above all they needed to be together. . . . They were not yet prepared to make love. They had tried once, but it had not gone well, so now they would hold each other and talk quietly about having babies and perhaps a house of their own. They pretended things were not so bad. (1–2)

What seems initially a conventional realist fiction, however, is subtly disrupted by a brief narrative intervention during an account of their sixth day together: "In less than thirty-six hours she would be gone, but now she lay beside him on the porch and talked about all the ways they could make it better" (3). And the chapter ends with a similar temporal fault line as they try to soothe each other on the cottage porch that evening:

> There was the steady hum of lake and woods. In the days afterward, when she was gone, he would remember this with perfect clarity, as if it were still happening. He would remember a breathing sound inside the fog. He would remember the feel of her hand against his forehead, its warmth, how purely alive it was.
>   "Happy," she said. "Nothing else." (7)

Here again, the modal verbs expand John Wade's consciousness beyond the scene being described. As we become aware of the narrator's presence, hypothesizing what Wade might have felt later, we also realize that Kathy is already gone forever before she says her final words here, making the already desolate scene a memory suffused with grief and loss. Near the end of the novel, the last trace of Wade's identity imagines her buried "beneath the surface of the silvered lake"—"[n]ot quite present, not quite gone, she swims in the blending twilight of in between" (291)—and the narrator repeats the initial image of the now-deserted cottage, standing "in the timber overlooking the lake" as if it had never known the couple's presence:

"There are many trees, mostly pine and birch, and there is a dock and a boathouse and a narrow dirt road that winds through the forest and ends in a ledge of polished gray rocks at the shore below the cottage" (291). What has transpired between the opening and closing scenes is a ghost story, an account of missing persons haunted by memories of vanished lives. The road ends at the edge of a lake in an empty wilderness.

Wade's being able to recall the final instant of happiness above is made even more traumatic by what he can't remember: his final moments together with Kathy on their last night in the cottage. "What He Remembered" (Chapter 4) are the events of the day, but "How the Night Passed" (Chapter 8) is reconstructed as the culminating breakdown of Wade's life, a psychic collapse that leaves his final moments with Kathy a blank. Awakening from terrible nightmares provoked by the ruin of his life, Wade curses what has happened to him and boils the houseplants in a state of near-traumatization that direly rewrites the opening of *Northern Lights*: "The election was only part of it. There were also those mirrors in his head. An electric buzz, the chemistry inside him, the hum of lake and woods. He felt the pinch of depravity" (49). As at Thuan Yen, only bits and pieces of the rest of the night come back to him later, as he feels himself "glide away" back into the bedroom. Tenderly spying on Kathy as she sleeps, Wade feels a need to finally shatter the mirrors and reveal what they have been hiding:

> It occurred to him that he should wake her. Yes, a kiss, and then confess to the shame he felt: how defeat had bled into his bones and made him crazy with hurt. He should've done it. He should've told her about the mirrors in his head. He should've talked about the special burden of villainy, the ghosts at Thuan Yen, the strain on his dreams. And then later he should've slipped under the covers and taken her in his arms and explained how he loved her more than anything, a hard hungry lasting guileless love, and how everything else was trivial and dumb. . . .
>
> In the days that followed, John Wade would remember all the things he should've done.
>
> He touched her shoulder.
>
> Amazing, he thought, what love could do. (50–51)

The doubly receding point of view prompted by the modal verbs increases Wade's subsequent sense of desolation and guilt. "In the days that followed," a futile search for Kathy Wade has begun; the last person to see her alive has been her husband, in the scene narrated above. The painful memory of what he should have done, whether seventeen years ago when he returned from Viet Nam or during their last night together, is further haunted by a sense of responsibility for her disappearance. Wishes not acted upon have become unfulfilled obligations that might have saved both of them.

Beyond his final touch of her shoulder, Wade can remember only disconnected images connected "with radical implausibilities":

> the teakettle and a wooden hoe and a vanishing village and PFC Weatherby and hot white steam . . . smoothing back her hair . . . pulling a blanket to her chin. . . . All around him . . . that furious buzzing noise. The unities of time and space had unraveled. There were manifold uncertainties, and in the days and weeks to come, memory would play devilish little tricks on him. The mirrors would warp up; there would be odd folds and creases; clarity would be at a premium. (51)

He can vaguely recall standing in the lake, later submerging himself, and his own self-investigation in the rest of the book includes a "pre-memory" of being in the boathouse (191). For the rest of *Lake*, Wade's overwhelming love for his wife—and the narrator's other hypotheses for her disappearance—struggle against the terrible possibility that he has murdered Kathy during a traumatic berserk episode, covered up the crime, and then almost completely hidden the evil from himself in further psychic repression.

Therefore, just as the chapters that seem to narrate Wade's past life represent it through the asynchronous fragmentation, repetition, and intrusion of traumatic recapitulation, Wade's part in the official investigation is marked by posttraumatic desolation, not only for what he has done to Kathy but for what he may have done. Tony Carbo recalls that John responded to press inquiries about his presence at My Lai with "that blank dead-man look of his" (296), and the election debacle completes his political execution. But after the loss of Kathy, the rest of his life is posthumous, an endless suffering of grief and guilt that intensifies his disconnection from others. During much of the search for Kathy, he is investigating himself, and other searchers comment on his curious detachment from what is going on around him: "Senator, you *with* us?" (236) his friend Claude Rasmussen asks during a lake search, snapping Wade out of one of his reveries. His terse and affectless responses to investigators' questions are not

simply attempts to avoid self-incrimination but also signs of his own bewilderment and symptoms of postbreakdown emotional constriction. So,
too, the apparent superficiality of characterization and dialogue in the narrative portions of *Lake*, even the lack of political details, reflect Wade's uninterest in anything other than his lost love. By the end of the novel, as he
pilots Rasmussen's boat north on a final solitary search, the details of Kathy's disappearance are as much a mystery for Wade as for anyone else,
but he has also come to realize his own culpability for whatever has happened: "Kathy was gone, everything else was guesswork. Probably an accident. Or lost out here. Something simple. For sure—almost for sure. Except
it didn't matter much. He was responsible for the misery in their lives, the
betrayals and deceit, the manipulations of truth that had substituted for
simple love. He was Sorcerer. He was guilty of that, and always would be"
(282–83). Earlier, dreading the worst, he had dived below the boathouse to
see whether he had buried Kathy there but nearly committed suicide anyway when he couldn't find her. His ultimate disappearance is not only an
act of dark justice but an acknowledgment that without her he has no reason to go on living. The narrator's final judgment may be his most plausible: "Sorrow, it seems to me, may be the true absolute. John grieved for Kathy. She was his world. They could have been so happy together. He loved
her and she was gone and he could not bear the horror" (305). The final
reference to Conrad's *Heart of Darkness* undercuts even the redemptive
possibilities of romantic tragedy by suggesting that Wade could not live
with the darkness inside himself, just as he could not accept traumatization as an excuse for evil at Thuan Yen: "This was not madness, Sorcerer
understood. This was sin. He felt it winding through his own arteries,
something vile and slippery like heavy black oil in a crankcase" (110).

The hypothesis of traumatization allows the narrator to reconstruct
what happened to his missing persons, but it also makes Wade harder to
understand. Because his downfall is a result of experiences that have been
both unconsciously repressed and actively covered up, they must remain
unclear and unassimilated. The moments of actual breakdown are abnormal psychic experiences that can be rendered only as peculiar sensations
—gliding, buzzing sounds, a "strange heaviness" (51), a "twitch and flutter,
like wings" (51), "sunlight suck[ing] him down a trail toward the center of
the village" (109)—where they have not been blacked out entirely. Furthermore, the repetition of painful scenes from the past does not make them

coherent or bearable any more than Wade's memories of pleasures shared with Kathy in the past bring happiness after her disappearance.

That the mere recollection of repressed trauma may not enlighten or redeem is most provocatively suggested by O'Brien's representation of the My Lai Massacre. References to or descriptions of the war appear in eighteen of *Lake*'s thirty-one chapters, although most of them are brief flashbacks by Wade or bits of testimony by others. Like Wade's Viet Nam service generally, the massacre emerges only gradually into the novel, as if the former were simply an appendage to a political career that lies in ruins and the latter the dark shame that underlies both. Wade's early thoughts about the secret of "Thuan Yen" paradoxically obscure his references with an actual fact, the Vietnamese name for the subhamlet of My Lai where the horror took place, as an excerpt from the Peers Commission investigation of the My Lai Massacre eventually makes clear in Chapter 16 (137–38). A full description of Wade's involvement at Thuan Yen appears only in Chapter 13, "The Nature of the Beast," and then the "Evidence" three chapters later reproduces chilling excerpts from the official army investigation and the court-martial of Lieutenant William Calley, the ground commander at Thuan Yen. By the end of *Lake*, the My Lai Massacre has been represented by direct testimony taken from Calley's court-martial; other eyewitness reports; other army investigations; Wade's own self-torturing flashbacks; the recollections of his friend, an American Indian named Richard Thinbill who killed only some water buffalo (a grotesquely benign revision of analogous episodes in O'Brien's previous works); direct representations of the massacre in which both Calley and Wade are characters; and footnotes by the narrator concerning his own service in Quang Ngai Province, including a visit to Thuan Yen two decades after he had left Viet Nam, part of his "research for this book" (149). The blending of fact and fiction—which includes a nonexistent transcript of Thinbill's court martial testimony (202) (found in the "U.S. National Archives, box 4, folder 8, p. 1734")—makes the unimaginable real and grounds O'Brien's account of the massacre in history. But it also leaves what he has called "the mystery of evil" incomprehensible, despite the parade of witnesses. The horror is described in unsparing detail but through an emotional constriction that registers the suppression of normal consciousness:

> Just inside the village, Sorcerer found a pile of dead goats.

He found a pretty girl with her pants down. She was dead too. She looked at him cross-eyed. Her hair was gone.

He found dead dogs, dead chickens.

Farther along, he encountered someone's forehead. He found three dead water buffalo. He found a dead monkey. He found ducks pecking at a dead toddler. (108)

Wade's affectless registration of the mass murder is an effect of his own unwillingness to believe it, but it is evident in the historical testimony of participants as well, as in Richard Pendleton's description of a ditch: "It was seven to ten feet deep, maybe ten to fifteen feet across. The bodies were all across it. There was one group in the middle and more on the sides. The bodies were on top of each other" (141); or Charles Hall's explanation of how he knew that victims were dead: "They weren't moving. There was a lot of blood coming from all over them. They were in piles and scattered. There were very old people, very young people, and mothers. Blood was coming from everywhere. Everything was all blood" (142). Lieutenant Calley, pressed to distinguish between the enemy and human beings, men and women, turns them all into an abstraction: "I didn't discriminate between individuals in the village, sir. They were all the enemy, they were all to be destroyed, sir" (143). Wade's repression of emotion alternates with psychic breakdowns, and Varnado Simpson's testimony reflects the other side of traumatization, berserk hyperarousal: "I just went. My mind just went. And I wasn't the only one that did it. A lot of other people did it. I just killed. Once I started the . . . the training [ellipsis in the original], the whole programming part of killing, it just came out. . . . It just came. I didn't know I had it in me" (145).

Despite all the testimony and the would-be explanations that they offer—racial and ideological demonology, being trained to follow orders and to kill, revenge for killed buddies, the nature of counterguerrilla warfare, ignorance and sadism—the massacre remains both inexcusable and inexplicable. In a postscript on My Lai ("The Nature of the Dark"), O'Brien imagines Wade's company settling into night positions "in the months after Thuan Yen" as they "wandered here and there, no aim or direction, . . . doing what they had to do because nothing else could be done," a collection of lost souls traumatized forever by what they didn't know they had in them:

The days were difficult, the nights were impossible. At dusk, after their holes were dug, they would sit in small groups and look out across the paddies and wait for darkness to settle in around them. The dark was their shame. It was also their future. They tried not to talk about it, but sometimes they couldn't help themselves. Thinbill talked about the flies. T'Souvas talked about the smell. Their voices would seem to flow away for a time and then return to them from somewhere beyond the swaying fields of rice. It was an echo, partly. But inside the echo were sounds not quite their own. . . . There were stirrings all around them, things seen, things not seen, which was in the nature of the dark. (270–71)

According to a *Boston Herald* item reproduced on page 265, Robert T'Souvas, acquitted of unpremeditated murder charges brought by the army, was shot to death in Pittsburgh over a bottle of vodka on September 13, 1988, after years as a homeless alcoholic. John Wade falls only after a successful political career initially enhanced by his Vietnam service. In the end, though, neither legal absolution nor cover-up could save either from the darkness within.

Tragic Revisions

Just after publishing *The Things They Carried* in 1990, O'Brien claimed that his forthcoming book was going to be different from anything he had yet written. In fact, *In the Lake of the Woods* combines important aspects of all his previous works: Set in rural Minnesota, like *Northern Lights*, it has the ambitious historical and political scope of *The Nuclear Age*; presents an intense story of married love like those two United States–sited novels; and follows a company of GIs as they make their way through the destructive moral and physical landscape of combat patrols in Quang Ngai Province, just like Alpha Company in *Combat Zone, Cacciato,* and *Things.* Nor is its metafictionality, though more pronounced than in any previous book, unprecedented; in particular, O'Brien had used an authorial persona extensively in *Things* before resuming work on the novel.

Unlike anything he had written, however, *Lake* is hopelessly bleak in its outlook, the redemptive possibilities of the earlier books effaced by endless trauma. Both the Viet Nam and domestic portions of the novel are a dark revision of all the earlier books, making Wade's fate inescapably tragic. His comrades are that Charlie Company which made history by massacring hundreds of civilians on March 16, 1968; his commanding officer is not Captain Johansen or Lieutenant Corson or even Jimmy Cross, but Rusty Calley; and his attempt to literally erase his nearly inadvertent killing of a Vietnamese farmer and PFC Weatherby in order to expunge his own guilt and shame is a black magic that stains his soul forever: "At higher levels, he reasoned, other such documents were being redrafted, other such facts neatly doctored. . . . The illusion, he realized, would not be perfect. None ever was. But still it seemed a nifty piece of work. Logical and smooth. Among the men in Charlie Company he was known only as Sorcerer. Very few had ever heard his real name; fewer still would recall it. And over time, he trusted, memory itself would be erased" (272). While Tim O'Brien in *Things* converts his trauma into true war stories, Wade tries to erase his, and the only fiction he creates is an untrue story that finally destroys him.

The historical circumstantiality of *Lake* turns what had been fictional atrocities in O'Brien's previous books into factual ones in *Lake*. For example, the physical obliteration of Hoi An after Pederson's death is revised with Calley taking on the role of Lieutenant Sidney Martin in Chapter 11 of *Cacciato* but uttering the words of Paul Berlin (*Cacciato* 99):

> Three weeks later, on March 14, a booby-trapped 155 round blew Sergeant George Cox into several large wet pieces. Dyson lost both legs. Hendrixson lost an arm and a leg.
>
> Two or three men were crying.
>
> Others couldn't remember how.
>
> "Kill Nam," said Lieutenant Calley. He pointed his weapon at the earth, burned twenty quick rounds. "Kill it," he said. He reloaded and shot the grass and a palm tree and then the earth again. "Grease the place," he said. "Kill it." (105)

The severed ear of *Combat Zone* and Oscar Johnson's grenade in *Cacciato*, badges of solidarity and silence used to validate the lesser crimes in those books, become a fistful of flies, attracted by the mutilated corpse of a young woman and used by Calley to enforce the My Lai cover-up the day after the atrocity has been committed:

> He scooped up a handful of flies and held them to his ear. After a second he smiled.

"You *hear* this? Fuckin' flies, they're claiming something criminal happened here. Big noisy rumor. Anybody else hear it?"

No one spoke. Some of them looked at their boots, others at the woman's body. (215)

Wade and his friend Thinbill, who are openly dissatisfied with Calley's "moral spin" on the massacre (209), yield to the company line when the lieutenant brushes their ears with the closed fist: "I don't hear it, sir. Nothing" (215), acknowledges PFC Thinbill; "Deaf, sir," Wade responds, and the scene ends with a postmortem operation by Calley and his men to justify what they have done:

He smiled at Sorcerer. "These folks here, they look like civilians?"

"No, sir."

"Course not." Calley crushed the flies in his fist, put the hand to his nose and sniffed it. "Tear this place apart. See if we can find us some VC weapons." (216)

Morally, Mad Mark's little atrocity was ugly and the burning of Tri Binh 4 murderous, but the scale of crime in this scene is incredible, although it has been documented. And while the fragging of Lieutenant Sidney Martin was more than a "sad thing," following orders here is even worse.

John Wade's breakdown after the massacre recalls Paul Berlin's collapse on his first day in the war, after Cacciato has reminded him of Billy Boy Watkins's death from shock after losing his foot:

He rolled onto his belly and pressed his face in the wet grass. "Not so loud," the boy said. But Paul Berlin was shaking with the giggles: scared to death on the field of battle.

"Not so loud." (*Cacciato* 259)

Eventually he recovers, aided by Cacciato's attempts to quiet him and a final placebo for his trauma: "The boy gave him a stick of gum. It was Black Jack, the precious stuff. 'You'll do fine,' Cacciato said, 'You will. You got a terrific sense of humor'" (262). Wade's hysteria rewrites Berlin's, but the breakdown is more complex, the circumstances more horrific. Sitting in darkness with Thinbill after the postmassacre cover-up, listening to the flies still buzzing like ghostly rumors or spirits over the corpses, Wade is urged to help report the truth to army authorities. But while his friend has

refrained from murder, Wade has the deaths of a Vietnamese farmer and a
marauding fellow GI on his hands:

> The buzz made it hard to think straight. There was his future to take into
> account, all the dreams for himself. . . .
>
> Thinbill nudged his arm. "No other way," he said. "At least we'll sleep at
> night."
>
> "I don't know."
>
> "We *have* to."
>
> Sorcerer nodded. An important moment had arrived and he could feel
> the inconvenient squeeze of moral choice. It made him giggle. . . . He cov-
> ered his face and lay back and let the giggles take him. He was shaking.
> In the dark someone hissed at him to shut up, but he couldn't quit, he
> couldn't catch his breath, he couldn't make the nighttime buzz go away.
> The horror was in his head. (218)

Like Paul Berlin's, Wade's loss of self-control is provoked by intrusive
trauma, but whereas Paul recalls Billy Boy Watkins's death, Wade suddenly
recalls his comrades with their weapons on full automatic blowing apart
Vietnamese civilians trapped in a ditch, and then, as "some elastic time
went by," he is now forced to recall "sunlight and screams, then later . . . a
falling sensation, and after a moment he found himself at the bottom of
the irrigation ditch. He was in the slime. He couldn't move, he couldn't get
traction" (219–20). "The giggles seemed to lift him up" as Thinbill finally
calms him, but not without one last intrusion:

> The giggles were mostly gone. He folded his arms tight and swayed in
> the dark and tried not to remember the things he was remembering. He
> tried not to remember the ditch, how slippery it was, and how, much later,
> PFC Weatherby had found him there. "Hey, Sorcerer," Weatherby said. He
> started to smile, but Sorcerer shot him.
>
> "That's the ticket," Thinbill said. "Looking good. Whole lot better." (220)

As the chapter ends, the Chippewa GI, like Cacciato, ironically converts
hysterical giggling into therapy through comradely encouragement:
"Thinbill sighed. 'I guess that's the right attitude. Laugh it off. Fuck the
spirit world'" (220). Laughing off what they have gone through, however,
means covering up the most notorious war crime committed by Americans in Viet Nam, whereas Paul Berlin is simply trying to forget a com-

rade's death. Paul is afraid of dying, as Billy Boy Watkins's fate indicates that just being afraid can kill you. Wade, on the other hand, has killed others himself, even though "he didn't blame himself—reflex, nothing else—but still the notion of confession felt odd. No trapdoors, no secret wires" (218). He is not afraid of dying but of living with the revelation of what he has done as well as what he has witnessed. Berlin ultimately lays Billy Boy Watkins to rest; but Wade's attempt to bury his experiences at My Lai leads to their return, destroying his career and his life. The passage also recalls another American Indian comforting a buddy in "The Man I Killed" (*The Things They Carried*), but Tim O'Brien's victim is an enemy soldier, and neither he nor Kiowa has been a witness of crimes ordered by their commander and carried out by their comrades.

The revision of earlier scenes from the war into an historical evil is also effected by the brutal, almost offhand narration of Charlie Company's activities throughout *Lake* that makes little attempt to particularize its actions or humanize individual soldiers, even when they are victims rather than murderers; for example: "On February 25, 1968, they stumbled into a minefield near a village called Lac Son. 'I'm killed,' someone said, and he was" (105). The premassacre casualties cited above are no more than names in a list, since Sergeant George Cox, Dyson, and Hendrixson do not appear elsewhere in the novel. A description of the war in general just before these affectless traumatic incidents lacks the detail or involvement of similar characterizations in *Cacciato*, *Things*, or even *Combat Zone*: "The war was aimless. No targets, no visible enemy. There was nothing to shoot back at. Men were hurt and then more men were hurt and nothing was ever gained by it. The ambushes never worked. The patrols turned up nothing but women and kids and old men" (104). Doc Peret's description in *Cacciato* of the frustration is stylish as well as astute: "Aimless, that's what it is: a bunch of kids trying to pin the tail on the Asian donkey. But no fuckin tail. No fuckin donkey" (131). The commander of Charlie Company's is neither: "'Like that bullshit kid's game,' Rusty Calley said one evening. 'They hide, we seek, except we're chasin' a bunch of gookish fucking ghosts'" (104).

Wade's earlier connivance with the violence that finally boils over at Thuan Yen also darkens O'Brien's account of the war, which is represented as an obscenity in *Lake*. The first direct reference to his war experience appears in the chapter describing his relationship with Kathy at the University of Minnesota: "He graduated in June of 1967. There was a war in progress, which was beyond manipulation, and nine months later he found himself at the bottom of an irrigation ditch. The slime was waist-deep. He couldn't move. The trick then was to stay sane" (36). Wade kills PFC Weatherby from the slime, and many of the massacred are also slaughtered in a ditch, an unquiet grave that contaminates even as it covers up. The image recalls the shit field of *Things*: Unlike Kiowa, Wade emerges alive, but the rest of his life cannot efface the filth.

As Sorcerer, Wade is initially popular with his comrades, a would-be healer, a magician, a fortune-teller, blessed with "incredible good luck," "plugged into the spirit world" (38). But as the war goes on, his feats become increasingly violent, and O'Brien renders them sardonically, as when Charlie Company is hit with mortar fire and Sorcerer rounds up the nearby villagers for a magic show:

> He displayed an ordinary military radio and whispered a few words and made their village disappear. There was a trick to it, which involved artillery and white phosphorus, but the overall effect was spectacular.
>
> A fine, sunny morning. Everyone sat on the beach and oohed and ahhed at the vanishing village.
>
> "Fuckin' Houdini," one of the guys said. (65)

After he kills the sniper while in a berserk state, "the men in Charlie Company couldn't stop talking about Sorcerer's new trick" (40). In the aftermath, the nearby villagers are "summoned at gunpoint" as "Sorcerer and his assistants performed an act of levitation, hoisting the body high into the trees, into the dark, where it floated under a lovely red moon" (41). In Chapter 10, an abridged version of "The Things They Didn't Know" from *Cacciato* uses the mysteriousness of Viet Nam not simply to define the naïveté, fear, and ignorance of American GIs but to emphasize that "Sorcerer was in his element" (72): "It was a place where decency mixed intimately with savagery, where you could wave your wand and make teeth into toothpaste, civilization into garbage—where you could intone a few syllables over a radio and then sit back to enjoy the spectacle—pure mystery, pure miracle. . . ." (73).

As Charlie Company's casualties mount up, however, Wade's magic begins to fray, along with his connections to others. His impulsive killing of PFC Weatherby reverses his first action in the war, an attempt to calm a GI named Weber, mortally wounded through the kidney; but it also registers his ultimate alienation from his comrades, whose savagery at Thuan Yen he instinctively repudiates. Instead of pursuing justice, however, Wade joins the cover-up. He "thought he could get away with murder" by blaming Weatherby's death on the VC, and by doing so, of course, he mimics Calley's creation of nonexistent enemies: "He was convincing. He had tears in his eyes, because it came from his heart. He loved PFC Weatherby like a brother" (68). In fact, Wade despises his comrades even more than he hates himself, and writing himself out of Charlie Company is not just an act of self-protective disappearance but also a gesture of moral fastidiousness. The lack of individual details and the bitter tone of the war narrative in *Lake* contrast markedly with Paul Berlin's imaginary attempts to create comradeship in *Cacciato* or O'Brien's fabrication of the narrator's closeness to his buddies in *Things*. It reflects the perspective of someone who has tried to wink at brutality and murder and can never forgive himself or his companions.

O'Brien's reworking of *Northern Lights* and *The Nuclear Age* is as bleak as his revisiting Viet Nam in *Lake*, which is primarily a love story, not a war story. Like Paul Perry, John Wade is haunted by a dead father whose love and respect he could never satisfy. Unlike Perry, however, Wade is unable to gain an understanding of his father's character that would free him from unresolved guilt, grief, and anger: "At the funeral he wanted to kill everybody who was crying and everybody who wasn't. He wanted to take a hammer and crawl into the casket and kill his father for dying" (14). The setting of *Lake* directly recalls that of *Northern Lights*. O'Brien's earlier tale of family breakdown and personal recovery developed against the austere and threatening background of the northeast Minnesota Arrowhead; in *Lake*, the Wades' marital crisis comes to a head in the northwest angle, "gorgeous country, yes, but full of ghosts," where "everything is present, everything is missing" (289–90). The harrowing but quasi-redemptive ski trip of *Northern Lights* is metamorphosed into the Wades' disappearance in the wilderness just outside their cottage that reflects the dark secrets of John's buried past.

The last known trace of the protagonist is his final radio broadcast from the Chris-Craft that he pilots north into a blizzard, a final disappearing act in quest of his missing wife:

He offered a number of rambling incantations to the atmosphere, apologies and regrets, quiet declarations of sorrow. His tone was confessional. At times he cried. At dawn, just before signing off, he seemed to break down entirely. Not his mind—his heart. There were garbled prayers, convulsive pleas directed to Kathy and to God. He spoke bluntly to his father, whose affection he now demanded, whom he begged for esteem and constancy, and then near the end his voice began to sink into the lake itself, barely audible, little bubbles of sentimental gibberish: "Only for love, only to be loved . . . Because you asked once, What is sacred? and because the answer was always you. Sacred? Now you know . . . Where *are* you?" (305) [ellipses in the original]

Besides revising the parodic heroism of *Northern Lights* into pathetic tragedy, Wade's desolate final journey ironically revisits O'Brien's failure to flee the army in *Combat Zone* and "On the Rainy River" (*Things*)—but even if Wade could reach Canada, it is too late to escape. Without Kathy, his life is already over, and unless his final breakdown is the greatest trick of his life, it ends in the throes of endless trauma.

Perhaps it is *The Nuclear Age* that O'Brien revises most traumatically in his fifth novel. Like William Cowling, John Wade is so desperate for his wife's love that he tries to control and monitor her life. The couple's love and marriage are the subject of the three *Lake*-related short stories that O'Brien published before the novel: "The People We Marry" (1992); "Loon Point" (1993), which describes a wife's affair with a dentist more directly than in the novel, although the troubled couple in the story are named Ellie and John Abbot; and "How Unhappy They Were" (1994). For Wade, from the very beginning of his relationship with Kathy, "[t]he trick . . . was to make her love him and never stop. The urgency came from fear, mostly; he didn't want to lose her. Sometimes he'd jerk awake at night, dreaming she'd left him" (32). "Here I am," she once reassures him, "and I'm not going anywhere," but Wade remains traumatized by an earlier disappearance: "John shrugged and looked away. He was picturing his father's big white casket. 'Maybe so,' he said, 'but how do we know? People lose each other'" (32). While Cowling's lunacy leads him to coercively imprison his family, Wade's insecurity drives him to spy on Kathy before their marriage so that he can confirm his own anxieties. Like using magic to substitute for his

father's love, the spying allows him to control circumstances and eventually becomes a game that he pursues for its own sake until it is replaced
by the greater magic of politics. Like Bobbi, Kathy Wade eventually con-
firms her husband's insecurities by having a brief affair, which simply
makes his need to control her all the more desperate. Like Cowling's, the
overwhelming force of Wade's love is matched by its self-regard, but its effects are even more devastating. Kathy has an abortion for the sake of his
Senate candidacy, since "they were near the top of that mountain they'd
been climbing, almost there, one last push and then they'd rustle up a
whole houseful of kids" (158). And although Cowling ultimately saves his
family after his daughter saves him from himself, Kathy and John make
each other disappear. The dangerous intensity of his passion is ominously
reflected by a peculiar image frequently invoked by Wade, derived from
the "bizarre circle of appetites" (61) of two snakes that he saw swallowing
each other's tails on a trail in Viet Nam until a GI chopped them apart with
a machete. His reflection on the incident at the end of Chapter 10 ("The
Nature of Love") as, hyperaroused, he watches Kathy lying asleep next to
him "all night" anticipates the mysterious end of the two lovers: "[F]irst the
tails, then the heads, both of them finally disappearing forever inside each
other. Not a footprint, not a single clue. Purely gone—the trick of his life.
The burdens of secrecy would be lifted. Memory would be null. They
would live in perfect knowledge, all things visible, all things invisible, no
wires or strings, just that large dark world where one plus one will always
come to zero" (76–77).

John Wade as Paradigm and Persona: Tim O'Brien's Trauma

By reconstructing the mystery of John Wade as a study in self-destruction, *In the Lake of the Woods* becomes O'Brien's fullest fiction of traumatization as well as his first tragic novel. The narrator replicates O'Brien's art
as a trauma writer, but the result is a doubly fictive biography that formally reflects his failure to ever find its missing subject. But what accounts
for the hypothesis of traumatization? Ultimately, it derives from the experiences of both the narrator and his creator, who are reconsidering themselves as they create John Wade, revising their trauma as they put together
his. As noted in Chapter 1, the narrator of *Lake* has felt intimately the sudden impulse toward vengeful violence that overcame Charlie Company at

Thuan Yen, and he recalls it in a footnote to the text. At the end of his final chapter of "Evidence," the would-be biographer notes that representing Wade's experiences in Viet Nam helps him to recover his own, which
remain only as a barely recalled series of traumatic fragments:

> On occasion, especially when I'm alone, I find myself wondering if these old
> tattered memories weren't lifted from someone else's life, or from a piece of
> fiction I once read or once heard about. My own war does not belong to me.
> In a peculiar way, even at this very instant, the ordeal of John Wade—the
> long decades of silence and lies and secrecy—all this has a vivid, living clar-
> ity that seems far more authentic than my own faraway experience. Maybe
> that's what this book is for. To remind me. To give me back my vanished life.
> (301)

The narrator's realization that Wade's life re-creates his own is complemented by a suggestion that Wade can be understood only by understanding himself. One of the pieces of "evidence" included just before the
meditation above is a statement by a friend of the Wades, Ruth Rasmussen, that "they're gone and they're not coming back. Both of them. I
mean, honestly, some things you best walk away from, just shrug and say,
Who knows? . . . sooner or later you should think about getting back to
your *own* life. Don't want to end up missing it" (297–98). Reflecting in a
footnote on her advice to give up his "craving to know what cannot be
known," the narrator admits that "I know something about deceit. Far too
much. How it corrodes and corrupts. In her gentle way, I suppose, Ruth
Rasmussen was trying to tell me something both hard and simple. We find
truth inside, or not at all" (298). This insight defines the act of reading as
well as writing, of course. If the truth must be found within each of us,
then Wade's evasions, self-delusions, and covering up must be viewed as a
product of the narrator's self-knowledge, just as his "forgotten" war has
been revisited through Wade's trauma.

Whereas the narrator's investigation can at least depend on trying to
understand himself in order to re-create Wade, his reconstruction of Kathy
Wade is more difficult. Her sister Pat Hood is exasperated by his absorp-
tion with only one side of the mystery: "Always John! You're driving me
nuts! I mean, wake up. I get tired of saying it—*Kathy* had troubles, too, her
own history, her own damn life!" (266). Both the Wades are missing persons, but each of the attempts to imagine Kathy's fate, to reconstruct her

thoughts and motivations as she left her husband forever, is explicitly labeled "Hypothesis," as if the narrator were reflecting not only the absence
of any witness to what happened to her but his own presumption in trying
to read her mind. (The penultimate "Hypothesis," Wade's murder of Kathy,
might also be seen as an act beyond the narrator's understanding of Wade
or of himself.)

Kathy's sister objects to an androcentric narrative that privileges the
trauma of husband and soldier over that of his wife. So the narrator's explicitly hypothetical versions of Kathy's tragedy acknowledge the difficulty
faced by a male biographer and author in understanding and representing
a woman's experience. This recognition of Kathy's radical otherness replicates Wade's ignorance of fundamental aspects of the person closest to
him: For example, the narrator has discovered that she secretly hated participating in John's campaigns and was not unhappy about the end of her
husband's political career. That they have both kept crucial secrets from
each other shows how covering up pervades and can taint or distort even
the most intimate of relationships. Thus, although these various possible
scenarios of Kathy Wade's end—narrated from her point of view—are the
most conventionally realistic and coherent chapters in the novel, they are
paradoxically the most uncertain because the narrator cannot even attempt to know Kathy in the same way that he can try to understand
Wade—by examining his own dark secrets.

Since John Wade is partly created in the image of a narrator who is a
persona of O'Brien, he is also the author's fabricated counterpart. Indeed,
aspects of O'Brien's life have gone almost directly into the representation
of Wade. He has acknowledged turning to magic as a child, just like Wade,
in order to gain "love and applause, and to feel you have some control"
(Mort 1990) during a lonely childhood. The distinction between author
and character actually collapses in a self-description that appeared three
years before the publication of *In the Lake of the Woods*. "As a kid, through
grade school and into high school, my hobby was magic. I enjoyed the
power; I liked making miracles happen," O'Brien wrote, going on to describe his childhood feats:

> In the basement, where I practiced in front of a stand-up mirror, I caused my
> mother's silk scarves to change color. I used a scissors to cut my father's best
> tie in half, displaying the pieces, and then restored it whole. I placed a penny

in the palm of my hand, made my hand into a fist, made the penny into a white mouse. This was not true magic. It was trickery. But I sometimes pretended otherwise, because I was a kid then, and because pretending was the thrill of magic, and because for a time what seemed to happen became a happening in itself. I was a dreamer, I liked watching my hands in the mirror, imagining how someday I might perform much grander magic, tigers becoming giraffes, beautiful girls levitating like angels in the high yellow spotlights, naked maybe, no wires or strings, just floating. (Baughman 137)

With minuscule changes and pronoun substitutions—"John Wade" and "he" for "I," "his" for "my"—the same description appears at the beginning of the early story "The People We Marry," later rewritten as Chapter 7 of *Lake*, "The Nature of Marriage." In reviewing the novel in 1994, Jeff Danziger suggested that "O'Brien has been walking around inside John Wade's head for years, trying to discover where a man who was at My Lai would have hidden his memories." The terms of the first clause might also be reversed, judging from the extraordinary mirroring of author and fictional character quoted above. Whatever O'Brien's own experiences as a boy sorcerer, the process of representing them here through writing has eliminated the distinction between Wade and his creator.

O'Brien has pointed out that "my dad determined my behavior as much as Vietnam" (Mort 1990), and Tobey Herzog has traced the motif of "fathers and sons" throughout his works, culminating in *Lake*. Herzog's extensive 1995 interview with O'Brien uncovered important personal details of the author's life that are reproduced in John Wade's, including his father's alcoholism (Herzog 1997: 7–8), O'Brien's turning to magic as a means of escaping feelings of rejection by his father (9–10), and even Wade's intrusive nightmares, his self-hatred, and his "Kill Jesus" refrain (158). Both of the fathers, Paul Wade and William T. O'Brien, are also World War II veterans, making it an intimate duty for each son to serve in the bad war. O'Brien described his own sense of personal obligation directly in *Combat Zone* and then rewrote it as a desire to satisfy the father in Harvey Perry, Paul Berlin, and Norman Bowker.

The father-son relationship in *Lake* realizes darker possibilities than O'Brien's personal experiences, however. John Wade's father spends days drinking at the American Legion Hall, has to be committed to a sanatorium, and eventually kills himself, and his personal demons forever remain a mystery for his wife and his boy. John Wade never has the opportunity to satisfy his father, to reconcile with him, or even to understand him. As a result, he remains troubled by his spirit, a disturbing presence more powerful and unappeasable than any living father could be. His haunting recalls the Perry brothers' similar trauma, but the suicide of Paul Wade makes this son's agony even more unresolvable, charged with bewildered grief, anger, and guilt. O'Brien provides only one motive for John Wade's going to Viet Nam, a desire—impossible of achievement or satisfaction—to fulfill his need for a dead father's affection and approval: "It was in the nature of love that John Wade went to the war. . . . He imagined his father, who was dead, saying to him 'Well, you did it, you hung in there, and I'm so proud, just so incredibly goddamn proud'" (59–60). As noted in Chapter 1 above, the motivation echoes O'Brien's own explanation of why he went to the war in "The Vietnam in Me": "I have done bad things for love, bad things to stay loved" (52).

Besides these direct parallels, smaller details point to the creation of Wade as a darker version of his creator. "Eleanor" is the name of Wade's mother and the second name of O'Brien's; the writer's sister is named Kathy. The narrator has interviewed one of Kathy Wade's classmates in O'Brien's hometown, Worthington, Minnesota (194). In "The People We Marry," the earlier version of Chapter 7, Wade goes to Viet Nam in 1969, like O'Brien; and thus his subsequent participation in brutal actions, just like the author's, occurs in Quang Ngai Province *after* the My Lai Massacre. In the novel, however, Wade arrives in Quang Ngai in 1967, but he extends his tour after Thuan Yen in order "to lose himself in the war" (271), thus coming home in November 1969, so that his time in-country incorporates about half of O'Brien's single-year tour. Like his creator, Wade spends the last several months of his service as a clerk, which gives him the opportunity to change his identity by altering military records, rewriting himself out of Charlie Company and into Alpha Company—O'Brien's own company. Thus, not only does O'Brien rewrite himself as Wade, but Wade tries to rewrite himself as O'Brien, the personnel clerk for a company that has killed civilians but not murdered them. Just like O'Brien at the end of *Combat Zone*, Wade changes clothes in the airplane bathroom at the end of his flight home: "The flight to Minneapolis was lost time. Jet lag, maybe, but something else too. He felt dangerous. In the skies over North Dakota he went back into the lavatory, where he took off his uniform and put on a sweater and slacks, quietly appraising himself in the mirror. After a moment he winked. 'Hey, Sorcerer,' he said. 'How's tricks?'" (273). Both tangibly divest themselves of their identities as soldiers, but whereas O'Brien finds that he's still wearing combat boots and has carried Vietnam through his subsequent career as a writer, Wade needs to make his bad war disappear in order to pursue his dream of a career in American politics. As he begins his metamorphosis here, however, his words echo a scene at Thuan Yen that he will never be able to efface, and his attempts to make it vanish will ultimately destroy him: "[H]e found himself in the slime at the bottom of an irrigation ditch. PFC Weatherby looked down on him. 'Hey, Sorcerer,'" Weatherby had said and "started to smile" before Wade used his M-16 to make him disappear (64).

The mirror in which Wade examines himself here is agent and symbol of changing one's identity throughout *In the Lake of the Woods*. Like the one that O'Brien used for his magic tricks as a boy, it allows the magician to perfect illusions that an audience will believe in. It also serves as a stage prop to help make such illusions seem real. But it is also an instrument of self-regard and multiple identity. In the passage cited above, Wade sees an image of himself, a superficial double that is not the real person. Or is it? The mirror presents a reality that can understand itself only through reflections and that may be as deep, dark, and finally unknowable as its simulacrum is one-dimensional, bright, and insubstantial. Like the deep lake that mirrors the tangled and infinite recesses of the woods that it can only reflect, O'Brien's novel pervasively demonstrates the unknowability of human identity. Wade's father is a puzzle to himself and his mother; Kathy and John never understand each other; and the protagonist is a mystery not only to others but also to himself. Although we are made aware of Sorcerer's deliberate self-representations, the essential John Wade, assuming that there is one, remains in absentia. At the end of Chapter 12 ("Evidence"), footnoting the category of "Other" from the primary election results that destroyed Senator Wade's career, O'Brien's narrator queries, "Aren't we all? John Wade—he's beyond knowing. He's an other. For all my years of struggle with this depressing record, for all the travel and interviews and musty libraries, the man's soul remains for me an absolute and impenetrable unknown," and he concludes with the further realization that "our lovers, our husbands, our wives, our fathers, our gods—they are all beyond us" (103).

As this final statement indicates, the researcher's frustration is not simply a self-conscious trick by O'Brien to remind us that fictional characters are self-evidently unknowable. After all, one of the traditional powers of stories is to create characters whom we seem to understand better than most people we meet in our everyday lives. But the multiple mirroring of author, narrator, and protagonist in *Lake* suggests that knowledge of another—and even of ourselves—is always a fiction. O'Brien creates a version of himself trying to reconstruct a deeply flawed protagonist whose character and actions reflect both his fabricators. Since this receding of selfhood is further incarnated in Wade, the book multiply enacts human identity as an empty space that has been vacated. Furthermore, underlying the reconstruction of author, narrator, and protagonist are shameful and traumatic secrets that may be inexplicable to others or even irrecoverable for the subject himself. "I have done bad things for love," O'Brien revealed in "The Vietnam in Me," but they can only be reflected, not recovered. And if we "find truth inside, or not at all," then understanding others depends crucially on self-knowledge. Whether we believe that John killed Kathy or that they both committed suicide or that they began a new life together in Canada (the final chapter, and "Hypothesis," of the novel) depends on what we can believe of ourselves. In any case, the happy romantic ending proposed by the narrator would violate—cover up?—the reconstruction of John and Kathy Wade that he has fabricated out of the available facts and his own self-investigation. In that reconstruction, *Lake* has also drawn on Tim O'Brien's own trauma; but the case of John Wade, like that of John Paul Vann in *Bright Shining Lie*, illuminates dark aspects of his country's political history and culture also.

Psychobiography, History, and Fiction

O'Brien has characterized the writing of *Lake* as a personal and professional struggle (Elsen; Lee 200; Herzog 1997: 145); as noted above, he put it aside in order to complete *The Things They Carried.* Just after the publication of *Lake*, he began to consider giving up fiction altogether (Elsen, Mort 1991). As "The Vietnam in Me" reveals, crises in O'Brien's life may be reflected in the novel, including divorce from his wife after two decades of marriage, the breakup of another relationship at about the time the book was finished, and near-suicidal despair. In his interview with Jon Elsen,

O'Brien suggested that Wade's secrets are a revision of his own, given larger significance by fiction: "The deceits I write about in the book are magnified versions of the secrecy and deceit I practice in my own life, and we all do." One of his other intentions in *Lake* was to "write a book where craving for love can make us do really horrid things that require lifelong acts of atonement" and, he added, "[t]hat's why I write about Vietnam. It was given to me, and I'm giving it back." *In the Lake of the Woods* incorporates and culminates the trauma that was indirectly represented in *Combat Zone* and *Northern Lights* and was variously redemptive in the three subsequent novels even as it came closer to reflecting O'Brien's personal regrets. But John Wade carries burdens that go beyond even those of the Tim O'Brien who was left "with faceless responsibility and faceless grief" because he was "afraid to look" (*Things* 203).

An exaggerated version of potential darkness in O'Brien himself, Wade is a significant contrast to William Cowling, that exaggerated representation of O'Brien's desires for peace and domestic tranquility. Whereas Cowling flees the draft to save his life and his principles, Wade not only goes to Viet Nam willingly and participates eagerly at first but extends his service for another year to cleanse his soul. Cowling's political activities are radically antiwar, whereas Wade capitalizes politically on his official war record. Both figures represent extreme choices not taken by O'Brien, who fought in the war while hating it and came home to refashion its trauma. Wade's roles as a combat radio operator and then an army clerk mirror O'Brien's own quasi-writerly functions in Viet Nam, just as each became a magician, making use of the war in their subsequent careers and creating illusions to gain the admiration of their audiences. But Wade uses mirrors to deceive others and himself, whether in Viet Nam, politics, or marriage, and his black magic ultimately destroys him; by contrast, O'Brien has transformed Vietnam into a literary career that has tried to redeem the trauma of the war. He has refabricated Vietnam but told true war stories; his counterpart simply lied. And whereas Wade's disguises ultimately reduce him and Kathy to zero, O'Brien has productively re-created himself through his art.

If Cowling's story allowed O'Brien to imagine the courageous choice of fleeing from the war that he rejected, Wade's life presents more terrible possibilities. Yet Wade's apparent moral cowardice is at least as complexly realized as Cowling's apparent courage. John Wade is spiritually damned by the cover-up of his actions at Thuan Yen, not necessarily by the actions themselves: He killed a Vietnamese farmer who was raising a hoe that Wade mistook for a weapon, and he killed a fellow American who had slaughtered Vietnamese civilians, and later blamed his crime—or act of justice?—on the Viet Cong. He kills while traumatized by a horror that he is trying to flee; if he has murdered Kathy, his crime is an even more profound breakdown, the culmination of a psychic twisting that began in childhood. O'Brien ends the book with four questions for us to consider and no final answers: "Can we believe that he was not a monster but a man? That he was innocent of everything except his life? Could the truth be so simple? So terrible?" (306).

Although the hypothesis of traumatization is another permutation of self-reflective moral analysis by O'Brien, it does not excuse Wade's crimes any more than Cowling's nuclear trauma excuses the abuse of his wife and daughter. Indeed, the two figures are complements as well as contraries: Each is traumatized in childhood, and each ends up doing terrible things for love. Although both protagonists engage themselves directly in politics, their motives are self-protective and the results ultimately insubstantial. Cowling not only abandons antiwar activity but political involvement altogether and retreats into his personal fief in Montana. Wade builds a successful but hollow public career on vaguely liberal instincts that mask an otherwise purposeless drive for self-validation, and he transforms Kathy's dreams and desires into an adjunct of his own ambitions. Like Cowling's, his retreat from politics ends in a self-destructive madness that threatens him and those he loves. For Wade and Kathy, a happy ending would be sheer fantasy, but the comic resolution of *The Nuclear Age* is also an uneasy one, dependent on Cowling's attempt to wish away warheads and his ability to survive Bobbi's leaving him.

The skepticism about politics suggested by Cowling's and Wade's failures may reflect O'Brien's decision to abandon a Ph.D. in political science for a literary career. Like *The Nuclear Age*, however, *In the Lake of the Woods* openly handles American political history, and the American Historian's Cooper Prize validates its attempt at political fiction. Like the trauma narrative as a whole, its method is indirect, depending on the reader's imagination to consider the "Evidence" that supports its fabrication of John Wade. Instead of the canned history and monomaniacal self-justification of William Cowling, we are presented with an elusive record of testimony and texts excerpted from memoirists, biographers, historians, and psychologists that makes the case of John Wade a compilation of fragments from U.S. history and psychobiography. As a result, his trauma and tragedy resonate as a more significant metonym than Cowling's idiosyncratic breakdown.

H. Bruce Franklin has noted that political circumstances in the narrative are sketchy (43–44), but they are prophetically astute nonetheless. Being well-liked; avoiding hard choices; covering up unpleasant and embarrassing private secrets and actions; and successfully uncovering, manufacturing, alluding to, suggesting, or denying scandals have come to replace principles as the sine qua non for electoral success with American voters, and for staying in office, whether as senatorial candidate or as president. History is irrelevant in articulating policy, except where triumphalist or self-congratulatory, and Vietnam, taboo. O'Brien's "Evidence" chapters provide a darker gloss on the present fatuity. The My Lai Massacre is not simply a nightmarish fiction but a fact, as the documentary record attests in sickening detail. Rather than being an exception, the disaster in Viet Nam replicates other ugly wars in our history, as the excerpts from accounts of Sand Creek and the Little Big Horn attest. The testimony of British participants at Lexington and Concord, ashamed at the brutal war crimes of their comrades (262–64 passim), remind us of our own guerrilla war for independence against a great power, and the cries of Custer's terrified men begging for mercy (145–46) offer a tragic view of our history, not simply polemics.

Wade's loveless childhood, the need to satisfy a scornful father, the trauma of electoral repudiation, Kathy Wade's unhappiness as a "spectacular" political mannequin for her husband (163) are all paralleled by testimony by and about other American politicians and their wives from Al Smith to Pat Nixon in O'Brien's "Evidence." But Woodrow Wilson's need for love (28–29, 197), Lyndon Johnson's lying and demands for others' affection (28, 198), and Nixon's cover-ups and near-breakdown after Watergate (267–68) are perhaps the most significant analogies to John Wade's tragedy. We are left to consider the connections between psychological instability or trauma and the crooked course of America's crusade to remake the world in its own superficial mirror image from Wilsonian idealism to "peace with honor" in Viet Nam to creating a "multicultural" Balkans. Reflecting on the art of writing a biography, Freud proclaims that "truth is not accessible" in another piece of "Evidence" (294), and it is even more difficult to truthfully tell a nation's story. But the case of John Wade at least provides some traumatic fragments that cannot be repressed if we are to fabricate a more honest account.

Besides its excerpts from nonfiction texts, O'Brien's "Evidence" includes brief literary citations, ranging from Sophocles to Thomas Pynchon. "Man is bound to lie about himself," the narrator of Dostoevsky's *Notes from Underground* asserts (148), and in Edith Wharton's *Touchstone* we are reminded that "we live in our own souls as in an unmapped region, a few acres of which we have cleared for our habitation; while of the nature of those nearest us we know but the boundaries that march with ours" (193). Such extracts provide a grounding for O'Brien's characterization of John and Kathy Wade, but they also pay tribute to the power of fictions to investigate human nature, even when what we discover is the residue of guilt, shame, and deceit that makes all of us mysteries even to ourselves. With *In the Lake of the Woods*, O'Brien provides his own testimony of that dark enlightenment.

Although the novel seems to continue O'Brien's pattern of alternating books sited in Viet Nam with books that are situated in the United States, the distinction between war books and books that leave Vietnam behind is dissolved by his focus on the survival of trauma as a condition of late-twentieth-century American life as well as his own. Although *Combat Zone* takes its protagonist from American Midwest pieties to the bad war that has forever darkened his view of himself and his nation, the book is fundamentally a combat memoir, whatever its refigurations of personal experience. By contrast, *Northern Lights* seems to deliberately leave the war behind, using it only as undeveloped background to a narrowly focused account of family conflict and struggle against the elements. On the other hand, as O'Brien's decision to publish the original "Speaking of Courage" as an independent story indicates (see "Notes," 180–81, in *The Things They Carried*), *Going After Cacciato* deliberately never leaves Viet Nam except in Paul Berlin's imagination. His attempt to go home again through memory and fantasy produces a partly sentimental journey that Americanizes Vietnam more humanely but no less futilely than the real war. Conversely, although none of *The Nuclear Age* takes place in Viet Nam and its protagonist flees from the war, Vietnam in the larger sense of a political, moral, and cultural breakdown nearly dominates the book and Cowling's consciousness. As noted above, the only real bombs that detonate fall on Southeast Asia, and it is only after they do that Cowling fitfully enters politics. Thus, whereas *Cacciato* and *The Nuclear Age* focus on protagonists whose situations and decisions about going to Viet Nam seem completely different, Berlin's imagination is as attracted to going home as Cowling's is distracted by the inescapability of Vietnam.

Vietnam as a mental rather than physical or temporal setting is even more apparent in *The Things They Carried*, which is a radically postwar book despite its true war stories. In this work, Vietnam has become a permanent reality for its writer-protagonist, whose presence throughout works against any assumption that what we are reading is a conventional narrative of things that happened or that its subject is war. In a sense, the fictional setting is indeterminate, but if we had to identify it rigorously, it would be the narrator's memory or imagination or his bedroom or study or a lecture hall at least as much as it would be Viet Nam. *In the Lake of the Woods* carries even further O'Brien's development of a fictional continuum that combines post-Vietnam America and the war that ended in 1975. Physically, the novel is set in Minnesota in 1986, but it intrusively resituates us in Viet Nam and, more particularly, in the middle of the My Lai Massacre on March 16, 1968. Psychologically, its protagonist has staked his soul on erasing his actions in Viet Nam, which are literally unforgettable.

With the creation of John Wade, O'Brien has courageously and hauntingly considered some of the darkest possibilities that he could have chosen for himself—or that might have been forced upon him if he had gone to Viet Nam one year earlier than he did and was assigned to Charlie Company. *In the Lake of the Woods* provides at least imaginative closure for the moral trauma that began in *Combat Zone*, was variously rewritten in every work that followed, and is most pithily expressed in "On the Rainy River": "I was a coward. I went to the war" (*Things* 63). With the traumatic tragedy of John Wade complementing the traumatic comedy of William Cowling, O'Brien has investigated the other possibilities that his difficult choice avoided: fleeing the war or going willingly. While "The Vietnam in Me" directly demonstrates the power of writing to save his own life once more, his self-fabrications from *Combat Zone* to *In the Lake of the Woods* have already established a literary monument that would make further autobiography superfluous. Perhaps this accounts for his comments to John Mort in 1994 that "I feel I've completed the things I have to say about myself and the world I've lived in, and also I've completed a kind of search. I can't see anywhere else to go beyond where John Wade is" (1991). To Jon Elsen, O'Brien expressed similar desires to give up writing novels or even fiction in general, possibly turning to essays or other forms of nonfiction, as W. D. Ehrhart has done. Such a postfictional new direction is intimated in *Lake*, with its metafictive fragments of American history and political biography as unexamined trauma. In the meantime, however, O'Brien's ability to refabricate his personal experiences traumatically has taken a new direction in *Tomcat in Love*, turning away from wherever John Wade is by reshaping important elements of O'Brien's first truly tragic novel into his first true comedy.

CHAPTER 8

GUYS JUST WANT TO HAVE FUN

Vietnam and the Age of Clinton

Tim O'Brien's most recent novel hilariously extends his fictional explorations of post-Vietnam America into the Age of Clinton and postfeminism without leaving the Vietnam war entirely behind. In form, genre, and traumatic register, *Tomcat in Love* most closely resembles *The Nuclear Age*, O'Brien's first deliberately comic novel. Each is narrated by a traumatized protagonist who has lost his mind, but the later book is less explicitly self-important and more successful than the *Strangelove*-like black comedy of William Cowling's story. That work, intended to be a funny book about a terrifying subject but poised uncertainly between political polemic and nuclear age picaresque, had been less critically successful than O'Brien had hoped and perhaps less funny than he had believed. Its portentous and ambitious title contrasts strikingly with *Tomcat in Love*, a phrase whose small irony proved more attractive to O'Brien than the two alternatives he was considering as he finished the book in 1997: "A Dictionary of Love" and "In Defense of Thomas Chippering" (telephone conversation, April 10, 1997). The two discarded titles remain fundamental to characterization and structure in *Tomcat,* however. The first not only alludes to the protagonist's detailed ledger of would-be romantic conquests but is also embodied in the book's chapter titles, nearly all of them a single word. Moreover, as a former linguistics professor, Chippering thinks lexicographically, and his inner dictionary comprises not only traces of personal trauma but also the freely associative structure of O'Brien's narrative. The second working title would have defined the book as fictional autobiography intended as explanation and self-justification, just as *The Nuclear Age* is William Cowling's apologia for entombing himself and his family in order to save them all.

It was Chippering's voice—minimaniacally solipsistic, preening itself fastidiously on its own pretensions to intellectual and erotic mastery when not breaking down into childish self-pity, resentment, or rage—that O'Brien found most compelling during his work on the book. As noted in the introduction above, he has been particularly pleased to have successfully imagined a figure so different from himself. Nonetheless, Thomas Chippering is the latest fictional revision of the author who has created him. O'Brien's divorce, the emotional desolation of losing his partner Kate Phillips, and the persistence of Vietnam as a psychic wound lie behind the fabrication of Chippering, who spends most of the novel plotting vengeance upon his first wife and her second husband while being haunted by the war and occasionally visited by its phantoms. Even Chippering's academic vocation was one of O'Brien's postwar professional options as he entered graduate school at Harvard in the 1970s. However, like Cowling's flight to escape the war and John Wade's political use of his status as a veteran, O'Brien rejected a possible career in academia in favor of writing about Vietnam.

The mutually corrosive experiences of Vietnam and lost love were at the heart of *In the Lake of the Woods*, of course, and in our April 1997 telephone conversation O'Brien characterized *Tomcat* as a rewriting of its predecessor. Like Wade, Chippering is an insecure and deceptive husband who suffers a professional and personal breakdown as his marriage crumbles. Instead of the bleakly tragic scenario of *Lake*, however, *Tomcat* has a cartoonlike quality that is appropriate to its hero's relatively buffoonish downward spiral and his ultimately soft landing. Dismissed from the University of Minnesota on charges of sexual harassment after his wife Lorna Sue has divorced him, Chippering is punished for his largely imaginary offenses through a series of public humiliations: a bare-assed spanking in front of his final class of undergraduates; being fired on the testimony of two coeds for whom he has written theses without being monetarily or sexually compensated; being reprimanded for trying to teach Shakespeare in his subsequent job at a day-care center, where he is apparently falsely charged with fondling toddlers; having a nervous breakdown on live public-access television as he competes for a position as host of a children's cartoon show; and, ultimately, being institutionalized in a state of self-willed, posttraumatic silence. "I begin with the ridiculous," Chippering intones in the first sentence of the novel, a word that he further defines in Chapter 9, and *Tomcat in Love* is unashamed to revel in the ridiculous even as it shows how seriously it may be taken.

The publication of *Tomcat* in fall 1998 coincided with another ridiculous yet serious subject that was to draw questions from O'Brien's audiences during his subsequent public readings from the novel. Like Bill Clinton, Thomas Chippering undergoes public humiliation as a result of erotic indiscretions and attempts to exculpate himself through idiosyncratic technical definitions of sexual relationships; like Clinton's, Chippering's claims to being an advocate for women are undercut by others' opinions that he is a sexual harasser; and just as Clinton disgraced himself with an intern young enough to be his daughter, Chippering's vocation includes variously ogling university coeds or any other younger woman whose eyes meet his. Unlike Chippering, Clinton did not lose his job, and his ordeal had important public and constitutional consequences. Yet the impeachment crisis of 1998–99 was very different from that of 1973–74. "Ridiculous" would not inaccurately define Clinton's deplorable conduct and self-defense, but it would be at least as applicable to his maladroit and fustian tormentors, from the puritanically voyeuristic, nationally despised "special counsel" to the often clownish House "managers."

Of course, the American news media and entertainment industries have contributed enthusiastically to the profitable spectacle of American politics in the 1990s. Long before the Monica Lewinsky follies, the president had presented himself on MTV, orchestrated phony "town meetings" that were broadcast to more important media centers, and seen himself become an object of entertainment. The novel *Primary Colors* presented a thinly disguised Clinton clone, and John Travolta became the presidential double in the movie version. Another film, *Wag the Dog*, was actually cited during impeachment hearings as an analogue to Clinton's poll-driven foreign policy, and its scenario of a video invasion of Albania became preternaturally prescient with Operation Allied Force, during which the film was repeatedly shown on Serbian television. Indeed, from a perspective that the White House must have hoped would someday become mythologized, Kosovo was Clinton's Vietnam, a successful mirror image of that failed "liberal" war. Here, by contrast, America righteously took the side of indigenous guerrillas, prevented the fall of Balkan dominoes, and redeemed the president's historical standing from the ridicule of Monicagate and the contempt aroused in right-wing covens by the president's earlier "draft dodging."

Whatever O'Brien's ostensibly narrower intentions in *Tomcat in Love*, Chippering's fall reflects something in the cultural and political air of millennial, post-Vietnam America that is both ridiculous and portentous. Playing war games as a seven-year-old, Tommy and his best friend Herbie Zylstra imagine bombing runs on the Zylstra home. Humiliated and traumatized in Viet Nam by his comrades, Thomas Chippering calls in an air strike on their own position to avenge himself and leaves just in time to award himself the Silver Star for valor after his act of terror. Divorced by his wife, the forty-something-year-old Tomcat plots to frighten her, her family, and her second husband with firebombs after an earlier plot against them has led to his public disgrace. Like the childhood mason jars intended to blow up the Zylstra household, Chippering's bombs never killed anyone, he assures us; they were intended merely to frighten, not murder. Nor would the later firebombing, which is ultimately aborted, have been lethal, Chippering insists: "I did not wish to kill. Only to rock the complacent Zylstra world, alert them to the consequences of tampering with the spiritual well-being of Thomas H. Chippering" (248).

However comically pathological O'Brien's protagonist might seem, a tendency to use or threaten to use bombs—or sawed-off shotguns, semiautomatic rifles, or handguns—to avenge perceived slights and grievances against others has become an American disease over the past two decades. The explosive fantasies of Herbie and Tommy are not simply child's play, as the periodic eruptions of "senseless" male violence by schoolboys, disgruntled employees, and former soldiers such as Timothy McVeigh make clear. Moreover, such rites to bear arms are complemented by what passes for effective American foreign policy these days. Chippering's desire for bombs that will destroy buildings but not people, terrorize but not kill, parodies the development of "smart" munitions technologies from the neutron bomb to laser-guided warheads of the sort that Americans have been dropping from Iraq and the Sudan to Belgrade. Clinton's cost-free interventions outnumber those of the preceding Reagan and Bush administrations, and if the Yugoslavian dead and wounded had only matched the number of NATO military casualties, Operation Allied Force would have been the "perfect war" (James William Gibson's phrase) that the United States failed to carry out in Viet Nam. Reviewing *Tomcat* for *The New Statesman,* Phil Whitaker identifies such "political dimensions" as part of its satiric force and suggests (perhaps a bit too categorically) that they reflect a contradictory state of foreign affairs that derives from the unresolved trauma of the bad war: "America today is governed by a generation still smarting from the ignominy of Vietnam; somewhere in her collective national psyche she longs for the chance to exorcise and avenge the shame of that humbling war. She also finds herself cast in the role of global police officer, intervening in ill-understood conflicts in far-off theatres" (45).

While government of, by, and for entertainment is only lightly reflected in Chippering's updated linguistics courses (e.g., "Your Thick Tongue," "Methodologies of Misogyny"), the aging Tomcat's erotic fiascoes also point to a new sexual politics that is only just emerging in American public life and that Clinton's ability to address women's issues and encourage his own wife's senatorial campaign has begun to define. At the same time, like millions of middle-aging male baby boomers, the impeached president and the terminated professor "just don't get it," to use the inescapable mantra of the Age of Clinton. Women's best friend turns out to be a dirty old man, an adherent to the Playboy Philosophy as well as the bridge builder to the twenty-first century. Chippering claims that he has "long and proudly marched" in the "ranks" of "the feminists of our world" (124). Defining himself later as a "lifelong victim of the most ferocious male jealousies and insecurities," he laments that "only women, alas, seem to appreciate my quirky virtues" and concludes his critique of gender with a grateful panegyric: "Thank heavens for the gentler sex. Politics and physique aside, I could cochair a NOW convention or take my seat at any midafternoon kaffeeklatsch" (276). The condescending terms of this rhapsody and the way it horns in on its objects of desire undercut the sincerity of the appraisal, however. Elsewhere, Chippering rails in Rush Limbaugh fashion against the "feminist flies buzzing at my buttocks, those jackbooted squads of Amazon storm troopers denouncing my indefatigable masculinity" (218), and typically vents his appreciation of the "weaker sex" (151) in brief catalogs of attracting body parts. In sum, Chippering is an incorrigible son of baby-boom America, like Clinton himself, an inheritor of male privilege who can only awkwardly adapt himself to the gender revolution. Whether playing with bombs or ogling cleavage, his gestures parody an old and young boys' network whose contradictions threaten its survival in the new century and whose dissolution may be both gracefully liberating and desperately destructive. *Tomcat in Love* is a brilliant lexicon of both alternatives.

A Dictionary of Love

Introducing his Ann Arbor reading from the novel in 1998, O'Brien claimed that "I've never been very interested in plots in my works." The fragmentary, asynchronous narratives of all of O'Brien's books after *Northern Lights* deliberately mimic the phenomenal and psychological condition of traumatization, however, and *Tomcat* is no exception. Even compared with his predecessors', however, Chippering's is a remarkably incoherent life story. Its first chapter ("Faith") begins with two traumatic childhood experiences in 1952, when Tommy was seven years old, fast-forwards to his divorce four decades later, and ends with a grammar school kiss at the age of twelve. The trauma of 1952 is supplemented later in the narrative by two earlier scenes from childhood, so that the life events of Chapter 1, like those throughout the book, have no clear and discrete point of origin or closure. *Tomcat* is the most formally "plotless" and "pointless" of O'Brien's trauma narratives, its employment of fragmentation, truncation, repetition, recovery, and re-covering even more extensive than in previous books.

Chippering justifies his digressiveness at the beginning of Chapter 7, which moves from springtime in Minnesota, sometime in the 1990s, to late fall in Viet Nam, 1969: "The shortest distance between two points may well be a straight line, but one must remember that efficiency is not the only narrative virtue. Texture is another. Accuracy still another. Our universe does not operate on purely linear principles" (56). This typically pedantic justification is followed immediately by an appeal to the experience of the reader, who is invoked here and elsewhere as a *female* counterpart to Chippering, traumatized by her husband's having abandoned her for a younger woman: "Bear in mind, too, the story of your own botched life, its circularities and meanderings, how your thoughts sometimes slide back to that dismal afternoon when you introduced your husband to a lanky

young redhead named Suzanne or Sandra or Sarah—let us settle on Sandra—and how you watched the two of them chat over coffee, and how at
one point it occurred to you that they might be getting along rather too
well. . . . We move forward by looping briefly backward" (56), he concludes,
a parodic epitome of trauma therapy, before finally beginning his Vietnam
narrative.

Throughout the novel, Chippering's endless lecturing irritates and
alienates his fictional audiences. Continuing his Vietnam testimony for
the benefit of a Tampa hotel janitor in Chapter 19, for example, the professor ultimately loses his listener, who, having been promised "sound and
fury" after he complains that Chippering's "tale . . . seems told by a goddamn idiot" (163), eventually falls asleep. This digressiveness can be taxing
for O'Brien's readers as well—Michiko Kakutani's impatient review called
Tomcat a "mangled mess." Her dissatisfaction with the novel, like her earlier dismissal of *The Nuclear Age* and its "tedious, long-winded hero," condemns the narrator as "not only a boor" but also "a big bore." Tim O'Brien
is neither, of course, and other reviewers, including other fiction writers,
have been surprised and delighted with his representation of a boring
boor. Jane Smiley was grateful that O'Brien has risked himself on a comic
novel for the new millennium (12), and the English novelist Phil Whitaker
found *Tomcat* "complex and enthralling" (46).

Despite their dissimilarities, however, the pedantic professor and his
creator are authorial equivalents. Chippering is represented as the writer of
his own testament by the end of the novel, somewhat to the reader's surprise. Divorced and disgraced but exiled in a Caribbean paradise with his
recently divorced bride-to-be, the aging Tomcat works on his life-in-prog-
ress: "Mrs. Robert Kooshof makes pottery. I prune the bougainvillea, culti-
vate vegetables, fine-tune this personal record. In the evenings we con-
sume fresh fish, a drink or two, and very often each other. . . . Occasionally,
should inspiration strike, I will jot down a memory or two, or a telling footnote to this volume. But for the most part I watch the aqua bay" (341–42).
As the compiler of the life history that we have just read, Chippering
enacts O'Brien's own activity, despite the obvious physical, ethical, and
professional differences between them. Moreover, telling phrases throughout the novel suggest a writerly correspondence between the "idiot" who
has told this tale and the trauma artist who has created him: "I had wanted
to be a cowboy, for God's sake, but here I was, a peddler of the English lan-

guage," Chippering laments after his first wife has divorced him (49); "I'm a
wordsmith . . . It takes time," (78) he explains to Mrs. Robert Kooshof, her
successor, to justify what seems to her another pointlessly digressive childhood narrative in Chapter 9; and near the end of his life story, Chippering
defines himself as "a man who lives by words, a man whose very being
amounts to little more than language" (339). Such self-identification defines
Tim O'Brien's own writerly identity as well as that of the former linguistics
professor, in whose "well-informed view . . . the dictionary stands as our supreme book of books, an embodiment of both civilization and the very
idea of civilization" (88). Lexicography fashions not only the novel's thirty-
seven chapter titles (from "Faith" [Chapter 1] to "Fiji" [Chapter 37]) but also
much of their content, the eighty or so entries that make up Chippering's
internal dictionary. In *Tomcat*, iconic, prenarrative fragments of traumatic
events have been reduced to solitary words, each the trace of a threatening
experience that remains a verbal wound within Chippering's psyche, a
trigger of past humiliations and present resentments that range from "An-
gel" (his wife's term for him before their divorce) to "Zylstra" (her maiden
name). Chippering's "dictionary of love" is thus a lexicon of trauma, each
word prompting past memories of self-diminishment, exposure, or betrayal
that are obsessively renarrated throughout the book. Its composition thus
becomes Chippering's personal posttraumatic therapy.

"Faith," the only portion of the novel to appear before its publication,
epitomizes this traumatic lexicology, presenting primal sites of traumatization that are never fully outgrown and that pervade the rest of the narrative. Its opening scenario ("in June 1952, middle-century Minnesota") has
serious ramifications, although Chippering now regards as "ridiculous"
"that silvery-hot morning when Herbie Zylstra and I nailed two plywood
boards together and *called it* [emphasis added] an airplane." The boys
spend the summer painting their airplane green and clearing a runway,
waiting for Mr. Chippering to deliver the "engine" that he has promised.
Whereas Herbie wants to bomb, Tommy simply wants to fly, inspired by
the magic associated with a single word: "At night, in bed, I would find myself murmuring that powerful, empowering word: *engine*. I loved its sound.
I loved everything it meant, everything it did not mean but should" (2). But
when his father finally brings home a pet turtle named Toby and invites
the boys to pretend that it is an engine, Herbie is contemptuous and
Tommy deeply embarrassed. His compensating ploy to drop Toby as a

bomb on the mailman is dismissed by Herbie, who bitterly reminds his chum that "your dad's still a liar, Tommy. They all are. They just lie and lie. They can't even help it. That's what fathers are *for*. Nothing else. They lie" (5). Herbie's hostility toward paternal authority—symptomatized by dreams of bombing his own house—is carried further by his scheme to convert the now discarded "airplane" into a "cross" and nail his seven-year-old sister Lorna Sue to it. More than forty years later, near the end of *Tomcat*, Herbie explains to Chippering that he was simply testing the ultimate Father to see whether he was as bogus as his earthly substitutes: "I didn't mean to hurt her, you know. It was like an experiment or something, like research. I was just so goddamned *curious*. Wanted to see if she'd go to heaven. If I'd go to hell. If the skies would open up. *Curious*" (320).

The abortive crucifixion of Lorna Sue Zylstra is the primal trauma of *Tomcat*, a wounding that never goes away for its participants. Tommy assists initially, but after his mother interrupts the first attempt, he receives a tongue-lashing from his parents while composing a silent apology "that I had never really believed in any of it, that I was almost positive that Herbie would not have hammered those nails through Lorna Sue's pretty brown hands" (7). But Herbie does nail his sister later—"the left palm. Halfway through. Almost dead center" (7)—although Tommy is "not there to witness it. All I can attest to is the sound of sirens. Voices too, I think. And maybe a scream. But maybe not" (8).

The psychic consequences of the crucifixion remain both pervasive and obscure throughout *Tomcat*, a trauma narrative that Chippering misinterprets but that neither he nor we can fully understand. Herbie is sent away to Jesuit reform school and comes back transformed: rigid with "a stern, self-flagellating religiosity" (38) and so closely tied to his sister, who becomes Tommy's wife, that Chippering comes to accuse him of incest. The wounding subversively parodies both the Crucifixion and prefeminist relationships between the sexes. Rather than fleeing from her brother's game, Lorna Sue is eager to participate. "Sunday school, . . . I get to be Jesus" (6), she enthusiastically informs Tommy's mother when Mrs. Chippering intervenes to interrupt the children the first time. The traumatic rite replaces male with female divinity, but it effects adoration through abuse and empowers by crippling. Heroine yet victim, Lorna Sue becomes an object of sacred devotion for the guilty brother who had wounded her as well as the husband who had failed to protect her.

The symptoms of Lorna Sue's traumatization are played out myste-
riously through the rest of the novel. She is damaged both physically and
psychically in ways that can never be fully understood or healed by either
brother or husband and that are both self-destructive and aggressive. The
tiny wound becomes a stigma that she picks at and reopens whenever she
is verbally censured by her first husband. Such self-mutilation is a characteristic posttraumatic symptom of childhood sexual abuse (van der Kolk
202), and in a footnote near the end of the novel Chippering approaches
the ineffable truth when he compares the relationship between Lorna Sue
("forever the maimed girl-goddess") and Herbie ("forever her guardian and
caretaker") to his own infatuation with Little Red Rhonda, one of his
countless objects of desire, who had been sexually abused by her father
yet continues to "keep chasing perverted old fruitcakes." "A common
phenomenon," Chippering is at last able to recognize, including himself
among the erotically dysfunctional: "I cannot exclude myself from this re-
dundant psychological paradigm. Again and again, over the course of a
lifetime, I seem to have repeated certain fundamental mistakes" (336).

In Chapter 16, mentally picking at the "scab" of their seventh wedding
anniversary, Chippering recalls how Lorna Sue had celebrated the occa-
sion with a surprise party arranged by Herbie to which he, her husband,
was not invited. Angrily taking her home after midnight, Chippering accuses her of hurting him again, only to have his wife pull out a fountain
pen and jab herself with it five times, licking the blood away and explaining that "sometimes I want to hurt *you* that way, Tom. And Herbie. Everybody" (133). The stigmata both repeat and reject the original wounding,
proliferating its violence both masochistically and aggressively. Her counterviolence expresses itself in periodic firebombings of Catholic churches
and the desecration of religious statuary with lipstick, including painting
breasts on images of Christ. Her brother conceals or takes responsibility
for Lorna Sue's public outbursts and evidently mitigates her private breakdowns so well that they remain enigmatic to Chippering until the end of
the novel. Her apparently pathological behavior, which radically extends
her brother's childhood rebellion against untrustworthy patriarchs, epitomizes the rejection of male erotic and ideological authority that Chippering encounters throughout the novel.

Herbie's love for his sister is ultimately not erotic, but neither is it successfully therapeutic. Intending to ensure Lorna Sue's happiness, to pro-

tect her from harming herself or others, he provides the grounds for her divorce from Chippering and takes responsibility for her violence against the Church. A second marriage, to a Tampa real estate magnate, seems much more successful than her first but ultimately leaves her no less unsatisfied. In the end, Herbie's protectiveness proves no more redemptive than his guilt, and he finally leaves her to find her own happiness, which is also the only way that he can begin to live his own life as an adult.

The bewilderment and resentments of Chippering within this traumatized triad take up the rest of "Faith." The abortive childhood bombing campaign concludes with the traumatic signifier *turtle*, whose "twin syllables still claw" (3) at the middle-aged narrator more than forty years later. Additional entries in Chippering's dictionary of love include *corn*, *Pontiac*, and *Indian* (all associated with his first, grotesquely uncomfortable experience of sex with Lorna Sue at the age of sixteen, sprawled upon the icy hood of his father's car in a deserted October cornfield, under the gaze of its Native American hood ornament); *tycoon* (the only name Chippering will use to refer to Lorna Sue's second husband, as if effacing his real name—"Kersten"—could make him disappear); *Tampa* (the new home of Lorna Sue and the tycoon, and a city that Chippering visits in order to spy on them and plot his revenge); *plywood*; and *engine*. The experiences recalled by these lexical wounds appear briefly as allusions or truncated scenes throughout Chapter 1; repetitively elaborated throughout the rest of the novel, such asynchronous fragments and intrusive recollections constitute the trauma narrative of *Tomcat* as a dictionary of past frustrations and embarrassments recalled in the present.

Thus, Chapter 6 ("Substance") is introduced by Chippering as a reflection on a single word and gradually assumes narrative sequence as it strings together a series of scenes from childhood up to his first encounter with Mrs. Robert Kooshof, his eventual partner, who has discovered him crying in the backyard of his childhood home—which she now owns—after Lorna Sue has divorced him. As the fragmentary narrative moves back and forth from childhood to the present, it also careens lexically from his father's *substance* in his memory to *lizard/crocodile/reptile* (alternative epithets for his disloyal former wife) to the man of *substance* for whom she has deserted him to the *assumption* of arson that he hopes will lead the Tampa police to question and thus traumatize Herbie for his church bombing—guilty or not—to *boring* (defined in Chippering's personal dictionary by his hometown) to the buxom woman of *substance* who admits him to her house, kitchen, and bed and with whom he is plotting further vengeance against Lorna Sue, Herbie, and the tycoon at the end of the chapter.

Chapter 9 ("Cat") also begins as if it were a classroom lecture: "Let us pause over the word *ridiculous*. It is worth noting—would you not agree? —that our lives are often sculpted by the absurd, the unlikely, the purely fortuitous" (70). The subsequent account of his accidentally dropping Lorna Sue's cat to her death when he was seven years old irritates Mrs. Kooshof, to whom it is narrated, because of its fixation on his former wife, tedious circumstantiality, and apparent meaninglessness. But it constitutes his first lie to his future wife—he tells Lorna Sue that he dropped Vanilla because the cat scratched him—as well as his first failure to live up to her expectations of him. It thus anticipates his losing her "four decades later" (77), when she discovers underneath their mattress her husband's secret love ledger of promiscuous infatuations for younger women as well as a collection of uncashed checks made out to a nonexistent psychiatrist whom Chippering has pretended to be seeing in order to treat his paranoid suspicions about Lorna Sue's relationship with her brother. Divorce follows the double discovery, which Herbie has revealed to his sister. Since Mrs. Kooshof has "missed the point" (78), Chippering concludes his ridiculous account by spelling out for the reader its traumatic affiliations:

> A pattern was established on that Saturday morning. Issues of trust, issues of faith.
>
> If necessary, we will lie to win love. We will lie to keep love.
>
> (*Cat* becomes *mattress*.) (78)

Yet the cover-up continues in "Cat"; Chippering dares not mention the ledger, which he is continuing to supplement, to Mrs. Kooshof, for fear of losing her. When she does find out about it later ("Ledger," Chapter 20), her fury with her incorrigible Tomcat forces him to meet the crisis by proposing marriage.

"Faith," the title of the first chapter, is the most important word in the novel and its most important value. The mock crucifixion establishes a posttranscendent world in which everyone is seeking love "in odd places" (Fasman) and bearing their own scars and wounds of infidelity and violated personal trust. While Chippering's erotic misadventures may deny that "love is all you need," O'Brien's parodic treatment of religious belief suggests that love is what most of us should settle for. "Catholicism" is a metaphor for pathology in the novel, and Chippering's only return to his lapsed faith occurs in a hotel chapel on his way back from a urinal to a hotel bar where he has been sobbing out the story of his life to two sympathetic prostitutes and his former departmental secretary:

> For some time I simply sat there: half inebriated, soul-sick.
>
> Dumbly, I murmured the word *faith*, as if the utterance itself might awaken something in me. But nothing much occurred, just an incoherent buzz in my blood. . . .
>
> A lifelong quest for love—a ledger full of names and dates—and it all ended here in the sad sanctuary of a Ramada Inn.
>
> I saw nothing blasphemous in removing my shoes and stretching out for a short nap. (229–30)

"Faith" enters the novel literally in the final episode of Chapter 1, preceded by the traumatic signifier *mice*, as Chippering recalls how he and Faith Graffenteen had kissed each other at the age of twelve. "[S]he puked *mice*," Lorna Sue tells her faithless boyfriend, accusing him of "suck[ing] out all her snot," while he claims innocence ("Faith *made* me," he protests) (17). The incident comically recalls, anticipates, and epitomizes a life that has been traumatized by the exposure of its own desperate and often dishonest search for love.

Chippering's dictionary of love includes not only the lexicon of erotic frustration that is *Tomcat* but also the ledger of erotic activity that he begins at least as early as middle school and that he has supplemented and revised for almost four decades. A detailed personal record of significant encounters, painstakingly categorized (name, date, phone number, body type, hair color, state of origin, a mystery ethnic identity, etc.), Chippering's scorebook ("an ego booster," he calls it) is prodigious only in its quantity: 1,788 meaningful gazes at the cost of 2,200 full-course meals, over 17,000 beverages, and 15 boxes of chocolates—but resulting in only four home runs ("Or three. Depending [160]") and one marriage (later dissolved) (figures from pages 160–61, 172, and 232). Parodying male pornography and phallic tall tales as well as erotic fiction, Chippering's pathetic personal record is sign and symptom of unhappiness and ineffectuality as well as emotional and gonadic faithlessness, and its final revelation to Lorna Sue becomes her final justification for divorce. Chippering's big black book continually intrudes past trauma and threatens a new breakdown in Chapter 20 ("Ledger") after Herbie has handed it over to Mrs. Robert Kooshof.

Chippering's relationship with her provides his dictionary with its only success. Separated from her abusive and imprisoned husband, a veterinarian and tax cheat, Mrs. Kooshof rescues Tom from his postdivorce despair by putting up with and outlasting his pathological adoration of Lorna Sue and his schemes to either win her back or avenge himself. Chippering only reluctantly gives up his obsessions, however. Not only must Mrs. Kooshof uncover and then forgive the half-truths and deceptions of her "sponging, freeloading, ungrateful, oversexed tomcat" (284), she must force him to accept his own happiness, which is marked by broadly comic sexual romps that O'Brien piquantly celebrates in Chippering's outrageously priapic verbal ejaculations (e.g., "She gummed and gnawed—did everything but swallow—and for ten momentous minutes we were most literally and thoroughly engaged. Cemented, in fact. Glued. At the ultimate moment, as I alighted in paradise . . ." [184]). His movement from cohabitation to proposal to ring to eventual wedding is digressive and vertiginous, however, and only at the end of the novel is his future wife's name—"Donna"—finally beginning to replace "Mrs. Robert Kooshof" in Chippering's dismal lexicon. His usual epithet defines her as a mistress, cook, and caretaker who is someone else's wife. The former, pedantically glossed by the linguistics professor as her "Christian, semi-Moorish name" (345), not only recognizes her independent identity, but its obvious Italian meaning is far more relevant than his etymology. At the age of at least forty-nine, the childish Tomcat has finally grown up enough to acknowledge his satisfaction with a "woman."

In Defense of Thomas Chippering

Like William Cowling's testament, Chippering's dictionary is also an apologia, an explanation and justification for his personal obsessions. Trying to explain his love ledger to the rest of us, the narrator treats his unsuccessful philandering as the nearly autonomic result of a short circuit in his erotic wiring, so that "like some horrid cancer, the need for affection multiplied into a voracious, desperate, lifelong craving. . . . In my defense, however," he continues, "I must quickly declare one other fundamental truth: the motive was never physical. Repeat: *never!* The motive was love. Only love" (160). Chippering's self-defense culminates in one of the balance sheets cited above, where the paltry total of "carnal relations" is immeasurably outnumbered by debits. "And yet," he concludes, "I had to keep fueling the furnace, refilling the hole, topping off my leaky love tank" (161). His pursuit of verbal intercourse with every coed, secretary, or shop girl that he finds attractive, during and after his marriage with Lorna Sue and even while he is luxuriating most nights in Mrs. Robert Kooshof's bed, is symptomatic of his dysfunction but also undercuts his self-defense. In all these cases, Chippering represents himself as both irresistible and victimized, imagining signs of immediate infatuation in every glance and vindicating himself as an innocent Tomcat pursued and continually betrayed by lovestruck females.

Chippering's language gives him away, however, because every one of his female interlocutors is hailed carnally despite his various protestations of innocence, victimization, need to be loved, or romantic sentiment. Thus, Toni, "with an *i*, short for Antonia with a pair of firmly bracketing *a*'s" (89), with whom Chippering conducts private seminars to advise her on her senior thesis (a comparative study of the language of marriage vows!), ultimately blackmails him into writing it for her by threatening him with sexual harassment charges. There *are* no overt gestures, words, or actions, but *we* are privy to her tutor's characterization of "the comely Toni," "worshipful," "erotic," a "little marshmallow," and "luscious little fraud" with "long and shapely legs" and "a black skirt cut high over waxy brown legs" (89, 93–95, 121). Although her lovemaking makes such blazons less fetishistic, even his bride-to-be is inventoried, from his first sight of her ("Mid-thirties. Blond hair. Blue eyes. Long legs. Busty as Nepal" [52]) to later appraisals: "Powerful Dutch thighs," "Breasts to float a navy" (68). Chippering's continual verbal ogling comically, tastelessly alerts us not only to his startling lack of self-awareness and his skill at self-serving rhetoric but also to his unreliability as a narrator. On a literal level, his jokes about his companion as a "Dutch treat" are not even etymologically correct, since "Kooshof" is her husband's name, after all, and he seems oblivious to her fuller identity until he discovers that she is actually an "O'Neill," the daughter of a governor of South Dakota and an heiress to her grandfather's fortune (249). As a "half-truth teller" (171), Chippering is so adept at "pondering the subtleties of that innocent-seeming syllable—*no*" (122) that when Mrs. Kooshof asks him if he loves her—"Even a little?"—he responds by discussing "the nature of love, the physics of infinity" before eventually "asking for a rain check." "I guess that means no," his lover sighs, but is reassured by the Clintonesque explanation that "no, . . . Even *no* doesn't mean no" (123). But as soon as she finds the relationship pointless, Chippering revises his answer to a "yes" that leaves her incredulous but blissful ("You mean it? . . . does *yes* really *mean* yes?") and her partner eager to change the subject: "'Got me,' I said. 'Let's have breakfast'" (124). A secret codicil provides a final gloss on the exchange, however:

> "Yes," I'd said, but was this a promise?
>
> Was this duplicity?
>
> Mrs. Kooshof's question, remember, had come in two parts. Did I love her? Even a little? My eventual response—which was pried out of me like a wisdom tooth—had addressed the interrogatory as a whole, not merely its unqualified first component. . . . Otherwise, I would have responded, "Yes, yes," or, more probably, "No, yes." (124)

Here as elsewhere, Chippering is incapable of giving his listeners straight, accurate, or direct answers or explanations.

Chippering's digressive and ambivalent testimony was recognized and evaluated by Lorna Sue at the age of twelve: "You're a liar, Tommy" (77), was her simple response to his denial of responsibility for dropping her cat to her death. As her husband, he is accused of being a "compulsive" and "pathological" liar (65). And even as she cuddles in bed with her middle-aging lover, Mrs. Kooshof ruefully concedes: "You're a scoundrel, right? All the lies. Just a hopeless, unreliable, old tomcat . . ." (83). "In truth, I will admit, I do at times incline toward exaggeration, especially in self-defense" (65), Chippering concedes, justifying his prevarications as simple protection. The need to cover up or fabricate his experiences in order to maintain the love of others calls into question nearly all of Chippering's self-flattery, many of his explanations and justifications, and even his factual descriptions. Such bad faith is particularly evident in Chapter 14 ("Virtue"), a nasty piece of business that ironically and opaquely catalogs Lorna Sue's admirable qualities through damning details of her domestic, erotic, and professional sterility and one of the incidents of self-mutilation. Even though a footnote acknowledges that this is only one side of the story, it extends her husband's hostility: "Lorna Sue, of course, would furiously defend herself . . . in that scolding, sanctimonious tone of hers" (113).

Few divorces are amicable, of course, but Chippering's extreme bitterness derives, paradoxically, from a near-pathological devotion to the failed redeemer whom he calls "the girl of my dreams—my Juliet, my eternal Magdalene, my Lorna Sue" (290) and the traumatic realization, when she walked out on him *and* married someone else, that "I was never sacred to her" (114). Instead of accepting Mrs. Kooshof's faithful and palpable affection, Chippering is driven toward bombing his way to revenge upon his "pious, God-infected, betraying little sweetie pie" (293) in order to finally gain her respect. His ceaselessly invoked memories of Lorna Sue and of fragmentary scenes from their childhood and marriage characterize traumatization, and Chippering's self-defense depends on his defining himself as victim. He explicitly uses the words "trauma," "traumatic," and/or "stress" to explain his behavior in several dubious instances (14, 23, 86, 235, 262), ranging from hiding his phony records of psychiatric counseling under the marital mattress to hitting a four-year-old girl under his supervision at a day-care center. His destructive schemes against his former wife, her new husband, and Lorna Sue's "incestuous" brother are similarly justified as responses to his own psychic wounding.

Chippering's increasingly lunatic plots of revenge make up the one continuous action in *Tomcat.* Intended initially as a self-defensive, postdivorce counterstrike that would "resuscitate the old virtues," Chippering glosses his "revenge" in heroic terms just before he begins flying from Minnesota to Tampa to spy on the newlyweds and plot his self-vindication: "The word comes to us from the Latin, *vindicare*, . . . and in its most primitive etymology is without pejorative shading of any sort. To vindicate is to triumph over suspicion or accusation or presumed guilt, and for the ancients, such triumph did not exclude the ferocious punishment of false accusers. . . . To be 'vindictive' implied qualities both honorable and heroic, a fineness of spirit, a moral readiness to strike back against falsity and betrayal" (24). In the event, Chippering's Roman virtue goes no further than placing sex shop lingerie in the tycoon's Mercedes in order to raise his wife's suspicions, and fabricating intimations of carnal desire between Herbie and Lorna Sue in order to infuriate the real estate executive against both of them. But the feeble success of the plotting is only temporary, nearly destroys his relationship with Mrs. Kooshof, and ultimately leads to a more decisive vindication by his enemies, who force the professor to expose and wiggle his bare buttocks and endure the ignominy of a painful whipping while publicly proclaiming himself a "horse's ass" (214) in front of his captivated and appreciative linguistics students. The trauma of this humiliation occurs nearly simultaneously with another exposure: Two coed "cupcakes" who had threatened him with sexual harassment charges unless he ghostwrote their theses for them disclose that he has sexually harassed them by ghostwriting their theses. Forced to resign tenure and employment in order to avoid public charges, having ended his career with his final—and his most memorable—class, Chippering beats a full retreat back to his hometown and, indeed, his boyhood house, escorted by Mrs. Kooshof, who allows him free room, board, and bed. Undeterred by complete failure, Chippering plots his final vindication for Independence Day, when all of the Zylstras will gather in Owago and he can blow "a hole in the Fourth of July" that will remind them that "you have been *fucking* . . . with a fucking war hero!" (304).

Chippering's vindications are of a piece with his vulgar double entendres: ineffectually wishful, farcical, and childish. The Owago explosions that he plots when he is at least forty-nine years old (he covers up his exact age) recapitulate almost precisely the mason jar firebombings that he had imagined at the age of seven. Spanked before his class, as if he were a naughty boy, Chippering is later tied up with his pants pulled down and left overnight by two bar maids offended by his ogling. One of his fiercest resentments against Lorna Sue is her final words to him before she walked out the door forever: "Don't be an eighteen-year-old" (19). "The world sometimes precedes itself," Chippering notes, introducing Herbie's initial invitation to Lorna Sue to be crucified at the age of seven (5). Such inescapable recurrence, Freud has pointed out, derives from the preconscious, involuntary, and contingent nature of childhood experience and the repetition of its trauma as constitutive of adult identity. More tangibly, it reflects Chippering's difficulty in growing up. His infantilization accelerates once he has returned to Owago, where he becomes a day-care school attendant and ambitiously tries to teach his pre-kindergartners phonemes through a study of *Macbeth* (e.g., "Out, damned *spot*" [255—emphasis added]) but finds himself being blackmailed by Faith Graffenteen's four-year-old daughter into auditioning to replace the recently deceased host of a children's cartoon show on Channel 19, the local public-access television channel. The hilariously traumatic account of his attempt to entertain toddlers comprises Chapters 28 and 29 of *Tomcat* ("Spot" and "Nineteen") and is one of O'Brien's masterpieces.

Chippering discovers that the late-lamented Captain Nineteen, alias Hans Hanson, was a middle-aging but still virilely attractive "small-town jeweler and weary space traveler" (258), from whose shop the disgraced Tomcat had reluctantly purchased Mrs. Kooshof's engagement ring. In deciding to assume his on-air identity as commander of a cardboard studio spaceship with a crew of twelve, ranging from weanlings to first-graders, Chippering anticipates reassuming his command authority publicly, particularly after detecting the telltale signs of female infatuation in Jessie, the "mouth-watering" producer whom he condescendingly mistakes for a stagehand (264). But his publicly broadcast tryout is a catastrophe. Too large for the Captain's old uniform, which makes him look and feel like "a can of moist and densely packed Spam" (266), Chippering is otherwise too small for the role. Changing from linguistic martinet to trauma victim within the course of a few minutes, he tearfully pours out the story of his ruined marriage, accusing Herbie of incest, fulminating against the tycoon, and pleading for Lorna Sue to respect the sacredness of his love while studio phones ring angrily in the background, Mrs. Kooshof looks down at the linoleum, and Jessie's face goes "phosphorescent" with what Chippering identifies as "hero worship" (270). "Inexplicably, then" he recalls, "the studio went upside down" and he enters the ineffable experience of traumatic breakdown: "An impossible thing to describe . . . but it was as if the last several months of my life had suddenly given way under the pressure of time and gravity. A psychic avalanche . . . [ellipsis in the original] I felt buried. Claustrophobic darkness descended upon me, succeeded by boiling heat, succeeded by a sharp popping sensation at the top of my skull. A brain plug came loose" (270). Moving off-camera in a haze, he pulls a firebomb out of his briefcase and hoists a four-year-old onto his lap after returning to the crew module, where he breaks down in tears, threatens suicide, and broadcasts an appeal to Lorna Sue to return to him. Escorted offstage by a cameraman, Chippering requires hospitalization after his collapse, which leaves him even more than usually delusional, feeling betrayed not only by Jessie (who has unaccountably chosen a used-car dealer as the new Captain Nineteen) but by his loyal companion: "It was all Mrs. Kooshof's doing—the revenge instinct—and I played along only because I had temporarily misplaced my capacity for speech" (271).

Lorna Sue's infuriating insult of her husband for acting like a teenager is thus validated by Chippering's abysmal failure to turn nineteen, which has joined *eighteen* as another of his traumatic lexicon entries. Moreover, his failure as Captain Nineteen reduces him to literal infancy, which is prolonged at the psychiatric hospital, where he refuses even to talk with his infuriated counselor, as well as by his subsequent stay with the mortified Mrs. Kooshof, who has seen and heard her fiancé humiliate himself *and* proclaim his devotion to Lorna Sue on public television. He lies in bed, expecting her to provide nursing, meals, mothering, and sex, and when he finally breaks several weeks of silence to complain about her failure to wait on him hand-and-foot—"'This,' I declared, 'is a disgrace'" (282)—she explodes in righteous rage and sorrow, informs him that she is planning a vacation by herself, and threatens to throw him out of her house. Chippering is naked as he argues with her (her iced tea has soiled his bathrobe), and so she forces him to wrap a dish towel around his waist. The infantile former professor thus looks like a middle-aging baby in his diaper as he begins to recover his power of speech, and his subsequent plot to blow up the Zylstras when the tycoon and Lorna Sue come home for the Independence Day holiday replicates the schemes of a seven-year-old. Forced to canvass Owago playgrounds and bargain with children in order to find illegal firecrackers to ignite his mason jars of gasoline, Chippering is ridiculed by one ten-year-old for his failure to fill heroic shoes: "I seen you on TV. Captain Nineteen, he isn't some stupid old crybaby" (302). "Who cried?" the would-be vindicator angrily responds to his arms merchant. Derided as "Captain Crybaby" by the "malicious little prick," Chippering has the last childish word:

> "Right on TV, man. You bawled and bawled."
> "Didn't."
> "*Did!*"
> "Absolutely did fucking *not*," I growled, then rapidly exited the playground, proud of myself, armed to the teeth, stalwartly whistling an old Vietnam marching ditty as I headed for the wars. July the Fourth. Call me patriotic. (303)

Although he has recovered his speech, Chippering is no more successful as a domestic soldier than as a spaceship commander, and post-Vietnam vengeance, like his failure as Captain Nineteen, turns out be both unsuccessful and retraumatizing.

PTSD as Comedy/Vietnam as Parody

When Faith Graffenteen accuses Chippering of corrupting her four-year-old daughter by teaching *Macbeth* in a day-care center and suggests "[out], darn, stupid spot" as a decent emendation for Lady Macbeth's execration (255), she also reaccuses him, forty years on, for forcing her to kiss him at the age of twelve. "I am forever astonished at the longevity of childhood," Chippering digresses in a footnote, "How it never ends. How we are what we were" (256). The persistence of childhood is reflected comically in Chippering's problems in growing up, which casually reflect how the adult subject is inescapably constituted by ideology—here, American Cold War militarism, religious faith, and sexual idealism—beginning irrevocably in childhood. O'Brien's handling of Vietnam in *Tomcat* suggests something childish in the ideology itself and satirizes male fortitude, a conventionally serious subject that had been handled so in earlier books. *Tomcat in Love* is O'Brien's most fully realized domestic novel since *Northern Lights*, yet the war in Viet Nam returns, though in darkly comic form, rather than being covered up or ignored. Chippering's ultimate self-vindication is modeled after his status as a "war hero" who has "won" the Silver Star after ordering a retaliatory air strike against his own comrades, and he puts on his thirty-year-old combat fatigues in order to carry out his revenge against his wife and her in-laws.

Like *In the Lake of Woods*, *Tomcat* is a trauma-saturated narrative that brings together crises of childhood, love and marriage, and the war. Here, however, childhood traumatization is enacted by children themselves, and the Law of the Father, which is undercut throughout the novel, plays little role in Tommy Chippering's crises. His father's turtle/engine *diminishes* his authority and provokes a fascination with the symbolic that calls language into question rather than validating it. Like John Wade's, Chippering's father dies suddenly, in 1957, the same year that his twelve-year-old son begins his first love ledger and kisses Faith, as if patriarchal expectations were early replaced with erotic ones. Wade went to Viet Nam to gain his dead father's love; Chippering, who describes himself as "the reactive type," goes out of inertia: "[T]he war sucked me in, and in January of 1969 I found myself filling sandbags at a forward firebase in the mountains of Quang Ngai Province" (57).

Like the childhood crises associated with bombing and crucifixion and Chippering's devastating divorce, the trauma of Vietnam is part of Chippering's initial self-presentation, but only through obscure traces. A comparison of the eight-year-old Herbie to unnamed murderous figures encountered later in Viet Nam is the only reference in Chapter 1. The third chapter ("Tulip") refers to Chippering's year in Viet Nam through enigmatically enumerating the words *tulip, goof, spider, wildfire,* and *death chant.* Chippering claims that he has "been ruthlessly pursued for many decades now, partly by a Tulip, partly by the word *tulip*" (22) and assures us that "in due course" he will explain further.

Only in Chapter 7 ("Jungle"), a "tactical transgression" (56) that intrusively interrupts his domestic narrative just after Mrs. Kooshof has first taken him in, does Chippering suddenly present an account of his only combat mission in Viet Nam, but he breaks it off at the point when six Green Berets seem to have abandoned him and he finds himself as "lost as lost gets" (62) in triple canopy jungle. Ten chapters later, "Lost" (Chapter 18) and "Found" (Chapter 19) complete Chippering's in-country narrative, a story of humiliation, multiple traumatization, and amazing grace that ends with self-vindication and the Silver Star for Valor. The five-word incantation in Chapter 3 turns out to identify the top-secret aliases of the Green Berets—*Bonnie Prince Charming* is the sixth—who provide the coordinates for an apocalyptic secret bombing campaign from their covert base camp, a luxurious villa deep in the Vietnamese cordillera provided with tennis courts, a swimming pool, native gardeners, and cooks. Finally, in Chapter 34, Chippering discloses what happened to him in Viet Nam after he had bombed his own comrades and reveals how the vengeful Spider finally caught up with him in Owago on the Fourth of July and looped piano wire around his neck before releasing him.

In short, Chippering's Vietnam experiences are presented as an almost classic trauma narrative, a fragmentary, initially iconic recollection, broken off repeatedly by the survivor, who recovers the terrible details only fitfully until, gradually, a whole story has been reconstructed. The intrusion of the trauma is represented by the sudden reappearance of former comrades as Chippering prepares to avenge himself on his former wife—a sudden glimpse of Goof on the University of Minnesota campus in Chapter 11, Spider's showing up in Owago.

Chippering's traumatization, which begins with his abandonment by the six Green Berets and leads to his walking in circles through the jungle, is so shattering an experience that he loses the sense of his own identity: "Except for an occasional whimper, I had lost my capacity for language, the underlying grammar of human reason; I had lost the *me* of me—my name, its meaning—those particularities of spirit and personality that separate one from all, each from other. I was a grubworm among grubworms. One more fly in God's inky ointment" (149). The subsequent trauma narrative proceeds centripetally as much as sequentially. Chippering uncovers more and more hidden details for himself and for us as he goes on—the identities of Tulip and the others, their mission, his vengeance against them, why he is being chased. Only in Chapter 34 does he reveal that the air strike he ordered as payback had only terrified his comrades, not killed them, and that they had eventually caught up with him in Viet Nam and conducted a mock execution. But their ultimate vengeance, he only now discloses, has been psychic. One unaccountable moment of "macho," "Roman" bravery ("for once, briefly, I loved myself as I so relentlessly wished to be loved by others" [306]), has traumatized the rest of his life—Chippering had not flinched when the command to "Fire!" had been uttered but drew no response from the six-man squad, lined up to execute him. Let off for the moment but threatened with eventual death, Chippering has suffered ever afterward from what Spider ironically labels "the burden of the brave" (307), a paranoid dread that he is being followed by his former tormentors and victims and will eventually be killed. Thus, he explains, a number of peculiarities of the life story that we have been reading—classic symptoms of PTSD: "unplugged telephones. Obscenities in my sleep. Separate marital bedrooms. A certain subtle frenzy to my life" (307).

Literally buried in the middle of Chippering's Vietnam revelations is an astonishing episode that helps him to explain and justify his lifelong fear of betrayal, sense of being used by others, and recourse to vengeance. Chippering was abandoned not only by the Greenies but by his first lover, an "unimpeachable and pure" (162) yet sexually adroit Vietnamese teenaged housemaid with whom he fell in love and had passionate sex in the villa until one night when their own explosive orgasm was complemented by "an impressive B-52 strike in the mountains to the west" (161). Bothered by Thuy Ninh's reactions to the sometimes sleep-interrupting air strikes and by his unreliable comrades' cryptically cynical comments about his love affair, Chippering discovers not only that the Green Berets are forward observers for a massively destructive, covert bombing campaign but that Thuy Ninh is their common lover (which explains her startlingly advanced erotic proficiency). To the suddenly outraged Chippering, the Green Berets are quasi-psychotic murderers who enjoy their violent mission—"search and scald" (163). Thuy Ninh is even worse: "She was a reptile. She was sick with treason" (165)—terms that he repeatedly applies to Lorna Sue. Vietnam thus becomes a traumatic site of love betrayal *and* violent self-vindication: He calls in an air strike close to the villa, abandons his companions to the vengeance of his terror bombing, and gives himself the Silver Star once he has returned to the firebase where he is awards clerk.

Chippering's representation of this terrible experience is used to explain his subsequent quest for nubile young coeds, a "sacred" marriage, and the need to vindicate himself by traumatizing others. Its significance as a deeply buried primal site is reinforced by its formal placement. Within O'Brien's thirty-seven-chapter novel, "Found" (Chapter 19), Chippering's account of finding and then abandoning Thuy Ninh and the Green Beret villa, occupies the exact center of the narrative, preceded by the proleptic Vietnam trauma narrative of "Lost" (Chapter 18). Like the My Lai sections in "The Vietnam in Me," Chippering's experiences are thus a traumatic source of subsequent grief buried precisely in the middle of the longer narrative. In my 1998 telephone interview with O'Brien, he confirmed that the placement of the Thuy Ninh episode was "absolutely deliberate."

Although the war is uncovered as a traumatic experience for Chippering, his own self-representation, his unreliability as a narrator, and even the pervasiveness of his traumatization subvert the conventional solemnity of the subject. Traumatic signifiers are almost *too* blatant in *Tomcat's* nearly manic unloading of failures, resentments, and emotional breakdowns, its dictionary of traumatic materials almost too numerous to take seriously. Thus Chippering variously explains his ultimate collapse as a consequence not only of his one combat mission in Viet Nam but also (among others) of mock bombings and a crucifixion in childhood, a childhood kiss, lying to Lorna Sue about her cat, a leaky love tank, a heroic mistake in Quang Ngai, and his failure, seven times, to win the Hubert H.

Humphrey Prize for Teaching Excellence, among other sources. Chippering confesses that "confession is not to my taste" (79), but his self-justifying explanations actually expose his own boorish folly rather than censoring or sanitizing it. Instead of covering up his experiences, Chippering broadcasts them to anyone who will listen, as on Channel 19, and his frantic pursuit of girls is only superficially erotic: His greatest passion is forcing the stories of his life on them. Even when he asks Mrs. Kooshof for an account of her first sexual experience, he interrupts her first sentence and launches into an account of his own ("Pontiac") that eventually leaves him without an audience.

Like Cowling's hyperaroused apologia, Chippering's trauma narrative is intended to make its readers laugh, but it is more effectively dramatized as comedy. Most of the sequential episodes are inflicted upon embarrassed, bored, unwilling, or offended listeners, from Mrs. Kooshof to a Tampa salesgirl who models S&M and bondage fashionware for Chippering, to the barmaids who finally tie him up and gag him and the Holiday Inn janitor who finds his Vietnam tale pointless, to the horrified viewers of Channel 19. Chippering's sob stories parody trauma therapy itself; they satisfy his need to justify or feel sorry for himself, but his mainly female listeners have problems of their own, including the early death of parents and abusive or unfaithful boyfriends or husbands.

Thus, the trauma of Vietnam becomes a self-pitying, self-validating tale told by an idiot in *Tomcat*, and it contrasts strikingly with the repressed and constricted Vietnam trauma narrative of John Wade. Both figures falsify their war records, but whereas Wade tries to literally expunge his own identity by removing himself from Charlie Company, Chippering awards himself the second highest U.S. combat decoration and keeps identifying himself as a "war hero" to all of his audiences. Nor can we be sure that this is a "true war story" even within the fictional universe that is the novel. At the same time that he misrepresents his aversion to confession, Chippering avers that "the truth, to put it squarely, is that I have always had trouble with the truth" (79). Chippering's unreliability as a narrator particularly infects his recollection of Vietnam. The episode with Thuy Ninh and the Green Berets seems almost fantastic, as in Chippering's description of the plantation mansion from which the "covert" air war is activated—"a villa, it seemed, or what I imagined a villa must be" (149). Although his old uniform is genuine enough, its Silver Star may be as ersatz as the "valor" he demonstrated in earning it. After all, Chippering's self-serving scenario represents himself as an irresistible but faithful "stallion" and "stud" betrayed by a Vietnamese lover, taking just vengeance upon six comrades who are devastating Viet Nam in a bad war from which he is otherwise detached. He is both a traumatized victim of violent comrades and an unfaithful girl, *and* an avenging Rambo—or Coppola's Captain Willard, as the bombing raid that he calls in resembles the ending of the movie *Apocalypse Now*.

The reappearance of Spider in the final Vietnam-related chapter of *Tomcat* is similarly fantastic. The original version of Chapter 37 had been too purely imaginary for his editor, so O'Brien had rewritten it as a scene involving the reappearance of Chippering's former comrade in Owago and a get-together in a local bar, with both old soldiers dressed in their Viet Nam jungle fatigues. That revision was too *factual* for O'Brien, so the final fabrication, both palpable and imaginary, invites us to consider what is real and what is hallucinatory (telephone interview, November 3, 1998). Spider catches up with his former victim and tormentor on the Fourth of July while he is stowing his firebombs in Mrs. Kooshof's garage, and although they later have beers in a tavern and Chippering sees him off at the local Greyhound station, the narrator wonders "if his presence was a product of my imagination, those feverish brain winds now gusting at hurricane velocity," because "he seemed to float toward me without ordinary means of locomotion" (308). Even after Spider has half-garroted him with piano wire and then "sighed, removed the wire, coiled it up, and returned it to his pocket" (310), Chippering is "very powerfully . . . struck by that sleepwalking sensation" (310).

Chippering is going through a posttraumatic breakdown throughout the final narrative sequence of the novel—the events from July 2 through the night of July 4—and this haunting by Spider is one of its symptoms. Beginning with the arrival of Lorna Sue, Herbie, and the tycoon in town for the holidays, Chippering descends into an increasingly ludicrous madness that begins with a traumatic blackout during the hours that he spends (or imagines he spends?) watching Lorna Sue and her second husband sleeping together after he has crept into his former wife's bedroom and that later includes climbing up into the Edenic apple tree next to the Zylstra residence to spy on them, dressed in his jungle fatigues. The "Velocity" (Chapter 32) of traumatization after his "Visitation" (Chapter 31) to Lorna

Sue's bedroom accelerates, and his world goes "G-force hazy" (312) until Chippering prepares to retrieve his firecracker-primed weapons on the night of the Fourth and "blow her to smithereens" (319): "It was full dark when I slipped out to the garage. After the strain of recent months, I now felt an electric sizzle in my bones, partly anticipation, partly dread. I was capable of anything. For a few seconds I stood there in the dark garage, envisioning a big yellow house afire, an exploding Mercedes, a family of turncoats running for their lives. The image made me snicker" (314). The "electric sizzle" deliberately echoes the traumatic breakdowns of John Wade in Viet Nam and in the cottage at Lake of the Woods. That Chippering's breakdown will be resolved more happily is suggested by the faux-apocalyptic details and the final snicker.

Spider's reappearance, whether posttraumatic psychic intrusion or actual visit embellished by Chippering's breakdown, is the fulcrum of his recovery. Spider is the ghost of the war, a figure like W. D. Ehrhart's three companions in *Busted*, but his message to the former army clerk is to give it up, not to keep replaying it: "For the rest of us, Tommy, the war's history—gonzo—but in this really nifty way you've kept it going. That life-and-death edge, man, it gives *meaning* to everything. Keeps you in contact with your own sinnin' self" (310). Chippering's attempt to restage Vietnam in Owago, Minnesota, and his manically repetitive insistence on being taken seriously as a "fucking war hero" by Spider, Lorna Sue and her clan, Mrs. Kooshof, the coeds and the working girls, the children in the playgrounds, and all of us as readers are undercut by Spider's childhood appellation. "Tommy" has never grown up, and his association of bombs with manly fortitude, retributive justice, and self-respect is childish, not heroic. When he finds his bombs missing, forces his way into the Zylstra household to accuse Herbie of stealing them, and reveals his lunatic schemes of vengeance, he suffers his final infantile breakdown, "a childish blubbering that mortified me even as it rushed from my throat. I sank to the floor. I was gasping; I hugged myself and rocked on my knees and tried to explain that the whole idea was to make her care, to make her remember" (323). Helped to his feet and to enlightenment by Herbie, Chippering comes to realize that the relationship between Herbie and Lorna Sue is custodial, not incestuous; that *she,* not her brother, has been the firebomber, a posttraumatic survivor herself not yet capable of love who both craves and feels oppressed by their attention. When, like some madwoman in the Zylstra attic, Lorna Sue threatens to destroy them all with the stolen bombs, Chippering's calm *"No"* to her demand for continued adoration is an act of courage and self-respect more significant than any explosive vengeance. "Did I love her? I did," he confesses. "Was she still sacred? She was not" (339). But Chippering leaves it to Mrs. Kooshof to disarm the "former girl of [his] dreams" (340) more palpably by seizing the firebombs and putting an end to her ultimate self-mutilation. He ends Independence Day by walking home with the woman whose underappreciated—and unaccountable —love has allowed him to start putting childish vindication behind him and begin to become a man, starting with following her instructions just before she prepares breakfast for two: "'Do the dishes,' she said, 'then pack your bags. This is history, Thomas'" (340).

This predawn scene on the Fifth of July is followed by "Fiji," a postscript to Chippering's narrative in the form of a posttraumatic tropical idyll that contrasts with the lunacies of Minnesota, Viet Nam, and the Fourth of July. Chippering's healing has begun much earlier, however, just after Spider's appearance and his final breakdown before Herbie. Its initiation is dramatized by a baptismal scene that replaces the initial comedy of the first encounter between Chippering and Mrs. Kooshof with an epiphany of self-awareness. Then, he had bawled next to the birdbath in her backyard. Now, he pulls off his Vietnam fatigues, strips naked, rinses his hands in the birdbath, wipes off the charcoal camouflaging his face, and lies down on the grass, looking up at the "lovely night" and the "stars":

> I stood up, naked as a baby, and let the Fourth of July bathe me.
> Each of us, I suppose, needs his illusions. Life after death. A maker of planets. A woman to love, a man to hate. Something sacred.
> But what a waste. (324)

Chippering's baptism rewrites Paul Perry's epiphany as he looks up to see the northern lights after his submergence in Pliney's Pond, but his more articulate enlightenment is both wiser and more melancholy: Whatever we have faith in (including the Fourth of July) is as illusory as it is necessary. Having realized that some illusions are not only unnecessary but crippling, Chippering moves beyond the traumas of divorce and Vietnam by begging Mrs. Robert Kooshof to marry him, meaning "virtually every word" and finally overcoming what he is now wise enough to realize is "her better judgment" (325). Since Chippering comes to his senses more than twenty pages before the end of the book, *Tomcat* is O'Brien's most satisfying narrative of recovery from trauma. This psychological reintegration is formally reflected by the last three entries in O'Brien's dictionary of love. After the intrusion and exorcism of Spider, the final chapter titles trace a narrative that is sequential, coherent, and therapeutic: "The Fourth (Late Afternoon, Evening)" (Chapter 35), "The Fourth (Late Night)" (Chapter 36), and "Fiji" (Chapter 37).

Chippering's transit from academia to paradise has not yet cured him of Vietnam, nor is the tomcat fully civilized. He has "spotted Death Chant . . . on the beach" (346); he spends his afternoons on "the pristine topless beaches" of a Club Med near the couple's bungalow (344); and although at Mrs. Kooshof's insistence he is finally cooperating with a psychiatrist, she is a "jolly young lady of African descent" who "speaks little English" (346) and treats him with amulets after listening to daily installments of his dictionary of love. "Like an invalid on the mend, hour to hour," he recovers his life "[a] step forward, a half step back. An appropriate pace in this sun-drenched zone" (344, 346). He is learning how to love, and in his daily conversations with his future bride, who insists that she be called *Donna*, he has "begun to master the high art of listening" (343). Having happily abandoned academia and his own pedantic and erotic obsessions, Chippering is beginning to understand, listen, and minister to women by patiently dressing their hair: "I specialize in corn rows. I envision a Rock Cornish Salon in my prairie future" (344). "Tonight," he concludes, "I will braid Mrs. Robert Kooshof's hair. Confess all. Begin again" (346).

Saving Tim O'Brien: *Tomcat in Love* as Countertherapy

Chippering's recovery actually takes place somewhere in the Caribbean, not in Fiji, which has been an imaginary destination throughout *Tomcat*, a paradoxically traumatic signifier for the presumed reader that he has been addressing in sporadic intrusions throughout the novel, beginning in Chapter 1: a happily married woman whose husband has abandoned her and gone off to Fiji with a "redhead barely half his age" (13). A site of betrayal rather than a paradise, Fiji's wounding implications are fabricated in twenty-two of *Tomcat*'s thirty-seven chapters, including all of Chapter 27 ("You"), an uninterrupted address to the love-wounded heroine that follows Chippering's own crisis-forced promise of marriage to Mrs.

Kooshof in Chapter 26 ("Ring"). "You" represents "every brokenhearted lover on this planet" (241), and the narrator imagines her flying to Fiji to spy and exact vengeance on her former prince and his lover but ultimately breaking down in tears and returning home alone again without a word. O'Brien's intention in these apostrophes is to directly summon the reader's experience and imagination, but originally the addressee was a male who had suffered abandonment in love, like Tom Chippering (interview, October 8, 1998)—and Tim O'Brien.[1] By extending his own posttraumatic survivordom to a female persona who is also his reader, Chippering is sympathetically imagining the suffering of a female Other who is not simply an object for ogling or adoration—or a therapeutic listener, attendant, or cook for himself. Indeed, insofar as Chippering's recovery involves listening to women, the Fiji digressions may be thought of as his culminating attempt to "fine-tune this personal record" (341).

Tomcat in Love ends with a final section of apostrophe where the narrator offers therapy to a woman rather than expecting it from her:

> He is in Fiji, with another woman, and will not soon be returning.
>
> But believe this: He loved you. He still does. He knows his transgression and feels it like a loosened tooth in his mouth on the morning of your anniversary, and on your autumn birthday, and when the snow does not come to Fiji on Christmas Eve. Believe too, that in those soft Pacific breezes, late at night, he wakes to think of you, hoping you are well, and that the image with which he finally finds reprieve is of someday returning to your door and knocking on it and begging admittance. A matter of faith. (346–47)

"You" had concluded with an ironic footnote suggesting that Tomcat's sympathy was insincere or self-validating ("So there. I have a sensitive side"—243). The empathy here, however, measures Chippering's progress toward maturity and recovery, not least because it may covertly reach out to comfort Lorna Sue with his love and to accept personal responsibility for what has happened. The "faith" required of the imaginary Other and all of O'Brien's readers is as necessary as it is mundane: We may never love again unless we can believe that we have been loved. The benediction that concludes the novel defines a courage more valuable than bombs and Silver Stars, a love more healing than adoration:

> Take heart.

Fiji, my lost princess, is but a state of mind. Embolden yourself. Brave the belief.

Bless you.

In 1994, a retraumatized and quasi-suicidal Tim O'Brien had also identified Vietnam as a "state of mind" before concluding "The Vietnam in Me" with the hope that "minds change," that "starting can start." He had also expressed a desire to give up fiction altogether after a public breakdown during a reading from *In the Lake of the Woods* in Ann Arbor (Weber B1). Four years later, when I asked him in Ann Arbor what had started him writing again (interview, October 8, 1998), his response both explained and characterized *Tomcat*, the work from which he had just been reading:

> I guess it was recovery, in a way, from all the nightmares I'd been going through four years ago. Now, you either laugh at yourself and the world involved with this dance between men and women that's been going on since Adam and Eve, or you can bawl or be angry. There's not much else you can do, and I thought it was time for me at least to lighten up a bit about myself and obsession and love and all that stuff and have a lot of fun with it. This book is not all funny, it's a savage, dark, kind of angry book in parts, but the other parts, I think, are funny . . . I guess that writing *Tomcat* for me was just about the far most enjoyable experience I've ever had as a writer.

Tomcat in Love is the result of what "started" in 1994, and in completing it O'Brien has not only "saved his life" once more with a story but produced his most original revision of his previous work and of himself.

The domestic details of *Tomcat* refabricate all of O'Brien's previous fiction, often unexpectedly. Even the guilt-edged toothache imagined at the end of "Fiji" reprises a peculiar symbolic detail from O'Brien's first piece of published fiction, "A Man of Melancholy Disposition," for Paul Perry is suffering from such pain throughout that rejected prototype of *Northern Lights*. Lorna Sue reincarnates Lorna Lou, O'Brien's childhood girlfriend who most transparently reappeared in "The Lives of the Dead," and "Kooshof" puns on Rat Kiley's misogynistic obscenity from "How to Tell a True War Story," an idiosyncratic joke that O'Brien noted in his Ann Arbor reading and that reappears in Chippering's impolitic term for the wife of the university president: "dumb cooze" (114). Chippering's dismantling Mrs. Kooshof's phone as well as her barricading herself behind closed doors when he becomes unbearable replicate similar domestic lunacies in *The Nuclear Age* involving Cowling and Bobbi. The trauma of Vietnam is revised in particularly unexpected ways. Thuy Ninh—her name tastelessly and ethnocentrically garbled by the future linguistics professor as "Take In"—is a sexually and culturally violated Sarkin Aung Wan as well as a reincarnation of Mary Ann Bell, the "Sweetheart of the Song Tra Bong." The Green Berets from that story are reinvented as Spider, Death Chant, and Chippering's other murderous comrades, and their cynical incantations of "Love bombs!" as they take turns with Thuy Ninh and obliterate the Southeast Asian landscape grotesquely recall O'Brien's melodramatic apology in "The Vietnam in Me": "We should have bombed these people with love" (50).

Additional striking revisions could be cited, but what is most interesting is how O'Brien is brilliantly parodying himself in *Tomcat.* A primal traumatic source of O'Brien's writing, his unheroic acquiescence to a bad war, is rewritten through Chippering's heroic vengeance upon his murderous companions but results in the same effect: endless bad dreams and trauma narratives. If O'Brien's authorial function is mimicked by Chippering's therapeutic rewriting of his life, then what is "ridiculous" in *Tomcat* includes the fictions that are revised. Chippering's comic frustration in finding a proper audience for his Vietnam tale recalls Tim O'Brien's serious instructions for "How to Tell a True War Story" in *The Things They Carried,* as does the disappointment or boredom of listeners who expect more "sound and fury" and less digressive soul-searching from the narrator. On the other hand, Spider's ironic praise of Chippering's inability or unwillingness to efface the trauma of Vietnam both validates and comically appraises O'Brien's career. Presenting himself as the haunting trace of the war, a gift that keeps on giving, Chippering's ghostly comrade notes, "'Thanks to me, you're still in the Nam, still up in those creepy mountains.... Lucky Tom,' he murmured. 'It's like this gift we gave you. Judgment Day. Most of us forget it's on the calendar'" (310). Chippering himself, here a stand-in for his creator, "Lucky Tim," silently acknowledges the benefits of trauma: "In a sense, I realized, he was right. For better or worse, the whole terrifying business had given definition to the past couple decades of my life. That pursued feeling—it was something to believe in, a replacement for Easter" (310). "You're in a special position, Tommy," Spider acknowledges, "[a]mong the elect, so to speak," and as he tightens the piano wire noose about the narrator's neck, he pays tribute to the moral value of true war stories that the posttraumatic survivor can never stop telling: "[T]he rest of us poor yo-yos, we're the Walking Numb, totally blind to our own pitiful mortality." "Weird thought," Spider concludes after he removes Tommy's (Timmy's?) noose and prepares to leave Owago, "but you make my world hum. Wouldn't want to lose my reason for living" (311). This deliciously ridiculous praise of the "sufferings and greatness" of the trauma artist both thanks and nearly strangles him for his contributions to our moral enlightenment.

Chippering's traumatic visitations and breakdowns also burlesque the trauma of love and the grief, guilt, regret, and anger that followed the dissolution of O'Brien's marriage and his abandonment by a younger partner. Just before his terrible classroom humiliation, as he delusively anticipates Lorna Sue's crawling back to beg his forgiveness, Chippering anticipates authoring what sounds like an academic version of "The Vietnam in Me" and *In the Lake of the Woods*: "It struck me, just in passing, that I might someday author a monograph on the eerie similarities between wartime combat and peacetime romance. Blood lust. Mortal fear. Shell shock. Despair. Hopelessness. Entrapment. Betrayal" (206).

O'Brien is not just having fun with himself, he is also laughing at conventional pieties of American maledom in *Tomcat*. Chippering's exhilarating description of his sexual congresses with Thuy Ninh and Mrs. Kooshof are so over-the-top that they undercut both his veracity and the unquestioned reverence and value paid to sexual prowess and pleasure in much American Vietnam fiction.[2] As a Tomcat on the prowl in postfeminist America, the professor's misadventures with variously foul-mouthed, previously abused, sexually provocative, and/or shrewdly manipulative predatory females reverse the normal myths of male control and conquest. And although Chippering loudly asserts his status as a "war hero" to anyone within earshot, his "heroism" keeps him sleepless, his Silver Star is a sham, and his "deviant" (303) recostuming in combat fatigues thirty years after he had left Viet Nam climaxes O'Brien's infantilizing subversion of the remasculinization of America. Chippering's characterization of his own mock execution in Quang Ngai by Death Chant and the others after his vengeance had "scorched their minds" (305) and "shrank their supersoldier testicles" epitomizes both follies: "[I]t was ridiculous—like the war itself, like the bulk of human experience as I have rather cynically come to know it. A pitiful, unfunny joke. Little boys playing war. (Or a little boy, in my case, playing love.)" (306). Breaking down even as he tries to violently vindicate himself as forsaken husband, academic Tomcat, and war hero, Chippering comes to appreciate the serial obsessions of Son of Sam, but his ultimate model is the bombastic self-promotion of a bogus spaceship commander with a crew of preschool and post-kindergarten admirers: "Once in every century, . . . there is born into this universe a special man. With the strength of Atlas. The wisdom of Solomon. The courage of a lion . . . *You* are that chosen individual. [Orchestral punctuation.] *You* are Captain Nineteen—today's man of the future" (257, 259).

The astonishing blend of absurdity and seriousness in *Tomcat*, the "funny" and the "angry," makes it O'Brien's most emotionally comprehensive work. Like *In the Lake of the Woods*, it integrates the traumatic triad of childhood, Vietnam, and eros but in a very different key. Chippering's comic recovery as well as his hyperaroused, naked confessional, a self-justification that hoists itself with its own regard, contrasts happily with the tragically constricted, painfully reconstructed trauma narrative of John and Kathy Wade. The cover-ups and repressed fragments of *Tomcat* eventually all come out, just as the narrative finally straightens itself out after literal infancy and futile hospitalization ("Nerves") and the intrusion of Spider, permitting a new start with Mrs. Robert Kooshof in a "Fiji" where Chippering is beginning to recover his faith and is putting together his posttraumatic memoirs.[3]

In the most repressed of its episodes, Chippering's attempt to re(-)cover astonishingly refabricates O'Brien's own. The brief traumatic fragment of "Eighteen" (Chapter 2) begins with his desperately taking Lorna Sue by the shoulders and pushing her up against their bed after she has told him that "there's someone else" and insulted his reaction: "Don't be an eighteen-year-old" (19). It ends with Chippering's standing ridiculously on the other side of the door that his wife shut behind her when she walked out of his life—"a creaking, ruined, desiccated, hollow old man in his underwear" (20) who will never be eighteen again. Only in Chapter 30 ("Nerves"), 260 pages later, does its immediate sequel appear, an incident that had been promised in Chapter 17 ("Tampa"). There, after Mrs. Kooshof has rejected his obsessive vengeance, reminding her companion that he is divorced and that Lorna Sue doesn't love him, he grabs his new partner in a dangerous state of hyperarousal ("a sudden rupture in the physics of time . . .

a powerful, aching dizzy feeling" [140]) and nearly pushes her over the edge of the balcony. Snapping out of his posttraumatic violence, he releases the betrayer/Thuy Ninh/Lorna Sue/Mrs. Kooshof, so bewildered and frightened by his breakdown that she temporarily "abandons" him. *Balcony* is the traumatic trigger here, and a footnote uncertainly promises to open the enigma: "Bad memories. Later in this narrative, if I am up to it, I will do my best to elaborate. For now, however, it is an act of courage merely to peck out the word *balcony* on this trusty old Royal" (141).

The earlier fragments of "Eighteen" and "Tampa" are finally supplemented and closed in "Nerves." Trying to defend himself from diagnoses of being "delusional" and "depressive" after his breakdown on Channel 19, Chippering concedes that he *has* been "suicidal" (279–80) and returns to the direct aftermath of Lorna Sue's walking out on him. On the other side of a temporary blackout, with the word *eighteen* reverberating as a voice on the radio intoned the word *Lexus*, with his world now reduced to lexical fragments (identified by italicized text), Chippering found himself in his underwear, wondering whether to remove his *socks* as he pulled one leg over the *balcony*, "high above University Avenue," and prepared the final jump of his life to the *pavement* below. But puzzled and irritated by hearing a word not already part of his vast personal dictionary, the cashiered professor engaged in etymological speculations ("plainly Greek") before waving to "a gathering of upturned heads below" and pulling himself back inside to consult his "*Webster's Third New International.* It was a professional relief," he concludes, "to find the word *Lexus* unlisted (Proper noun, it turns out)" (281).

Chippering concedes something "ridiculous" about both the "awkward pose" of his abortive suicide attempt and his rescue-by-dictionary, but the entire series of *balcony* episodes therapeutically refabricates Tim O'Brien's breakdown in the summer of 1994 and/or in "The Vietnam in Me," when he sat in his underwear, traumatized by his return to Viet Nam and his loss of Kate, only partly pacified by his pharmacopoeia of antidepressants (Chippering's "only true and faithful companions"—279), unaffected by his sleeping pills, and labored at "this unblinking fool of a computer" (see Chapter 1, "O'Brien's Art of Trauma," above) to complete his narrative of near-suicidal depression. Like Chippering, he was saved by words themselves (Λεξισ/*lexis*), not simply one word (*Lexus*), not only through the memoir of his crisis but also through the new "start" that was to eventually emerge as *Tomcat in Love*, refabricating nightmare as traumatic carnival and recovering beyond the "ridiculous" side of his own obsessions.

After he has seen "Fire" (Chapter 25) and seen "Rain" (Chapter 21), lost his public dignity and his job, "everything signified nothing," Chippering laments at the end of "Ring" (240). His premature despair marks the ineffability of trauma itself and what John Wade might have ultimately concluded even as it parodies Shakespeare's most traumatized but most resonantly articulate observer of his own self-destruction as soldier and husband. Things will actually get worse before they get better for O'Brien's antihero, who is too foolish for tragic anagnorisis but too wise for full comic resolution. Happily, *In the Lake of the Woods* did not fulfill O'Brien's feelings in 1994 that he had said everything he needed to say about himself and his world, that he had "completed a kind of search" (Mort 1991). Whatever its ultimate reception, *Tomcat* continues O'Brien's personal fictional quest for survival beyond trauma even as it introduces a new tone within which to refabricate it. And its concluding apostrophe, as well as the narrator's earlier addresses to the "lost princess" of Fiji, anticipates a new direction altogether.

C O N C L U S I O N

A Trauma Artist

Posttraumatic Nation

He was so young, barely four, when he was scarred by abuse that he can't even take it out and look at it. There was terrible conflict between his mother and grandmother. A psychologist once told me that for a boy being in the middle of a conflict between two women is the worst possible situation. There is always the desire to please each one. (Franks 174)

That Hillary Clinton could so publicly uncover her husband's pain in the early stages of her own senatorial tryout illustrates how childhood and other traumas have become officially validated paradigms for explaining human behavior within the media spectacle of millennial American public and political life. Her comments also suggest the prescience of Tim O'Brien's recent fictions as tropes of American posttraumatic culture in the 1990s. They would have been appropriate "Evidence" if their subject, the Comeback Kid, had been the protagonist of *In the Lake of the Woods* instead of John Wade and if O'Brien's sixth work had been a comedy. After all, similar psychobiographical passages about the early lives of Woodrow Wilson, Lyndon Johnson, and Richard Nixon appear in the novel's footnotes, and although the disorders that they implicate might seem more serious than girl chasing, Bill Clinton was the only one of these four potentially great but damaged leaders to be impeached.

That the deeply religious Mrs. Clinton cites "a psychologist" as her authority illustrates as well how reliably she could count on Americans' faith in ego psychology to explain everything from sexual peccadilloes to mass slaughters like the one that had occurred in two on-line day-trading offices in Atlanta three days before the inaugural issue of *Talk* magazine appeared in August 1999. But clinical explanation did not preclude her right to call upon a much older paradigm as well despite its virtual usurpation by the Reaganite counterrevolution: She, and we, can and must forgive Bill if we wish to imitate the most significantly wounded victim in (traumatic) history; after all, "Peter betrayed Jesus three times and Jesus knew it but loved him anyway. Life is not a linear progression. It has many paths and challenges. And we need to help one another" (Franks 248). The intimation of Hillary Clinton's imitating Christ and a boy being scarred by the love of two women may remind us of O'Brien's most recent and most digressive novel, of course, even without reference to the parallels between O'Brien's Tomcat and the former First Philanderer. Although Thomas Chippering is unwilling or unable to uncover exactly what punctured his "leaky love tank" at an early age, an explanation something like the former First Lady's very public testimony would seem to account for his case at least as plausibly as it might explain Monicagate and its appendices of additional national scandal and innuendo.

"What abuse? What actually happened?" was the immediate cry of a skeptical media and those who hounded the president through two administrations, and even Clinton's press secretary was quick to deny any *physical* harm. Whatever Mrs. Clinton's own credibility, such demands for facts ignore the radical inexpressibility and ineradicability of traumatic experiences. O'Brien has characterized *Tomcat in Love* as "a novel about a guy with a huge [w]hole in his heart that he desperately spends life filling. I don't know exactly what caused it, and I wrote the novel" (telephone interview, November 3, 1998). The ineffability and the absent presence of trauma are what writing it out (or writing out of it) recovers. Like many survivors, Chippering denies his disorder as much as he uses it in his own self-defense. After his public breakdown, he tries to refute diagnoses of his behavior—delusional, depressive, and suicidal—refuses to talk to his "Nazi" psychiatrist, and defines his condition as "existential" rather than "nervous" (281). Earlier, the breakup of his marriage to Lorna Sue is accelerated by his refusal to seek help for his jealousy, paranoia, and postwar nightmares, and it is finally effected by the uncovering of fourteen uncashed checks made out to a counselor whom her husband has never seen, because he doesn't exist. Such a figure, who would combine older and newer faiths, might provide a final healing—but a "Dr. Ralph Constantine" can only be imagined, particularly if posttraumatic survivorship is an "existential" condition.

For Lacanians, of course, our very existence is posttraumatic, the symbolic order—whether of Λογοσ, Λεξισ, or *Lexus* ("the Word"/"any word"/a word)—the sign of that inescapable sundering from the M/other but also the means through which a prediscursive Real may be recognized. The gaps, silences, fragments, and elaborate re-coverings and self-refabrications of O'Brien's fiction mark a distinctively American posttraumatic disorder as imaginative truth. Although Tim O'Brien's works are intensely (though covertly) personal, a self-revision of nearly thirty years that has gyred out of an ethical choice with endless consequences—"I was a coward. I went to the war"—they also reflect the traumatic circumstances of American postwar life more generally. By "postwar," of course, I mean post-Vietnam, which has already replaced World War II as a generational marker defining the present U.S. political and business establishment. Even as the traumatizing demonology of the Cold War and the threat of nuclear apocalypse recede, however, Vietnam remains a nightmare that can be only repressed or displaced, despite the shattering of the Berlin Wall and the fin de siècle spread of Wall Street's international marketplace. Margot Henriksen's formidable study of post–World War II American popular culture illustrates the variously inventive forms that public traumatization has taken, just as the current search for an enemy or a number of small enemies or a technological or biological catastrophe to replace international Communism symptomatizes the need of our national security state to perpetuate itself through civic retraumatization. Even as it capitalizes upon our own insecurity, spectacular media coverage of Y2K scenarios, Internet viruses, or "going postal" in all its terrifying manifestations, from middle schools to brokerages to Honolulu Xerox offices, at least suggests that the enemy may be us.

The Nuclear Age was O'Brien's first novel in which the end of the world, the end of a marriage, and childhood terrors were equivalent for the protagonist, and the first in which connections between public and private pathologies were made explicit. It was also his first novel to be categorized as a non-Vietnam book, often to its detriment, for it disappointed many reviewers after the triumph of *Going After Cacciato*. But just as *Cacciato* marked a crucial break from the documentary realism of *If I Die in a Combat Zone* and *Northern Lights*, the hyperbolic and parabolic fiction of its successor crucially extended O'Brien's evocations of traumatization and posttraumatic recovery beyond the personal and individual. Reviewing *In the Lake of the Woods* for the *Guardian* in 1995, Claire Messud noted that its author "has wrung exceptional, universal fiction from his experience as an infantryman." But he has also refabricated his childhood and his relationships with women to create a traumatic triad that O'Brien has defined as "the war of life itself" (McNerney 24) and that ironically provides formal coherence for his posttraumatic fictions. What Don Ringnalda has called the "understood confusion" (90) of O'Brien's work exposes what the writer first discovered for himself through Vietnam: the fragility of selfhood, inevitably subject to physical, psychic, and moral ruin and the cultural paradigms that form and deform our lives as Americans. Although Messud narrows the site of trauma to combat, O'Brien would probably be pleased with her recognition that he has *used* Vietnam rather than trying to merely *represent* it, that the war was the terrible resource out of which he has constituted himself as a writer of fictions engaged with the challenges of personal integrity, ethical choice, and mortality.

Whether or not O'Brien's focus is "universal," it is central to twentieth-century literature. "Modernist literature is a literature of trauma" Karen DeMeester begins a recent article on *Mrs. Dalloway* in a special fall 1998 issue of *Modern Fiction Studies* on "Modernisms and Modern Wars." By grouping its twelve articles under the headings of "The Home Front," "Trauma," and "Ethics," editor Margot Norris acknowledges Tim O'Brien's insistence that "true war stories" are not about "war." David Jarraway's study of trauma and recovery in O'Brien's work explicitly acknowledges its importance in the author's treatments of Vietnam, and its appearance along with DeMeester's essay and an article by Anne Whitehead on Pat Barker's *Regeneration* suggests that trauma is central to postmodern fiction as well. Indeed, trauma theory is increasingly becoming an important prism through which one can see varieties of contemporary writing from a number of perspectives. In the past three years, such work includes J. Brooks Bouson's book on racial trauma in Toni Morrison's novels; Christine van Boheemen's work on Joyce, Derrida, and Lacan; Suzette Henke's study of trauma in women's life-writing; and Efraim Sicher's collection of articles on the post-Holocaust generation of writers in Israel. Earlier studies by Shoshana Felman (1992) and David Aberbach (1989) on literary witnessing of traumatic crises also attest to how trauma is becoming a personal and literary matrix of increasing importance within the academy. A session of the Northeast Modern Language Association in March 2001 titled "Residues of War in America" will examine war as a posttraumatic phenomenon and invites papers on such writers as Wharton, Faulkner, Ellison, Mailer, Flannery O'Connor, Joy Ogawa—and Tim O'Brien, among others.

O'Brien's own "war of living" has been most fully explored in his most recent novels, the tragic and comic love stories, respectively, of *In the Lake of the Woods* and *Tomcat in Love*. But while John Wade's life seems to be over, Thomas Chippering's seems to be *starting* over, and the same may be said for O'Brien's work itself, which continues to find new post-Vietnam subjects. Chippering's mysterious "hole" may be psychic or existential, but the most important wound in the novel is quite tangible, yet even more mysterious and relatively unexplored. The hole in Lorna Sue's hand cannot be filled or repaired any more easily than Chippering's, but since *Tomcat* is his story, hers can be only imperfectly imagined and healed through his posttraumatic apostrophes to the "lost princess" for whom "Fiji" represents pain and loss. O'Brien's categorization as a Vietnam writer and Chippering's inability to imagine his wife's story are starting places for considering O'Brien's present critical reputation and for speculating upon his future evolution as an artist of our disorder.

Academic Polemics

Exactly two decades after its end, the furor over Robert McNamara's penitential judgment that the American war in Viet Nam was "wrong" and unwinnable and that he knew this even at the very time that he was administering it reignited briefly a national debate that has never been resolved and that lies under the surface of the body politic like a shameful wound that seems dangerous to expose. George McGovern, whose unsuccessful presidential campaign in 1972 characterized Vietnam as a failed and immoral enterprise, was kinder than most to McNamara's duplicity, noting that the war remains unassimilable within the settled body of national myth: "In a sense, this is our second civil war. We're going to be fighting this war for the rest of our lives" (Fisher). The continuing war over the war within academic criticism has gone through what might be categorized as three phases since the late 1970s: the *representational*, or mimetic; the *canonical*, or literary proper; and the *cultural*, or ideological. Although they overlap in particular studies, the terms are generally useful in distinguishing critical emphases and assumptions. Representational criticism evaluates whether or not a work effectively conveys the reality of the war; canonical, whether it contributes significantly to the body of American literature, national myth, and civil religion; and cultural, how it exposes or covers up ideologies of race, gender, and class that characterize American society generally and normally go unremarked in an age of indiscriminate consumption, commodified popular culture, and specular politics.

From the very beginning of the Viet Nam war, truth was a casualty, so the question of mimesis—whether a work represents Vietnam authentically—initially assumed an importance that went beyond simply reproducing details of combat or portraying the American presence in Viet Nam. The most common purpose of most American Vietnam literature, whatever the writer's political position, was to expose the untruths of official policy, progress reports, and propaganda, media sound bites, and popular mythology that misrepresented the reality of Vietnam until the war was lost. But the literary value of war fiction does not depend on mimetic representation or experiential authority. It doesn't have to describe the battlefield at all; Homer's similes in the *Iliad* are powerful because they describe peace or nature, not war. Nor is experience as a soldier necessary: *The Red Badge of Courage*, the archetypal American war story, was written by a journalist who never saw combat, and Susan Fromberg Schaeffer has written one of our best Vietnam war novels (*Buffalo Afternoon*; see Jason 1993). Canonicity is determined by extramimetic factors, including whether a work participates in, extends, or rewrites literary tradition. Finally, since Vietnam was not just a war but also a significant American historical, political, and cultural *episteme*, a work may be valuable for what it shows us about the end of the American century and the ideological writing and rewriting of our own lives within and beyond it.

The movement from representational to cultural criticism is well illustrated by the work of Philip Beidler, whose two important critical surveys of Vietnam literature have different purposes. The very title of *American Literature and the Experience of Vietnam* (1982) epitomizes its project: Nearly twenty-five writers are discussed in some detail and recognized for giving significant literary form to the realities of the war in Viet Nam. Many of the same writers, having been canonized by Beidler and subsequent critics, are reconsidered in *Re-Writing America: Vietnam Authors in Their Generation* (1991). As the title suggests, Beidler would claim that these authors haven't simply written books; they have revised American culture through their writings. Their ultimate subject turns out to be America, not the war (and certainly not Viet Nam). O'Brien is among the twelve writers handled extensively in both studies, and his position as a first among equals is implicit in the second book: He is the first writer to be treated in *Re-Writing America*, and a citation from *The Things They Carried* is Beidler's initial epigraph. The careers of writers who have continued to treat Vietnam for the past twenty years have also moved from Viet Nam to America and from the war to its cultural and ideological contexts, as Beidler's second study demonstrates. Looking at the broader cultural context of American Vietnam war literature has characterized other studies of the 1990s, including those of John Carlos Rowe and Rick Berg, Andrew Martin, and Philip H. Melling.

This movement from representing Vietnam to reconsidering America (and Viet Nam) is an inevitable function of generational change, of course. Beidler, like most Vietnam fiction writers and poets, was himself a soldier in the war, whereas many of the cultural critics began their careers after it was over or were never in Viet Nam during the American intervention. Negative critical reevaluations of O'Brien's work share a general unease about valorizing combat narratives by direct participants rather than other representations of Vietnam. But they also reflect a shift within the profession of literature itself as the war years recede from personal memory into history and younger scholars move from literary criticism to cultural studies. For such academic writers, the Vietnam author is less important as witness or artist than as symptomatic reproducer or subversive disrupter of dominant ideologies that the critic seeks to expose. All texts become political vehicles for use in the present. Thus, Susan Jeffords has argued in *The Remasculinization of America* that "the arena of warfare and the Vietnam War in particular are not just fields of battle but fields of gender, in which enemies are depicted as feminine, wives and mothers and girl friends are the justifications for fighting, and vocabularies are sexually motivated" (xi). While Jeffords critiques its gender discourse, Renny Christopher censures the ethnocentric bias of canonical American literature dealing with Vietnam. Nearly all such works represent the war falsely or partially, and such attempts to authenticate it through literary aestheticization simply mystify their contradictions and evasions.

The combat metaphor invoked in Jeffords's introduction is entitled to more explicit prominence in the three most recent book-length cultural critiques of American Vietnam literature, Don Ringnalda's *Fighting and Writing the Vietnam War* (1994), Milton Bates's *The Wars We Took to Vietnam* (1996), and Jim Neilson's *Warring Fictions* (1998). The polemics pursued in such studies typically target Vietnam writers and other critics. For example, Ringnalda defines and praises the work of "blue-collar postmodernist" writers (xii) whose methods are configured with the successful battlefield tactics of the Viet Cong. He contrasts these literary guerrillas with the more numerous "warrior realist" writers (27), whose assumptions and procedures are denounced for being infected by the same linear thinking and mechanistic paradigms that the American military applied so futilely in waging the war. Ringnalda's approach and his combative title enlist him in the culture wars of the post-Vietnam American academy on the winning side: His chief culprits among the successful realist writers, James Webb and John Del Vecchio, have denounced the postwar Vietnamese government and believe that the United States was right to fight the war but used the wrong means to fight it. Like Renny Christopher and Susan Jeffords, Ringnalda is also dissatisfied with the first generation of Vietnam literary critics—Beidler, John Hellmann, Thomas Myers—insofar as their denunciation of the war is less critical of "mythic junk" (44), American cultural paradigms that their writing revalidates. Yet Jeffords herself is also criticized for being insufficiently postmodern in her criticism. More strikingly, in Ringnalda's analysis of his works, O'Brien is recanonized as one of the supreme literary guerrillas; statements by the writer are used to support the critic's own point of view; and Doc Peret, one of O'Brien's characters in *Going After Cacciato*, is interpreted as a guru of the metafictional consciousness that is the touchstone of the most valuable Vietnam texts for the critic. In turn, Jim Neilson's neo-Marxist critique finds Jeffords (and the publishing industry generally) insufficiently working-class but particularly denounces Ringnalda and others whose false faith in postmodernism ignores its cover-up of material realities. Besides discovering that the United States is an aggressively capitalist society infected with liberal pluralism, *Warring Fictions* outdoes previous critiques of previous academic criticism by Jeffords, Christopher, Ringnalda, and Kali Tal by focusing primarily on Vietnam literary criticism rather than on literature. For Neilson, *The Things They Carried* is characterized by "elaborate and elusive self-consciousness" (193), a "self-referentiality" (194) that approving critics have praised as a reflection of the "surreality and unreality of Vietnam" (195), thus mystifying the criminality of the war by "confusing its perceptual experience with its material fact" (195). Renny Christopher, a cultural critic more concerned with ethnocentric distortions, has criticized O'Brien's *Cacciato* for failing to teach us anything about Viet Nam (229) and being fixated on the "minutiae of individualism" (230). Although Jeffords barely refers to O'Brien's work, other important feminist critics, including Lorrie Smith and Tal, have been unsatisfied with his genderized, largely instrumental representation of female characters, which they find typical of most American Vietnam War narratives. Thus, Tal (1990) defines Sarkin Aung Wan as simply a figural aspect of O'Brien's protagonist: "Both more and less than a human being, the Asian woman character represents the reconciliation of contradictions within the author" (77). Since Paul Berlin ultimately rejects his fantasized Asian girlfriend, he "succumbs, in the end, . . . to the traditional myths of male romance. . . . The division between men and women in this novel is unbreachable, and it is the male half which must triumph" (78).

Whether criticized as typically ethnocentric/solipsistic/sexist or praised as mythopoeic/postmodernist, O'Brien's status as the most well-known American writer on the war makes him an essential subject for other writers to illustrate and validate their own critique of Vietnam. If the author had any interest in academic warfare, he would probably deny that his subject is Vietnam or Viet Nam, regard the charge of ethnocentrism as irrelevant or unfair, and claim that while his works both represent and enact self-consciousness, they undercut, satirize, and repudiate solipsism. Claiming to speak for the Vietnamese point of view would be "hubris," he has noted, just as the Vietnamese writers that he met in 1994 would never claim to represent the American point of view (McNerney 17). Ultimately, a less ethnocentric, less personal, and less traumatic view of Vietnam and Viet Nam is not O'Brien's responsibility. It is already being effected by Vietnamese and Vietnamese exile writers such as those treated by Christopher and reviewed in Philip Jason's recent survey of "Vietnamese in America." It will also derive from the work of women and other noncombatants, including later writers. Two recent college anthologies of Vietnam

literature valuably broaden the focus and extend the canon of Vietnam literature in such directions. Wayne Karlin, Le Minh Khue, and Truong Vu
provide "postwar" fiction and emphasize Vietnamese and Vietnamese
American writers. H. Bruce Franklin, the dean of antiwar American ac-
ademics, presents a large number of women Vietnam writers, many of
them relatively unknown. Linda van Devanter and Joan Furey's collection
of poetry written by women who served in Viet Nam whether in military
or humanitarian organizations, and anthologies edited by American and
Vietnamese writers, such as *Mountain River* (modern Vietnamese war poetry; Bowen), provide other examples. Karlin has also edited and published
English translations of the poetry of Le Minh Khue (1997) and the fiction of
Ho Anh Thai (1998) as part of Curbstone Press's "Voices from Vietnam" series. Larry Heinemann is currently writing a book on the Vietnamese railroad system that will also consider cross-cultural perceptions of the war
by Vietnamese and Americans. For O'Brien, however, who found it difficult
to swallow the legacy of Nuoc Man when he returned to Quang Ngai in
1994, Vietnam is a traumatic resource, not the subject of his writing.

Questions about ignoring or weakly representing women, which have
been prominent in recent interviews (e.g., Kaplan, Bourne, McNerney),
seem to be more significant charges for the writer. Just after finishing *The
Things They Carried*, he told Brian McNerney and Catherine Calloway that
his numerous appreciative letters from women readers are even more satisfying than those from Vietnam veterans: "The joy is not the joy of touching veterans or touching people who have lived what you have lived. The
joy is just the opposite. Maybe that's what hurts me when I hear that articles are being written by women saying I am anti-feminist. The whole
creative joy is to touch the hearts of people whose hearts otherwise
wouldn't be touched" (McNerney 15). *Tomcat in Love* seems an ironic response to such criticism. Chippering is both victim and epitome of the
minicontestations and follies of academic life, which are broadly bur-
lesqued in the novel. In a footnote on page ninety-seven, he refers to *Critique*, a cultural studies journal in which O'Brien's work has been praised
but also criticized, as in Lorrie Smith's attack upon the "gendered subtext"
of the *Esquire* stories that were later incorporated into *The Things They
Carried*. Less oblique references to feminist critics make up Chapter 24,
"Noogies," a gleefully chauvinist riposte to "demagogues of gender" by
Chippering. In Chapter 36, once he has given up his lunatic schemes of

vengeance against his former wife, the former professor suffers a late
Fourth of July night dream in which he is executed by Jane Fonda for his
failure to treat all the "girls" he has known as "individuals" while Lorna Sue
burns up his love ledger. A chauvinist's worst nightmare, O'Brien's apocalyptic vision is the culmination of Chippering's being "womanhandled"
(327) throughout the novel. The distance between O'Brien and Chippering
as a caricature of his creator needs to be emphasized, however. Whereas
the professor's academic career flames out spectacularly, O'Brien happily
spent the year after finishing *Tomcat* as a visiting writer within the academy at Southwest Texas State University and currently holds the Mitte
Chair in Creative Writing there. By risking his readers' patience with a protagonist whom even male reviewers have found "crazy" (Fields-Meyer),
"obnoxious" (Sterling), and "arrogant" (Kloszewski), of course, O'Brien is
able to satirize both sides of the gender divide as well as comically refabricate his own pain, anger, and retraumatization. At the same time, an episode like Chippering's being bound and gagged while he tries to tell his
Vietnam trauma story reflects O'Brien's personal dissatisfaction with having his work canonized or criticized simply because it fulfills or fails to fulfill extraliterary criteria for significance or value. "The world wants to tie
me up or shut me up with every book," he joked during our telephone interview (November 3, 1998). Even a glowing review of *Tomcat* in the *Tor-
onto Globe and Mail* was headed by a title that the author found irritating
("O'Brien Does Vietnam Better") because he was not trying to "do Vietnam"
again (telephone interview, November 3, 1998). Each book creates its own
world and explores new territory, O'Brien would claim, and none of them
since *Combat Zone* is a book about Vietnam.

Responsible Dreams

Asked during his 1998 Ann Arbor reading about what territory he
might wish to explore next, O'Brien confessed an ambition to write from a
woman's point of view, a feat of ventriloquism that he had tried only once
in his career. The short story "Loon Point" tells the story of a wife's infidelity and the accidental death of her secret lover by representing her trauma
from within. Abridged and radically rewritten as Chapter 24 of *In the Lake
of the Woods* ("Hypothesis"), it is the sixth of the eight attempts to imagine
what might have happened to Kathy Wade. As noted in Chapter 7, the title

itself confesses the male narrator's/author's diffidence as he arrogates the power to enter a woman's mind and understand her as she might understand herself. Like Chippering's apostrophes to his female counterpart in *Tomcat* (who was originally a jilted man like himself—and like O'Brien), these tentative approaches to fabricating a woman's soul may reflect O'Brien's honest reluctance both as an artist and as a survivor of divorce and heartbreak to enter such unexplored and self-annihilating territory and emerge with true stories.

Such narrative prosopopoeia, which would be an even more radical reinvention of himself than the pedantic lunatic of *Tomcat,* is at the heart of some of O'Brien's post-*Tomcat* fiction, three short stories that have appeared in *The New Yorker* and *Esquire.* In "Nogales" (perhaps partly encouraged by O'Brien's move to Texas), the spinster Karen Burns is both sexually attracted to and betrayed by the young man who drives the van for a Tucson retirement community that she directs. In "The Streak," Amy, a thirty-six-year-old lawyer and newlywed, realizes that she has made a terrible mistake even as she watches her fifty-one-year-old husband ride a $240,000 lucky streak at an Indian-owned casino in northern Minnesota. "Class of '68," a one-page minifiction, is told from the point of view of a jilted former lover who encounters his old flame at a class reunion. But its central figure is the fifty-one-year-old woman, just diagnosed with breast cancer and drinking heavily for reasons that her resentful and self-pitying former lover may lack the imagination to understand. In addition to their focus on women in distress, the stories are notable for their lack of Vietnam references (although "Billy" in "Class of '68" seems to have fled to Canada during the war and been "betrayed" by his female classmate's failure to go with him) and for their straightforward, naturalistic prose style and details. Whatever their eventual fate—whether as stories or as part of the book that O'Brien is currently putting together—they suggest that their author has summoned himself to fabricate a female "other" who is independent of his own self-revision. Whether this latest "new start" is being pursued as a consequence of his personal and professional recovery, in unacknowledged response to criticism of his representations of women, or simply as an artist's challenge, it extends O'Brien's focus on the breakdown, fragmentation, and questioning of the self that accompanies traumatic experiences. Karen and her party of senior citizens are kidnapped and left for dead in the Mexican desert by two young drug smugglers;

Amy feels a desperate need to walk out on her husband four days after marrying him in order to save her own life; the cancer-stricken "sensible woman" of "Class of '68" may be haunted by a "sense of a foreshortened future," a diagnostic criteria for PTSD (see appendix: C.7) that has been traumatically extended in the age of AIDS.

O'Brien's most recent true fictions—"Winnipeg" and "July '69"—continue the refabrication of himself, his work, and other writers that we have seen in all his previous fiction. The former extends the brief sketch of "Class of '68" by narrating the life history of Billy McMann, who has lost his country, his college sweetheart, his wife, and his most recent lover. This series of traumata began with his flight to Canada in 1969 to escape Vietnam and ends in this story with his return to the United States with his daughter Susie and a bitter encounter with the first love of his life, Dorothy, the figure in "Class of '68" who stayed in the States rather than accompany him to Canada, and who has married well. McMann has also attended his mother's funeral in Minnesota but remains a figure in exile from America and his own painful past, emotionally constricted and sullen. Billy McMann is the latest refabrication of O'Brien's romantic and political trauma, but he also combines elements of Cowling, Wade, and Chippering in a new, unsatisfied posttraumatic survivor. Such refashioned elements of autobiography are even evident in the earlier stories. O'Brien has revealed to Lynn Warton that not only does "Nogales" partly reflect the work of Flannery O'Connor, it is also based on an incident involving his own parents during an earlier vacation trip to Arizona. And while Amy is the protagonist of "The Streak," her husband's almost fanatical pursuit of gambling in a Minnesota casino reflects one of O'Brien's own small pleasures, exemplified in Bruce Weber's interview of the author in 1998.

Perhaps the masterpiece among this post-*Tomcat* fiction is "July '69," which focuses on Lieutenant Dave Todd, the only survivor of a platoon that he has led to annihilation in an enemy ambush. While the platoon radio intermittently broadcasts reports of the first American moon landing, Dave Todd spends July 16, 1969, crawling away from the carnage, shot through both feet, mortally wounded, imaginatively revisiting his life until another voice with a Texas accent seems to come over the radio, offering to order him a dustoff if he has the courage to accept what he must endure after that final helicopter ride. Like the postmortem decision of Ted Lavender in "The Lives of the Dead" and pacified by his last Syrette of morphine, Dave chooses to "fly," to live as a posttraumatic survivor who will be crippled forever physically and psychically by the trauma he has gone through—or does he simply accept death? An exquisitely moving yet off-beat synthesis of the worst obscenity of war with a minitriumph of the human spirit, "July '69" seamlessly combines symbolic associations derived from O'Brien's own wounding in Viet Nam and his experiences as a platoon radio carrier; the ironic juxtaposition of America's triumph in space with its terrible failure on the ground; and elements of Paul Berlin, Ted Lavender, Jimmy Cross, and Oedipus in the characterization of Dave Todd (*tod*—"dead"). Trauma is first fabricated and then refabricated into art so that death has no dominion, and the "burden of the brave" becomes simply continuing to go on after the worst has already happened.

Valuable in themselves, the post-*Tomcat* stories are on their way in August 2000 to becoming O'Brien's first book of the new millennium, a fiction with the tentative title "July, July." The title suggests, as always, O'Brien's fascination with overall form and ideas even in a collection of short stories. Billy McMann fled to Canada on July 7, 1969; Dave Todd (and Neil Armstrong) left this earth on July 16, 1969; the United States of America was born on July 4, 1776; and on other Fourths, Norman Bowker considered suicide, Thomas Chippering gave up his obsession with Lorna Sue, and, of course, Tim O'Brien revisited, survived, and re-created "The Vietnam in Me" in 1994. Whether the new work resembles *The Things They Carried* in repeating, elaborating, and cross-referencing its fictions and fragments as a whole or juxtaposes them more loosely, it seems that traumatization will once again be at the center of any form that may be fashioned from it.

What began as one young man's moral trauma—choosing to participate in what he knew was evil—has exfoliated in O'Brien's fictional world to include love as well as war, childhood and marriage and the death of parents, individual moments of crisis and the violence of American history and culture, personal and national nightmares. His work, which was made possible by Vietnam, has extended beyond the battlefield to the war of life itself. It continues the author's attempt to achieve the universality that O'Brien believes is both the privilege and the responsibility of true fiction. Just as its vehicle has been the artfully organized representation of traumatic symptoms, the tenor of O'Brien's fictional world has been what we have come to accept as the traumatic conditions of survival in postmodern society. "It would be hard to estimate the plasticity and the elemental power of the concept," Kirby Farrell notes in *Post-traumatic Culture*. "People use trauma as an enabling fiction, an explanatory tool for managing unquiet minds in an overwhelming world. But it has that explanatory power because, however overstated or implausible the concept sounds, people feel, or are prepared to feel, whether they are aware of it or not, as if they have been traumatized" (x). Like Kali Tal, who introduced *Worlds of Hurt* by revealing that she had suffered sexual abuse at the age of twelve (1996: 4), Farrell locates personal experiences within his critical paradigm: the sudden death of an elderly neighbor when he was nine years old and "suddenly [understanding] that one day I was going to die" (ix); memories of Cold War childhood "war games in sunny New England backyards, dimly aware of the satanic Communists supposedly hiding under every bed"; their intrusion into his experience as a Peace Corps consultant forty years later in Kazakhstan where he watched schoolchildren playing about a rusting and discarded Soviet war plane (x). Yet the loss of personal and cultural certainties that is an aftermath of traumatic experiences "can spur imagination to new creativity" whether in Don DeLillo's "white noise of background dread," cited by Farrell (xiii), or in the world that Tim O'Brien has created.

Tomcat in Love reminds us that there are degrees of trauma, of course, that it can be abused as well as fabricated, used either as an excuse for irresponsibility or as a starting point for personal and cultural interrogation. That trauma can be a resource for growth is exemplified not only by O'Brien's career and Kali Tal's study of the literature of trauma but by countless personal triumphs. Thus, Eric Shinseki, who grew up on Kauai as an officially identified "enemy alien" during World War II and was nearly killed twice in Viet Nam, where he lost part of his foot, was to become the first Asian American four-star general in American history before being chosen the army's thirty-fourth chief of staff on June 22, 1999 (Kakesako). But although trauma may painfully make us stronger and wiser sometimes, it can never be effaced. The D-Day celebrations of 1994 were marked much less by the triumphant pride and satisfaction of the American heroes in what they had accomplished than by the breakdown of aged veterans into tears as they recalled their failure to save lost comrades, a reassertion of trauma used by Stephen Spielberg to bracket the narrative of *Saving Private Ryan* in 1998.

That both men and women break down and cry in the face of unbearably wounding experiences testifies not only to the universality of trauma but to the potential of postmodern traumatic fiction in uniting at least its readers beyond the everyday fractures of gender and political or national enmity that are the breeding ground of our smaller and greater wars. Jane Smiley's praise of *Tomcat in Love* in the *New York Times Book Review* (1998) is preceded by Richard Berke's review of ideological boilerplate from Bill Bennett (*The Death of Outrage: Bill Clinton and the Assault on American Ideals*) but also followed by Richard Shweder's review of Nancy Venable Raine's *After Silence: Rape and My Journey Back*, an account by a thirty-nine-year-old divorcee of being assaulted in 1985 that is also a testament of recovery. For Shweder, "*After Silence* is a book that dignifies the human spirit. It should be read by *everyone*" [emphasis added]. O'Brien's fiction seems appropriately placed between Bennett's tendentious "morality" and Raine's authentic "happening-truth," sharing their ethical seriousness but fabricating experience into a posttraumatic narrative that might be enjoyed by anyone. Judith Kitchen's 1996 meditation on *In the Lake of the Woods* and Edna O'Brien's 1994 novel *The House of Splendid Isolation* also suggests the resonance of Tim O'Brien's traumatic fictions for another writer and reader, who interweaves John Wade's tragedy with other texts, including the Irish novel, and intrusions of "our shame": the Irish Republican Army bombing campaign, the Vietnam War/Democratic Convention in 1968, and the April 1995 bombing of the Murrah Building in Oklahoma City, where Kitchen had conducted a writing workshop for survivors by invitation of the Oklahoma Arts Institute.

In another review of *In the Lake of the Woods*, Alan Davis referred to O'Brien as "still a hunger artist, struggling with the aftermath of Vietnam" (328). Although the author might disagree with the categorization of his subject, he might welcome being recognized as a heartland Kafka, a postwar trauma artist of the American century as it dissolves into a new millennium. To whatever extent the feast of folly that is *Tomcat in Love* and the tentatively gynocentric direction of some of O'Brien's latest fiction represent a fresh start, they also extend the everyday abnormality of posttraumatic experience that has shaped and been reshaped in all of his work. During a public reading tour of *The Things They Carried* at Claremont McKenna College more than ten years ago, O'Brien became fascinated with Delmore Schwartz's collection *In Dreams Begin Responsibilities* and spent one night reading the copy lent to him by one of his faculty hosts. The haunting title story might have struck him with the shock of self-recognition and furnishes this study with a final epitome of O'Brien's traumatic art.

Schwartz's narrator, a thinly fabricated version of the author himself, enters, or dreams he enters, a motion picture theater in 1909 and watches his mother's and father's courtship developing on the screen. Breaking down uncontrollably, he tries to efface his destiny by breaking up the engagement, shouting aloud at the screen and spoiling the movie for the rest of the audience: "Don't do it. It's not too late to change your minds, both of you. Nothing good will come of it, only remorse, hatred, scandal, and two children whose characters are monstrous" (6). Loudly interrupting it again at the point when their future together, including his own life, are about to be revealed by a fortune teller, he is forcibly ejected from the theater by an angry but wise usher who scolds him for his irresponsibility just before he wakes up "into the bleak winter of [his] 21st birthday": "What are *you* doing? Don't you know that you can't do whatever you want to do? . . . You can't act like this even if other people aren't around! You will be sorry if you do not do what you should do, you can't carry on like this, it is not right, you will find that out soon enough, everything you do matters too much" (8–9). Besides reflecting typical O'Brien themes such as the permeability of fiction and experience, dreams and reality, and childhood and adulthood, the story dramatizes the later artist's lifelong attempt to rewrite his own life while still remaining true to the obligations of his imagination by not interfering irresponsibly. Schwartz's parodic rewriting of Job's desire that he might never have been born sees life itself as a posttraumatic experience, beginning with the wound of birth. But, whether in life or its fictive fabrication, we must accept the conditions under which everything we do matters too much since we can't do what we want to do and ought to do what we should. Suspended like Paul Berlin at the Paris peace talks between desires and obligations, O'Brien's characters and his various fictive selves are faced with the responsibility of making choices that, at best, can recover trauma but can never bury it. It may have been "twisted" from the first, like the "magic" apple tree in which Tommy, Lorna Sue, and the eight-year-old Herbie are first inspired to make firebombs (*Tomcat* 253–54), but the show must go on.

From the *Diagnostic and Statistical Manual of Mental Disorders, Fourth Edition* [*DSM-IV*]. Washington, D.C.: American Psychiatric Association, 1994: 427–29.

A. The person has been exposed to a traumatic event in which both of the following were present:

(1) the person experienced, witnessed, or was confronted with an event or events that involved actual or threatened death or serious injury, or a threat to the physical integrity of self or others.

(2) the person's response involved intense fear, helplessness, or horror. **Note:** In children, this may be expressed instead by disorganized or agitated behavior.

B. The traumatic event is persistently reexperienced in one (or more) of the following ways:

(1) recurrent and intrusive distressing recollections of the event, including images, thoughts, or perceptions. **Note:** In young children, repetitive play may occur in which themes or aspects of the trauma are expressed.

(2) recurrent distressing dreams of the event. **Note:** In children, there may be frightening dreams without recognizable content.

(3) acting or feeling as if the traumatic event were recurring (includes a sense of reliving the experience, illusions, hallucinations, and dissociative flashback episodes, including those that occur on awakening or when intoxicated). **Note:** In young children, trauma-specific reenactment may occur.

(4) intense psychological distress at exposure to internal or external cues that symbolize or resemble an aspect of the traumatic event.

(5) physiological reactivity on exposure to internal or external cues that symbolize or resemble an aspect of the traumatic event.

C. Persistent avoidance of stimuli associated with the trauma and numbing of general responsiveness (not present before the trauma), as indicated by three (or more) of the following:

(1) efforts to avoid thoughts, feelings, or conversations associated with the trauma

(2) efforts to avoid activities, places, or people that arouse recollections of the trauma

(3) inability to recall an important aspect of the trauma

(4) markedly diminished interest or participation in significant activities

(5) feeling of detachment or estrangement from others

(6) restricted range of affect (e.g., unable to have loving feelings)

(7) sense of a foreshortened future (e.g., does not expect to have a career, marriage, children, or a normal life span)

D. Persistent symptoms of increased arousal (not present before the trauma), as indicated by two (or more) of the following:

(1) difficulty falling or staying asleep

(2) irritability or outbursts of anger

(3) difficulty concentrating

(4) hypervigilance

(5) exaggerated startle response

E. Duration of the disturbance (symptoms in Criteria B, C, and D) is more than 1 month.

F. The disturbance causes clinically significant distress or impairment in social, occupational, or other important areas of functioning.

Specify if

Acute: if duration of symptoms is less than 3 months

Chronic: if duration of symptoms is 3 months or more

Specify if

With Delayed Onset: if onset of symptoms is at least 6 months after the stressor

Introduction

1. In Philip Jason's superb 1992 annotated bibliography of articles and books on Vietnam War literature, the two works with the greatest number of individual entries are *Dispatches* (nineteen) and *Cacciato* (twenty-three). They have been handled together in important articles by Dale Jones and John Jakaitis as well as in Thomas Myers's seminal book on American Vietnam fiction, which pairs them as exemplars of "dazzling alchemistic operations within a revised American romanticism" (Myers 1988: 33). *Dispatches* ironically intersected with O'Brien's first published work. His combat memoir, *If I Die in a Combat Zone, Box Me Up and Ship Me Home*, was initially submitted to Knopf, where it was well-received. But because the publisher was already preparing to bring out Herr's work on Vietnam, O'Brien was advised to contact Seymour Lawrence, his future editor (Lee 198).

2. The problem of cultural misreading is further complicated and enriched by the peculiar provenance of written Vietnamese itself, the only Asian tonal language written and read in Western romanized scripts by native speakers. A product and vehicle of Western colonization, written Vietnamese is perhaps the most tangible manifestation of how codependent Viet Nam and the West have been from the seventeenth century onward, tragically so during the past two centuries. The "national language" (*quoc-nhu*), which replaced the earlier written language, a transliteration of Vietnamese words into Chinese characters, was an invention of Catholic missionaries that culminated in the work of Alexandre de Rhodes, whose Annamese [Vietnamese]–Portuguese–Latin dictionary was published at Rome in 1651 (Thompson 54). As a result, Vietnamese looks like something familiar to an American reader, even though it differs profoundly from English in all

other ways. See my discussion of "The Things They Didn't Know" (*Going After Cacciato*) in the introduction and the accompanying note below.

3. Without the proper intonation, reading the Western-derived letters of Vietnamese simply produces meaningless sounds. But even the presence of tonal diacritics in a dictionary would further bewilder a nonnative speaker. "*Lùi lại*," "step back," must be pronounced in two descending tones, the second significantly more abrupt than the first. An American soldier threatening villagers with his M-16 would probably speak the two-word phrase with abruptly ascending intonation. "*Nằm xuống đất*," "lie down on the ground" (Stink would probably like to say "hit the dirt!"), follows one descending tone with two ascending ones; the vowels [ă], [ô], and [â] are distinctive phonemes; and [đ] represents the English sound [d], whereas the letter [d] in Vietnamese has a very different sound than [d] in English, more like [y] in southern areas and [z] in the north. Much more radically than other foreign languages written in Western script, Vietnamese cannot simply be read aloud by Americans; it must be experienced through contact with native speakers and be communicated through entirely different habits of articulation. (Tonal diacritics are taken from the *Vietnamese-English Dictionary* edited by Nguyen Dinh-Hoa.)

1. Fabricating Trauma

1. Even those not directly in combat were often traumatized. Over one-fourth of the women who served in Viet Nam developed full PTSD, and one-third of them were still victims in 1990, fifteen years after the end of the war. (Comparable figures for men were 30 percent and about one-half.) Vietnam veterans' PTSD rates were about eight times those of Vietnam-era veterans who had not been in Southeast Asia, and about fifteen times the rate for the American civilian population (figures from Kulka, xxvii–xxviii).

In both the Viet Cong and the North Vietnamese Army (NVA), of course, the "tail" of noncombat support troops was much smaller, and traumatization must have been the "usual experience" for the majority of Vietnamese, who incurred enormous physical and psychological devastation, whether they were civilians or combatants. Bao Ninh's *The Sorrow of War*, the most celebrated North Vietnamese novel of the war that has been translated into English, is a powerful fiction written by an NVA combat veteran whose narrator's postwar responsibility is to find and bury dead comrades, whose bodies have often been nearly obliterated beyond physical recovery. The Vietnamese protagonist is so deeply traumatized that he eventually commits suicide without finishing his tragic memoir. The emphasis on unresolvable trauma in this novel made it profoundly controversial in Viet Nam, as it suggested that the war had resulted in inescapable and endless suffering for the victors as well as the losers.

2. Ehrhart's writings are finely analyzed in Chapter 4 of *Worlds of Hurt*, but Kali Tal focuses mainly on the poetry, and her emphasis on trauma differs from mine. Ehrhart's *Busted*, discussed above, was published in 1995, after the completion of Tal's book, along with reprintings of *Passing Time* (originally titled *Marking Time*) and *Vietnam–Perkasie*.

2. A Bad War

1. O'Brien published a revised version of the work in 1989, an early literal rewriting of himself that followed his first three fictional refabrications. Since I argue that even the original form of the combat memoir self-consciously rewrites personal experience as quasi-fictional paradigm, all citations are from the 1973 text, O'Brien's first published book, and the one most readily available to readers.

2. Here and elsewhere my references to O'Brien's works published before 1993 are based on the valuable bibliographies of his work compiled by Catherine Calloway.

3. The original Italian in O'Brien's text is the following: *"lo maggior don che Dio per sua larghezza / fesse creando . . . / . . . fu de la volontà la libertate"* (10).

4. As O'Brien explains in "My Lai in May" (118), this name for the general area of the Batangan Peninsula that included the villages of My Lai was overdetermined. It was colored pink on American military maps, signifying a built-up area, but the soil as well was "sandy red clay." A Viet Cong stronghold, the name was obviously politically appropriate as well.

3. The Old Man and the Pond

1. I count twenty-six specific references to Vietnam in Part One of the novel, six in Part Two; descriptions of Harvey's eye decrease from fourteen in Part One to eight in Part Two, which is thirty-seven pages longer.

2. Marie Nelson notes that O'Brien's dedications show regard for the values of community and family (*Combat Zone* was dedicated to his family, for example). O'Brien's work certainly emphasizes such values, but they are not well-represented in the Arrowhead people of *Northern Lights*, who are largely satirized, like O'Brien's own hometown in *Combat Zone*. Using an ironic tactic that goes back at least as far as Chaucer and Boccaccio, O'Brien fends off resentment by reminding local readers that this is not the truth but "just a story."

3. In fact, referring to the protagonist is a problem that curiously reflects Paul's own undefined sense of identity as O'Brien has styled him. Rosellen Brown's *New*

Republic review of the novel used the family name (Perry) alone instead of "Paul," whereas Roger Sale used "Perry" as if it were the proper equivalent of "Harvey," thus confusing Paul's given name with the patronymic. My own use of "Paul" is largely a practical convention to distinguish the younger brother from "Harvey," but it is literally misleading because the narrative voice in *Northern Lights* never uses the name.

4. The fictional chronology, like so much else about the book, both intimates and rejects autobiographical referentiality. O'Brien returned to Minnesota in the same year that Harvey did, and both had been wounded in the war. But whereas *Combat Zone* ends in late winter, with O'Brien looking down on the bleak Minnesota landscape through his plane window, Harvey arrives in the stifling heat of mid-July. Harvey's damaged eye can't help but be visible; O'Brien's wound was partially hidden, however, as he was hit by grenade shrapnel on his hand, arm, and the back of his legs.

5. Only twenty reviews of *Northern Lights* are listed in Catherine Calloway's two O'Brien bibliographies despite the critical success of its predecessor, *Combat Zone*, with its thirty reviews. With the acclaim given to *Going After Cacciato*, of course, reviews of that novel and the following books are far more numerous. *Northern Lights* is usually not discussed by critics who define O'Brien as a Vietnam writer. In his earlier book, for example, Philip Beidler analyzes *Combat Zone* and *Cacciato* extensively but makes no mention of O'Brien's first novel. In *Re-Writing America*, it is given two and one-half pages in a twenty-six-page discussion of O'Brien's first five books.

6. In fact, the book was reviewed in the journal *Western American Literature* along with Richard Martin Stern's *Power*, a piece of popular fiction about real estate deals in northern New Mexico. O'Brien's novel, judged to be the more significant work, was praised as a "consideration of the ingrained myths of a disappearing northern frontier" (Roripaugh 179).

7. The title page itself is iconographic, arranging the headings of the nine sections in a circular pattern around the image of an arrowhead whose apex points downward to "Blizzard." The image maps the trajectory of the brothers' narrative, spiraling downward from Harvey's return from the war to the nearly fatal ski excursion, and then rising to their imminent departure from the Arrowhead.

8. She notes that the fictional time frame of *Northern Lights* occurs about two years after that of *Combat Zone* and the later novel, treating it as a successor to *Cacciato* chronologically. Her argument that *Northern Lights* presents a more ma-

ture ethical resolution than the other two books admirably revalues O'Brien's first novel but leaves unacknowledged the great differences between the circumstances of Paul Perry and the soldier protagonists of the Vietnam-sited books as well as the more effective literary achievement of the memoir and the subsequent novel. It also overstates the positive comic resolution of *Northern Lights* and understates its irony. Although they don't affect her demonstration of chronological priority, the fictional time frames presented are inaccurate: She dates O'Brien's Viet Nam service in *Combat Zone* about a year too early, and the narrative of *Northern Lights* runs from summer 1970 to the following summer, not the spring.

9. The story focuses on a traumatic stillbirth out of wedlock. As the preacher at Damascus Lutheran Church, Reverend Perry provides ineffectual counseling for a flirtatious young girl about to give up her baby for adoption. Paul witnesses the grisly parturition and officiates with his wife at a private burial service for the stillborn infant. His wife's name is Grace, but Harvey, Addie, and the "old man" are not mentioned in the story, nor is Sawmill Landing; there is no overt apocalypticism; and Paul seems less alienated from the community.

4. A Soldier's Dream

1. For a chronology of fictional events, see McWilliams (245, 247–48), who dates Paul's night of guard duty precisely: November 20, 1968. For an argument that the observation post episodes are as fully imagined by Paul Berlin as the fantasy trip to Paris, see Raymond, 99–100.

2. The stories, listed in order of publication, include the following (the relevant chapter numbers in *Cacciato* are included in parentheses): "Where Have You Gone, Charming Billy?" (Chapter 31), "Landing Zone Bravo" (Chapter 20), "Going After Cacciato" (Chapter 1), "Speaking of Courage," "The Way It Mostly Was" (Chapter 25), "Keeping Watch by Night," "Fisherman" (Chapters 34 and 35), and "Calling Home" (Chapter 24). Besides Catherine Calloway's article on these earlier stories, Albert Wilhelm contrasts O'Brien's use of ballad allusions in "Where Have You Gone, Charming Billy?" with its revised version in "Night March" (Chapter 31 of *Cacciato*).

3. Catherine Calloway's earlier checklist (1991) mistakenly identifies the *Washington Post* piece as a future chapter of *Cacciato*. It is instead an early version of Chapter XVII of *Combat Zone*, as her corrected entry in the 1993 bibliography indicates. Its actual title, "The Enemy at My Khe," is an ironic one because the enemy's maiming and killing of GIs is made possible by the incompetence of O'Brien's commanding officer, the Captain Smith who replaced Captain Johansen

(see my discussion in Chapter 2, "Moral Combat"). A note to the piece in the *Post* (where O'Brien was a staff writer in 1972) identifies it as forthcoming in "Fire in the Hole," a book "to be published in March, 1973, by Delacorte Press/Seymour Lawrence." In the end, "Fire in the Hole" became *If I Die in a Combat Zone*; "The Enemy at My Khe" became its seventeenth chapter, "July"; and the memoir's original title was given to Chapter 11 of *Going After Cacciato*.

5. The Bombs Are Real

1. The most extensive single treatment of the novel is Steven Kaplan's chapter in *Understanding Tim O'Brien*, which perceptively shows how game playing replaces politics in the book but otherwise largely describes the plot at length. Tobey Herzog, who provides significant biographical parallels between O'Brien's childhood and Cowling's, summarizes the plot as a tripartite bildungsroman. In his treatment of O'Brien's work through *Things*, Philip Beidler (1991) provides a much shorter summary than either, while Daniel Zins's brief review of O'Brien's career finds the writer's fourth book his weakest. In the only article treating *The Nuclear Age* exclusively, Lee Schweninger praises its critique of patriarchal thinking, but nearly half the short essay focuses on identifying proponents of ecofeminism in general and briefly recapitulating their ideas.

Recent books on nuclear-age fiction have not given *The Nuclear Age* the attention it would seem to deserve, either. The novel was published too late for inclusion in Paul Brians's *Nuclear Holocausts* (1987), a survey with bibliography that does not even include the four earlier stories published before 1985, including "The Nuclear Age." But even the later books by David Dowling, Joseph Dewey, and Patrick Mannix barely mention O'Brien's work, although Dowling sees Cowling's accommodation as parabolic or typical of life under nuclear terror. Albert Stone's *Literary Aftershocks* (1994) handles *The Nuclear Age* in more detail, however. The best single study of the novel is Peter Schwenger's Lacanian analysis in *Letter Bomb*, which treats Cowling's activities as both metaphor and symptom of psychic processes related to writing.

2. Cowling's meditations in the shelter are not simply an internal monologue. Melinda hears the "hole" cackle "Dynamite!" just after she awakens (352–53) as well as "No survivors!" (356) just before Cowling disables the firing device. Her father's denials of his own words make his more plausible denials to her of lethal intent seem just as hollow, and make clear his temporary insanity in the final chapter of *The Nuclear Age* until his daughter rescues him from himself. Although most of what he thinks to himself and says to his wife and daughter in the shelter-digging chapters makes sense, we don't have to imagine him raving aloud when alone to realize that Cowling is nearly psychotic by the time he carries Bobbi and Melinda into the family tomb.

3. As noted in Chapter 3, Carl Anthony reveals in his recent biography of Jackie Kennedy that the president sent his family to the deep shelters at Camp David during the Cuban Missile Crisis of 1962. The danger of "defensive" missiles becoming agents of mass homicide if not national annihilation is literally a national security secret, of course. *Hostile Waters*, a 1997 BBC-produced film starring Rutger Hauer and Martin Sheen, details the crisis that occurred when Soviet and American nuclear submarines collided off North America while Reagan and Gorbachev prepared for their Reykjavik summit to consider outlawing nuclear weapons in 1982. The Soviet sub was eventually scuttled after receiving damage that could have launched its scores of MIRV'd nuclear warheads against the East Coast of the United States if its crew had not been so adept at averting the potential catastrophe. The incident was publicly revealed only in 1996.

4. "Civil Defense" was first published as a short story in the August 1980 *Esquire*, where it is so designated in the editor's introductory footnote (82).

5. The symmetrical characterizations are a product of revision between the early story "The Nuclear Age" and the completed novel that turned O'Brien's original antiwar protesters into caricatures or types to suit the parodic mode of the novel. In the fuller narrative of *The Nuclear Age*, Sarah not only is the recipient of William's sexual fantasies and imaginary phone calls from high school on but also mimics and goes beyond Jane Fonda in her transformation from campus golden girl to antiwar guerrilla. There are a larger number of former antiwar activists in O'Brien's first version of "The Nuclear Age," eight altogether, and they are not as broadly defined as they are in the novel. The Sarah of the short story is the Sarah of the novel, but Ned and Ollie are indistinguishable from the others, and with the exception of "Richard," dropped from *The Nuclear Age*, everyone else has a doctorate or is about to enter graduate school. Tina is missing from the group altogether.

6. O'Brien's replaying of that nightmare of the nuclear age was uncannily resurrected in June 1999 by the "capture" in St. Paul, Minnesota (O'Brien's home state!), of Kathleen Ann Soliah, one of two remaining members of the SLA who were still fugitives from justice twenty-five years after the kidnapping of Patty Hearst.

7. Cowling's graphic warning seems to rewrite, combine, and more capably effect O'Brien's own antiwar activity at Macalester College and his abortive, nearly comic attempt in Chapter II of *Combat Zone* to broadcast his anger at being drafted (noted above in Chapter 2, pp. 52–53).

6. True War Stories

1. "The Ghost Soldiers" appeared in *Esquire* in 1981 (March) and was reprinted in the 1982 O. Henry Award *Prize Stories* volume. "The Things They Carried" first appeared in the August 1986 *Esquire* and won the 1987 National Magazine Award in Fiction. "How to Tell a True War Story" (October 1987), "The Lives of the Dead" (January 1989), and "Sweetheart of the Song Tra Bong" (July 1989) also appeared in *Esquire*, while four other sections of *Things* appeared first as short stories: "Speaking of Courage" (*Granta*, Winter 1989), "In the Field" (*Gentleman's Quarterly*, December 1989), "On the Rainy River" (*Playboy*, January 1990), and "Field Trip" (*McCall's*, August 1990). Six other shorter pieces in *Harper's* (March 1990) and *Mānoa* (Spring 1990) were to be slightly altered when they appeared shortly afterward in *The Things They Carried.* (For bibliographical details, see Calloway 1991 and 1993.)

2. In turn, O'Brien noted to Martin Naparsteck, "the Tim character" is "transformed again" into the character Norman Bowker (7). Here as elsewhere, O'Brien's self-revisions are at the center of his fiction making. The transformations of O'Brien into Norman Bowker (and Paul Berlin) in "Speaking of Courage" are discussed below.

3. As Calloway (1995) notes, the hunting hatchet in the original 1990 edition of the story is replaced by moccasins in the 1991 paperback editions (Penguin and Flamingo [U.K.]). Perhaps "burying the hatchet" was too flagrant a symbol for the narrator's attempted therapeutic gesture.

7. The People We Kill

1. Wade's nightmares transform O'Brien's earlier, matter-of-fact explanation of "Pinkville" in *Combat Zone* (see Chapter 2, note 4) into an ominous phantasmagoric anticipation of collective murder.

2. Hemingway's novel begins similarly: "In the late summer of that year we lived in a house in a village that looked across the river and the plain to the mountains. In the bed of the river there were pebbles and boulders, dry and white in the sun, and the water was clear and swiftly moving and blue in the channels" (3). Like Kathy Wade, Catherine Barkley is already dead, but at least the narrator, her lover, knows her fate. A later reflection by Frederic Henry suggests Wade's circumstances at the beginning of the novel as well as his final desolation: "The world breaks every one and afterward many are strong at the broken places. But those that will not break it kills. It kills the very good and the very gentle and the

very brave impartially. If you are none of these you can be sure it will kill you but there will be no special hurry" (249). Wade, like most us, is "none of these."

3. Interviewed by Daniel Bourne in 1991, and with about one-fourth of the novel completed, O'Brien identified its starting place as a single sentence containing the word "unhappy," just as *The Things They Carried* had germinated with the simple phrase, "This is true" (80–81, 90). O'Brien published "How Unhappy They Were" as a short piece in the October 1994 *Esquire*.

8. Guys Just Want to Have Fun

1. In its original short story form, "Faith" retains the trace of O'Brien's initial intention in its first apostrophe, just after Chippering has noted that *turtle, corn,* and *Pontiac* are personal triggers of pathos: "Have you ever loved a woman, then lost her, then learned she lives on Fiji with a new lover? Is Fiji still Fiji? Coconuts and palm trees?" (62). Subsequent turnings away from the narrative are addressed to a woman, however, as in the novel. In *Tomcat,* the revised version of what has been cited simply switches gender: "Have you ever loved a man, then lost him, then learned he lives on Fiji with a new lover? Is Fiji still Fiji? Coconuts and palm trees?" (4).

2. A particularly striking example is *They Whisper* (1994) by Robert Olen Butler, one of the most significant and prolific American Vietnam fiction writers and virtually the only one who has effectively provided convincing and sympathetic representations of the South Vietnamese, including *A Good Scent from a Strange Mountain,* his Pulitzer Prize–winning collection of postwar stories about Vietnamese exiles in America. The deadly seriousness of the narrator's lyrical, wistful tone in *They Whisper* as he intimately reviews his encounters with what might be labeled "all the girls I've ever known," Vietnamese or American, seems ridiculously pompous when juxtaposed with O'Brien's more ironically aroused ogling and bedroom acrobatics. Chippering's encounter with Spider also parodies the reverence or pathos afforded to fictional ghosts of the war in works such as Ehrhart's *Busted.*

3. Ironically, in the wake of the May 2000 nativist coup by George Speight against Fiji's elected government and the subsequent imposition of military control after his arrest, Fiji itself is no longer "Fiji": The political unrest, despite its small scale and the present reimposition of law and order, has ruined the visitor industry and sullied Fiji's reputation as a "paradise" for wealthy foreign tourists.

REFERENCES

Aberbach, David. *Surviving Trauma: Loss, Literature, and Psychoanalysis.* New Haven: Yale Univ. Press, 1989.

American Psychiatric Association. *Diagnostic and Statistical Manual of Mental Disorders.* 4th ed. Washington, D.C.: American Psychiatric Association, 1994.

Anthony, Carl Sferrazza. *First Ladies: The Saga of the Presidents' Wives and Their Power, 1789–1961.* New York: William Morrow, 1990.

Auden, W. H. "The Shield of Achilles." *Selected Poetry.* 2d ed. New York: Vintage, 1970.

Bao Ninh. *The Sorrow of War.* Translated by Phan Thanh Hao. New York: Pantheon, 1995.

Bates, Milton. "Tim O'Brien's Myth of Courage." *Modern Fiction Studies* 33, no. 2 (Summer 1987): 263–79.

———. *The Wars We Took to Vietnam: Cultural Conflict and Storytelling.* Berkeley: Univ. of California Press, 1996.

Baughman, Ronald, ed. *American Writers of the Vietnam War: W. D. Ehrhart, Larry Heinemann, Tim O'Brien, Walter McDonald, John M. Del Vecchio.* Detroit: Layman/Gale, 1991.

Beidler, Philip D. *American Literature and the Experience of Vietnam.* Athens, Ga.: Univ. of Georgia Press, 1982.

———. *Re-Writing America: Vietnam Authors in Their Generation.* Athens and London: Univ. of Georgia Press, 1991.

Berke, Richard L. "Conduct Unbecoming." Review of *The Death of Outrage: Bill Clinton and the Assault on American Ideals,* by William J. Bennett. *New York Times Book Review,* 29 September 1998, 11.

Bonn, Maria S. "A Different World: The Vietnam Veteran Novel Comes Home." In *Fourteen Landing Zones: Approaches to Vietnam War Literature.* Edited by Philip K. Jason, 1–14. Iowa City: Univ. of Iowa Press, 1991.

Bourne, Daniel. "*Artful Dodge* Interviews Tim O'Brien." *Artful Dodge* 22.3 (1992): 74–90.

Bouson, J. Brooks. *Quiet as It's Kept: Shame, Trauma, and Race in the Novels of Toni Morrison.* Albany: State Univ. of New York: 2000.

Bowen, Kevin, Nguyen Ba Chung, and Bruce Weigl, eds. *Mountain River: Vietnamese Poetry From the Wars, 1946–1993. A Bilingual Collection.* Amherst: Univ. of Massachusetts Press, 1998.

Bowie, Malcolm. *Lacan.* Cambridge, Mass.: Harvard Univ. Press, 1991.

Brians, Paul. *Nuclear Holocausts: Atomic War in Fiction, 1895–1984.* Kent, Ohio: Kent State Univ. Press, 1987.

Brown, Constance A. "Severed Ears: An Image of the Vietnam War." *War, Literature, and the Arts* 4.1 (Spring 1992): 25–42.

Brown, Rosellen. Review of *Northern Lights. New Republic* 174 (7 February 1976): 27–28.

Broyles, William, Jr. *Brothers in Arms: A Journey from War to Peace.* New York: Alfred A. Knopf, 1986.

Butler, Robert Olen. *A Good Scent from a Strange Mountain.* New York: H. Holt, 1992.

———. *They Whisper.* New York: H. Holt, 1994.

Buttinger, Joseph. *The Smaller Dragon: A Political History of Vietnam.* New York, Washington, D.C., and London: Praeger, 1958.

Calloway, Catherine. "'How to Tell a True War Story': Metafiction in *The Things They Carried.*" *Critique* 36 (Summer 1995): 249–57.

———. "Pluralities of Vision: *Going After Cacciato* and Tim O'Brien's Short Fiction." In *America Rediscovered: Critical Essays on Literature and Film of the Vietnam War.* Edited by Owen W. Gilman and Lorrie Smith, 213–24. New York: Garland, 1990.

———. "Tim O'Brien: A Checklist." *Bulletin of Bibliography* 48.1 (March 1991): 6–11.

———. "Tim O'Brien (1946–): A Primary and Secondary Bibliography." *Bulletin of Bibliography* 50.3 (September 1993): 223–29.

Caputo, Philip. *A Rumor of War.* New York: Holt, Rinehart, and Winston, 1977.

Christopher, Renny. *The Viet Nam War/The American War: Images and Representations in Euro-American and Vietnamese Exile Narratives.* Amherst: Univ. of Massachusetts Press, 1995.

Coffey, Michael. "Tim O'Brien." *Publishers Weekly* 237 (16 February 1990): 60–61.

Conrad, Joseph. "Heart of Darkness" and "The Lagoon." In *The Portable Conrad.* New York: Penguin, 1975.

Couser, G. Thomas. "*Going After Cacciato*: The Romance and the Real War." *Journal of Narrative Technique* 13, no. 1 (Winter 1983): 1–10.

Dante. *Paradiso.* Translated by John D. Sinclair. New York: Oxford Univ. Press, 1939.

Danziger, Jeff. "The Vietnam War Comes Lurching From the Past." Review of *In the Lake of the Woods. Christian Science Monitor,* 4 November 1994, 13.

Davidson, Jonathan R. T., M.D., and Edna B. Foa, M.D., eds. *Posttraumatic Stress Disorder: DSM-IV and Beyond.* Washington, D.C., and London: American Psychiatric Press, 1993.

Davis, Alan. "The Purest Wilderness: Feasting and Fasting in Fiction." Review of *In the Lake of the Woods,* et al. *Hudson Review* 49 (Summer 1995): 325–32.

Del Vecchio, John M. *The 13th Valley.* New York: Bantam, 1982.

DeMeester, Karen. "Trauma and Recovery in Virginia Woolf's *Mrs. Dalloway.*" *Modern Fiction Studies* 44.3 (Fall 1998): 649–73.

Dewey, Joseph. *In a Dark Time: The Apocalyptic Temper in the American Novel of the Nuclear Age.* West Lafayette, Ind.: Purdue Univ. Press, 1990.

Dostoevsky, Feodor. *Notes from Underground.* Translated by Richard Pevear and Larissa Volokhonsky. New York: Knopf, 1993.

Dowling, David. *Fictions of Nuclear Disaster.* London: Macmillan, 1987.

Ehrhart, W. D. *Busted: A Vietnam Veteran in Nixon's America.* Amherst: Univ. of Massachusetts Press, 1995.

———. *A Generation of Peace.* New York: New Voices, 1975.

———. *Going Back: An Ex-Marine Returns to Vietnam.* Jefferson, N.C., and London: McFarland, 1987.

———. *Passing Time: Memoir of a Vietnam Veteran Against the War.* Amherst: Univ. of Massachusetts Press, 1995. Reprint of *Marking Time.* New York: Avon, 1986.

———, ed. *Unaccustomed Mercy: Soldier Poets of the Vietnam War.* Lubbock, Tex.: Texas Tech Univ. Press, 1989.

———. *Vietnam–Perkasie: A Combat Marine Memoir.* Amherst: Univ. of Massachusetts Press, 1995. Reprint. Jefferson, N.C., and London: McFarland, 1983.

Elsen, Jon. "Doing the Popular Thing." Interview with Tim O'Brien. *New York Times Book Review,* 9 October 1994, 33.

Fallowell, Duncan. "Bangs and Shingles." Review of *Northern Lights. Spectator* 3 (April 1976): 22.

Farrell, Kirby. *Post-traumatic Culture: Injury and Interpretation in the Nineties.* Baltimore and London: Johns Hopkins Univ. Press, 1998.

Fasman, Jonathan. "Love in odd places." Review of *Tomcat in Love. Times Literary Supplement,* 14 May 1999, 24.

Felman, Shoshana. *Testimony: Crises of Witnessing in Literature, Psychoanalysis, and History.* New York: Routledge, 1992.

Fields-Meyer, Thomas. Review of *Tomcat in Love. People Weekly,* 26 October 1998, 43.

Fisher, Marc. "Response to McNamara Shows Wounds Haven't Healed." *International Herald Tribune,* 21 April 1995, 2.

Franklin, H. Bruce. *M.I.A., or Mythmaking in America.* New York: Lawrence Hill, 1992.

———. "Plausibility of Denial." Review of *In the Lake of the Woods. The Progressive,* December 1994, 40–44.

———, ed. *The Vietnam War in American Stories, Songs, and Poems.* Boston: Bedford/St. Martins, 1996.

Franks, Lucinda. "The Intimate Hillary." *Talk* 1.1 (August 1999): 166–74, 248–51.

Gibson, James William. *The Perfect War: Technowar in Vietnam.* Boston: Atlantic Monthly Press, 1986.

Giles, Jeff. "Murder, Mystery, and Memories of My Lai." Review of *In the Lake of the Woods. Newsweek* 124 (24 October 1994): 78.

Gold, Charles H. Review of *Northern Lights. Booklist* 72 (15 September 1975): 116.

Graham, Judith, ed. "Tim O'Brien." In *Current Biography Yearbook,* 441–45. New York: H. W. Wilson, 1995.

Harris, Michael. "Almost Like Two Novels in One." Review of *Northern Lights. Washington Post,* 14 August 1975, C12.

Heberle, Mark A. "Correspondent Visions of Vietnam." *War, Literature, and the Arts* 1.1 (Spring 1989): 4–18.

———. Unpublished interviews with Tim O'Brien. Honolulu, Hawaii, 14 November 1996; Ann Arbor, Mich., 8 October 1998; Austin, Tex. (by telephone), 3 November 1998.

Heinemann, Larry. *Close Quarters.* New York: Farrar, Straus, and Giroux, 1977.

———. *Paco's Story.* New York: Farrar, Straus, and Giroux, 1986.

Heller, Joseph. *Catch-22, A Novel.* New York: Simon and Schuster, 1961.

Hellmann, John. *American Myth and the Legacy of Vietnam.* New York: Columbia Univ. Press, 1986.

Hemingway, Ernest. *A Farewell to Arms.* 1929. Reprint, New York: Scribner's, 1957.

———. *In Our Time.* 1925. Reprint, New York: Scribner's, 1958.

———. *The Sun Also Rises.* 1926. Reprint, New York: Scribner's, 1954.

Henke, Suzette A. *Shattered Subjects: Trauma and Testimony in Women's Life-Writing.* New York: St. Martin's, 1998.

Henriksen, Margot A. *Dr. Strangelove's America: Society and Culture in The Atomic Age.* Berkeley: Univ. of California Press, 1997.

Herman, Judith Lewis, M.D. *Trauma and Recovery.* New York: Basic Books, 1992.

Herr, Michael. *Dispatches.* 1977. Reprint, New York: Random House, 1991.

Herzog, Tobey C. "*Going After Cacciato*: The Soldier-Author-Character Seeking Control." *Critique* 24.2 (Winter 1983): 89–96.

———. *Tim O'Brien.* New York: Twayne, 1997.

Ho Anh Thai. *Behind the Red Mist: Fiction.* Edited by Wayne Karlin. Translated by Nguyen Qui Duc, et al. Willimantic, Conn.: Curbstone Press, 1998.

Howes, Craig. *Voices of the Vietnam POWs: Witnesses to Their Fight.* New York: Oxford Univ. Press, 1993.

Hutcheon, Linda. *Narcissistic Narrative: The Metafictional Paradox.* Waterloo, Ontario: Wilfred Laurier, 1980.

Huxley, Aldous. *Brave New World.* New York: Harper, 1950.

Jakaitis, John. "Two Versions of an Unfinished War: *Dispatches* and *Going After Cacciato.*" *Cultural Critique* 1.3 (Spring 1986): 191–210.

Jarraway, David R. "'Excremental Assault' in Tim O'Brien: Trauma and Recovery in Vietnam War Literature." *Modern Fiction Studies* 44.3 (Fall 1998): 695–711.

Jason, Philip K. "'How Dare She?' Susan Fromberg Schaeffer's *Buffalo Afternoon* and the Issue of Authenticity." *Critique* 24.3 (Spring 1993): 182–92.

———. *The Vietnam War in Literature: An Annotated Bibliography of Criticism.* Pasadena, Calif.: Salem Press, 1992.

———. "Vietnamese in America: Literary Representations." *Journal of American Culture* 20.3 (Fall 1997): 43–50.

Jeffords, Susan. *The Remasculinization of America: Gender and the Vietnam War.* Bloomington and Indianapolis: Indiana Univ. Press, 1989.

Jones, Dale W. "The Vietnams of Michael Herr and Tim O'Brien: Tales of Disintegration and Integration." *Canadian Review of American Studies* 13.3 (Winter 1982): 309–20.

Journal of Traumatic Stress. London and New York: Plenum, 1983–.

Joyce, James. *Ulysses.* 1934. Reprint, New York: Modern Library, 1961.

Kakesako, Gregg K. "Chief of Staff Gen. Eric Shinseki. Native son joining ranks of eminent Army Leaders: Born an 'enemy alien,' a Japanese-American from Kauai perseveres." *Honolulu Star Bulletin,* 21 June 1999, A-1, A-6.

Kakutani, Michiko. "Shell Shock on the Battlefields of a Messy Love Life." Review of *Tomcat in Love. New York Times,* 15 September 1998, E7.

Kalevala: The Land of Heroes. 2 vols. Translated by W. F. Kirby. New York: Dutton, 1907.

Kaplan, Steven. "An Interview with Tim O'Brien." *Missouri Review* 14.3 (1991): 93–108.

———. *Understanding Tim O'Brien.* Columbia, S.C.: Univ. of South Carolina Press, 1995.

———. "The Undying Uncertainty of the Narrator in Tim O'Brien's *The Things They Carried.*" *Critique* 35.1 (Fall 1993): 43–52.

Karlin, Wayne, Le Minh Khue, and Truong Vu, eds. *The Other Side of Heaven: Post-War Fiction by Vietnamese and American Writers.* Willimantic, Conn.: Curbstone Press, 1995.

Keats, John. *Selected Poems and Letters.* Edited by Douglas Bush. Boston: Houghton Mifflin, 1959.

Kitchen, Judith. "Out of Place: Reading O'Brien and O'Brien." *Georgia Review* 50.3 (Fall 1996): 477–94.

Kloszewski, Marc A. Review of *Tomcat in Love. Library Journal,* 1 September 1998, 216.

Kovic, Ron. *Born on the Fourth of July.* New York: McGraw-Hill, 1976.

Kuberski, Philip Francis. "Genres of Vietnam." *Cultural Critique* 1.3 (Spring 1986): 168–88.

Kulka, Richard, et al., eds. *Trauma and the Vietnam War Generation. Report of Findings from the National Vietnam Veterans Readjustment Study.* New York: Brunner/Maazel, 1990.

Kurzweil, Edith. *The Freudians: A Comparative Perspective.* New Haven and London: Yale Univ. Press, 1989.

Langer, Lawrence. *Holocaust Testimonies: The Ruins of Memory.* New Haven: Yale Univ. Press, 1991.

Lawson, Jacqueline. "Telling It Like It Was: The Nonfiction Literature of the Vietnam War." In *America Rediscovered: Critical Essays on Literature and Film of the Vietnam War.* Edited by Owen W. Gilman and Lorrie Smith, 363–81. New York: Garland, 1990.

Le Minh Khue. *The Stars, the Earth, the River: Short Stories.* Edited by Wayne Karlin. Translated by Hoai Tran and Dana Sach. Willimantic, Conn.: Curbstone Press, 1997.

Lederer, William J., and Eugene Burdick. *The Ugly American.* New York: Norton, 1958.

Lee, Don. "About Tim O'Brien." *Ploughshares* 21.3 (Winter 1995–96): 196–201.

Legacies of Vietnam: Comparative Adjustment of Veterans and Their Peers. Edited by Arthur Egendorf, Charles Kadushin, Robert S. Laufer, George Rothbart, and Lee Sloan. Washington, D.C.: GPO, 1981.

Leland, John G. "Writing About Vietnam." *College English* 41.5 (January 1980): 739–41.

Lifton, Robert Jay. *Home From the War: Vietnam Veterans: Neither Victims nor Executioners.* New York: Simon and Schuster, 1973.

Lomperis, Timothy J. *"Reading the Wind": The Literature of the Vietnam War.* Durham, N.C.: Duke Univ. Press, 1987.

Maclean, Alastair. "Brotherly Lusts." Review of *Northern Lights. Times Literary Supplement,* 23 April 1976, 498.

Mannix, Patrick. *The Rhetoric of Antinuclear Fiction: Persuasive Strategies in Novels and Films.* Lewisburg, Pa.: Bucknell Univ. Press, 1992.

Martin, Andrew. *Receptions of War: Vietnam in American Culture.* Norman and London: Univ. of Oklahoma Press, 1993.

Mason, Bobbie Ann. *In Country.* New York: Harper and Row, 1985.

Mason, Robert. *Chickenhawk.* New York: Viking, 1983.

McCaffery, Larry. "Interview with Tim O'Brien." *Chicago Review* 33.2 (1982): 129–49.

McInerney, Peter. "'Straight' and 'Secret' History in Vietnam War Literature." *Contemporary Literature* 22.2 (Spring 1981): 187–204.

McNerney, Brian C. "Responsibly Inventing History: An Interview with Tim O'Brien." *War, Literature, and the Arts* 6.2 (Fall 1994): 1–24.

McWilliams, Dean. "Time in O'Brien's *Going After Cacciato.*" *Critique* 29 (Summer 1988): 245–55.

Melling, Philip H. *Vietnam in American Literature.* Boston: Twayne, 1990.

Messud, Claire. "Vet Cemetery." Review of *In the Lake of the Woods. Guardian Friday Review*, 7 May 1995, 7.

Milton, John. *The Riverside Milton.* Boston: Houghton Mifflin, 1998.

Mort, John. "The Booklist Interview: Tim O'Brien." *Booklist* 90 (August 1994): 1990–91.

Myers, Thomas. "Tim O'Brien." In *Dictionary of Literary Biography.* Vol. 152, *American Novelists Since World War II, Fourth Series.* Edited by James D. Giles and Wanda H. Giles. Detroit, Washington, D.C., and London: Bruccoli Clark Layman/Gale: 1995.

———. *Walking Point: American Narratives of Vietnam.* New York: Oxford Univ. Press, 1988.

Naparsteck, Martin. "An Interview with Tim O'Brien." *Contemporary Literature* 32.1 (1991): 1–11.

Neilson, Jim. *Warring Fictions: American Literary Culture and the Vietnam War Narrative.* Jackson, Miss.: Univ. Press of Mississippi, 1998.

Nelson, Marie. "Two Consciences: A Reading of Tim O'Brien's Vietnam Trilogy." In *Third Force Psychology and the Study of Literature.* Edited by Bernard J. Paris, 262–79. Rutherford, N.J.: Fairleigh Dickinson Univ. Press, 1986.

Nguyen Dinh-Hoa, ed. *Vietnamese-English Dictionary.* Rutland, Vt., and Tokyo: Charles Tuttle, 1991.

Norris, Margot. "Introduction: Modernism and Modern Wars." *Modern Fiction Studies* 44.3 (Fall 1998): 505–9.

O'Brien, Tim

BOOKS

———. *Going After Cacciato.* New York: Dell, 1978.

———. *If I Die in a Combat Zone, Box Me Up and Ship Me Home.* New York: Dell, 1973.

———. *In the Lake of the Woods.* New York: Houghton Mifflin, 1994.

———. *Northern Lights.* New York: Delacorte/Seymour Lawrence: 1975.

———. *The Nuclear Age.* New York: Dell, 1985.

————. *The Things They Carried.* Boston: Houghton Mifflin/Seymour Lawrence, 1990.

————. *Tomcat in Love.* New York: Broadway, 1998.

STORIES, NONFICTION, READINGS

————. "Calling Home." *Redbook* 150 (December 1977): 75–76.

————. "Civil Defense." *Esquire* 94 (August 1980): 82–88.

————. "Class of '68." *Esquire* 129 (March 1998): 160.

————. "The Enemy at My Khe." *Washington Post,* 20 August 1972, C.3.1.

————. "Faith." *The New Yorker* 71 (12 February 1996): 62–67.

————. "Fisherman." *Esquire* 88 (October 1977): 92, 130, 134.

————. "Going After Cacciato." *Ploughshares* 3.1 (1975): 42–65.

————. "How Unhappy They Were." *Esquire* 122 (October 1994): 136–38.

————. "July '69." *Esquire* 134 (July 2000): 102–9.

————. "Keeping Watch by Night." *Esquire* 148 (December 1976): 65–67.

————. "Landing Zone Bravo." *Denver Quarterly* 4 (August 1975): 72–77.

————. "Loon Point." *Esquire* 119 (January 1993): 90–94.

————. "A Man of Melancholy Disposition." *Ploughshares* 2.2 (1974): 46–60.

————. "Night March." In *Prize Stories 1976: The O. Henry Awards.* Edited by William Abrahams, 211–19. Garden City, NY: Doubleday, 1976.

————. "Nogales." *The New Yorker* 75 (8 March 1999): 68–73.

————. "The Nuclear Age." *Atlantic Monthly* 243 (June 1979): 58–67.

————. "The People We Marry." *Atlantic Monthly* 269 (January 1992): 90–98.

————. "Speaking of Courage." *Massachusetts Review* 17 (Summer 1976): 243–53.

————. "Step Lightly." *Playboy* 17 (July 1970): 138–39.

————. "The Streak." *The New Yorker* 74 (28 September 1998): 88–91.

————. "The Things They Carried." *Esquire* 106 (August 1986): 76–81.

————. "The Vietnam in Me." *The New York Times Magazine,* 2 October 1994: 48–57.

————. "The Vietnam in Me." *The Observer Sunday Magazine,* 2 April 1995: 14–20.

————. "The Way It Mostly Was." *Shenandoah* 27 (Winter 1976): 35–45.

————. "Where Have You Gone, Charming Billy?" *Redbook* 145 (May 1975): 81, 127–32.

————. "Winnipeg." *New Yorker* 76 (14 August 2000): 72–77.

————. Public reading from *Tomcat in Love.* Ann Arbor, Mich., 18 October 1998.

Orwell, George. *Nineteen Eighty-Four: A Novel.* New York: Harcourt, Brace, and World: 1950.

Owen, Wilfred. *Collected Poems.* Edited by C. Day Lewis. New York: New Directions, 1964.

Plato. *Laches and Charmides.* Translated by Rosamond Kent Sprague. Indianapolis: Indiana Univ. Press, 1973.

Pochoda, Elizabeth. "Vietnam, We've All Been There." *The Nation*, 25 March 1978, 344–46.

Pound, Ezra. *Selected Poems*. New York: New Directions, 1957.

Proust, Marcel. *Remembrance of Things Past*. Translated by C. K. Scott Moncrieff. New York: Random House, 1981.

Pynchon, Thomas. *Gravity's Rainbow*. New York: Viking, 1973.

Raymond, Michael W. "Imagined Responses to Vietnam: Tim O'Brien's *Going After Cacciato*." *Critique* 24.2 (Winter 1983): 97–104.

Reischauer, Edwin O., and John K. Fairbank. *East Asia, The Great Tradition*. Boston: Houghton Mifflin/Tokyo: Charles E. Tuttle, 1960.

Remarque, Erich Maria. *All Quiet on the Western Front*. Boston: Little, Brown, 1929.

Ringnalda, Don. *Fighting and Writing the Vietnam War*. Jackson, Miss.: Univ. Press of Mississippi, 1994.

Roripaugh, Robert A. Review of *Northern Lights* and Richard Martin Stern, *Power*. *Western American Literature* 11 (Summer 1976): 177–79.

Rowe, John Carlos, and Rick Berg. *The Vietnam War and American Culture*. New York: Columbia Univ. Press, 1991.

Sale, Roger. "Fathers & Fathers & Sons." Review of *Northern Lights*. *New York Review of Books* 22 (13 November 1975): 31.

Schroeder, Eric James. "Two Interviews: Talks with Tim O'Brien and Robert Stone." *Modern Fiction Studies* 30.1 (Spring 1984): 135–64.

———. *Vietnam, We've All Been There*. Westport, Conn., and London: Praeger, 1992.

Schwartz, Delmore. *In Dreams Begin Responsibilities and Other Stories*. New York: New Directions, 1937.

Schwenger, Peter. *Letter Bomb: Nuclear Holocaust and the Exploding Word*. Baltimore and London: Johns Hopkins Univ. Press, 1992.

Schweninger, Lee. "Ecofeminism, Nuclearism, and O'Brien's *The Nuclear Age*." In *The Nightmare Reconsidered: Critical Essays on Nuclear War Literature*. Edited by Nancy Anisfield, 177–85. Bowling Green, Ohio: Bowling Green State Univ. Popular Press, 1991.

Searle, William J. "Walking Wounded: Vietnam War Novels of Return." In *Search and Clear: Critical Responses to Selected Literature and Films of the Vietnam War*. Edited by William J. Searle, 1–12. Bowling Green, Ohio: Bowling Green State Univ. Press. 1988.

Shakespeare, William. *The Riverside Shakespeare*. 2d ed. Edited by G. Blakemore Evans. Boston and New York: Houghton Mifflin, 1997.

Shay, Jonathan, M.D., Ph.D. *Achilles in Vietnam: Combat Trauma and the Undoing of Character*. New York: Touchstone, 1994.

Sheehan, Neil. *A Bright Shining Lie: John Paul Vann and America in Vietnam*. New York: Random House, 1988.

Shweder, Richard A. "To Speak of the Unspeakable." Review of *After Silence: Rape and My Journey Back*, by Nancy Venable Raine. *New York Times Book Review*, 20 September 1998, 13.

Sicher, Efraim, ed. *Breaking Crystal: Writing and Memory after Auschwitz*. Urbana: Univ. of Illinois Press, 1998.

Sinfield, Alan. "Cultural Imperialism and the Scene of U.S. Man." In *Faultlines: Cultural Materialism and the Politics of Dissident Reading*, 254–302. Oxford: Clarendon Press, 1992.

Slabey, Robert M. "*Going After Cacciato*: Tim O'Brien's Separate Peace." In *America Rediscovered: Critical Essays on Literature and Film of the Vietnam War*. Edited by Owen W. Gilman and Lorrie Smith, 206–12. New York: Garland, 1990.

Slotkin, Richard. *Gunfighter Nation: The Myth of the Frontier in Twentieth-Century America*. New York: Atheneum, 1992.

Smiley, Jane. "Catting Around." Review of *Tomcat in Love*. *New York Times Book Review*, 20 September 1998, 11–12.

Smith, Lorrie N. "'The Things Men Do': The Gendered Subtext in Tim O'Brien's *Esquire* Stories." *Critique* 36.1 (Fall 1994): 16–39.

Sterling, John. Review of *Tomcat in Love*. *Publishers Weekly*, 13 July 1998, 61.

Stone, Albert. *Literary Aftershocks: American Writers, Readers, and the Bomb*. New York: Twayne, 1994.

Tal, Kali. "The Mind at War: Images of Women in Vietnam Novels by Combat Veterans." *Contemporary Literature* 31.1 (Spring 1990): 76–96.

———. "Speaking the Language of Pain: Vietnam War Literature in the Context of a Literature of Trauma." In *Fourteen Landing Zones: Approaches to Vietnam War Literature*. Edited by Philip K. Jason, 217–50. Iowa City: Univ. of Iowa Press, 1991.

———. *Worlds of Hurt: Reading the Literatures of Trauma*. Cambridge: Cambridge Univ. Press, 1996.

Tayler, Christopher. "At Sawmill Landing." Review of *Northern Lights*. *Times Literary Supplement*, 22 January 1999, 23.

Taylor, Mark. "Tim O'Brien's War." *Centennial Review* 39.2 (Spring 1995): 213–30.

Tegmark, Mats. *In the Shoes of a Soldier: Communication in Tim O'Brien's Vietnam Narratives*. Studia Anglistica Upsaliensia 105. Uppsala, Sweden: Uppsala Univ. Library, 1998.

Thompson, Laurence C. *A Vietnamese Reference Grammar. Mon-Khmer Studies XIII–XIV: A Journal of Southeast Asian Philology*. Edited by Stephen O'Harrow. Honolulu: Univ. of Hawai'i Press, 1987.

Updike, John. "Books: *Going After Cacciato*." *The New Yorker* 54.6 (27 March 1978): 128–30, 133.

van Boheemen, Christine. *Joyce, Derrida, Lacan, and the Trauma of History: Reading, Narrative, and Postcolonialism*. Cambridge and New York: Cambridge Univ. Press, 1999.

van der Kolk, Bessel A., Alexander C. McFarlane, and Lars Weisaeth. *Traumatic Stress: The Effects of Overwhelming Experience on Mind, Body, and Society.* New York and London: Guilford Press, 1996.

Van Devanter, Linda, and Joan A. Furey. *Visions of War, Dreams of Peace: Writings of Women in the Vietnam War.* New York: Warner, 1991.

Vannatta, Dennis. "Theme and Structure in Tim O'Brien's *Going After Cacciato.*" *Modern Fiction Studies* 28, no. 2 (Summer 1982): 242–46.

Warton, Lynn. "Journeying from Life to Literature: An Interview with American Novelist Tim O'Brien." *Interdisciplinary Literary Studies: A Journal of Criticism and Theory* 1.2 (Spring 2000): 229–47.

Webb, James. *Fields of Fire.* New York: Prentice-Hall, 1978.

Weber, Bruce. "Wrestling with War and Love: Raw Pain, Relived Tim O'Brien's Way." *New York Times*, 2 September 1998, B1, B4.

Whitaker, Phil. Review of *Tomcat in Love. New Statesman*, 10 May 1999, 45–46.

Whitehead, Anne. "Open to Suggestion: Hypnosis and History in Pat Barker's *Regeneration.*" *Modern Fiction Studies* 44.3 (Fall 1998): 674–94.

Wilhelm, Albert E. "Ballad Allusions in Tim O'Brien's 'Where Have You Gone, Charming Billy?'" *Studies in Short Fiction* 28 (Spring 1991): 218–22.

Zins, Daniel. "Imagining the Real: The Fiction of Tim O'Brien." *Hollins Critic* 23.3 (June 1986): 1–12.